The United Nations

An Introduction

Sven Bernhard Gareis
and
Johannes Varwick

Translated by Lindsay P. Cohn

Originally published in German by Leske & Budrich, Opladen

This adapted and updated translation of the 3rd German edition
(2003) published 2005 by
PALGRAVE MACMILLAN
Houndmills, Basingstoke, Hampshire RG21 6XS and
175 Fifth Avenue, New York, N.Y. 10010
Companies and representatives throughout the world

PALGRAVE MACMILLAN is the global academic imprint of the Palgrave
Macmillan division of St. Martin's Press, LLC and of Palgrave Macmillan Ltd.
Macmillan® is a registered trademark in the United States, United Kingdom
and other countries. Palgrave is a registered trademark in the European
Union and other countries.

ISBN-13: 978–1–4039–3539–7 hardback
ISBN-10: 1–4039–3539–4 hardback
ISBN-13: 978–1–4039–3540–3 paperback
ISBN-10: 1–4039–3540–8 paperback

This book is printed on paper suitable for recycling and
made from fully managed and sustained forest sources.

A catalogue record for this book is available from the British Library.

A catalog record for this book is available from the Library of Congress.

10   9   8   7   6   5   4   3   2   1
14 13 12 11 10 09 08 07 06 05

Printed and bound in China

Contents

List of Figures and Tables

Figures

Tables

Preface

The United Nations (UN) plays a singular role in the discussion regarding the future of international politics. Although founded in 1945 and thus at the time of writing, some six decades old, the organization sometimes gives the impression that it is still in need of a foundation. Whether it be peacekeeping, strengthening human rights, dealing with problems of the global environment or the struggle against international terrorism and its manifold causes, there hardly seems to be a global problem in the world today in which the United Nations is *not* expected to play a key role. On the other hand, it is always pointed out in the very same breath that, for the UN to play its role adequately, it stands in need of reform and renewal. Moreover, a fundamental change in perspective – especially on the part of the more powerful member states – is necessary for the UN's success. A further complaint often heard is that on especially important issues – such as the recent war in Iraq – the UN is frequently avoided or even deliberately shoved aside. It is obvious that a great gulf still exists between the UN's actual capabilities and the strong organization that many desire it to be.

That the United Nations is sought-after in its capacities as agent and as a forum in such a wide spectrum of political issues is attributable primarily to the fact that the organization can boast almost perfect universality (with 191 states as members). Also important, however, is the UN's self-understanding as a broad global forum for international co-operation. The United Nations was created to be a comprehensive organization not only in terms of its membership, but also in terms of the breadth of its competencies. Each aspect of its work – peacekeeping, human rights, development co-operation, environmental protection and so on – will be emphasized in turn by the people for whom those tasks take precedence. Since the very beginning, the work of the United Nations has been based on a broad concept of peace; one that goes beyond the mere prevention of war to include the improvement of the humanitarian and social condition of humankind, the strengthening of international law, and concerns regarding sustainable development. In this sense, at least, the UN has been astonishingly modern.

It is because of this broader concept of peace that the goals of the UN Charter comprise a much broader field of responsibility than the mere possibility of using military force against an aggressor. Other areas include the resolution of disputes by peaceful means, the search for co-operative solutions for economic, social, cultural and humanitarian problems, and the encouragement of behaviour that accords with the principles of international law. This ambitious catalogue of goals makes it quite clear that the UN does not understand itself as a mere means to the fulfilment of a specific task, but rather envisions a qualitative change in international relations in general. The UN's concrete fields of activity have broadened considerably since the founding, without requiring changes to the Charter. In the words of the current Secretary-General, Kofi Annan, for the first forty-five years of its existence, the UN stood in the shadow of the Cold War, which prevented the organization from fulfilling some of its core responsibilities, but also led to the discovery of other essential tasks. But now, even the core tasks have undergone some changes of their own. For example, at the time of the founding, inter-state warfare was the greatest threat to international peace and security, but at the start of the twenty-first century, internal conflicts and a fundamentally different concept of war are on the agenda.

It is also impossible to overlook the fact that the UN in its present form is unable to play its role adequately as motor and agent of a comprehensive politics of world order. It is thus no coincidence that reform of the UN has a prominent position on the international agenda. Within the reform debate, a distinction can be made between reforms of organizational law, which can be made without any changes to the Charter, and constitutional reforms, which require the Charter to be amended. While numerous important projects falling under the first heading have been implemented during Kofi Annan's tenure, the hurdles facing changes of the second kind remain extremely high. Thus, with reliable regularity, some portion of the list of reform proposals is to be found on the agendas of diverse working groups of the General Assembly and Security Council without there ever being a consensus in sight. Although there exist plentiful fundamental disagreements over the organization's precise future form and function, there is a general consensus that the UN stands in need of comprehensive reform. Both the Charter and the organization itself require a basic overhaul, and what all the reform exigencies have in common is that the measures necessary to implement them can be decided upon and put into practice only by the member states themselves. In such a situation as this, it is almost impossible to make predictions about the chances for success of central projects such as Security Council reform.

The world organization's persistent need for reform should not, however, distract anyone from the fact that the United Nations is indispensable for the stability of the international system. Political practice unfortunately does not usually keep pace with the demands of an ever more complex listing of international problems. Sustainable solutions to humanity's chief problems in the twenty-first century are most likely to be found multilaterally, and the UN plays a prominent role in the warp and woof of international regimes and organizations. However, it is also true that if the existing institutions do not succeed in solving the problems of international politics, states will seek other types of solutions. Thus it is necessary for the UN to deliver realistic contributions to the solution of problems if the organization does not wish to sacrifice its significance. If the member states fail to support the organization more strongly and consistently, however, success will not be possible.

This book approaches its subject in nine steps, each presented in a separate chapter. The individual chapters may be seen as self-contained pedagogic units, but they do, of course, build on one another, and a truly substantiated picture of the UN's potentialities emerges only when the book is taken as a whole.

The first chapter presents a basic introduction to the structure of the UN. Along with an overview of the organization's historical development, the UN Charter and the principal organs, programmes, funds and specialized agencies will be introduced, and their functions and decision-making processes explained. How the UN is financed will also be explained.

In the second chapter, the theoretical perspective takes precedence. Here we ask how an international organization's work can be classified and explained conceptually, and address the challenges that arise from increasing globalization and their impact on the main tasks and functions of the UN.

The third chapter focuses on the principle of collective security – one of the key elements of the UN in the area of securing international peace and security. Both the limitations and possibilities of this principle are explained, as well as the development of the general prohibition on the use of force and the way in which that principle is anchored in the Charter itself.

The fourth chapter assesses the practical side of UN peacekeeping. We provide an overview of all UN peacekeeping operations to date, as well as of the strengths and weaknesses of peacekeeping generally. We also address the role of the UN in relation to disarmament, arms control and prevention. Finally, two short case studies (the impact of international terrorism and the Iraq War) will be used to illustrate current challenges in the area of peacekeeping.

Chapter 5 is about the protection of human rights in the framework of the UN. As in Chapter 3, with peacekeeping, we here discuss the basic questions of the normative development, codification and definition of human rights.

In the sixth chapter, the practice of human rights protection and the relevant treaty bodies take centre stage. Newer approaches to the protection of human rights are discussed, along with so-called humanitarian interventions and international criminal jurisdiction.

Chapter 7 addresses an area of the UN that is often neglected because of the far higher profile (at least in the Western world) of peacekeeping and human rights. None the less, we argue, development work and efforts on environmental issues has also become a core task of the United Nations.

Chapter 8 moves on to consider the issue of reform, and in particular the necessity and prospects for change in relation to the areas described in the preceding chapters. Along with conceptual questions of the extent and limitations of the reformability of the various UN organizations, this chapter will introduce and analyse several concrete reform proposals.

In the final chapter, we attempt to pull all these strands together to produce a balance sheet of the work of the UN. This chapter raises the fundamental question of how possible it is to steer and direct international politics, introduces new concepts of global governance and multilateral co-operation; and assesses the prospects and outlook for the UN in the twenty-first century.

Overall, our central purpose is to provide an introduction to the UN's central fields of activities, to evaluate the chances of reform in these fields, and to discuss the role of the organization in international politics. The book is addressed primarily to students of the political and social sciences, but also to teachers and lecturers involved in political education as well as a broader circle of interested readers in politics, journalism and society at large. It is conceptualized in such a way that the most important organs, committees and mechanisms of the United Nations will be described in terms of their legal and institutional composition, but will also be subjected to a political science treatment of their strengths and weaknesses. Thus the book should be useful even to readers who are not yet well acquainted with the United Nations organization.

A review of the original German-language version of this book in the periodical *Vereinte Nationen* ('United Nations') concluded that the book 'conveys a clear and readable synopsis of the potentialities, advantages, weaknesses, and problems of the UN, and it is to be presumed that anyone who has read this book is now in possession of a well-founded understanding of the United Nations'. If this is in fact the case, then we, the authors, have achieved our goal: to produce a challenging but readable, comprehensive but not too detail-obsessed, critical but not unfair, political science analysis of the organization with all its potential and limitations.

In 2004, this book went into its third edition in the German language, and has enjoyed a widespread and positive reception in the German-speaking world. For this English version, the book has been further revised and substantially recast in line with the rather different style and approach of Anglo-American textbooks. We very much hope that the book is as well received in the English-speaking world! We shall of course, be grateful for any suggestions for improvement or for any information that could be useful in preparing the next edition – and particularly for any feedback arising from the use of this book on university and other courses.

The English edition has a companion website at www.palgrave.com/politics/gareis-varwick which includes links to other relevant websites: the complete text of the UN charter; a full list of member states with their accession dates and current budget contributions; and more detailed information on the United Nations system and its constituent organizations. We also plan to provide updated material reflecting substantial changes in the organization and functioning of the UN since completion of the book.

We would like to express our heartfelt thanks to Lindsay Cohn, who not only transformed the German manuscript into idiomatic English with great dedication and competence, but whose understanding of political science has also contributed to the clarity and readability of the content.

SVEN BERNHARD GAREIS
JOHANNES VARWICK

List of Abbreviations

ACABQ	Advisory Committee for Administrative and Budgetary Questions
ASG	Assistant Secretary General
AWACS	Airborne Warning and Control System
CAT	Convention against Torture
CC	Committee on Conferences
CCPR	Committee under the International Covenant on Civil and Political Rights
CEDAW	Convention on the Elimination of all Forms of Discrimination against Women
CERD	Convention on the Elimination of all Forms of Racism
CPC	Committee on Planning and Coordination
CRC	Convention on the Rights of the Child
CSD	Commission on Sustainable Development
CTBT	Comprehensive Test Ban Treaty
DPA	Department of Political Affairs
DPKO	Department of Peacekeeping Operations
ECA	Economic Commission for Africa
ECE	Economic Commission for Europe
ECLAC	Economic Commission for Latin America and the Caribbean
ECOMOG	Economic Community of West African States-Mobile Group
ECOSOC	Economic and Social Council
ECOWAS	Economic Community of West African States
ECPS	Executive Committee for Peace and Security
ESCAW	Economic Commission for Western Asia
EU	European Union
FAO	Food and Agriculture Organization
GA	General Assembly
GEF	Global Environmental Facility
IAEA	International Atomic Energy Agency
IBRD	International Bank for Reconstruction and Development
ICC	International Criminal Court
ICCPR	International Covenant on Civil and Political Rights
ICESCR	International Covenant on Economic, Social and Cultural Rights
ICJ	International Court of Justice
ICTR	International Criminal Tribunal for Rwanda
ICTY	International Criminal Tribunal for the Former Yugoslavia
IFAD	International Fund for Agricultural Development
IFOR	Implementation Force

IGO	International Governmental Organization
ILC	International Law Commission
ILO	International Labour Organization
IMF	International Monetary Fund
INGO	International Nongovernmental Organization
INSTRAW	International Research and Training Institute for the Advancement of Women
ISAF	International Security Assistance Force
KFOR	Kosovo-Force (NATO)
MIGA	Multilateral Investment Guarantee Agency
MINUCI	United Nations Mission in Cote d'Ivoire
MINURSO	United Nations Mission for the Referendum in Western Sahara
MONUC	United Nations Organization Mission in the Democratic Republic of Congo
MoU	Memorandum of Understanding
NATO	North Atlantic Treaty Organization
NGO	Nongovernmental Organization
OAS	Organization of American States
OAU	Organization of African Unity
OCHA	Office for the Coordination of Humanitarian Affairs
OECD	Organisation for Economic Co-operation and Development
OIOS	Office of Internal Oversight Services
ONUC	United Nations Operation in the Congo
P5	Permanent Five
PKO	Peacekeeping Operation
RDMHQ	Rapidly Deployable Mission Headquarters
SC	Security Council
SFOR	Stabilization Force
SHIRBRIG	Stand-by High Readiness Brigade
SRSG	Special Representative of the Secretary General
UNAMIR	United Nations Assistance Mission for Rwanda
UNAMSIL	United Nations Mission in Sierra Leone
UNAVEM	United Nations Angola Verification Mission
UNCED	United Nations Conference on Environment and Deployment
UNCHS	United Nations Centre for Human Settlement
UNCRO	United Nations Confidence Restoration Operation in Croatia
UNCTAD	United Nations Conference on Trade and Development
UNDCP	United Nations International Drug Control Programme
UNDG	United Nations Development Group
UNDOF	United Nations Disengagement Observer Force
UNDP	United Nations Development Programme
UNEF	United Nations Emergency Force
UNEP	United Nations Environmental Programme
UNESCO	United Nations Educational, Scientific and Cultural Organization

UNFICYP	United Nations Peacekeeping Force in Cyprus
UNEPA	United Nations Fund for Population Activities
UNHCHR	United Nations High Commissioner for Human Rights
UNHCR	United Nations High Commissioner for Refugees
UNICEF	United Nations Children's Fund
UNIDIR	United Nations Institute for Disarmament Research
UNIDO	United Nations Industrial Development Organization
UNIFEM	United Nations Development Fund for Women
UNIFIL	United Nations Interim Force in Lebanon
UNIKOM	United Nations Iraq-Kuwait Observation Mission
UNITAR	United Nations Institute for Training and Research
UNMEE	United Nations Mission in Ethiopia and Eritrea
UNMIBH	United Nations Mission in Bosnia and Herzegovina
UNMIK	United Nations Interim Administration Mission in Kosovo
UNMOGIP	United Nations Military Observer Group in India and Pakistan
UNMOP	United Nations Mission of Observers in Prevlaka
UNMOVIC	United Nations Monitoring, Verification and Inspection Commission (Iraq)
UNO	United Nations Organization
UNOMIG	United Nations Observer Mission in Georgia
UNPREDEP	United Nations Preventive Deployment Force
UNPROFOR	United Nations Protection Force
UNRWA	United Nations Relief and Works Agency for Palestine Refugees in the Near East
UNSAS	United Nations Stand-by Arrangement System
UNSCOM	United Nations Special Commission (Iraq)
UNTAC	United Nations Transitional Authority in Cambodia
USA	United States of America
UNTAES	United Nations Transitional Administration for Eastern Slavonia, Baranja and Wstern Smyrnum
UNTAET	United Nations Transitional Administration in East Timor
UNTAG	United Nations Transition Assistance Group
UNTSO	United Nations Truce Supervision Organization
UNU	United Nations University
USG	Under Secretary-General
WEU	Western European Union
WFP	World Food Programme
WHO	World Health Organization
WMO	World Meteorological Organization
WTO	World Trade Organization

1

The United Nations System

The United Nations Organization (UN) is an international organization bringing together 191 states which have committed themselves voluntarily to a mutual obligation to safeguard peace and humane living conditions for the peoples of the world. The UN reached this level of membership – an unusually high one for an international organization – in September 2002 with the accessions of Switzerland and East Timor (see Table 1.1). These accessions finally allowed the UN to realize its claims of universality for its goals, norms and principles, as even the one very small and exceptional state (the Vatican) which does not officially belong to the UN still engages itself in multiple ways as an active non-member.

The Charter of the United Nations was signed in June 1945 by fifty founding members. Poland, which had not been able to participate in the founding conference, later entered as the fifty-first founding member. Since the UN's foundation, a further 140 states have become members, and this expansion of the membership has had fundamental effects on its work (see Table 1.1). New issues such as development were drawn into its remit, new organs, organizations and programmes were created, and the developing countries reached a two-thirds majority in the General Assembly (GA). The main reasons for this increase in membership lie in the increase in the number of states following decolonialization (through the 1970s), and in the establishment of a new international order following the end of the Cold War in the 1980s and 1990s. Moreover, during the East–West conflict, there were often disputes over the accession of any given state, so that many applications for admission came to grief on the alternating vetoes of the USA and the USSR. Such blocked states often obtained admission only during phases of eased political tension. Considering the possibility of further disintegration and creation of states, the possibility that UN member rolls may increase further cannot be entirely ruled out.

Acquisition and loss of membership are covered in Articles 3–6 of the Charter. According to these articles, 'all peace-loving states' may become members. The content of the concept of 'peace-loving' is not, however, defined any more closely, and is thus only minimally useful as far as political practice goes. So states may become members as long as they 'accept the obligations contained in the present Charter, and, in the judgment of the Organization, are able and willing to carry out these obligations'. No right of exit or withdrawal is provided for in the Charter, but Indonesia did withdraw from the UN from March 1965 to September 1966 – the

TABLE 1.1
UN membership

Founding members	51 states
Joined 1945–54	9 states
Joined 1955–74	78 states
Joined 1975–84	21 states
Joined 1985–2002	32 states
Total members 2004	**191 states**

Source: Information compiled from United Nations website.

only country to have done so. The General Assembly may, upon the recommendation of the Security Council and if certain conditions have been met, withdraw a country's right to exercise the rights of membership for a certain period of time. The GA could even foreclose a country's chances of membership, although this has never happened in practice.

State admission into the United Nations follows formally on a decision of the General Assembly based on the recommendation of the Security Council. Only sovereign states may become members. Thus it is that newly-emerged states consider admission to the United Nations the most visible symbol of their statehood. Almost unavoidably, however, disputes have arisen continually about what qualifies a state for admission, or what form a state must take to be entitled to the right to enter the United Nations. One example is the representation of China, which took place for quite some time through the Republic of China (Taiwan), but which – following a decision of the General Assembly in 1971 – has since been administered through the People's Republic of China. Another example of problems with membership was the refusal of the General Assembly between 1974 and 1994 to recognize the government of South Africa as the legitimate representative of that country on the grounds of its policies of racial discrimination (apartheid). In Germany's case, it was not until September 1973 that the admission of two German states, the Federal Republic of Germany (FRG) and the German Democratic Republic (GDR), was even possible. The GDR's membership lapsed when it was unified with the Federal Republic in October 1990. Further problems arise out of the dissolution of states or through secession, when 'pieces of states' demand sovereignty under international law. The modalities of accession are inadequately regulated in the Charter, but legal commentaries as well as countless decisions of the International Court of Justice and other international treaties and agreements offer assistance in the interpretation of those regulations that do exist. Nonetheless, it is in the nature of international law that recognition is primarily a political right, the practical implementation of which often runs into limitations. The international system has nothing at its disposal comparable to the binding legal instruments that a national political system enjoys.

It has already been mentioned that the work of the UN is based on a broad conceptualization of the notion of peace, which goes beyond the mere prevention of war to the improvement of the humanitarian and social conditions of mankind, the strengthening of international law, and extensive concerns of development. Thus the UN Charter contains a number of regulations according to which the principal organs can create appropriate secondary or special organs for the realization of their tasks, or can work together with other organizations and actors. It is in this way that a densely interwoven fabric of institutions and co-operative relationships has arisen around the UN in the course of its history, for which the term 'the UN system' has found its way into the lexicon. The elements of this system, which differentiates itself according to various functional and regional criteria, can be subdivided into two categories:

(i)   The special organs, programmes and regional arrangements created by the UN itself and assigned to the authority of the General Assembly, the Social and Economic Council, or the Secretariat; and

(ii) The specialized agencies: independent bodies that have bound themselves to the UN through agreements, which enjoy legal standing and which fall into a 'family of organizations'.

This system is rounded out by manifold, more-or-less formalized connections to other areas and actors, such as international civil society, the world of business, and the world of science. Thus there are approximately 2,000 NGOs registered with the Social and Economic Council with consultative status, and the special organs and programmes maintain fully independent co-operative relationships with committees of experts and state as well as non-state institutions worldwide. The system of the United Nations is a dynamic image, difficult to define precisely and defying even experts to maintain an overview of the whole.

   Along with their differing legal natures, the participating institutions also have different competencies. This variety of form and function makes both the vertical steering and horizontal co-operation of their work anything but easy. Complexity, redundancy and at least partial inefficiency are among the most common accusations laid at the UN's door. These accusations, however, tend to overlook two things:

(i)   This convoluted structure did not emerge on its own, but was produced through the decisions of the most important actors in this system, the member states. It is their responsibility to adjust what was seen as appropriate under other political circumstances to the challenges of the present and the future, even if it means closing significant interest gaps – for example, between industrial and developing countries; and

(ii) In the course of nearly six decades, a unique system has arisen which offers a forum for the common analysis of problems and the development of solution options for every ever-more-global challenge that presents itself. It is less the deficiencies of the system that prevent its decisive use by the member states than it is their relatively weak will to engage in multilateral co-operation.

Thus, when one sees the terms 'UN system' or 'UN family' in the technical literature, this is correct in reference to the description of the extensive network of institutions the UN has cultivated over the course of its history. Such a description,
however, obscures the lack of co-ordination within and among these networks, as
well as the real power structures through which the member states play a decisive
role. The UN system is therefore best characterized as a 'complicated-diffuse
structure', which 'is characterized more as a network of very loosely-coupled
institutions which act autonomously – some *de jure*, some *de facto*' (Hüfner 2002,
p. 636).

A Short History of the United Nations

At the time of writing, the United Nations Organization can look back on nearly
sixty years of history in a world full of turbulent change. The emergence of the UN
in the end-phase of the Second World War was tied up inextricably with the experiences of that conflict. The mounting East–West conflict, however, made it
largely impossible for the organization to be engaged effectively in its original
core task of maintaining international peace: its primary decision-making body,
the Security Council, was trapped in a de facto permanent gridlock because of the
antagonism of the superpowers. Thus, for decades, such deep-rooted processes as
decolonization, and the conflicts accompanying or following from it, stood in the
shadow of the Cold War. It was also during this time, however, that the UN experienced a continuous increase in its membership, institutional expansion, differentiation in its fields of activity, and the development of new political instruments in
the realms of, for example, peace-maintenance and the protection of human rights.

It was not until the USA–USSR détente and the Cold War's eventual end,
however, that the UN was able to realize its claims to universality for its norms and
values, and achieved the status of a true world organization. The self-destruction
of the USSR and the rest of the socialist bloc created yet another wave of appli-
cants for membership, the Security Council experienced an unprecedented freedom of action, and the UN's spheres of responsibility and regulation expanded
dynamically until they included numerous domestic affairs of the member states.
This explosive increase in the number and types of tasks, taking place in the
context of globalization, pushed the United Nations to the very limits of its capabilities. Following the failures of a few of the larger peacekeeping missions,
phases of marginalization alternated with phases of brief renaissance. Since 11
September 2001 and the 2003 Gulf War, the United Nations has stood at a decisive
point in its development: it must, with the support of its member states, master the
institutional and normative reforms necessary for its continual functioning in a
complex world. Should it fail in this undertaking, its seventh decade may very well
be its last.

This short history of the United Nations will present an overview of the major
phases of the organization's development. It should be noted that such generaliza-
tions are never exact, and that the various phases often overlap in some ways. This

historical summary will avoid comprehensive analysis and discussion, as Chapters 2 to 8 go into the genesis and historical context of the UN's various areas of responsibility in much more detail.

Phase 1: The Founding (1941–45)

Thought had been given to the possible founding of a world organization long before the Second World War. In view of the unabated aggression of the German Reich, Italy, and Japan, US President Franklin D. Roosevelt was convinced as early as 1937 that another huge war was unavoidable, and that the USA would have to be involved in it. The isolationist mood of large segments of the American population, however, required the creation of a political framework in which American involvement – even with the likelihood of great sacrifice – might find widespread acceptance. The lessons emerging from the fate of the League of Nations were an important point of contact. That organization, founded at the end of the First World War in an attempt to eliminate war and violence gradually from international relations, had been defunct for many years, and had been in no position to oppose the impending catastrophe of the Second World War. Many weaknesses of the League were responsible for this state of affairs, from inadequate normative provisions, through a lack of sufficient authority, to the unhappy linkage of peacekeeping tasks with the implementation of the Treaties of Versailles, Trianon and Neuilly. The decisive element, however, was that the League was never able to bring all the great powers into its Permanent Council to take responsibility for world peace. Germany and Japan – permanent members of the Council – left the organization in the 1930s, and the Soviet Union was expelled in 1939 after its attack on Finland. The USA, despite the fact that the whole project had been initiated largely by President Wilson, never became a member.

Roosevelt wanted to make sure that the USA did not repeat this mistake. In the summer of 1941, he proposed to the British prime minister, Winston Churchill, that a security organization for monitoring the conquered enemy states should be set up, and that this organization should not belong to the USA alone, but should be led in concert with the United Kingdom. Churchill anticipated problems from the rest of the states about an organization led by two powers only. He therefore supported some version of a further-developed League of Nations with a strengthened representation for the various regions of the world. In the Atlantic Charter, presented by Roosevelt and Churchill on 14 October 1941, the functional tasks of a future order of world peace were outlined clearly, but the organization that was to create this world order was mentioned only indirectly in its eighth point: 'Since no future peace can be maintained if land, sea or air armaments continue to be employed by nations which threaten, or may threaten, aggression outside of their frontiers, they believe, pending the establishment of a wider and permanent system of general security, that the disarmament of such nations is essential'. After the entry of the USA into the Second World War, in the 'Declaration by United Nations' of 1 January 1942, a further twenty-six countries joined themselves to the Atlantic Charter, obligating themselves at the same time to support the alliance against Germany, Italy and Japan. This declaration, too, avoided a concrete announcement of the creation of a new institution. The self-definition of this group as the 'United Nations' was, however, to become the name of the institution.

Whereas in 1941 Roosevelt believed firmly in a post-war order led by the United Kingdom and the USA, by 1942 he was willing to add the Soviet Union and China to the circle of powers responsible for world peace (Russell, 1958, p. 96). He still believed that the greatest threat lay in the enemy states of the Second World War, and that these could be controlled through the co-operation of the 'Four Policemen'. Churchill objected that future co-operation with the Soviet Union would prove very difficult, and that a China weakened by civil war and Japanese occupation would not be able to meet its responsibilities (Luard, 1982, vol. I, p. 19). However, Churchill's vision of a more strongly regionalized organization (he suggested regional councils for Europe and Asia under the leadership of a common organization) was not implemented. In October 1943, at the conference of foreign ministers in Moscow, China was in fact co-opted into the circle of the four responsible powers. In their concluding declaration, the four powers stated '[t]hat they recognize the necessity of establishing at the earliest practicable date a general international organization, based on the principle of the sovereign equality of all peace-loving states, and open to membership by all such states, large and small, for the maintenance of international peace and security' (Joint Four Nation Declaration, 1943, Point 4).

The Moscow Conference was the breakthrough point in the creation of the United Nations. Following the Teheran Conference of November 1943, the USA as the lead-state drafted an Outline Plan for the world organization, which placed the creation of an executive council – later to be called the Security Council – at the centre of the decision-making mechanisms. In a further step, over the course of 1944 the US State Department developed Tentative Proposals for a General Organization, and cleared them with the other three powers. Among the most important of these proposals were the expansion of the permanent members' circle to include France, and the inclusion of regional arrangements in the collective security system. These Tentative Proposals then formed the basis for the Dumbarton Oaks Conference, where from 21 August to 9 October 1944, experts met to produce the first draft of a statute (for a comprehensive treatment, see Hilderbrand, 1990). It was in fact possible for the powers to reach agreement on a large number of the proposed provisions at Dumbarton Oaks, and these were then incorporated into the United Nations Charter.

A few controversial points were left open, which had to be negotiated personally by Roosevelt, Churchill and Stalin at Yalta in February 1945. In view of the increasingly evident dominance of the American camp in the organization, the Soviet Union insisted upon the inclusion of its sixteen unified Republics as equal members. A compromise was made in which the Ukraine and Byelorussia (now Belarus) received their own memberships, and the voting procedure in the Security Council was arranged so that, for non-procedural questions, a quorum of seven out of ten votes, including all five permanent members, was necessary. This Yalta formula formed the basis of the Permanent Five's right of veto. The Soviet Union was even able to insist that the decision on whether the question at hand was procedural or not was also subject to the veto. Furthermore, with respect to the issue of limiting the right of veto to situations where the member was not affected directly by the decision, Roosevelt and Churchill were unable to win their point. Only in processes of peaceful dispute resolution under Chapter VI are permanent members expected to withhold their votes in matters pertaining to their own affairs. Finally, the American initiative to anchor human rights in the Charter was wrecked on Stalin's opposition at Yalta, as he refused to recognize any connection between human rights and world peace.

After the Yalta agreements, four of the five permanent members (France was insulted at its non-inclusion in Yalta) invited the forty-five states that had opposed Germany and Japan in the war to the founding conference of the United Nations in San Francisco. Poland was allowed to enter as the fifty-first founding member once its political representation was sorted out to the satisfaction of the Soviet Union. At this meeting, lasting from 25 April to 26 June 1945, the double privilege of the Big Five through permanent representation and right of veto came under particular criticism. The great powers made it very clear from the beginning, however, that this was the price for their participation in the responsibility for world peace. With such a choice set before them – either to accept the elevated position of the Permanent Five or to give up the project of a world organization for peace – the founding states resolved to accept the lesser evil. The Charter, with nineteen chapters and 111 articles of detailed provisions, came into force on 24 October 1945 with the deposition of the Soviet Union's instruments of ratification.

This Charter represented the success of a remarkable compromise, achieved in the exceptional context of the Second World War. The UN thus exhibits much stronger egalitarian tendencies and characteristics borrowed from the League of Nations than Roosevelt had intended. This evolution from an efficiently-run security institution to an inter-state organization with a broad spectrum of tasks was also carried along by the growing recognition – expressed early on by Churchill – that the level of agreement necessary among the Permanent Five for the sake of taking responsibility for world peace would in fact be nearly impossible to achieve. The looming contradiction between democratic and socialist camps threw too heavy a shadow over the negotiations for the United Nations. Rather than burdening themselves with such responsibility, the great powers concentrated on making it impossible for the rules of the collective security system to be used against them. Under the auspices of the Cold War, this led to stagnation in important areas such as the Security Council. On the other hand, this state of affairs also ensured that the United Nations could not be instrumentalized directly for the East–West conflict. Had the organization been put to such a test, it would surely have collapsed. Thus the UN was in many ways prevented from meaningful action of any kind, but was in some areas able to develop initiatives and instruments that would never have come to pass without such an organization.

Phase II: Start-up and Stagnation in the Cold War (1945–54)

Even before the Charter came into force, the UN had begun work on its organizational and institutional formation. A preparatory committee including all member states was created, but the important conceptual work was done by an executive committee of fourteen states, including the Permanent Five. The structure of the General Assembly was quickly agreed upon, as it was relatively simple to fall back on the model of the League of Nations, and in addition six main committees were created. Against the wishes of the Soviet Union, which was in favour of a decentralized secretariat structure for each of the main bodies, a single centralized UN Secretariat was created. After a few East–West skirmishes, the Norwegian foreign minister, Trygve Lie, was installed as the first UN Secretary-General on 1 February 1946. In the course of choosing the Secretary-General, it was also agreed that this office should not be occupied by a representative of any of the Permanent Five. Following the dissolution of the League of Nations on 18 April 1946, the UN took over not only its offices in Geneva, but also its social and economic working panels. Special agreements were made with pre-existing specialized agencies such as the International Labour Organization (ILO), while others, such as the Food and Agriculture Organization (FAO), were newly created. The 'first-aid' organizations, such as UNICEF (1946) and the Economic Commission for Europe (ECE) (1947), were also founded. After the inclusion of human rights in the Charter failed because of the opposition of the Soviet Union, the UN Human Rights Commission (1946) began to develop an International Bill of Human Rights which would be independent of the Charter. The first milestone was reached on 10 December 1948, when the General Declaration on Human Rights was passed as Resolution 217 A (III).

The maiden session of the General Assembly took place on 10 January 1946 in London, at which point the question of where the organization would have its main base had still not been decided. Most of the European states wanted the new organization to be anchored in Europe. Secretary-General Lie, however, pointing to the tragic fate of the League of Nations, supported a completely new start in the USA. This would also, he hoped, tie the Americans into the organization more tightly: 'The challenging question of the future was how to secure the fullest possible US participation in whatever international organization might emerge. A repetition of the tragedy of the League of Nations, stemming not least from the US's refusal to join, could not be permitted' (Lie, 1954, p. 54). After a discussion lasting more than a month and sometimes becoming very dramatic indeed, the decision was induced by a gift from John D. Rockefeller, Jr. He declared himself willing to provide the sum of US$8.5 million for the purchase of real estate on New York's East River. The offer was accepted, and the following years saw the erection of the UN Headquarters. Until their first session in the new buildings, in October 1952, the General Assembly and Secretariat were housed temporarily at Lake Success in New York State.

Several of the organizational decisions in this initial phase of UN activity were already showing signs of the influence of the growing East–West conflict. In view of the West's clear majority in the General Assembly, where there was, of course, no veto, that bloc was able to push through many of its programmes. The situation was different, however, in the Security Council. There, vetoes and threats of vetoes were a constant presence in every discussion (Patil, 1992). In the Security Council, it became very clear just how limited the justification for Roosevelt's optimism about the responsibilities of the 'Global Policemen' had really been.

The first major conflict emerged in the debate over the admission of new members. Article 4(1) provides that 'Membership in the United Nations is open to all other peace-loving states which accept the obligations contained in the present Charter and, in the judgment of the Organization are able and willing to carry out these obligations.' The decision based on these conditions is, according to Article 4(2), to be made by the General Assembly on the recommendation of the Security Council. Therefore every Permanent Member also possesses a practical veto right over the admission of new members. In the years following the organization's founding, the Superpowers watched particularly closely to make sure that the other camp did not enjoy any major increases in member numbers. Thus only a small group of states was admitted, including Afghanistan, Iceland, Sweden and Thailand (1946); Yemen and Pakistan (1947); and Burma (1948), which were regarded by both sides as being neutral. Several other states failed repeatedly in their overtures. Israel, which was admitted in 1949, was the last state allowed in for a period of six years. Only after 1955 was the blockade at last overcome, and the way opened for a stream of new members.

Conflicts also developed very quickly over the zones around the fault-lines between the two blocs. In Iran, Greece and Czechoslovakia, the Soviet Union attempted to extend its sphere of influence. Finally, in the Berlin crisis of 1948/9, it challenged the Western powers directly. The UN offered mediation services, started its own initiatives and played an altogether constructive role, but without exercising any decisive influence on the course of the political process between the two Great Powers. For the conflict in Palestine, the UN created cease-fire and observer commissions (the UN Truce Supervision Organization – the oldest UN peace mission still functioning – evolved out of the cease-fire commission created in 1948). This, together with the UN Military Observer Group in India and Pakistan, UNMOGIP, created in 1949 in Kashmir, constituted the foundation for a concept of peacekeeping on the edges of the Superpowers' spheres of interest which respected their sovereignty, but was none the less relatively successful.

The young collective security system faced a difficult ordeal on 25 June 1950, when North Korea invaded South Korea. The Security Council met immediately and was able on that same day to pass Resolution 82, which demanded more than just the 'immediate cessation of hostilities' and the withdrawal of the North Korean armed forces behind the 38th parallel: in Section III, the Security Council required all member states 'to render every assistance to the United Nations in the execution of this resolution and to refrain from giving assistance to the North Korean authorities' (S/RES/82, 25 June 1950). The Resolution was passed with nine 'yes' votes and Yugoslavia's abstention. The Soviet Union was not present at this 473rd meeting of the Security Council, as it was boycotting the organization in protest at the General Assembly's decision to recognize the nationalist Chinese government – which had fled to Taiwan after the Chinese Civil War – instead of the communist People's Republic government as the legitimate representative of China. Disregarding the Soviet absence, the Security Council determined two days later to use force against North Korea: in Resolution 83, it recommended 'that the Members of the United Nations furnish such assistance to the Republic of Korea as may be necessary to repel the armed attack and to restore international peace and security in the area' (S/RES/83, 27 June 1950).

Thus the collective security mechanism of the UN was set in motion for the first time. This was not done, however, according to the provisions of the relevant Chapter VII, but rather in the form of a Security Council recommendation legitimizing the use of military force. Furthermore, when the Soviet Union returned to take over the rotating presidency of the Security Council on 1 August 1950, the blockading began. As President of the Council, the Soviet Union was able to hinder votes through creative use of the order of business, and in September 1950 it began to use its veto on all Korea resolutions. None the less, on an American initiative, on 3 November 1950, the General Assembly passed its famous Uniting for Peace Resolution (A/RES/377 V), which stated in the very first paragraph that

if the Security Council, because of lack of unanimity of the permanent members, fails to exercise its primary responsibility for the maintenance of international peace and security in any case where there appears to be a threat to the peace, breach of the peace, or act of aggression, the General Assembly shall consider the matter immediately with a view to making appropriate recommendations to Members for collective measures, including in the case of a breach of the peace or act of aggression the use of armed force when necessary, to maintain or restore international peace and security.

A commission was then set up, the activities of which did finally contribute to the ending of a bloody war that had stretched out over three years (on the role of the UN in the Korean War, see Luard, 1982, vol. I, pp. 229 et seq.).

This action heralded a power struggle between the General Assembly and the Security Council. After all, according to Article 12(1) of the Charter, the General Assembly enjoys only a subsidiary competence to address issues of international conflict with which the Security Council is already occupied. The Uniting for Peace Resolution threw serious doubt on the validity of this rule, and it has in fact over the years lost all significance. The General Assembly's right to give recommendations is now essentially uncontested, and has been confirmed in ten Emergency Special Sessions called on the basis of GA Resolution 377. On the other hand, the hopes the USA nurtured at the time of establishing the General Assembly as an alternative decision-making forum for those times when the Security Council was gridlocked were not fulfilled. The authority of the General Assembly has never gone beyond the making of recommendations. Even the authority taken by the General Assembly in the Suez Crisis (1956) or in Irian Jaya (1962) to send peacekeeping troops immediately, became the Security Council's affair.

For a time at least, under the auspices of a US-friendly majority, the General Assembly was in fact able to act as a corrective for the Security Council. The Western bloc's interest in such a function for the General Assembly disappeared immediately, however, when the decolonization process began to cause a shift in the balance of power.

Phase III: Decolonization and the Emergence of the 'Third World' (1955–74)

The death of Joseph Stalin in March 1953 had led to a sort of détente between the two Superpowers, including improved co-operation, and thus also to a partial overcoming of the stagnation in the United Nations. The Soviet Union began to co-operate in a number of UN organizations, such as the ILO and UNESCO, but maintained its distance with respect to others – for example, the World Bank Group. A series of international conferences had led to a far more relaxed international climate, and agreement over the status of Austria, along with the 1955 Geneva Summit Conference of the USA, the USSR, the United Kingdom and France brought the great powers into closer dialogue with one another. This new willingness to co-operate found its most important expression in the acceptance of several candidates for UN membership. By the beginning of the 1960s, the number of members had climbed to 118, necessitating an increase in the number of non-permanent members on the Security Council from six to ten. This was achieved through a General Assembly regulation (A/RES 1991A (XVIII) of 17 December 1963), which came into force in 1965.

The decisive movement of the UN's second decade was, of course, the independence of numerous colonies, particularly in the southern hemisphere. As a consequence, the affairs of these new states began to take up central importance in the work of the United Nations – its funds, programmes and specialized agencies. The changing balance of majorities in the General Assembly ensured that the interests of the developing countries would be taken into account appropriately in the organizational and institutional development of the UN. The establishment of a number of subsidiary organs focused in particular on development issues (for example, the World Food Programme (WFP, 1961); the UN Conference on Trade and Development (UNCTAD, 1965); and the UN Industrial Development Organization (UNIDO, 1966)) also arrived during this period. The political organization of the developing countries also progressed significantly: in April 1955, in Bandung, Indonesia, representatives of a group of twenty-nine Afro-Asian states met. This meeting became the platform for the Non-Aligned Movement (NAM) which was to form itself six years later at the Belgrade Conference. At the time of writing comprising 113 members, the NAM is numerically the strongest group of states within the UN, and without its support no decisions affecting the organization itself can have any hope of being passed. The Bandung Conference was also the starting point for the emergence of the so-called 'Third World' of developing countries, which joined the 'First World' Western Bloc and the 'Second World' Eastern Bloc. Beginning in 1961, the UN initiated its first 'Development Decade', which was followed immediately by a second, starting in

1971. The General Assembly's recognition of the communist People's Republic of China on 25 October 1971 can be seen as an important step in this context. With that decision, the permanent seat in the Security Council was removed from Taiwan after twenty-five years and transferred to Beijing.

The role and function of the United Nations in the countless conflicts plaguing this period was extremely dependent on the constellations of Superpower interests. In October/November 1956, in the Suez Crisis, France, the United Kingdom and Israel employed armed force against Egypt following Egyptian President Nasser's nationalization of the Suez Canal, even though the Security Council had declined to label Egypt's actions a threat to peace. After draft resolutions for ending the conflict failed on the French and British vetoes, Yugoslavia proposed the calling of the first Emergency Special Session of the General Assembly based on the Uniting for Peace Resolution. This session produced demands for an immediate cease-fire and the withdrawal of the British, French and Israeli forces. The day after this agreement was reached, Secretary-General Dag Hammarskjöld proposed the creation of a peacekeeping force to monitor the cease-fire. On 4 November 1956, the General Assembly determined to send the United Nations Emergency Force (UNEF I) to act as a buffer between the conflicting parties. Thus the most important peacekeeping instrument of the United Nations, the 'blue-helmet missions', was called into being. For eleven years, UNEF I succeeded in maintaining relative stability in Sinai. When Nasser demanded the withdrawal of the blue-helmets in 1967, the Six Day War followed on their heels.

A second spectacular blue-helmet mission was not far behind. In the summer of 1960, a province (Katanga) within the recently independent former Belgian colony of Congo in turn declared itself independent. Belgium supported Katanga, and Congolese President Patrice Lumumba called on the United Nations for help. Secretary-General Hammarskjöld recommended the undertaking of an *Opération des Nations Unies pour le Congo* (ONUC). This operation did succeed in negotiating the withdrawal of Belgian forces, but was then drawn into the maze of Congolese domestic politics, which were sliding quickly towards civil war. It was only after serious loss of life and with massive intervention on the part of the USA that the Congo was eventually unified. Secretary-General Hammarskjöld, who had supported this controversial mission in the Security Council and in the third Emergency Special Session of the General Assembly, and had engaged himself actively in its implementation, was killed when his plane crashed in the Congo on 12 September 1961. Although ONUC was considered an overall success, the mission had in fact thrown not only the idea of blue-helmet missions but also the entire UN organization into a serious crisis. The Soviet Union in particular, but also a large number of other states, refused to pay their regular contributions following this unusual mission, thus bringing the organization to the edge of financial ruin.

When the Soviet Union crushed the uprising in Hungary in 1956, and during what was probably the most dangerous episode of the entire post-war period, the 1961/2 Cuban Missile Crisis, on the other hand, the United Nations was largely powerless. Although the General Assembly called its second Emergency Special

Session because of a Soviet veto in the Security Council, and that session produced a number of declarations and recommendations, it could not influence the course of events. The same was true of the Cuban Missile Crisis, during which Secretary-General U Thant sought to bring both sides closer together without a loss of face. It was none the less clear that it had become impossible for an organization such as the UN to act as a mediator between the Superpowers. This limited influence also evinced itself in the many-faceted disarmament and arms control efforts with which the UN was constantly occupied through General Assembly panels. The breakthroughs (for example, the Non-Proliferation Treaty of 1968–70) and the important talks on strategic arms limitations (for example, SALT I and II) were all affairs of the Superpowers.

Phase IV: The Dominance of the North–South Conflict (1975–84)

For a long time, the East–West opposition had constituted the central world conflict. With the numerical increase in the number of states from the 'Third World', however, which was quickly approaching a two-thirds majority in the General Assembly, this group of states also developed a much stronger self-consciousness. The North–South conflict, in which questions of a just world economic order and a balancing of the interests of industrialized and developing countries stood at the top of the agenda, began to have phases where it overshadowed even the East–West conflict. Besides basic demands for a New International Economic Order, these states' efforts found their most potent expression in the Charter of Economic Rights and Duties of States, adopted by the General Assembly in 1974 (A/RES/39/163). Article 1 of this Charter states that the General Assembly

> decides to undertake a thorough and systematic review of the implementation of the Charter of Economic Rights and Duties of States, taking into account the evolution of all the economic, social, legal and other factors related to the principles upon which the Charter is based and to its purpose, in order to identify the most appropriate actions for the implementation of the Charter that would lead to lasting solutions to the grave economic problems of developing countries within the framework of the United Nations.

The dominance thus attributed to the Group of 77 – a sort of labour union for developing countries – in both the General Assembly and several of the UN's funds, programmes, and specialized agencies, was met with serious criticism from the Western states. Some of these – above all the USA, as both the leading Western and leading economic state – reacted by withholding payments and contributions, and by withdrawing from certain specialized agencies such as the ILO and UNESCO. Furthermore, the UN was at the same time involved in a number of long-term conflicts, the most important of which were in the Middle East. In 1973, following on the 1967 Six Day War, a third attack on Israel was made. In its wake, new blue-helmet missions were begun in the Golan Heights (UNDOF, 1974) and in the Sinai Peninsula (UNEF, II, 1974–9). The partition of Cyprus also required a peacekeeping mission (UNFICYP, 1974), and in Lebanon in 1978, the UNIFIL was added to the list.

At the end of 1979, however, the Soviet invasion of Afghanistan once again made it clear to the world just how narrow the limits of its collective security system really were. The Security Council was gridlocked, and while the urgently-called special emergency session of the General Assembly condemned the aggression, it was still essentially powerless. The UN's fourth decade had begun with a hopeful explosion of multilateralism and co-operation, but as both sides of the North–South conflict continued to intensify the political-ideological opposition, and as the NATO decision to catch up on nuclear armaments led to a dramatic worsening of relations between East and West, the UN was left with very little room for manoeuvre. It was not until 1985 that a fundamental change in this situation took place, when Mikhail Gorbachev became Secretary-General of the Communist Party in the Soviet Union and there began a lasting thaw between the two blocs that led eventually to the end of the East–West conflict and opened up a playing field for the UN wider than any it had ever known.

Phase v: Renaissance, Crisis and Attempts at Reform (1985 to Present)

The final phase of UN history will be dealt with in very cursory fashion here, since its developments are the central topics of the following chapters of this book. The Superpowers' mutual approach to one another led to a strengthening of the central decision-making mechanism of the UN, namely the Security Council. The nearly habitual use of the veto became a thing of the past, although the veto itself by no means disappeared from the stage. The number of new peacekeeping missions matched the number of newly-emerging forms of conflict that began to appear all over the world following the end of the all-encompassing Cold War. Within the space of approximately fifteen years, the number of peacekeeping missions rose from fourteen to fifty-seven (as of March 2004). New tasks in the areas of post-conflict management or transitional situations (for example, in Namibia and Cambodia) required new concepts, but attempts at peace enforcement such as those in Somalia and Yugoslavia proved more difficult. The 1990–1 Gulf War for the liberation of Kuwait, conducted on the basis of a Security Council mandate, fuelled hopes for a new world order built on the foundation of the UN. World Conferences on every imaginable global issue followed one another in rapid succession, from the rights of the child (New York, 1991), sustainable development and protection of the global environment (Rio de Janeiro, 1992), human rights (Vienna, 1993), women's rights (Beijing, 1995), and all the way to world population (Cairo, 1999).

Against the hopes of a more strongly multilateral world, however, stood a number of setbacks and crises. During the Kosovo conflict in 1999, a lack of willingness to cooperate in the Security Council led to the first lasting marginalization of the UN through NATO's unmandated action against the former Yugoslavia. Not least, the attacks of 11 September 2001 and the 2003 war in Iraq showed that the United Nations was in need of a fundamental reform of its decision-making structures, as well as both its normative and operational apparatus. Secretary-General Boutros Boutros-Ghali undertook the first steps toward reform in these areas. His successor, the current Secretary-General Kofi Annan, has made decisive progress since 1997 with reforms of the Secretariat and of the peacekeeping machinery. On the other hand, however, the member states' willingness to push through those innovations that are impossible without their consent – such as a reform of the Security Council – remains extremely weak.

This short look at the history of the United Nations has shown that the UN as an international organization is, and always has been, totally dependent on external conditions. These include first the international fault lines that determine and limit its work. Both the East–West and the North–South conflicts, as the two major international struggles since the founding of the United Nations, have defined the UN's scope of action and left structural impressions on the organization's work:

> The major industrialized countries tend to be interested in promoting order in the international system and managerial and financial efficiency in multilateral institutions like the UN. The developing countries tend to be more concerned with promoting justice, that is, achieving greater economic and political equity through redistribution of resources and enhanced participation in key decision-making (Mingst and Karns, 2000, p. 44).

The second important circumstance influencing the UN's work was the considerable difference among the various member states' expectations for the organization, and in particular the divergent understandings of how broad a scope of action nation-states should allow international organizations (see Chapter 2). Inter-governmental organizations (IGOs) such as the UN 'have been created largely to promote and protect the interests of states. They enhance the opportunities for participation and influence by small states, coalitions of states, and NGOs. They have also facilitated their own emergence as actors in the international system' (ibid.).

Since the end of the East–West conflict, the UN has found itself in the most demanding phase of its development to date. The chances and opportunities, but also the problems and challenges, facing the UN will be subjected to a deep and comprehensive analysis in the following pages. The reader who is truly familiar with the nearly six decades of the UN's history is far less likely to be concerned by the constantly fluctuating world political conditions influencing the organization's use. A look at the UN's history makes it very clear that phases of marginalization have alternated consistently with phases of renaissance. In fact, this history can be formulated very simply: crisis is always followed by renewal, until the next crisis comes along.

The UN Charter: Purposes and Principles

The Charter of the United Nations is the founding document of the world organization. It emerged as an answer to the failure of a weak League of Nations, which had enjoyed very little respect from its member states, and which had not been in a position to prevent the Second World War. This catastrophe, the dimensions of which overshadowed all previous wars, led necessarily to the contemplation of a new world order, one that would attempt to prevent further war altogether.

The Charter can be seen from many perspectives as an odd compromise and one that could only have been accomplished in the exceptional situation that followed the Second World War. The USA, the United Kingdom and the USSR accepted their different views on the proper form of the new world organization, which had emerged so clearly during the negotiations over the preliminary documents. They agreed on a concert of the great powers, into which they would co-opt two more participants, who were more the primary victims of the war rather than its victors. The overwhelming majority of the fifty-one founding member states were forced to recognize that the effective world organization they wished to have was achievable only at the cost of a dramatic lowering of expectations regarding the ideal of equal rights of sovereign states. The collective security system that emerged thus carried with it as a birth defect an internal contradiction: on the one hand, the aspiration was to subject states to a universal regime for securing peace, but on the other, the great powers were still unwilling to accept the rules of that regime for themselves. Notwithstanding, with the Charter of the United Nations, a sort of 'constitution of the world community' was created (Ress, 2002) which has shown itself to be robust and flexible enough not only to survive the political processes and changes of the second half of the twentieth century, but also to give it a generally accepted foundation of international law and an organizational framework. That said, the Charter's legal classification of the UN's goals and principles remains in many ways unclear. Neither the degree of bindingness nor the consequences for violations of the Charter are articulated precisely. No unambiguous prioritization of the goals can be inferred, and even the assignment of competencies to individual organs, and with that the regulation of responsibilities, remain open to interpretation. The 111 articles of the Charter, divided into nineteen chapters and a Preamble:

- Bind the behaviour of states in their intercourse with one another, and to an increasing degree in their internal politics, to norms and rules;
- As the organization's statute, clarify all legal questions relating to the organization, from the conditions of membership to the process of emendation;
- Define the competencies and modes of operation of the primary organs; and
- Limit the responsibilities of the organization with respect to the member states and other international bodies.

In the Preamble, which was first drafted and added to the Charter at the San Francisco Conference, general avowals of the future form of international relations are given in very lofty terms. 'We, the peoples of the United Nations' are determined to 'save succeeding generations from the scourge of war', to 'reaffirm faith in fundamental human rights, in the dignity and worth of the human person, in the equal rights of men and women and of nations large and small'.

Furthermore, it aims 'to establish conditions under which justice and respect for the obligations arising from treaties and other sources of international law can be maintained', as well as to 'promote social progress and better standards of life in larger freedom'. For these purposes, states should 'practice tolerance and live together in peace with one another as good neighbours', 'unite our strength to maintain international peace and security', 'ensure, by the acceptance of principles and the institution of methods, that armed force shall not be used, save in the common interest', and 'employ international machinery for the promotion of the economic and social advancement of all peoples'. The purposes of the United Nations are codified in Article 1 of the Charter in the form of normative obligations for the organization as well as for the member states that comprise it. The basic instruments and guidelines for action through which these goals are supposed to be realized are also named. Article 1 reads:

The purposes of the United Nations are:

(1) To maintain international peace and security, and to that end: to take effective collective measures for the prevention and removal of threats to the peace, and for the suppression of acts of aggression or other breaches of the peace, and to bring about by peaceful means, and in conformity with the principles of justice and international law, adjustment or settlement of international disputes or situations which might lead to a breach of the peace;

(2) To develop friendly relations among nations based on respect for the principle of equal rights and self-determination of peoples, and to take other appropriate measures to strengthen universal peace;

(3) To achieve international co-operation in solving international problems of an economic, social, cultural, or humanitarian character, and in promoting and encouraging respect for human rights and for fundamental freedoms for all without distinction as to race, sex, language, or religion; and

(4) To be a centre for harmonizing the actions of nations in the attainment of these common ends.

The primary goal of the United Nations is the maintenance of international peace and security, and all other goals are to serve this primary purpose, which in the end is the sole justification for the existence of the world organization (Cede, 2001). Although the concept of 'peace' is of central importance for the work of the United Nations as a whole, and the word is used fifty-two times in the Charter – of which thirty-two instances come under the description of 'world-' or 'international peace' (Dicke and Rengeling, 1975, p. 15), in the entire treaty there is no precise definition of this concept. The discussion about how to interpret the term has been conducted with predictable controversy, because the implications of differing views of 'peace' permeate and affect the interpretation of the entire body of rules contained in the Charter, and cause the various areas of United Nations' competency to be evaluated differently. A narrow construction of 'peace' would constrict severely the spectrum of possible actions for the prevention of war and the use of force in the international arena. However, the list of purposes laid out in Article 1 seems to make it clear that a very broad construction of 'positive peace' is the Charter's basic concept, which places human dignity and human rights, as well as the creation of social justice, explicitly in the central position. Thus, the UN – unlike the League of Nations – consciously and from the very beginning connected the idea of maintenance of the peace closely with several other areas. The practice of the UN also accords with this wider concept of peace, in that it has constantly exerted itself in an attempt to remove the structural causes of war and violence, not only through the creation of new special organs, but also through a large number of specific programmes and actions. Furthermore, and in increasing measure, it sees its future tasks to be of this kind (Annan, 2000). The development of the United Nations into a central forum of interaction for the formation of global governance processes would hardly have been possible had it been working from a narrow, 'negative' concept of peace.

On the other hand, this orientation on a positive concept of peace raises the question of precisely how broad that concept is, and which rights and duties should be inferred from it for both the organization itself and the member states. Thus, in the history of the United Nations – and in particular in the 1990s – humanitarian problems and questions of self-determination of peoples have come into conflict with the principle of sovereignty and the prohibition on intervention enshrined in Article 2 of the Charter. Even during the early 1990s some authors spoke from the perspective that the mere existence of the principles articulated in Article 2 indicated that the states had not intended the purposes of the United Nations to be pursued at *any* price. On the other hand, since the beginning of the twenty-first century – following a good number of UN interventions for humanitarian reasons – there has been an intensive debate over whether the protection of human rights and the right of self-determination of peoples should not perhaps be regarded as having equal weight with the principles of sovereignty and non-intervention. In the context of global governance, the Preamble of the Charter has also received renewed attention. The Preamble contains a number of formulations that might also be considered to be purposes of the organization, but since it assigns no basic duties to the member states, it has in practice usually been regarded more as an aid to the interpretation of the provisions in the main body of the Charter. The Millennium activities of the United Nations were, however, carried out under the leitmotiv of the first three words of the Preamble: 'We the Peoples'. This was intended to express the fact that the United Nations was not simply an organization dedicated to the realization of the interests and concerns of states, but that the activity of states is also bound up in responsibility towards the people who inhabit them. This return to the original *raison d'être* of the organization emphasizes the orientation on a positive concept of peace, which not only legitimizes, but practically demands the United Nations' competencies in the areas of economic and social development as well as in the realm of protection of human rights and humanitarian concerns.

Article 2 of the Charter establishes the principles according to which the organization should, in concert with its member states, pursue and realize its goals. For this purpose, the positions of the member states in the organization are clarified,and their respective rights and duties specified; the basic structure of the organization is defined; and the competencies of the United Nations in relation to the member states are limited. The principles are described as follows in the seven paragraphs of Article 2:

(1) Sovereign equality of all members of the organization;
(2) Good-faith fulfilment of all obligations assumed in accordance with the Charter;
(3) The duty to settle international disputes by peaceful means in such a manner that international peace and security, and justice, are not endangered;
(4) Prohibition on the threat or use of force, either inter-state or other kinds of force incompatible with the purposes of the United Nations;
(5) The duty to assist in any action taken by the organization, and to refrain from giving assistance to any states against which the organization is implementing preventive or enforcement measures;
(6) The duty of the organization to ensure that states which are not members act in accordance with the principles in the Charter so far as may be necessary for the maintenance of international peace and security;
(7) The exclusion of any right of the organization to interfere in matters which are essentially within the domestic jurisdiction of a state except of cases of measures under Chapter VII.

These seven principles, of which a few are specified more precisely in further chapters and articles of the Charter, are not equally relevant in practice for the United Nations. Paragraph 2, for example, is merely a declamatory emphasis of the old legal principle of *pacta sunt servanda* (treaties must be fulfilled). This was intended to express the importance of the general international law principle of 'good faith', and the expectation that the members would take seriously their obligations arising out of the Charter. Very little significance remains to Paragraph 6 now that membership is essentially universal; and the obligation to assist the United Nations in Paragraph 5 contains no new obligations above and beyond those already set down in Paragraph 2. This duty relates to enforcement measures which the Security Council may take under Chapter VII of the Charter, and is further specified to that effect in Article 25: the member states are bound to accept and implement the decisions of the Security Council. However, no duty to provide troops in the case of military actions is contained in this paragraph, as this obligation could arise only from a special agreement under Article 43. In practice, every use of national personnel for UN actions has been based on the principle of voluntary participation.

On the other hand, the obligation contained in Paragraph 3 to settle disputes using peaceful means, which is further specified in Chapter VI and is constantly re-emphasized in one UN declaration after another (see in particular the Manila Declaration on the Peaceful Settlement of Disputes Among States, of 15

November 1982, and the Declaration on the Prevention and Elimination of Conflicts and Situations which might threaten World Peace and International Security, of 5 December 1988), is one of the main pillars of the United Nations. The peaceful settlement of disputes aims at a comprehensive and lasting end to conflict as a necessary prerequisite to peaceful coexistence. The means available for use in this framework of peaceful dispute settlement are more far-reaching and differentiated than the classical military instruments of security precautions. An orientation on consensus, confidence-building, co-operation, increasing interdependence and legalization of relations are some of the long-term effective measures of peaceful dispute settlement. On the basis of this principle, and following Chapter VI of the Charter, the United Nations developed their most successful instruments for a sustainable peace, among which the peace missions (the so-called blue-helmet missions), based on the consensus of the belligerent parties, have acquired particular significance. The duty of the peaceful resolution of disputes is intimately connected to the general prohibition on the use of force (Paragraph 4), which has become a central compulsory norm of international law and is often called the heart of the Charter (Cede, 2001).

The general prohibition on the use of force is the United Nations' answer to the failed attempt of the League of Nations to banish war and violence from international relations through only a partial prohibition. Such attempts began with the Kellogg–Briand Pact of 27 August 1928, but that document's attempt to prohibit war still involved and allowed the threat and use of military force. The Charter's general prohibition on the use of force is a negative right for all states, whose comprehensive form and clarity of meaning are above all an attempt to prevent the victimization of smaller or weaker states in the service of an 'overarching interest of peace' (as, for example, in the case of Czechoslovakia in the Munich Agreements of 1938). According to this paragraph of the Charter, violence is fundamentally impermissible in international relations. Should it indeed be used, it thus stands in need of exceptional legitimization. The only two grounds of justification on this point that are still relevant are the right to individual and collective self-defence, as anchored in Article 51 of the Charter, and the authority of the Security Council according to Chapter VII to take measures of enforcement using military force in the case of a threat to or breach of the peace, or an act of aggression. While the Security Council's controversial practices were, before the 1990s, limited largely to the Korean War, the right to self-defence, especially in regard to its scope, has been discussed actively and controversially throughout the organization's history. Examples include the case of interventions to protect one's own citizens (for example, Israel in Uganda, 1976; and the USA in Iran, 1980); of pre-emptive measures (for example, Israel in Egypt, 1967); of retaliatory measures (for example, USA against Libya, 1986; and the USA against Afghanistan and Sudan, 1998); of attempts to recover 'lost territories' (for example, Argentina in the Falklands, 1982); and most recently in the debate on the US National Security Strategy of 2002 and its postulate of the right of pre-emptive self-defence. In the case of terrorist threats – especially in connection with weapons of mass destruction – a society must (according to, for example, US security strategy) be able to defend itself through early action if need be, possibly of a military nature (see Chapters 4 and 8).

With the new capacity for action that the Security Council began to enjoy in the 1990s, the number of interventions mandated on the basis of Chapter VII increased dramatically. The Kosovo crisis of 1998–9 highlighted the grey zones between the prohibition on the use of force, military intervention in the case of humanitarian catastrophes such as genocide or ethnic cleansing, and the use of military force according to national definitions of interest without following the established rules of international law. The Spring 2003 military engagement of a US-led alliance in Iraq, conducted against the expressed will of the Security Council, also put the Charter's system for the maintenance of international peace to a serious test. These conflicts have drawn both the general prohibition on the use of force and the ostensible monopoly of the Security Council over the legitimization of the use of force in non-self-defence cases into crisis. The general prohibition on the use of force claimed to be a compulsory norm of international law, but the threshold for breaching it legitimately has been lowered (see Chapter 4).

Paragraphs 1 and 7 of Article 2 are closely related, together forming the decisive constitutional principle of the Charter. Paragraph 1 makes clear that states in no way abrogate their sovereignty by joining the United Nations. This is precisely because they are, of their own free will, taking certain limitations upon themselves over their sovereign rights associated with particular regulations. These limitations do not encroach on the core of the member states' constitutional sovereignty. Additionally, they emphasize the principle of sovereign equality of all UN members, which corresponds to a fundamental principle of international law. The prohibition on intervention contained in Paragraph 7 arises out of the principle of sovereignty. It creates a negative right for states against the possibility of interference by the organization in matters that 'are essentially within the domestic jurisdiction of a state'. The only limitation on this negative right to be left alone is found in the Chapter VII power to take enforcement measures for the sake of protecting world peace. At that point, the principle of sovereignty and the prohibition on intervention give way to the collective interest in peace. The question of the extent of the constraints on state sovereignty that arise from entry into the United Nations, as well as that of the competencies of the organization's active organs, belong to the most controversial issues in the relationship between organization and member states. This is even more so in so far as the United Nations is not a type of world government or world court, under the rule of world law, but rather a political union whose decisions are dominated by considerations of political opportunity.

In practice, it seems that the UN has always considered the discussion of, and making of, recommendations on internal events in a member state compatible with the prohibition on intervention. Should any doubt have remained, however, the Security Council delivered two emphatic illustrations of the legitimacy of such actions in the case of human rights abuses when it sanctioned Southern Rhodesia and South Africa in the 1960s and 1970s. In both instances, the Security Council based its interference on the fact that internal affairs in the affected countries were endangering world peace. Beginning with the so-called 'Kurd Resolution' (Res. 688, 5 April 1991), the Security Council expanded its competence systematically over the course of the 1990s to carry out or authorize interventions for humanitarian purposes or in cases of civil war. These interventions included not only a whole gamut of newly-created instruments, from criminal tribunals to transitional governments, but also the use of military force to implement agreed-upon measures. This expansion of the concept of security in general and the understanding of 'international security' in particular caused the dynamic development – possibly even the redefinition – of some of the Charter's central principles:

> The difficulty of precisely delimiting in individual cases the scope of what, in the current status of international relations, belongs exclusively to the realm of an individual state's sovereignty, in which neither the UN nor other states may involve themselves, arises from the fact that the relevant political understandings have changed fundamentally over the past 50 years (Cede, 2001).

At its core, the principle of state sovereignty remains, but the *domaines reservées* of the member states have grown noticeably smaller. It remains an open question whether this development should be regarded as a real change in the principle; and whether there now exists some sort of global domestic politics. At any rate, the broad interpretation – especially of Paragraph 7 – which has been current since the early 1990s points to a progressive erosion of state sovereignty, above all in the areas of humanitarian issues and internal conflict.

The Principal Organs: Competencies, Functions and Decision-making Processes

The United Nations system – as already mentioned – consists of various, sometimes independent, decentralized organizations and programmes, each with its own by-laws, membership, structure and budget. According to Article 7 of the Charter, the central organization – the actual international organization called 'the United Nations' – encompasses six principal organs relevant to the decision-making processes. The composition, competencies and decision-making processes of these organs are each regulated in separate chapters, while their functioning and policy are codified in the respective by-laws. The six primary organs are:

- The General Assembly (Chapter IV of the Charter);
- The Security Council (Chapter V);
- The Economic and Social Council (Chapter X);
- The Trusteeship Council (Chapter XIII);
- The International Court of Justice (Chapter XIV); and
- The Secretariat (Chapter XV).

With the exception of the International Court of Justice in The Hague, the Netherlands, all principal organs (also referred to in this text as 'main bodies') of the organization are based in New York. Article 7(2) makes it possible for these organs to create secondary and assistant bodies as they consider it necessary for the fulfilment of their tasks. The main bodies have made frequent and multifarious use of this right, to the extent that there are now hundreds of secondary organs at work worldwide in the form of commissions, boards, standing conferences, funds, offices, high commissioners and missions. These derivational structures have grown organically, and have over the course of time freed themselves in varying degrees from the organizational structure foreseen in the statutes. They thus exhibit various peculiarities, in particular with respect to their configuration, their degree of independence from the main bodies, and their financing (Trauttmansdorff, 2001).

The character of the United Nations as an inter-state entity finds clear expression in the configuration of its main organs. Those bodies authorized to make political decisions comprise member state delegations bound by instructions from their respective governments, while the Secretariat and International Court of Justice are staffed by UN employees or independent judges. Both the position of the various organs and their relationships to one another are regulated fundamentally by the relevant provisions of the Charter. That said, certain changes in the role and meaning of certain of the main bodies have taken place in the actual practice of the United Nations, so that the current constellation is also at least in part the result of the organization's historical development. The main bodies and overall structure of the United Nations are set out in Figure 1.1. For our purposes it will suffice to limit the treatment here to a brief sketch of their functions within the organization and their relationships with one another.

The General Assembly

The General Assembly is the organizational centre of the United Nations. It is the only major body in which all member states of the organization are in fact represented equally on the principle of 'one state, one vote'. Representation of the members is accomplished through delegations of up to five representatives of the respective governments. Lacking a vote, but none the less active, a number of observers also participate in the work of the General Assembly. Observers are primarily states that do not belong to the United Nations, or special organizations on the basis of special agreements, as well as other international organizations and national relief organizations resulting from special decisions of the General Assembly. In spite of the frequent use of the term, the General Assembly is not a 'world parliament', but rather an inter-governmental forum for consultation and co-operation. The work of the General Assembly takes place primarily in its six main committees, in which the decisions are prepared in plenum. In these committees, as in the General Assembly itself, all member states are represented. The committees are currently responsible for dealing with:

- disarmament and international security (First Committee);
- economic and financial issues (Second Committee);

FIGURE 1.1
The UN system: principal organs

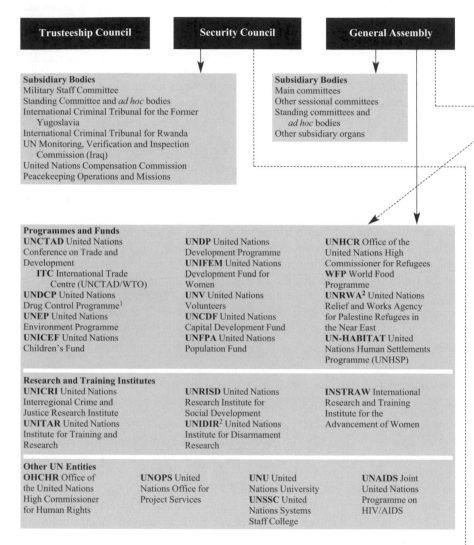

Notes: Solid lines from a Principal Organ indicate a direct reporting relationship; dashes indicate a non-subsidiary relationship. 1. The UN Drug Control Programme is part of the UN Office on Drugs and Crime; 2. UNRWA and UNIDIR report only to the GA; 3. The World Trade Organization and World Tourism Organization uses the same acronym; 4. IAEA reports to the Security Council and the General Assembly (GA); 6. SPecialized agencies are autonomous organizations working with the UN and each other through the co-ordinating machinery of the ECOSOC at the intergovernmental level, and through the Chief Executives Board for co-ordination (CEB) at the inter-secretariat level.
Source: Reproduced from UN website (www.un.org); version DP1/2342 – with the permission of the UN Department of Public Information, March 2004.

Economic and Social Council	International Court of Justice	Secretariat

Functional Commissions
Commissions on:
Human Rights
Narcotic Drugs
Crime Prevention and
 Criminal Justice
Science and Technology for
 Development
Sustainable Development
Status of Women
Population and Development
Commission for Social
 Development
Statistical Commission

Regional Commissions
Economic Commission for
 Africa (ECA)
Economic Commission for
 Europe (ECE)
Economic Commission for Latin
 America and the Caribbean
 (ECLAC)
Economic and Social
 Commission for Asia and the
 Pacific (ESCAP)
Economic and Social
 Commission for Western
 Asia (ESCWA)

Other Bodies
Permanent Forum on Indigenous
 Issues (PFII)
United Nations Forum on
 Forests
Sessional and standing commit-
 tees
Expert, *ad hoc* and related
 bodies

Related Organizations
WTO[3]   World Trade
         Organization

IAEA[4] International Atomic
         Energy Agency

CTBTO Prep.com[5]
         PrepCom for the
         Nuclear-Test-Ban-
         Treaty Organization

OPCW[5] Organization for the
         Prohibition of
         Chemical Weapons

Specialized Agencies[6]
ILO   International Labour
         Organization
FAO   Food and Agriculture
         Organization of the
         United Nations
UNESCO   United Nations
         Educational,
         Scientific and
         Cultural Organization
WHO   World Health
         Organization

WORLD BANK GROUP
IBRD   International Bank for
         Reconstruction and
         Development
IDA   International
         Development
         Association
IFC   International Finance
         Corporation
MIGA   Multilateral
         Investment Guarantee
         Agency
ICSID   International Centre
         for Settlement of
         Investment
         Disputes
IMF   International
         Monetary Fund
ICAO   International Civil
         Aviation
         Organization
IMO   International
         Maritime
         Organization
ITU   International
         Telecommunication
         Union
UPU   Universal Postal
         Union
WMO   World Meterological
         Organization
WIPO   World Intellectual
         Property
         Organization
IFAD   International Fund for
         Agricultural
         Development
UNIDO   United Nations
         Industrial
         Development
         Organization
WTO[3]   World Tourism
         Organization

Departments and Offices
OSG   Office of the
         Secretary-General
OIOS   Office of Internal
         Oversight
         Services
OLA   Office of Legal
         Affairs
DPA   Department of
         Political Affairs
DDA   Department for
         Disarmament
         Affairs
DPKO   Department of
         Peace-keeping
         Operations
OCHA   Office for the
         Coordination of
         Humanitarian
         Affairs
DESA   Department of
         Economic and
         Social Affairs
DGACM   Department for
         General
         Assembly and
         Conference
         Management
DPI   Department of
         Public
         Information
DM   Department of
         Management
OHRLLS   Office of the High
         Representative
         for the Least
         Developed
         Countries,
         Landlocked
         Developing
         Countries and
         Small Island
         Developing States
UNSECOORD Office of the
         United Nations
         Security
         Coordinator
UNODC   United Nations
         Office on Drugs
         and Crime
UNOG   UN Office at
         Geneva
UNOV   UN Office at
         Vienna
UNON   UN Office at
         Nairobi

- social, humanitarian and cultural affairs (Third Committee);
- special political questions and issues of decolonization (Fourth Committee);
- administrative and budgetary affairs internal to the organization (Fifth Committee); and
- legal issues (Sixth Committee).

Every issue of international significance can be discussed in these committees with the intention of producing recommendations. This basic structure of the General Assembly is supplemented by a number of secondary and assistant organs, which can be activated as necessary.

The General Assembly begins its yearly sessions in September with the election of its leading councils and the general debate, which is usually led by the foreign ministers (or secretaries of state) of the member states. While in the past the sessions used to be finished by the third week of December, for some time now the General Assembly has continued to hold meetings throughout the year. Decisions of the General Assembly usually require a simple majority. For important questions (those listed in Article 18(2)), however, such as the selection of non-permanent members of the Security Council or the acceptance or rejection of members, a two-thirds majority is required. The number of resolutions adopted by consensus or acclamation has increased dramatically since the 1990s, so that an overwhelming number of decisions are now reached through consensus proceedings rather than through a formal vote. With respect to the political work of the General Assembly, a distinction can be made between internal and external competencies. While the General Assembly functions something like a legislature within the organization itself and can make decisions that are binding on the other main bodies (such as the Secretariat) and the subsidiary bodies (such as those pertaining to the budget), it enjoys no such authority in its external relations. Its recommendations create no binding obligations under international law and thus have no claim on the obedience of member states. The Assembly's right to discuss any issue does not have any corresponding authority to constitute binding resolutions. According to the statute, the General Assembly merely enjoys the privilege of issuing recommendations on all issues falling under its purview (Trauttmansdorff, 2001). That said, Article 10 empowers the General Assembly to concern itself with practically every question of international relevance, as specified in a number of later articles. The once-significant constraint in Article 12, according to which the General Assembly may not issue any recommendations on a problem that is still being discussed in the Security Council, has in practice lost all meaning.

Although the General Assembly may lack hard instruments such as sanctions, it does not mean that its decisions and declarations remain utterly without effect. Public pressure, together with the political and moral authority of the world community, has helped countless General Assembly declarations and recommendations to reach nearly universal acceptance, and promoted the development of political and legal standards worldwide. Other instruments of the General Assembly for the creation of public awareness in questions of world peace and international security are their emergency sessions, which meet in situations of acute crisis or conflict when the Security Council is unable to act. This right to bypass the absolute primacy of the Security Council is based on the Uniting for Peace Resolution of 3 November 1950, when the General Assembly took on the Korea question. What in 1950 constituted a dangerous raising of tensions in the relationship between the General Assembly and the Security Council has now developed into an accepted mode of coexistence. This finds expression in particular in the fact that six of the ten emergency sessions that have taken place have been called by the Security Council. This special form of meeting, the last of which met in April 1997 at the request of Qatar to consider the question of Israeli occupation politics in the Palestinian autonomous provinces, remains reserved for situations where Security Council action under Chapter VII is impossible because of a veto by a permanent member. Even in the case of emergency sessions, however, the decisions of the General Assembly are restricted to recommendations, and no enforcement measures are available.

The first emergency session, called in November 1956 to deal with the Suez Crisis, produced the United Nations Emergency Force (UNEF I) on the basis of the General Assembly's recommendation and the agreement of the parties to the conflict. This was not only the first UN peace-keeping force, but was also the embodiment of the standards for a new instrument for keeping the peace that would prove successful over the long term (see Chapter 4). Thus, at the request of the General Assembly, special meetings may be called to handle current and urgent problems.

The Security Council

The Security Council consists of fifteen member states of the United Nations, of which the USA, the United Kingdom, France, Russia and the People's Republic of China are permanent members. The People's Republic of China replaced the debarred Republic of China (Taiwan) in 1971, and Russia succeeded to the membership of the Soviet Union when that entity dissolved in 1991. The ten non-permanent members are elected by the General Assembly for two-year terms, and may not serve two consecutive terms. Since five non-permanent member seats are up for election every year, the Security Council's composition changes annually. In January 1966, the number of non-permanent members was increased from six to ten, bringing with it a need for an appropriate geographic distribution of the seats. In practice, a rough system has been established whereby there are always three African, two Asian, two Latin American, one East European and two West European or Other states represented on the Security Council.

The Security Council's mode of operation is regulated in its rules of procedure – which are still provisional. It is organized to be able to perform its functions at any time, meaning that all its members must be represented at all times at the organization's main base. The president calls a session whenever s/he considers the situation requires it, or when a Security Council member, the General Assembly, a UN member state or the Secretary-General directs the president's attention to an issue. The by-laws require that two sessions must not be separated by a period of longer than fourteen days. In practice, the Council meets nearly every day, and frequently more than once a day. The presidency of the Security Council changes every month, following alphabetical order according to the English version of the countries' names. The Security Council reaches a decision when nine of the fifteen members are in agreement. Article 27, however, does differentiate between procedural questions and all other types of question. For the latter, the agreement of all the permanent members is required (Art. 27(3)), which is the basis of the permanent members' veto power. The abstention of a permanent member does not hinder the taking of a decision. For the realization of its duties, the Security Council may create subsidiary organs (Art. 29), which may be classified under three headings:

(i)   Committees (General Staff Committee, Committee of Experts on Rules of Procedure, Committee on Admission of New Members, and *ad hoc* committees for the execution of sanctions and other measures imposed by the Security Council);
(ii)   Peace missions; and
(iii)   The International Criminal Tribunals for the Former Yugoslavia and for Rwanda.

The Security Council is by far the most powerful of the UN's main bodies, and is a unique instrument in international politics as a whole. The Charter assigns it primary responsibility for world peace and international security (Art. 24), and bestows upon it far-reaching powers for the administration of this responsibility. Thus, within the framework of peaceful settlement of disputes (Chapter VI), it has the power to investigate any situation (Art. 34), and may give recommendations for the peaceful settlement of any dispute determined to have implications for international peace and security (Art. 36 et seq.). The Security Council's role, according to Chapter VI, remains one that is merely advisory or moderative; and Chapter VII regulates the Security Council's use of coercive power. According to Article 39, it is for the Security Council to determine whether a situation constitutes a threat to the peace, a breach of the peace, or an act of aggression. Should the Security Council come to such a determination, it may then recommend appropriate measures to address the situation. It may also itself take measures for the forceful execution of its decisions. According to Article 41, such measures may consist of gradations of non-military – primarily economic – sanctions, and Article 42 allows the use of military measures. For the execution of enforcement measures under its own authority, the Security Council may call on regional organizations such as the OSCE (Chapter VIII, Art. 53). According to Article 25, all member states must accept and implement the decisions of the Security Council.

The special position of the Security Council is also apparent in its competencies within the organization. For example, a number of important decisions – especially those of the General Assembly – are contingent on an antecedent vote of the Security Council. This affects primarily the acceptance or rejection of new members, as well as the choice of Secretary-General and the judges of the International Court of Justice.

While the double privilege of permanent membership and veto rights for five states is already problematic in theory with respect to the principle of sovereign equality of all UN members, the use of the veto also led to a decades-long period of *practical* impotence for the Security Council. For a time, this even led to conflicts of competence with, and even a partial shifting of gravity towards, the General Assembly. Only when the East–West conflict began to subside in the late 1980s, and the willingness to co-operate among the permanent members improved with the end of the bipolar world order in the 1990s, did the Security Council regain its capacity to act. Formal vetoes became rare exceptions. Although the threat of a veto still belongs to the normal proceedings of consultations, the Security Council has been able to reach decisions, even in new and difficult situations such as civil wars, and to develop its instruments further. At the end of the 1990s, and again in 2003, the Security Council experienced a crisis of authority and ran the risk of losing its monopoly on the legitimization of the use of force. Although all problems of international peace and security were treated rhetorically as being within the competency of the Security Council, it remained clear that, in a number of cases, such problems were not in fact being handled under that authority. Above all, in the case of the former Yugoslavia, it was a group of states that worked out the drafts, which the Security Council then merely implemented through resolutions. In the 2002–3 Iraq crisis, there was a concentrated attempt to find a solution within the framework of the Security Council. When this failed, however, the central organ of the UN was simply bypassed by two permanent members (the United States and the United Kingdom) and even declared irrelevant by the US administration (see Chapter 4).

The decisive factor will be whether the Security Council can overcome its division and find its way back to a mode of trusting co-operation among its members. The future of the Security Council as the centre of an effective system of collective security on the basis of the Charter will depend primarily on its reform and the support of its work through the member states (Teixeira, 2003).

The Economic and Social Council

The Economic and Social Council (or ECOSOC), after a two-stage expansion, at the time of writing encompasses fifty-four members, elected by the General Assembly. Its main task is to take responsibility, together with the General Assembly, for those tasks in the economic and social realm enumerated in Chapter IX of the Charter. In accordance with this task, its system of regional representation is weighted towards developing countries. Fourteen members come from the African continent, eleven from Asia, ten from Central and South America, and six from Eastern Europe. Thirteen members come from the Western European and Other States group. Every year, a third of the members are selected for a three-year term. Since there is no bar to serving consecutive terms, some states have served for a long time, becoming semi-permanent members. Since 1997, ECOSOC has met once a year for a four-week session, to which non-members and representatives of special organizations or relief organizations recognized by the General

Assembly may also be invited as observers with the right to make suggestions, but not to vote. According to Article 63, ECOSOC – which also forms a link to the special organizations with membership status – may be active in issues of economics, social entities, culture, education, health and related areas.

A large part of ECOSOC's work is accomplished through its countless subsidiary bodies, which has led to the accusation that ECOSOC is a sort of 'organizational jungle' (Trauttmansdorff, 2001). These bodies comprise of nine functional commissions, among which are the Human Rights Commission; the Commission on the Status of Women; the Commission on Crime Prevention and Criminal Justice; the Commission on Sustainable Development; Social Development; and Population and Development; five regional economic organizations; four permanent committees, which handle the ongoing work between sessions; and a constantly fluctuating number of working groups and expert commissions. Of particular importance are the five regional economic commissions. Furthermore, ECOSOC co-operates constantly with a large number of subsidiary organs, and maintains consultative relations with more than 2,000 non-governmental organizations. In accordance with the goals of the United Nations as expressed in Article 1(3) and the concerns listed in Article 55, ECOSOC concerns itself primarily with questions of development in poorer countries (see Chapter 7). Its capacities are, however, limited, and subject to the authority of the General Assembly, and ECOSOC has in fact appeared to be evolving increasingly into a mere helper-organization for the General Assembly (Verdross and Simma, 1984, p. 110). What is more, the General Assembly has withdrawn further areas of competence from ECOSOC through the creation of special bodies such as the UNDP (UN Development Programme) and the UNCTAD (Conference on Trade and Development), so that hardly anything outside the area of human rights remains within its purview.

The Trusteeship Council

The Trusteeship Council is the only principal organ of the United Nations to have suspended its work; this occurred following the transition of the last trustee territory to independence (Palau on 1 October 1994). The roots of the trusteeship system (Chapter XII) and the construction of the Trusteeship Council (Chapter XIII) go all the way back to the Mandate system of the League of Nations, through which the colonial possessions of the German and Ottoman Empires were given to mandate states to administer after the end of the First World War. While the mandate system confined itself exclusively to territory that had belonged to the 'enemy' states, the trusteeship system of the United Nations Charter expanded the scope of the types of territory coming into question. According to Article 77 of the Charter, possible candidates for trusteeship status were those that were mandate territories at the time the Charter came into force, those territories separated from 'enemy' states during the Second World War, and any territories placed voluntarily under the trusteeship system by the governments currently responsible for them. For the last category, it must be said, there is no historical example. The basis for trusteeship status was a trusteeship treaty, the execution of which the Trusteeship Council was to oversee. The Council was made up of those states that were administering trusteeship territories, plus the permanent members of the Security Council, as well as enough other UN members to make the numbers of trusteeship-holders and non-trusteeship-holders equal (Art. 86). With the gradual release of the eleven trusteeship territories, the number of members of the Council also shrank, such that by the end of its work, only the permanent members of the Security Council were still represented on it. Chapters XII and XIII have not been struck from the Charter; nor, however, has the Council been entrusted with new duties, such as the administration of failed states, despite serious considerations of this option (Caplan, 2002).

The International Court of Justice

The International Court of Justice (ICJ) in The Hague is the primary juridical organ of the United Nations (Art. 92), and comprises fifteen independent judges. The judges are appointed through a procedure involving both the Security Council and the General Assembly. The Court's competencies and duties are enumerated in Chapter XIV of the Charter as well as in its own statute. This statute, which is essentially the same as that which had governed the Permanent Court of International Justice of the League of Nations, is an integral part of the UN Charter. Thus, every state that signs on to the UN Charter automatically becomes a party to the ICJ. Furthermore, non-members of the UN may become parties to the ICJ, as Switzerland did in 1948, or they may place themselves under ICJ jurisdiction in specific cases. Only states may be parties to disputes before the ICJ (Article 34(1) of the ICJ statute), in contrast to the two other courts with their seats in The Hague. Individuals may be called to account in the International Criminal Tribunal for the Former Yugoslavia, called into being in 1993 as a subsidiary organ by the Security Council. The same is true of the International Criminal Court, which, since the July 2002 entry into force of its 1998 statute, possesses jurisdiction over the prosecution of crimes against humanity (for the work of the ICC and its limiting factors, such as complementarity and so on, see Chapter 6).

The role of the ICJ cannot be compared to that of a domestic court. There is in international law no legal rule from which an obligatory international jurisdiction could be inferred. On the contrary, the co-operative nature of international law would seem to require that any subjection to an international court must arise from an agreement among all the parties. If even one state is unwilling to submit itself, the ICJ cannot take action in a dispute. Furthermore, the judgments of the ICJ are binding only on the parties to the dispute; its decisions do not have a general juridical effect. With the so-called facultative clause in Art. 36(1), states may subject themselves voluntarily to the jurisdiction of the court, either unrestrictedly or subject to certain conditions, for the purposes of determining questions related to the interpretation of treaties, or international law, or the violation of international obligations, as well as of compensation for such violations. In practice, however, only a small number of states have lodged declarations on the basis of this clause with the Secretary-General, so the development of an exercise of obligatory international jurisdiction through the ICJ remains unlikely. With only seventy-eight decisions (as of March 2004) in over five decades, the ICJ has not played a very active role in international politics, but it has certainly – through its decisions and its twenty-four advisory opinions – performed considerable service in the further development of international law in the areas for which it is responsible. Its significance lies in its special position as the 'universal juridical organ, and the resulting authority of its jurisprudence' (Trauttmansdorff, 2001). Furthermore, the ICJ remains the only international juridical instance that can interpret international law without being restricted to a particular treaty system.

The Secretariat

The secretariat is the main administrative organ of the United Nations. In accordance with Art. 97 of the Charter, it is composed of the Secretary-General and any other public servants the organization requires. The Secretary-General is chosen by the General Assembly on the recommendation of the Security Council. That way, neither of those organs has full control over the decision of naming a candidate. Since 1946, when the General Assembly issued a decision on this subject, the Secretary-General has served a five-year term of office, with the possibility of one second term. With the exception of Secretary-General Boutros Boutros-Ghali, whose re-election was prevented by a US veto in November 1996, all Secretaries-General have been elected for a second term (see Table 1.2).

Since January 1997, Kofi Annan of Ghana has stood at the head of the Secretariat hierarchy. In 2001, his term of office was extended to 2006. The Secretariat is organized into branches or divisions and departments, the latter of which are headed by under-secretaries or appointed general secretaries. In March 1998, Louise Frechette of Canada took over the newly-created office of Deputy Secretary-General. The Deputy Secretary-General is appointed by the Secretary-General according to Art. 101 of the Charter, just like all other public servants in the Secretariat.

TABLE 1.2
Secretaries-General of the UN

Term of office	Name	Country of origin
1946–53	Trygve Lie	Norway
1953–61	Dag Hammarskjöld	Sweden
1961–71	U Thant	Myanmar (Burma)
1972–81	Kurt Waldheim	Austria
1982–91	Javier Perez de Cuéllar	Peru
1992–96	Boutros Boutros-Ghali	Egypt
1997–Present	Kofi Annan	Ghana

As of the end of the year 2000, around 8,900 personnel from 170 member states were working in the Secretariat (of those, 3,750 were in higher-level service). These public servants, however, owe their occupational loyalty not to their states, but to the United Nations, and they must not receive instructions from any other source. The Secretariat has its primary base in New York, and enjoys the use of three subsidiary offices in Geneva, Nairobi and Vienna. Employees of the Secretariat are active in a large number of other offices worldwide. Among the tasks the Secretary-General must carry out in conjunction with the Secretariat are both political and administrative responsibilities. S\he must also co-ordinate the work of the other main bodies (with the exception of the ICJ), s/he is responsible for the construction of the budgetary plan and the execution of the financial administration; s/he registers and publicizes the treaties and notifications deposited with him/her by UN member states, and represents the organization as a whole both in the international realm and with respect to each of the member states.

One of the Secretary-General's original political tasks, according to Art. 99, was to steer the attention of the Security Council to all matters s/he considered to be possible threats to the peace. Various Secretaries-General have made very different uses of this rather non-specific duty. Boutros Boutros-Ghali undertook during his term of office to define the political position of the Secretary-General more clearly, and did not shrink from reminding member states emphatically of their responsibilities towards the peace of the world. After Boutros-Ghali's shipwreck on the American veto, Kofi Annan has managed to walk the thin line between his different roles as supreme administrative official and moderator or catalyst of international politics with comparative success. The mandate given to him by the General Assembly and Security Council grants him and his staff of experts more room to manoeuvre and a greater opportunity to influence the decisions of those main bodies than any Secretary-General has ever enjoyed before. The high international respect Annan has won for himself and his position as Secretary-General contributed greatly to his early re-selection. In December 2001, the United Nations as an organization and Kofi Annan, personally, were awarded the Nobel Peace Prize. The need to manage the delicate interplay between the collective concerns of the organization and consideration for the individual or group interests of the member states ensures that the office of Secretary-General remains 'the toughest job in the world'.

Immediately on taking office, Annan enacted the most far-reaching reform the Secretariat – long considered to be ponderous and over-manned – had ever experienced, not only in its structure, but also, and above all, in its modes of work and communication. The introduction of a completely new management culture was to ensure that the capacities of the various offices were used to maximum efficiency, and that all redundancy was to be eliminated. Aside from the already-mentioned institution of an office of Deputy Secretary-General, a high-level management group was also created to support the Secretary-General in the realization of his operative and administrative tasks. Attached to this group is a strategic planning unit whose task is to evaluate changes in global trends and then to give appropriate recommendations on them to the Secretary-General. Four executive committees were called into being for the purpose of co-ordinating the work of the departments of the Secretariat with that of the special organs and programmes; these committees are concerned with the central interest areas of the United Nations: peace and security; economic and social issues; development co-operation; and humanitarian issues. The question of human rights was made into a cross-cutting responsibility of all the core interest areas. The ten departments of the Secretariat were streamlined and adjusted to fit into the new structure. As the technological basis of the new management and communications culture, an integrated information management system was introduced, which was up and running by September 2000 (see Chapter 8). The process of internal optimization of the Secretariat's work was also pursued in the core areas of interest, above all in peace-maintenance, where new planning and leadership structures were created.

The Secretariat, whose workforce was reduced by around 20 per cent in the space of only a few years, is clearly on the way to becoming a more streamlined and powerful administrative organ, able to fulfil its many administrative tasks and delegated political functions in a modernized way. Admittedly, however, the number of challenges in the realm of peace-maintenance, which has been rising since 1999, is showing up serious personnel deficits, especially in the Department of Peacekeeping Operations. These deficits weigh even more heavily because it was impossible to replace fully the loss of relevant competence that took place through the removal of the so-called 'gratis personnel'. These 'gratis personnel' were specialists, on loan, so to speak, from a number of member states. Because only the richer states could afford the costs associated with the provision of such personnel, the developing countries – which control a majority in the General Assembly and which found the practice discriminatory – put an end to it in 1999. Even with the pressure for lean management, in the realization of its tasks – especially in the area of peace-maintenance – the United Nations will not be able to avoid at least a sectoral enlargement of personnel resources.

Programmes, Funds and Specialized Agencies

In the system of the United Nations, a number of functional institutions concerned with the accomplishment of specific tasks are integrated around the core organization. As has been indicated already, these institutions may be differentiated into two categories:

(i)   Programmes and funds, (also referred to in this text as 'subsidiary organs') created by the organization itself; and

(ii)   Specialized agencies, international organizations with their own legal personalities with which the United Nations co-operates on the basis of contractual ties.

The subsidiary organs are constituted by the General Assembly and regulated by it, sometimes directly, and sometimes through the Economic and Social Council.

In contrast to the specialized agencies, these programmes and funds enjoy no international legal personalities and are bound to the recommendations they receive from the General Assembly. They have no budgetary authority, even though most of them enjoy their own income through the voluntary, earmarked allocations of member states, or through private donations. If the subsidiary organs are thus often described as quasi-autonomous institutions, it is because they appear to be autonomous in comparison with their partners outside the UN, having a differentiated internal structure and their own political steering organs. The subsidiary organs' areas of responsibility (see Chapters 7 and 8) fall primarily into three categories:

(i)   Development aid programmes (for example, the UNDP, the UN Environmental Programme (UNEP), the UN Children's Fund (UNICEF), the UN Conference on Trade and Development (UNCTAD);
(ii)   Humanitarian issues (for example, the United Nations Relief and Works Agency for Palestine Refugees in the Near East (UNRWA), the High Commissioner for Refugees (UNHCR), or the World Food Programme (WFP)); and
(iii)   Educational and research activities (for example, the UN University (UNU), or the Institute for Training and Research (UNITAR)).

Most of the programmes and funds emerged in the decolonization period, when the states of the 'Third World' achieved a majority in the General Assembly and consequently engaged that body primarily with the economic and social problems of developing countries. With its principle of the formal sovereign equality of all states, the General Assembly became the central forum for the articulation of the interests of the newly-formed states. Furthermore, the General Assembly remained capable of action – at least in the areas of issues affecting the organization itself – while the Cold War rendered the Security Council largely impotent. The formidable number of subsidiary organs created in the first forty years of the UN's existence is an expression of the desire of developing countries to defend themselves against a world economic order they considered to be unjust, and which worked only to the advantage of the industrialized countries. Although they were indeed able, in this way, to ensure the place of the North–South conflict on the UN agenda, this did not lead to a successful treatment of the problem, which would have manifested itself as a structural improvement in the position of the developing countries (see Chapter 7). Thus the operative subsidiary organs of the United Nations continue to bear the character more of fire-fighting programmes, providing punctual assistance in latent and acute emergency situations, rather than instruments of sustainable improvement of the situation of those lands and groups of people for whose sake they were originally created.

The specialized agencies, some of which work in the same areas of operation as a number of the subsidiary organs, are inter-state institutions, resting on the basis of their own international law treaties, having their own membership and organizational structure, and their own budgets. The specialized agencies' scope of action reaches across practically all technical, economic, social, educational and environmental areas looked after and acted on under global auspices. A few of these organizations are significantly older even than the UN's predecessor, the League of Nations. Others were created by their member states at the instigation of the United Nations. Their status as specialized agencies with the United Nations is based on special agreements under Art. 63. The goal of this co-operation is to contribute to the achievement of the economic and social goals laid out in Art. 55 of the Charter, which are necessary for the maintenance of peaceful coexistence among states. These special agreements, which are all substantively similar, are made by the Economic and Social Council with the permission of the General Assembly, and regulate the forms of co-operation as well as the rights and duties of both parties. These organizations are commonly divided into three categories:

(i)   Technical bodies (for example, the Universal Postal Union (UPU), the World Meteorology Organization (WMO), or the International Labour Organization (ILO));

(ii)   Specialized agencies in social, cultural, and humanitarian areas (for example, the World Health Organization (WHO), the United Nations Educational, Scientific, and Cultural Organization (UNESCO), the UN Industrial Development Organization (UNIDO), or the Food and Agriculture Organization (FAO)); and

(iii)   Financial organizations (for example, the International Monetary Fund (IMF), the World Bank, and the International Fund for Agricultural Development (IFAD)).

In total, there are sixteen of these specialized agencies operating worldwide (September 2004). Further important institutions, such as the World Trade Organization (WTO), the International Atomic Energy Agency (IAEA), and the World Tourism Organization, co-operate extensively with the United Nations. Because these have made no Article 63 agreements with the UN, they do not count as special organizations, but rather as autonomous organizations within the UN system. As is the case with the subsidiary organs, the conflict of interests between industrialized and developing countries is reflected in the field of the specialized agencies. The richer states are more likely to view the financial bodies – where they dominate because of the voting weighted according to contribution size – as effective. In contrast, the developing countries put more weight on organizations for multilateral development co-operation – which are none the less equally dependent on the support of industrialized countries. Even the work of the powerful specialized agencies has barely been able to contribute to overcoming this difficulty.

Effective co-operation among the specialized agencies is made more difficult by the fact that the responsibility for the activities of the various members of the organizations lies primarily with the respective functional departments, so that the inter-state co-ordination problems are compounded by intra-state difficulties. What is true for the UN as a whole is also true for the specialized agencies: the success of their work depends largely on the will of the member states to engage in multilateral co-operation.

Financing of the United Nations System

The work of the United Nations is financed primarily through the contributions of its member states. These contributions fall into three categories:

(i)   Obligatory dues for the maintenance of a regular budget;
(ii)   Obligatory dues for UN peace missions and for the International Criminal Tribunals for the Former Yugoslavia and Rwanda; and
(iii) Voluntary contributions to funds and programmes of the UN.

The regular budget pays primarily for the personnel, administrative and property expenses of the UN. To a lesser extent, monies are expended from this budget for the work of the subsidiary organs and programmes; at the time of writing, two observation missions are being funded (as exceptions) out of this budget: UNTSO and UNMOGIP. The budget procedure involves the submission of a budget plan by the Secretary-General to the Coordination and Programming Committee (CPC) for examination, from where it proceeds to the Advisory Committee for Administrative and Budgetary Questions (ACABQ) for further examination. Once finally approved by the Fifth Committee, the budget goes to the General Assembly, where it must be approved by a two-thirds majority. For the two-year period covering 2004 and 2005, the regular budget has been fixed at US$3.16 billion – a figure that, considering the complex tasks involved, appears relatively modest, and which has grown almost imperceptibly from the previous period (In this book all references to billions and trillions are according to US style) (see Table 1.3).

In fact, this budget covers barely a third of the total expenses of the UN (see Table 1.4). Member states pay their dues into this budget on the basis of a scale of assessments that is subject to re-approval every three years. The standard for measuring the extent of a country's dues is the state's economic capacity, computed on the basis of the average per capita GNP during a given reference period of (usually) three to six years. Both the level of the state's debt and the variance in actual distribution of income are taken into account and these may lower the expected contribution. Detailed technical determinations of all financial aspects are contained in the 'Financial Regulations and Rules of the United Nations', the new version of which came into effect in January 2003. According to the scale of assessments from 23 December 2003, the upper limit of obligatory dues was set at 22 per cent and the lower limit at 0.001 per cent of the regular budget. According to this schedule, the poorest states would have payment obligations in the order of US$14,360, and the USA would have obligations of around US$270 million. In total, forty-seven of the member states provide 99 per cent of the regular budget.

TABLE 1.3
The UN programme budget, 2004–5

Section	US$ (000s)
Overall policy-making, direction and co-ordination	593 884.9
Political affairs	349 252.2
International justice and law	70 245.4
International co-operation for development	336 495.3
Regional co-operation for development	388 613.7
Human rights and humanitarian affairs	170 670.5
Public information	155 869.9
Common support services	516 168.9
Internal oversight	23 227.2
Jointly financed administrative activities and special expenses	102 445.3
Capital expenditures	58 651.3
Staff assessment	382 270.7
Development account	13 065.0
Total	**3 160 860.3**

Source: Data from A/RES/58/271, 23 December 2003.

The peace-maintenance measures taken by the UN are also financed through obligatory dues from the member states. However, each peace mission has its own financial framework, so that the total expenses for peace missions change constantly according to their number and scope. The Secretary-General creates a cost-plan for each mission, which must be approved by the Fifth Committee. If it receives this approval, the Secretary-General opens a unique account for the mission and sends requests for payments to the member states. The level of these contributions is basically orientated on the same schedule of payments as for the regular budget, but reductions are allowed for the poorer states. The system of dues for peace maintenance, reformed on 23 December 2000 and reaffirmed in 2003, anticipates ten categories (A–J) into which the member states are grouped according to their degree of financial power. Those states in categories C to J receive reductions of between 7.5 per cent and 90 per cent on the level of their dues for the regular budget, while the countries in category B must pay their normal dues. The deficits resulting from the reductions given to the C–J countries are redressed by the countries of category A – the five permanent members of the Security Council. The budgets thus produced must pay for the running costs of the missions, such as personnel (both UN personnel and those support personnel recruited locally), rents, transportation costs and so on. Member states who 'donate' personnel receive repayments of around US$1,000 per person per month, as well as compensation for any materials used. According to the actual costs to a country providing either troops or personnel, this form of 'reimbursement' can lead to further expenditures for the wealthier states and positively attractive profits for the poorer states. The voluntary contributions for the project work of the programmes and funds

TABLE 1.4
Expenditures of the UN system US$ millions

Year	UN regular budget	UN Peace-keeping	UN Agencies	Total assessment spending	Total voluntary spending	Grand total
1986	725	242	1 142	2 109	4 026	6,135
1987	725	240	1 178	2 143	4 197	6,340
1988	752	266	1 349	2 367	4 997	7 356
1989	765	635	1 359	2 759	5 260	8 019
1990	838	379	1 495	2 712	5 782	8 494
1991	999	449	1 509	2 957	6 761	9 718
1992	1 008	1 697	1 731	4 436	7 159	11 595
1993	1 031	3 005	1 713	5 749	7 307	13 056
1994	1 087	3 357	1 826	6 270	7 093	13 363
1995	1 181	3 281	1 847	6 309	6 937	13 246
1996	1 112	1 522	2 057	4 691	6 054	10 745
1997	1 112	1 226	2 033	4 371	5 993	10 364
1998	1 086	995	1 792	3 873	5 411	9 284
1999	1 217	1 321	1 787	4 325	5 423	9 748
2000	1 090	2 139	1 766	4 995	4 978	9 973
2001	1 074	2 700	1 772	5 546	6 374	11 920
2002	1 149	2 284	no data	no data	no data	no data
2003	1 409	no data	no data	no data	no data	no data

Note: The tables offer a summary of total UN system expenditures. Assessed contributions expenditures are funded by payments assessed to all UN member states. Voluntary contributions are payments made to specialized UN organs and agencies not included in the assessed contributions of member states. The data presented does not include assessed contribution expenditures for international tribunals, which are a separate but relatively small item, nor do they include the Bretton Woods Institutions, which are in practice quite distinct and rarely included in UN system data, since both their governance and their source of funds are very different. The major specialized agencies include the IAEA, ILO, FAO, UNESCO, WHO, UPU, ITU, IMO and UNIDO. The major programmes, funds, and other Organs include UNCTAD, UNDP, UNEP, UNFPA, UNHCR, UNICEF, UNIFEM and UNU. In evaluating these numbers, it must be kept in mind that the UN's scope of action has expanded significantly over time and thus the real expenditures have decreased. Detailed information on the expenditures of the UN system may be found in the report entitled *Budgetary and Financial Situation of Organizations of the United Nations System* (A/55/525) of 26 Oct 2000.
Source: Data from Global Policy Forum (www.globalpolicy.org).

remain at the discretion of the member states. The personnel and administrative costs of these subsidiary organs are defrayed through the regular budget. The sum of the voluntary contributions significantly outstrips that of the regular budget, and makes the operative work of the subsidiary organs possible.

Financial crises brought the UN close to the brink of financial ruin in the early 1960s, and have been a steady companion of the Organization ever since then (Schlesinger, 2001). Through the whole decade of the 1990s, the financial situation of the UN ranged from precarious to catastrophic, not least because of the USA's attempt to force UN reform via unilateral reduction or withholding of dues for peace-maintenance measures. And other states fell so far behind with their payments that, in accordance with Art. 19 of the Charter, they lost their right to vote in the General Assembly. Because of the tense situation with the regular budget, monies were drawn from the funds for peace-maintenance measures, which led to serious debts on the part of the UN to the poorer troop-contributing countries. Fundamental financial reform of the UN remains to be accomplished: recommendations the Secretary-General included in his 1997 programme of reform have never been implemented. The adjustment of the scale of assessments in December 2000 was successful in settling a long-standing dispute with the USA, but the fundamental problem of the organization's complete dependence on its more powerful contributors and their willingness to pay could not be solved.

Further Reading

Annan, Kofi (2000) *We the Peoples: The Role of the United Nations in the Twenty-first Century*, New York UN-Document (A/54/2000).

Cede, Franz and Lilly Sucharipa-Behrmann (eds) (2001) *The United Nations: Law and Practice*, The Hague: Kluwer.

Claude, Ines L. (1970) *Swords into Plowshares. The Problems and Progress of International Organizations*, New York: Random House.

Mingst, Karen A. and Margaret P. Karns (2000) *The United Nations in the Post-Cold War Era*, Boulder, CO: Westview Press.

New Zealand Ministry of Foreign Affairs and Trade; *United Nations Handbook*, Wellington (published annually).

Simma, Bruno (ed.) (2002) *The Charter of the United Nations: A Commentary*, Oxford: Oxford University Press.

United Nations Department of Public Information; *Yearbook of the United Nations*, Leiden, Boston: Martinus Nijhoff Publishers (published annually).

Volger, Helmut (ed.) (2002) *A Concise Encyclopedia of the United Nations*, The Hague: Kluwer.

Wolfrum, Rüdiger, with Christiane Philipp (eds) (1995) *United Nations: Law, Policies and Practice*, 2 vols, Dordrecht, Boston, London: Martinus Nijhoff Publishers.

2

Institution-building, Regime Impact and Globalization: The Role and Function of the UN

For centuries, the history of international relations (in both the practical and academic senses) has been shaped by attempts to contain and overcome the competitive nature of the states system, the principal actors of which recognize no power higher than themselves. The fundamental question of how states can be brought to settle their differences peacefully is as old as the roots of the modern states system itself (Griffiths, 1999), and has occupied thinkers from Niccolo Machiavelli (1469–1527) and Immanuel Kant (1724–1804) to Jürgen Habermas (b. 1929). As might be expected, their solutions were somewhat divergent.

Since time immemorial, there have been two primary views regarding appropriate ways of preventing war and securing peace, which may be described as the dispute between the *children of light* and the *children of darkness*. Out of the European Enlightenment comes a view that focuses on humankind's goodness, reason and aptitude for learning; thus, democratization, because of the demonstrable connections between the internal constitution of a state and its external behaviour, is the best way to head off international conflict. The other side sees the world as anarchically structured and ruled by the worst of human elements; only national strength and adherence to the principle of self-help can prevent conflict: one should reach not for the lofty goal of 'peace', but for the more moderate goal of 'security'. Standing thus opposed to one another are a multilateral world, where bargaining, persuasion, consensus-seeking and diplomatic solutions predominate; and a unilateral world, where there can be in the final analysis no reliance on international rules, and in extreme cases coercion must prevail over persuasion. To put it more dramatically: 'Those who desire peace must prepare for peace' versus 'Those who desire peace must prepare for war'.

Given the far-reaching implications of this fundamental disagreement, it seems necessary for a better understanding of the United Nations as one possible model of world order to consider the most important theories of states' behaviour in international relations.

Theories of International Organizations

The United Nations Organization (UN) was the second practical political attempt – after the failure of the League of Nations – to bring order to international disorder, to minimize the often-described 'perils of anarchy', and to entrust a global organization with the protection of world peace and international security. In the more than half a century since its founding (the Charter came into force on 24 October 1945), the UN has expanded its constitution and fields of action significantly, without the need for major changes to its foundational document. The UN has grown from fifty-one members at its founding to 191 (September 2004), and it should be noted that two-thirds of the present members were not even sovereign states at the time of the founding. From an organization whose primary purpose was to proscribe inter-state warfare as a political means, the UN has evolved into a multifunctional global forum where all the world's fundamental problems can be discussed and even, to some extent, brought closer to solution.

Independent of their judgements of the UN's work up to this point in time, there is a consensus among observers, analysts and practitioners of international politics that the organization must be reformed. Even those who stood on different sides of the disputes over actions in Kosovo (1999) and Iraq (2003) agree that the UN's structures and procedures are no longer appropriate for the political reality of the twenty-first century. The goal of reform, however, requires an answer to the question of what role the member states of a global organization are willing to accept in the shaping of international politics, and in what measure they are ready to use the instruments and opportunities of such an organization for the implementation of a multilateral, compromise-orientated politics. Only after this question has been answered can the debate begin over which means are the most appropriate for reaching these goals. At the same time, demand is rising for the UN to fill a gap in the politics of order in a globalized world. This contradiction between the realistic possibilities for UN action and the sometimes extremely high expectations for it creates a climate of excessive demands, and sometimes leads to an unfairly negative judgement of the UN's work.

In the following attempt to outline the theories, the main purpose is to understand their implications for the various conditions for; courses of activity for; and expected effects of international co-operation with respect to the United Nations, and not to provide a detailed explanation of all the theoretical principles at stake (for comprehensive treatments, see Claude, 1970; Griffiths, 1999; Viotti and Kauppi, 2001; and Zangl and Zürn, 2003).

The adherents of the so-called *Realist School* are of the opinion that the struggle for power and the achievement of the state's own interests constitute the most important categories for understanding international politics, because the sovereign nation-state is not subject to any higher authority with sanctionary power, and indeed *could* not be subject to such an entity. The lack of an overarching authority in the international system which could guarantee compliance with common decisions and basic principles leads states to seek to secure their existence as sovereign units through the accumulation of power. In such a situation, 'a feeling of insecurity born out of mutual fear and mistrust [drives] the units into a competition for power, in which for the sake of their own security they seek to pile might upon might; a struggle which remains vain, because perfect security is impossible to attain' (Herz, 1961, p. 130). Nation-states would have to give up their power-politics demand for sovereignty and subject themselves to a common decision-making process in order to face up to these historical exigencies. The nation-state of the old stamp can no longer fulfil what is required of it – especially in the realm of peace-maintenance. Quite the reverse, in fact – it is these states that are the central problem, as the anarchical situation of the international system implies that war is a necessary, natural and unavoidable product of this order (Claude, 1970, p. 372). Because of the security dilemma in this anarchical international self-help system, war and zero-sum conflicts arise almost of necessity, except when there is a fragile and continuously threatened balance of power. This is why the realists see pure inter-governmental collaboration as the only possible way of maintaining the balance of power, avoiding war and promoting co-operation. From this perspective, international organizations fill 'merely derivative functions, which arise out of the sovereignty and interests of their members; in their setting of goals and capacity for action, they are thus clearly determined by the readiness of their members to act' (Siedschlag, 1997, p. 227). Realists recommend traditional means of achieving security, such as national armed forces, alliances, and *ad hoc* collective proceedings of the rich and powerful against potential trouble-makers.

For those coming from the *Idealist School*, on the other hand, international organizations represent an analytical construct that is not so much the designation for a particular type of institution, but rather a normative-teleological image of the development of international relations (Rittberger, 1995). They make relatively little of the supposedly anarchical state of the international system, where there is no central, super-state authority, but focus instead on forms of co-operation that are intended to regulate that anarchy. They are of the opinion that international co-operation benefits all participants, and that relations between and among individuals, various types of organizations, and states, gradually lead to a sort of universal community, which by its nature tends to aid the cause of peace. This school also believes that variable-sum rather than zero-sum games are characteristic of many situations in international politics. Thus the actors enjoy gains they never could have obtained through unilateral action. Through the creation of a binding body of rules and regulations, the argument goes, there could emerge a civilized world community which, because of its common learning process, no longer solved its problems through force. This is why, for example, Klaus Dicke (1994, pp. 317–33) understands international organizations as the 'catalyst, forum, and form' of inter-state co-operation, which on the one hand serve states as the instruments of co-operation, and at the same time provide an ordered framework containing the rudimentary duties necessary for co-operation and normatively determining the idea of co-operation. With this idea, Dicke is also indicating the normative aspect of the concept of an international organization, comprising the ideas of law or justice and peace:

In this regard, the normative content of the concept of international organiza-tions is that they represent the imperatives of peace and the rule of international law, while at the same time offering the possibility of realization. These possi-bilities for realization, meanwhile, are indeed conditioned by manifold interests and political experiences. (ibid., p. 332)

In the past several years, the so-called *Institutionalist School* – standing firmly in the Idealist tradition but accepting key tenets of the Realist position – has grown steadily in influence. In contrast to Realists, Institutionalists believe that interna-tional co-operation is possible, and they ascribe international institutions (which provide normative regulation in specific areas of politics) a great deal more influ-ence over the interests and behaviour of states than do the Realists. Institutionalism's relevance depends, however, on two preconditions: first, the actors must have some common interests (that is, they must see or be able to expect material advantage from co-operation). Second, variations in the degree of institu-tionalization must have substantial effects on the behaviour of states, because if the degree of institutionalization were minimal or constant, it would make no sense to try to analyse state behaviour in terms of institutional change. The basic thesis of Institutionalism is that variations in the degree of institutionalization of interna-tional politics have significant effects on the behaviour of governments. This does not mean that states ignore the Realist power premises in their actions. Co-opera-tion and integration are not understood here as they are by Idealists, as 'rational' and therefore relatively easily achieved processes, but rather as difficult both to initiate and to maintain. State action, nevertheless, is seen as depending to a considerable extent on the existing institutional order. This institutional order influences:

- The flow of information as well as the capacity to bargain;
- The governments' opportunities to observe whether other states adhere to their agreements and carry out their duties and responsibilities, which is a pre-condi-tion for the decision to carry out one's own obligations; and
- The dominant expectations of how stable international agreements are.

According to Robert Keohane (1989, p. 150 et seq.), these institutions have both regulatory and constitutive aspects: they make certain actions possible for states, which would otherwise have been unimaginable, reduce costs, and influ-ence the role behaviour of states in relation to their concepts of self-interest. States also receive reliable information about the behaviour of other states from interna-tional organizations, which feeds back into the creation of trust and the reduction of anxiety. It is assumed that there is a tight connection between the form – that is, the member structure and rules – and the function – that is, the out-working activ-ities – of institutions: changes in form lead to changes in function, and vice versa. In Table 2.1, we present the basic assumptions of the three schools more schemati-cally.

Modern political science offers several very different answers to the question of

TABLE 2.1

Realism, idealism and institutionalism

	Realism	Idealism	Institutionalism
The international system is primarily characterized by . . .	The structural feature of international anarchy	. . . also through the structural feature of interdependence	. . . also through international arrangements
The actors in international politics are . . .	Primarily states that orientate themselves on their self-interests	. . . also various international organizations, balancing many different interests	. . . also various international organizations, balancing many different interests
The actions of actors are regarded as . . .	Rational action based on the interest of maintaining power	Rational action based on welfare interests	Rational action based on interests specific to each particular problem area
Peace on an international level can be secured by . . .	Through balance of power and national strength	Through the spread and support of democracy and insight into interdependence	Through international institutions and balance of interests

Source: Based on discussion in Zangl and Zürn (2003, p. 140 et seq.).

the emergence and functioning of international organizations. Analytically, we must first distinguish between IGOs (inter-governmental organizations – that is, organizations whose members are state governments) and INGOs (or sometimes NGOs: international non-governmental organizations, whose members are non-state actors). A more precise survey would then look at criteria-bundles such as geographical, sectoral or functional scope or degree of organization, as well as many other characteristics of typology or classification – coming from many scientific disciplines including political science, law, psychology, social psychology, and many more.

According to a minimal consensus definition, an IGO may be understood as a grouping of states created through multilateral international law contracts and having its own organs and competencies. Its goal is to facilitate co-operation among at least three states (if there were only two, it would be bi- rather than multi-lateral) in the political and/or economic, military, cultural, social and so on arena(s). Usually, the founding compact or treaty will set down not only the goals and methods of the co-operation, but also the permanent organizational structure by which these tasks are to be accomplished. These criteria differentiate international organizations from so-called international regimes, which represent a comparatively informal type of international co-operation in certain areas of politics, lying just under the threshold of true organization (Hasenclever *et al.*, 1997). The innovative element of research into regimes is to be seen particularly in the fact that forms of co-operation that are *not* formally institutionalized are also considered, as long as they are identified by a certain set of principles, norms, rules and decision-making processes. This approach allows a better understanding of processes of international governance beyond the nation-state than would be possible with a purely organization-centric analysis. These regimes include *inter alia* the many UN World Conferences in the 1990s on topics such as the environment and development, human rights, the rights of women and children, social development, population issues, human settlements, and nutritional security, some of which have in fact produced institutionalized forms of co-operation.

The degree to which states transfer sovereignty varies significantly from one IGO to another. As differentiating factors, it is useful to consider the ideal-typical concepts of *inter-governmental* versus *transnational* relations. Whereas with the former there is no giving up of direct sovereignty rights and the final decision authority remains with the individual states, with the latter, aspects of sovereignty are transferred to a supra-national body, and states must reckon with the possibility of being overruled in individual cases. Supra-nationality is also manifested when an international organization can enact binding resolutions on the member states.

The United Nations is an international organization based on the principle of multilateral inter-governmental co-operation. This means that the states belonging to the organization work closely together, but have not transferred any direct rights of sovereignty to the organization. One exception to this is in the realm of peace-maintenance, in which the Security Council may make decisions that are formally

FIGURE 2.1
Supra-national integration and inter-governmental co-operation

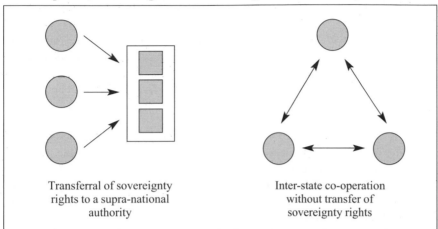

Transferral of sovereignty rights to a supra-national authority	Inter-state co-operation without transfer of sovereignty rights

binding on all member states and can in fact be enforced with the application of military force. Fundamentally, however, the UN is not a supra-national organization like those present in some fields of European Union (EU) politics. It must work towards amicable solutions for every issue that is raised; its medium is that of voluntary co-operation among sovereign states. The principle of multilateralism, however, as opposed to bilateral (two-sided, inter-state) forms of co-operation, means that several states must co-operate with each other, and that this co-operation follows established principles determining appropriate behaviour for the participating states (see Figure 2.1).

But who are the decision-makers in international organizations? If it is true that the member states have the final say, and make decisions according to their own national interests, then a more precise answer is needed to the question of what 'the state' in fact is. First, it must be noted that the actors involved in international organizations can be divided into various categories. Governments may be the primary actors in international politics, and their representatives may have the last word, but their actions will be influenced in turn by many other actors (for example, parliaments, interest groups, NGOs, advisers, the mass media and so on). The theory of foreign policy decision-making processes (Haftendorn, 1990; Hill, 2003) distinguishes among three concepts for the analysis of this complex process, which give different weights to these other sources of influence:

(i)   The attempts at explanation that start from the assumption of rational, goal-orientated behaviour on the part of the actors involved (above all Realist games, rational choice models);

(ii) The contextual attempts at explanation, which incorporate the operative milieu (such as social and organizational structures) more strongly in their form of analysis (above all organizational theory); and

(iii)   Attempts to explain decisions with the help of the psychological context, including perceptional, adjustment and attitudinal variables (above all political psychology).

According to the Realist model of rational politics, foreign policy events are conscious decisions of the governments of sovereign nation-states, made with the goal of achieving national interests. According to the organizational process model, they are the product of an organizational process that does not necessarily emerge from a clear understanding or idea of goals to be achieved. They result far more

> firstly, from the need such organizations have to produce acceptable results in order to achieve self-legitimation, and secondly from a mixture of the expectations and demands of other organizations within the government, legal authority, demands from citizens and interest groups, and not least from a bargaining process internal to the organization. (Lehmkuhl, 1996,136)

The parameters of this organizational process remain largely constant and are definable in each national context. In the bureaucratic politics model, more emphasis is placed on the idea that government decisions increasingly are the result of trans-governmental bargaining processes. In this model, it is neither the nation-state nor the various organizational units that are the sole actors to be analysed, but rather the actors constitute themselves out of a multiplicity of persons and levels representing specific offices or bureaux. The result of this bargaining process is not necessarily what was sought as the optimal solution to the problem, but rather the result of compromise, coalition-building and competition. Contrary to classical approaches, which regard the state as a rational, unitary actor capable of autonomous action, newer decision-theory approaches (for example, Neack *et al.*, 1995) start from the premise that foreign policy decisions can be defined as 'the product of a psychological selection process fully contained within the organizational complex, which purports to ascertain out of a limited and socially-defined set of problematic alternatives the one project which is supposed to bring about one of the particular end-states of things envisaged by the decision-makers' (Meyers 1981: 72). The so-called 'interpretative' approaches of Political Science, which build on the assumption that 'social reality is accessible to us only as a truth-construct; realities are socially negotiated, and arise in complex interactions as the result of interpretational struggles and understandings about common knowledge' (Nullmeier 1997: 101), take this statement more seriously. These assume, in contrast to the Neorealist Rational Choice approaches, that it is not only national power interests which influence the calculations and bargaining strategies of states, but also the institutional context. Interests and identities 'are not the independent variable through which political processes can be explained. They are themselves far more the product and expression of international interactions and institutions. Inter-subjectively shared convictions, expectations, and collective meanings construct those structures which determine the actions of the political actors' (ibid., p. 119).

From a functional perspective, IGOs can be viewed three ways (Archer, 2001, pp. 65–111; Rittberger and Zangl, 2003, pp. 33–48):

(i)   The first view sees international organizations primarily as *instruments of state diplomacy*, meaning that states instrumentalize international organizations in order to achieve their own interests in an anarchical environment. Agreements are not to be relied upon, because partners might at any time, according to their interests, break the agreement and take advantage of the co-operative behaviour of the other side;

(ii) The second view interprets international organizations primarily as *arenas of international politics*, which, as lasting diplomatic structures, can address different fields of politics on different levels of co-operation. Unlike the instrumental view, here international organizations are seen more as frameworks than as means of achieving given goals; and

(iii) The third view attributes to international organizations the independent quality of being *actors in international politics*, which, as causal factors, are also in a position to change the basic pattern of international politics in the sense of reducing the anarchy of its basic state.

Thus, if on one side, the analytical emphasis is placed on the co-operation-limiting structural anarchy aspect of the international system, national interests are the primary reference, and the chances of co-operation are – on balance – judged to be negative. Other perspectives tend to place the heightened chances of co-operation, with the help of international institutions, in the central position, and start from the assumption that organizations matter. Thorsten Benner and Jan Martin Witte (2001) have suggested that a new model of international organizations ought to be developed. As theme-focused interfaces, they argue, international organizations could realize three different roles:

(i)   As negotiating platforms, they could use their scope to bring different actors together;

(ii) As managers of knowledge, they could collect information, enable learning processes, and offer advisory services; and

(iii) As implementation agents, they could implement agreements and oversee their observance.

In the future, the essential function of international organizations is likely to consist in forming 'bridges in the international system' among various actors and issue areas.

When evaluating the work of the United Nations, it is essential to remember that it was constructed on inter-governmental principles, by which the member states are the 'Masters of the Treaties', and have the last word (and expect to be consulted) on practically every decision. As we hope to show, it is also essential to differentiate by political issue area, since 'the' United Nations as an international organization is in fact not a unitary actor, but rather a complex network of primary, secondary and special organs, exhibiting both various competencies and areas of responsibility, and different organizational structures. Not surprisingly, the roles of the United Nations (or, to put it more accurately the systems of the United Nations) in international politics vary along with these things. Depending on the issue area, they might function primarily as an instrument, an arena or an independent actor. Perhaps the principal characteristic of the UN, however, is its function as a forum, in which the 'most disparate interests can be formulated and discussed in the attempt to come closer to the development of global solutions to problems. This function is regarded by every state in the world as an indispensable service. In individual issue-areas, such as (e.g.) human rights, it is possible to ascertain the beginnings of actor-orientation . . . significant UN autonomy in various issue-areas, however, remains restricted to tightly circumscribed exceptional cases, even today' (Rittberger, 1994, p. 581).

Challenges of Globalization

A crucial backdrop to the functioning and analysis of the UN in the world today is the phenomenon of globalization. The term 'globalization' (Michie, 2003; Baylis and Smith, 2001) has become a buzz-word, inflated by over-use in political, publishing and scientific debates. What is more, the meaning of the term and its effects on international organizations such as the UN, as well as the question of what differentiates 'globalization' from 'internationalization' and the general loss of meaning that nation-state borders have been undergoing, all remain contested. Thus Michael Zürn (1998) has argued that the concept of 'uneven de-nationalization' should take precedence over that of globalization, and Ernst-Otto Czempiel (1999) speaks of a 'self-internationalizing politics'. In the scientific/academic debate, the dividing line seems run above to all between those who see globalization as sounding the death-knell of the nation-state, complete with its established steering and legitimization mechanisms, and those who continue to attribute the central role in international politics to the nation-state. Globalization is, however, a dynamic historical process, which may be developing asymmetrically in various regions of the world, but which must in spite of this be understood as a worldwide trend.

Globalization can generally be defined as a process in which the bonds or interactions among societies and issue areas increase in such a way that events in one area of the world touch societies and issue areas in other parts of the world to an ever-greater degree. These interactions have increased first in absolute quantity, second in qualitative intensity, and third in their spatial scope. Thus there has also been increasing erosion of that congruence of state territory, state citizens and state power, of territoriality and sovereignty, which were the markers of the nation-state. Action-relevant spaces are thus defined functionally, and extend beyond nation-state boundaries. Alongside states and international organizations, new actors such as multinational corporations and a transnationally-networked civil society have entered the stage of world politics.

There are different accounts as to the causes of increased globalization. In the thicket of research from many disciplines and at many levels of analysis, two paradigmatic positions may be discerned:

(i)   The first sees globalization as an exogenous process with its own logic. The driving forces are above all technological progress, the development of productive capacity, and the far-reaching changes in production relationships that come with the rise of multinational corporations, the differentiation of the international division of labour, and basic social and cultural change. Thus understood, globalization is a constituent part of a process of 'modernization' or 'Westernization', in which a transition – global in tendency – from 'traditional' to 'modern' societies takes place. This process is characterized, to a certain extent, by the fact that it takes its course relatively independently of political decisions.

(ii) The other paradigm emphasizes that it is states that have created the general framework in which the process of globalization is taking place. Globalization thus occurs not according to some law of nature, but following a political logic in the Idealistic tradition of international relations theory, which aims at a universal world-state with horizontal stratification. Even the networking of markets, for example, given all technical prerequisites, would have been impossible without politically-willed deregulation.

But in whatever way the individual causes are evaluated, it is at least uncontested that the process of globalization – once it is set on its path – possesses its own dynamic. The next task of a rational discourse on globalization is, therefore, to decipher its various dimensions. For every dimension there is, of course, a whole list of the exceptions that make generalization so difficult. The degree of globalization varies with region and issue area (Scholte, 1997, p. 18):

*   First, not all regions of the world are subject to globalization to the same degree. The diminishing meanings of time and space affect primarily, if not exclusively, the newly-industrialized Asian countries and the rest of the OECD world. Phenomena such as multinational corporations and the use of the World Wide Web are largely confined to this region, even though other regions may be affected by these things;
*   Second, globalization does not mean global unification or sameness. On the contrary, cultural diversification may even be a reaction particularly encouraged by hegemonial cultural trends in the course of globalization;
*   Third, globalization has not brought on the 'end of geography'. Much more likely is the creation of new, supra-territorial spaces, which do not allow standing borders to become meaningless, but rather complement and overlay them;
*   Fourth, mono-causal explanations which take, for example, technological advances, modernization, developments in productive capacity and deregulation as their point of reference, all fall short; and

- Fifth, globalization is neither a comprehensive explanation for all international politics, nor is it synonymous with the victory procession of liberal-democratic government systems that has been described as the 'end of history', and is supposed to herald a stable world free of war.

The first and most obvious dimension of globalization is found in the realm of economics and business. The central feature of economic globalization is a shift from an understanding of the world as being divided spatially, primarily by state borders, to one in which the world is divided primarily by economic barriers. Economic globalization manifests itself mainly in the ever-closer integration of national political economies. In order to understand this economic aspect, it is helpful to subdivide it into dimensions such as trade, capital investment, finance markets and actors. For years, world trade has grown more than world production, investments are planned globally, a growing number of multinational corporations – the so-called 'global players' – shape the face of the economic process, products and services are produced for a worldwide market, and capital can flow freely all over the globe and seek out the most economically efficient conditions. Between 1948 and 2000, trade increased by an average of 6.1 per cent (in real currency) every year, whereas production increased by a mere 3.9 per cent per year. Twenty-three countries account for 75 per cent of world trade. The portion of world trade accounted for by trade among the industrialized countries has since the 1980s increased even more (from 45 per cent in 1980 to nearly 50 per cent in 2000). International capital flows also increased enormously in the last decades of the twentieth century. External direct investments increased more than fivefold in the 1990s. The daily revenues on the foreign exchange markets are around US$1.2 billion, and are thus many times higher than would be required for the development of trade flows. The finance markets are so tightly interwoven that the entire international finance structure can be unbalanced by national financial crises – such as those that occurred in Mexico (1994), Asia (1997/8), Brazil (1999), or Argentina (2002/3) – and forced to confront the question of necessary reforms.

The increasing degree of interdependence among economies and the related broadening of world trade, along with the internationalization of production and the growing meaninglessness of time and space, also have significant implications for cultures, identities and lifestyles. The worldwide processes of modernization may be followed by growing commonalities in terms of a recognized and universal understanding of values, but they can also cause processes of cultural and ideological fragmentation, which theoretically can culminate in the destruction of political structures. This threat to historically-developed identities doubtless advances certain tendencies which find their expression in fundamentalist and ethno-nationalistic movements. Finally, globalization – understood as a worldwide interlinking of problem areas – has become a very important phenomenon in the realm of ecology. This dimension is characterized not merely by the obvious fact that harmful substances do not stop moving at state borders, but above all by an awareness of the ultimate limits on the global eco-system's carrying capacity. The risks of industrial development may be as old as industry itself, but in the age of globalization, these risks take on a new quality. The place of *origin* is no longer identical to the place of *effect*. Increasingly, the risks of industrial development are abrogating the traditional categories and boundaries of state-centred politics.

The development of the dimensions of globalization outlined briefly above cannot fail to affect international politics. The central aspect of political globalization is the erosion of nation-state sovereignty. The unity of decision-making *power* or *authority* and the *effects* of decision-making, which lie at the base of the all-encompassing dispositional power of the state over social conditions, is now in many areas a thing of the past. Today, the spaces relevant to action are determined primarily by function rather than by sovereign territory. The components of this process are:

- First, the growing significance of internationalized forms of political co-operation, which can in individual cases lead to the development of supranational decision-making mechanisms; and
- Second, the increasing sectoralization of international politics into border-crossing issue areas with the prefix 'global', such as security politics, environmental politics, finance politics and so on, which demonstrate that the nation-state as the sole arena for action has outlived its usefulness.

At the beginning of the twenty-first century, the international system consists of fewer than 200 states, of which – with an upward trend – somewhat more than 60 per cent may be described as electoral democracies (Freedom House, 2001). Using Freedom House's high standards concerning respect for human rights and the rule of law, however, only eighty-five states (44 per cent) can be considered to be liberal democracies, comprising only about 38 per cent of the world's population (see http://www.freedomhouse.org/reports/century.html). In addition to that, according to the Union of International Associations (UIA), which publishes the *Yearbook of International Organizations* annually, there are around 26,000 international treaties, 5,200 inter-governmental organizations, more than 15,000 non-governmental organizations, and some 40,000 multinational corporations. These numbers become a bit less extreme if calculation is done according to the traditional method: in which case, for the year 2002, the UIA estimated that there were 251 inter-governmental organizations with international legal standing, and 6,076 NGOs with worldwide or regional membership.

Ernst-Otto Czempiel (1993, 2002) suggested some time ago that the analysis of world-wide political processes should be orientated on the basis of the three 'worlds' of business, society and states. Under this rubric, the competence of international politics to develop solutions is largely restricted to the 'world of states'. However, the increasing global interconnectedness of the areas of business, culture, environment, technology, communication, transportation and migration have at the same time led to a decrease in the ability of the individual state to control events. A large number of problems remain stuck halfway on the road to a solution through international co-operation. Even in those fields of politics in which the political responsibility must remain for the foreseeable future in national hands, the traditional patterns of international relations among sovereign states are changing to a pattern of reflexive interactions among members of a community of states conscious of their mutual dependence, their mutual vulnerability, and their responsibility to consider the effects on their neighbours of proposed solutions to national problems. (Scharpf, 1999, p. 181)

Global Governance as a Possible Solution?

What, then, does this roughly-sketched portrait of the globalization process mean for the role and function of the United Nations, which conceives itself as being at the centre of attempts to realize the manifold goals of the Charter, ensuring world peace and friendly relations among nations, and promoting international co-operation?

A significant part of the present discourse of world order consists of the question of whether binding regulations on inter-state politics can and ought to be made. Such regulations would both further relativize national sovereignty (which is already eroding in many fields) in the global interest, and win back the UN's capability to control and influence problems that cross borders. In a world that is getting smaller, as Volker Rittberger (2000, p. 188) has maintained, there is a still need for those capabilities that traditionally were exercised by the state, but which today's states are no longer capable of exercising:

> A growing number of actors whose activities cross borders requires generally binding rules and other public capabilities which put them in a position to pursue both their individual and common interests, and which prevent conflicts of interest from producing effects which are destructive for either of the parties as well as for third parties.

How this is to be accomplished is a matter of some controversy among political scientists. Granting that globalization may change significantly economic, social and cultural life, representatives of the above-mentioned Realist School see no need for action because they see the nation-state remaining the central entity of international politics. Members of the Idealistic School evaluate the facts differently. For them, globalization means a fundamental transformation of global political processes, which make the Realists' visions look increasingly obsolete. For Idealists, international relations are like a spider's web, in which the state is understood as one (important) actor among many, but an actor that is no longer in a position to define what takes place on its own territory in an isolated fashion. Since, at the same time, Idealists acknowledge a great need for regulation in border-crossing issues, they seek alternative steering models for the globalized world.

One attempt to meet these global challenges goes by the name of global governance. By this term, political scientists understand an alternative steering model for the international system that includes international organizations as well as informal rules and norms. The concept is not to be confused with similar-sounding ideas such as global government, but is best understood as a particular form of a politics of world order. In this difficult process, the United Nations plays a central role, to which we shall return in the section discussing the various areas of UN action (on the concept of global governance, see Chapter 9).

Globalization may be understood as an indication of the accelerating, earth-spanning interconnection of actors and fields of action. In particular, the number of issue areas which do not (or no longer) allow for a national solution is a reliable indicator of the stage that globalization has already reached. Thus the central challenge for the discipline of international relations is to search for border-transcending substitutes for the dwindling steering capacities previously found at the nation-state level. How democratic and effective governance beyond the nation-state may be possible under these conditions remains one of political science's unanswered questions. The very demand for 'intelligent' mechanisms for this issue area is clear evidence that none have as yet been found. We shall return to this question, and the role of the United Nations in this area, in more detail in Chapter 9.

The Primary Tasks of the United Nations and the Expansion of the Concept of Security

Should one ask what the concrete areas of responsibility and chief tasks of the United Nations are, one is likely to receive several different answers. This is partly because the UN understands itself to be a global forum for international co-operation whose more precise responsibilities are somewhat difficult to pin down. The United Nations was created as an all-encompassing organization in so far as it was promised far-reaching competence. Its area of responsibility was the whole world, and all human problems calling for international attention must therefore fall under its purview (Claude, 1970, p. 67). Those interested in the politics of development will thus emphasize development issues, those interested in the environment, environmental issues, those interested in security, the security aspect, and so on.

At the foundation of the work of the United Nations lies a broad concept of peace that includes not only the desire to hinder the occurrence of war, but also the improvement of mankind's humanitarian and social status, the strengthening of international law, and long-term development concerns. The nearly-six-decades-old UN Charter thus anticipated a debate that has been occupying political scientists at least since the work of Johan Galtung on structural violence, and since the 1960s discussion of positive versus negative concepts of peace. However, this debate became much more intense in the 1990s, and has since been classified under the heading of the 'expansion of the concept of security'. This is about a horizontal broadening of the parameters of security, as well as a vertical increase in the reference points of security. It comprises three dimensions:

(i)   Economic interdependence and military-technological developments have led to the dissolution of the classical definition of security in relation to the

3

The Core of the United Nations: Collective Security

If one accepts the notion that Article 1 of the UN Charter does indeed represent a positive concept of peace, as discussed earlier, an apparent incongruity soon emerges. The provisions of the operative chapters concentrate expressly on the avoidance and ending of classical inter-state conflicts and wars. Attempts aimed at the sustainable elimination of the many economic, social or humanitarian causes of violence and war – as would be expected from a broader understanding of peace – are treated with comparative brevity. This fixation on inter-state conflict is understandable in light of the context, overwhelmingly influenced by the experience of the Second World War, in which the United Nations came into existence. The general inference drawn from the Second World War was the urgent need to eliminate war as a tool of international relations as a necessary prerequisite for the development of a comprehensive global peace. The basic principle on which all the United Nations' efforts to ensure peace are built is that of 'collective security'. Before we go into the normative and organizational development of this principle through first the League of Nations and then the United Nations, it seems appropriate to lay out and discuss this idea of collective security with respect to its assumptions, its intrinsic problems, and its practical potential for the maintenance of global peace.

The Principle of Collective Security: Limitations and Possibilities

The history of international relations has always been characterized by the fact that states use force to pursue their interests. As the countries of the world have moved closer together as a result of increasing political, economic and cultural linkage and interdependence, there have been ever more frequent attempts to avoid, or at least to limit, the damage and disruption of war, both for the states involved directly and for the international system as a whole. Non-aggression pacts, defensive alliances, reassurance treaties and careful balanced constellations among the great powers all showed themselves – in the catastrophe of the First World War – to be far too fragile to create durable constraints on the will of states to pursue their interests with force. Above all, the lack of internationally accepted norms forbidding the use of force, and authoritative bodies for the maintenance of a peace built upon such norms, allowed states to appeal to their sovereignty and to fall back constantly upon the *ultima ratio regum*: war.

The attempt at collective security, as it was first introduced into international politics with the League of Nations following the First World War, was an attempt to address these deficits. It was based on the assumption that all states might be capable of, and willing to, subordinate their own sovereign rights, and their own particular interests and needs, to a common interest in peaceful and stable international relations, and to take part in the creation of a global system capable of restraining its members from the threat or use of force. In contrast to a system of collective defence, whose members assure one another of aid in the case of threat or aggression from outside, a collective security system is orientated towards the states organized within it, using obligations and the threat of sanctions to influence them. In its ideal form, such a system would approximate a world state with a monopoly on the use of force and executive authority with respect to the individual member states. Because the creation of such a world state is a rather unrealistic goal, the only option left in practice for the realization of collective security is the voluntary self-limitation of states on the basis of an international treaty which:

- Obliges the parties to settle their disputes in a peaceful manner;
- Creates an organ with the authority to make judgements about the type and degree of possible violations of duties, as well as the consequences of such violations; and
- Contains clear provisions for measures for the enforcement of such judgements.

The capacity for effective action enjoyed by such a system, however, still depends on a whole string of prerequisites. First, all states must be ready to subject their interest in a forceful alteration of the political and territorial status quo to a general prohibition on the use of force (Claude, 1970, p. 250), even if they still consider themselves to be entitled to the use of force. They must also be ready to act collectively against a violator of the peace, even if that means once again disregarding their own interests. In any case, such a system would need an institutionalized process of peaceful dispute resolution as well as a central instance equipped with sufficient power – including military power – to implement any decisions taken. All states must agree upon not only the legal norms and rules, but also the procedures for the further development of them, for the purposes of dealing with violations of the peace and the measures to be taken to address them. The decisive factor for the functional capability of a system of collective security, however, which cuts through all the prerequisites mentioned so far, is trust. Every state must be able to rely upon at least the overwhelming majority of the other members of the system to abide by the rules in a more or less permanent way. Furthermore, every peace-loving state must be able to rely on the expectation of assistance from the others in case of aggression. Such reliance involves great demands not only on the other member states, but also on the effectiveness and impartiality of the central adjudicatory and enforcement body.

Most of the criticism of the idea of collective security arises from these complex prerequisites. From the Realist side, the objection is that, although the attempt at collective security superficially accepts a picture of international anarchy with egoistic states as the principal actors at its starting point, it fails to provide a conclusive solution to the problem of why states should overcome their mutual mistrust and the need for individual security sufficiency that arises from it. In the end, any attempt at collective security still begins from the assumption that there are in fact states that intend to behave aggressively, and thus strengthens the Realist precept of lingering inter-state insecurity and the permanent security dilemma (Mearsheimer, 1994, p. 30 et seq.). Further concerns about the effectiveness and efficiency of a system of collective security will accrete to that fundamental objection. For example, in a system made up of states, with institutions controlled by those states, decisions are always dependent on the interests of those states. Even a distinction between aggressor and victim – which becomes absolutely necessary at some point – is never easy, since the causes of war are usually very complex, and there is nearly always direct or indirect involvement of a large number of other states. Clientelism and a lack of congruence of interest among the states represented in the decision-making situation make international panels look particularly unsuited to playing the role of mediator or impartial referee. Moreover, even in relatively unambiguous cases, although many states may be interested in the cessation of hostilities, they quickly part ways on how to apportion the burdens of that undertaking. The phenomenon of free-riding, such a constant accompaniment to collective undertakings, undermines common actions even when there is widespread agreement about the needs and goals. The refusal of even a relatively small number of members to support an action leads to the deceleration, and sometimes even the paralysis, of the collective security mechanism. This problem is made even more acute when the system has to deal with several violations at the same time. Comprehensive and obligatory norms cannot endure selectivity without some loss to their obligation and credibility. On the other hand, if an attempt is made to meet every instance of aggression with the same decisiveness and unanimity, the system will very quickly find itself at the outer limits of its capacity (Roberts, 1993, p. 5).

It must in fact be admitted that collective security seems to be able to promise success only against relatively small, weak states. Should a great power, with the corresponding military potential, appear as the aggressor, the costs of engagement will quickly overtake the expected benefits. Their special position can even lead great powers to abuse a system of collective security, in that they usurp its decision-making body and conduct their politics under a veil of action in the collective interest (Hurrell, 1992, p. 45; Butfoy, 1993, p. 494). If it is not possible, however, to bind great powers into a system of collective security and the rules that go with it, the only option remaining from the Realist perspective is to fall back on the classical defensive alliances, balance of power arrangements, or concerts of the great powers. Thus, followers of the Realist school tend to conclude that because every state – and especially every great power – decides on a case-by-case basis according to its own interests whether and how a victim of aggression is to be assisted, and because democracies in particular make such decisions dependent upon the often tedious deliberation and (uncertain) consent of parliamentary bodies, the concept of collective security proves itself to be highly unrealistic. (Link, 1998, p. 106)

Liberal theorists, too, criticize the concept as inappropriate for the practice of international politics. According to Ernst-Otto Czempiel (1994, 25 et seq.), the idea of collective security is a great leap forward in terms of the history of theory, but has shown itself to be rather ineffectual in the logic of politics. Politics relies on a mechanism that does not work on a global scale. While these criticisms tend to remove the idea of collective security, with its complex and manifold prerequisites, into the realm of political utopia, other critics point at the incipient problems of a *functioning* system of collective security. If violence in international relations is considered to be basically and fundamentally wrong, but a collective security system endows its central effective body with the power to legitimize the use of force, or to empower others to use force legitimately, there is always the danger of an abuse of this authority. It is only natural that, in a global system, the norms underlying that system must be relatively abstract, and in any given case would require interpretation in order to facilitate a decision. Thus, in a complex world, conflicts of value and interest are practically programmed in: what is for one group of states a legitimate action in pursuit of peace, may for another group be an attempt to impose foreign ideas. This could present a dangerous opportunity for crusaders, warns Stanley Hoffmann (1981, p. 61). Through external involvement, limited conflicts could turn into altercations covering massive areas.

This is even more the case, as it becomes more common for the domestic affairs of states to be put on the agenda of the collective security system. Interventions on the part of the system in smaller, chronic conflicts could lead to these conflicts becoming incapable of fulfilling their function, which is to produce the conditions for a sustainable peace accord. In place of an order created by the parties to the conflict, there will be an order created by the organization, for which it must be responsible and must sustain, possibly even against the protracted opposition of one or more of the original parties to the conflict. The resulting international protectorates tie up the strength and resources of both the system and its member states in significant measure, and severely limit its ability to act in other conflicts.

The multifarious and serious objections against a system of collective security can all be concentrated into the question of whether the goal might not in the end simply be impossible to achieve; whether the creation of a global interest absorbing all particular needs and safeguarded by a central organ with a sustainable claim to legitimacy is at all feasible. Is 'collective security' in fact a myth, one that has never functioned and can never function (Czempiel, 1994, p. 25 et seq)? Should states preferably concentrate on the formulation and realization of their national interests (Nye, 1999), and through the clever use of their power and the application of tried and proven methods ensure that global stability results – in some sense – as the sum of these counter-balancing interests?

A large part of the criticism is in fact aimed at a straw man – a very idealized version of what collective security is meant to achieve. The concept would shed a great deal of its ostensible utopianism if it were understood with respect to its normative function as a target value for international relations and to its organizational design as a rule-based framework for the ordering of international relations. A system of collective security does not necessarily have to set institutions in the place of states as the central actors of international politics, and does not necessarily make classical security precautions superfluous. Instead, such a system may contribute to the creation of conditions that make the peaceful resolution of conflicts easier and more likely to enjoy success than they would under the conditions of international anarchy.

From this perspective, a system of collective security is complementary to rather than a replacement for other forms of, or attempts at, global and regional peace-maintenance; a 'value added' (Kupchan and Kupchan, 1995, p. 54). It offers alternative ways of handling conflicts, involving the use of institutions that may not be perfectly impartial, but whose initiatives and decisions do rest on compromises and the co-ordination of interests among very different powers, which limits the effects of arbitrariness. The advantages of such a system lie in the institutionalization of appropriate forums for consultation and in the tendency to reduce arbitrariness in the decision mechanisms. A system lacking comparable structures must rely exclusively on *ad hoc* measures. A collective security arrangement can also form the basis of a much more extensive system of co-operative security, in which social, economic, humanitarian or ecological problems can also be addressed through institutions. Through international consultation and co-operation, a broad palette of organizations, institutions, treaties or looser regimes can be developed which, with their varying levels of obligation, can set the standard or point to the proper direction for state activity.

The UN constitutes such a system of collective security. It has on the one hand made a number of departures from its original ideal because of the constraints of reality, but on the other has actively used opportunities to broaden the scope of its responsibilities and activities, even into the realm of co-operative security. With Art. 51, the Charter allows for the continuing need for individual and collective self-defence, but with its general prohibition on the use of force and the conditions laid out in Chapter VII, it has subjected every other form of violence to a Security Council monopoly on the legitimization of force, and anchored it solidly in the order of international law. The elevated position of the five permanent members of the Security Council represents the concept of a concert of responsible powers, which should – at least in theory – lead to largely acceptable decisions on the basis of compromises among enormously heterogeneous interests. It was in fact only on this basis that the decisive powers could be convinced to take part in the organization, although after more than fifty years of UN existence, that construction may be in dire need of reform (as will be seen below).

At any rate, the UN is still more of a forum than an actor, even in its primary purpose of securing peace through collective measures. Furthermore, it is a forum whose potential is used selectively, or in many cases not at all, by its member states. This hesitation on the part of the states is based on the one hand on the pervasive problems and contradictions between the Charter and the actual practice of the organization, but above all on a lack of trust in multilateral institutions. Before the following sections elaborate on the possibilities available for address-ing this deficit, and for developing new confidence in the potential and competen-cies of the world organization, the normative and organizational development of the collective security system of the UN as explained in the Charter must first be described.

Still a Challenge: The Exclusion of War from International Relations

In order to use its agency effectively, a collective security system needs a set of general norms and rules, against which its members are to measure their behaviour and through which the decisions and measures of the responsible instances of the system are legitimized. In the Charter of the United Nations, Art. 2(4)'s general prohibition on the use of force stands out among these general norms as the funda-mental norm of international law: 'All Members shall refrain in their international relations from the threat or use of force against the territorial integrity or political independence of any state, or in any other manner inconsistent with the Purposes of the United Nations.' This general prohibition on the use of force, which finds its complement in Art. 2(3)'s duty to resolve conflicts peacefully, represents the most extensive attempt yet to create a global order of peace on the basis of norms of international law. This apparently unambiguous and comprehensive legal princi-ple, however, provokes a number of questions arising from its origin, its legal scope and its practical political application. These questions will be discussed below.

The Development of the General Prohibition on the Use of Force

Although it is true that attempts to regulate inter-state relations in both war and peace through legal norms go back far into human history, practical efforts based on an attempt to banish war from the realm of international relations did not emerge until the twentieth century. Even the First World War was begun on the basis of the conviction that war and peace were naturally alternating conditions of inter-state relations. For centuries, the efforts first of moral theory and then of international law were aimed at restraining the effects of war (or, as Carl Schmitt said, 'die Hegung des Krieges'), but not at removing it altogether.

The religiously influenced early medieval ideas of Augustine (354–430 AD), formulated in the thirteenth century by Thomas Aquinas into the *bellum iustum* or the doctrine of just war, allowed recourse to war only under very strict conditions: first, it required *auctoritas principis*, or the auspices of a legitimate authority. Second, the war had to be waged for a just cause (*iusta causa*) such as the punishment of injustice. Finally, it should be waged with the good intention (*recta intentio*) of furthering the just and fighting evil. However, the theological and scholastically-influenced teachings of Aquinas leave open the question of according to what standard of practical worldly politics the 'just cause' was to be determined. In the conflicts of the late Middle Ages and the Early Modern period, marked especially by their confessional character, the *iusta causa* was usually claimed by all sides. Since, however, only one side could possibly be the true possessor of justice and truth, the appeal to the *iusta causa* led not only to the demonization of the foe, but also required a type of warfare that made it necessary not merely to subdue the enemy, but to bring about its near total destruction.

In view of these grave difficulties, the focus on a *iusta causa* slipped increasingly into the background, and attention was turned to the existence of certain formal conditions: in particular, the *auctoritas principis*, the sovereign power of the ruler which legitimized the waging of a just war; the war must also be declared, and certain rules about the way it was conducted must be observed. With the disappearance of a generally accepted overarching authority on questions of good and evil (because of the schism in Christendom and the disintegration of the medieval idea of empire), justice and injustice started down a new path. Following the intermediate idea of a war that might be just on both sides (*bellum iustum ex utraque parte*), found primarily in the writings of Francisco de Vitoria (1486–1546) and Alberico Gentili (1552–1608), there developed a morally indifferent concept of war, and finally the notion of a right to war (*ius ad bellum*) deriving from the sovereignty of the state. As predicted by Hugo Grotius (1583–1645) in 1625, in the world order created by the Peace of Westphalia (1648), war and peace became morally neutral legal situations in the intercourse of sovereign states among one another. There arose an anarchical system of international politics, which imposed no legal or moral limitations on a state's use of power. The cabinet wars of the eighteenth century and the wars of imperial conquest of the nineteenth could be waged equally well under the generally accepted and poignantly formulated Clausewitzian understanding of war as the continuation of politics by other means. Even in 1918, the Netherlands refused to extradite Emperor Wilhelm II to the victorious allies on the justification that, with the unleashing of the First World War, the Emperor had merely been using the *ius ad bellum* to which a sovereign state was entitled.

As problematic as the war-legitimizing effects of the principle of unlimited sovereignty must be seen in hindsight, it is equally true that, without this principle as the foundation of the morally neutral system of classical international law, the development of international relations among units with equal rights would hardly have been imaginable. The decline of the tendency to think in categories of good and evil also had consequences for the conduct of war, which was freed from the need to punish the loser comprehensively. With the understanding of war as a legitimate instrument of the pursuit of interest, the need also arose for the legal regulation of its inception, its conduct and its cessation, as well as for the protection of the civil populace. The law of war (*ius in bello*) became, next to the law of peace, the second pillar of international law. Although the *ius in bello* was in no way aimed at preventing war, its progressive drawing of warfare into the realm of legal norms, and its gradual dismantling of war's function of arbitration in international conflicts, created serious hurdles for any head of state who might wish to follow that route. Above all, in the efforts of the law of war to limit the damages and consequences of war for both soldiers and uninvolved civilians lay the seeds of international humanitarian law. The Hague Conventions on the Laws and Customs of War on Land, resulting from the peace conferences of 1899 and 1907, are the most important documents of this epoch (and are still valid as part of international humanitarian law at the time of writing). These attempted to regulate the laws and customs of land warfare according to humanitarian considerations.

The catastrophe of the First World War provided a dramatic demonstration of the deficiencies of an international regime that merely regulated the actual course of warfare, and caused a fundamental change in the way the major powers thought about war. It was recognized that the vast dimensions and total nature of modern warfare constituted an existential threat to the international structure and to humanity in general. With the constitution of the League of Nations, based on the fourteen points of American president Woodrow Wilson, the establishment of a partial prohibition on war was undertaken, to be guaranteed by a collective system of peace maintenance.

Article 11 of the League of Nations Charter disestablished the *ius ad bellum* as a subjective right of individual states: 'Any war or threat of war, whether immediately affecting any of the Members of the League or not, is hereby declared a matter of concern to the whole League, and the League shall take any action that may be deemed wise and effectual to safeguard the peace of nations.' However, in 1919, the states were still unable to push through a general prohibition on war, much less on the use of force as such. The preamble held only that '[t]he high contracting parties, in order to promote international co-operation and to achieve international peace and security by the acceptance of obligations not to resort to war, by the prescription of open, just and honourable relations between nations, by the firm establishment of the understandings of international law as the actual rule of conduct among Governments, and by the maintenance of justice and a scrupulous respect for all treaty obligations in the dealings of organized peoples with one another, Agree to this Covenant of the League of Nations'. Article 12 of the Convenant also requires merely that disputes that are 'likely to lead to a rupture' should be submitted to arbitration, judicial settlement or enquiry by the Council. During the phase in which the League was addressing the issue – being in the case of a Council enquiry less than six months, and in the cases of arbitration or judicial settlement, within 'a reasonable time' – and for a period of three months after the proceedings were closed, the parties were not allowed to resort to war. In practical terms, this clause created a 'cooling-off period' of about nine months' duration (Weber, 1995), after which, if the situation were still unresolved, recourse to war was possible. Only in the case of a unanimous recommendation by the Council, to which the parties to the conflict were willing to submit themselves, was there an actual prohibition on war (Art. 15(6)). If, on the other hand, the recommendations should have been merely those of the majority, 'the Members of the League reserve[d] to themselves the right to take such action as they shall consider necessary for the maintenance of right and justice' Art 15 (7)). Even this delaying effect, however, related only to the waging of war, and not to any use of force below that threshold, as long as it was declared as a measure of self-help (Guggenheim, 1932, 109).

In the first half of the 1920s, a number of initiatives attempted to close the loopholes and normative grey zones created by this partial prohibition on war. At the centre of these efforts stood the completion of the League's statute, especially with respect to the banning of aggressive war, which was still theoretically permissible. However, the Geneva Protocol of 2 October, 1924, which described aggressive war as an 'international crime' and intended to implement obligatory arbitral jurisdiction, never came into force (Wehberg, 1927). In the framework of the Western Pact, the Locarno Treaty of 16 October 1925 established a regional prohibition on aggressive war between Germany and Belgium, and between Germany and France, as well as obligatory arbitral jurisdiction between Germany and Poland and Czechoslovakia. A long list of exceptions made these agreements as full of holes as the others, but the Locarno Treaties accelerated a much more ambitious process of development that led finally to the general prohibition on war in the Kellogg–Briand Pact of 27 April 1928.

This Pact, arising out of a Franco–American initiative and named after the two Foreign Ministers, Aristide Briand and Frank B. Kellogg, represented a decisive breakthrough. Whereas the Statute of the League of Nations forbade war only under certain circumstances, and the Locarno Treaties forbade only aggressive war among specifically enumerated states, Article 1 of the Kellogg–Briand Pact finally made the unambiguous statement that 'The High Contracting Parties solemnly declare in the names of their respective peoples that they condemn recourse to war for the solution of international controversies, and renounce it, as an instrument of national policy in their relations with one another.' The only exceptions to this prohibition remained war for self-defence and collective measures of the League of Nations. These exceptions did not, however, represent a weakening of the general prohibition on war, but rather a confirmation of it. As forceful self-defence and forceful emergency aid are permissible in domestic law only against criminal actions, the rights to self-defence and collective aid at the international level worked to confirm the criminal nature of the actions against which they might be directed. In all, sixty-three countries joined the Kellogg–Briand Pact, comprising the overwhelming majority of the states existing at the time. The general prohibition on war was thus already a part of Customary International Law in the 1930s, and as such enjoyed worldwide legal validity independent of membership of the Pact.

In spite of its clear formulation and uncontested legal validity, however, even this general prohibition on war could not prevent the outbreak of the First World War. For one thing, the Kellogg–Briand Pact had not included 'measures short of war' in the scope of its prohibition, thus leaving the problem of grey areas unsolved. For another, the implementation of the prohibition on war had been left to the inadequate collective security system of the League of Nations. In 1945, the framers of the UN Charter planned to overcome these structural weaknesses. At the organizational level, a system for securing peace was created with at least the potential for being powerful. In the normative realm, the regulations of the Kellogg–Briand Pact with respect to the general prohibition on war were comprehensively expanded: not only the use, but also the threat of force in international relations were declared impermissible. This development's effect on the shape of modern international law cannot be overestimated. No international treaty with peace- or security-political goals, but lacking some reference to the Charter's general prohibition on the use of force, is even imaginable. The UN's realization of universal membership also lends the general prohibition a universal legitimacy, which would continue to apply even if the United Nations is dissolved, since the principle has entered into general international law.

The Prohibition on the Use of Force: Concept and Extent

The regulations found in Art. 2(4) of the UN Charter are less unambiguous than their language might lead one to suspect at first glance. The concept of 'force' is in particular need of a more precise explanation, in order to enable a distinction between the legitimate use of power by states in international relations and the illegitimate use of force. This clarification becomes even more urgent in light of the fact that a violation of the general prohibition on the use of force can justify both individual and collective reactions, which may in their turn employ force.

According to currently dominant legal opinion, the application of Article 2(4) is restricted to the use of military force between states (Randelzhofer, 2002). This interpretation does not, however, reduce the general prohibition on the use of force to a mere prohibition on war, which was already present in general international law, because it also includes the use of military force not amounting to war. The 'Declaration on Principles of International Law Concerning Friendly Relations and Co-operation Among States in Accordance with the Charter of the United Nations' of 24 October 1970, a declaration of principles by the General Assembly, is very telling on this point. In pursuing its goal of the further development and codification of basic norms of international law, it considers the general prohibition on the use of force to be the primary principle of state behaviour, far outweighing all others. In a thorough comment on the general prohibition on the use of force, the following rules and duties are set out:

- Aggressive wars are branded as crimes against peace;
- States may not use or threaten the use of force in order to harm the existing status of international borders, and may not make use of a propaganda of aggression;
- They may not use force in measures of retaliation;
- They may not involve themselves in the formation or the support of the formation of irregular armed forces or armed bands which have as their purpose the violation of the sovereign territory of another state;

- They must refrain from the organization, incitement, or support of acts of civil war or terrorism in another state, and may not suffer the support of such actions to take place in their sovereign territory;
- They may not obtain the sovereign territory of another state through the use of force. ('Declaration on Friendly Relations' A/RES/2625(xxv))

These comments confirm that the general prohibition on the use of force applies only to military or paramilitary force. At the same time, they also make it clear that indirect forms of the use of force that are carried out through the support of violent actions in another state also fall under this prohibition. That said, however, there still remains the question of which forms and levels of support to rebel organizations or parties to civil wars qualify as violations. In its decision on the military and paramilitary activities in and against Nicaragua, the International Court of Justice referred expressly to the Declaration on Friendly Relations, and described the USA's arming and training of the 'Contra' rebels, but not its financial support for them, as a use of force. Thus the Court recognized that there are permissible and impermissible forms of intervention in civil wars and uprisings, but failed to provide clear criteria for determining the difference between the two (Randelzhofer, 2002).

According to the specifications of the Declaration on Friendly Relations, all forms of economic pressure are expressly excluded from the prohibitions in Art 2 (4) of the UN Charter. This remains the case even though socialist and developing states made constant calls during the Cold War and the phase of decolonization to include them in the prohibition on force. However, the Declaration also includes a prohibition on intervention, which not only reinforces the ban on military activities, but also makes some economic, political and other non-military forms of pressure illegitimate, as well. Given that economic and military pressure often go hand in hand, however, a strict limitation of the general prohibition on the use of force to only the classical military application seems problematic, at least (Arangio-Ruiz, 1979, p. 99 et seq). In practice, therefore, it is best left to the Security Council, with the broader perspective on what might constitute a threat to the peace, to decide in individual cases which forms of economic or other non-military pressure are permissible or not.

Exceptions to the General Prohibition on the Use of Force

Although the declared purpose of the United Nations lies clearly in the utter displacement of war and violence from the realm of international relations, the Charter none the less does not entirely rule out the possibility of legitimate uses of force. The Charter considers the fact that there are states which, in the pursuit of their interests and intentions, may use military or other forceful measures, and that the use of force in defence against such states may indeed be necessary. Once again, the existence of permissible uses of force do not emasculate the prohibitory norm, but rather strengthen it in its basic character. The exceptions to the general prohibition which have their basis in the Charter are orientated exclusively on defence against illegal force, and thus do not constitute a covert attempt to reintroduce a *ius ad bellum*. This is made express above all in the fact that these exceptions are not unlimited, and their validity is subject to a whole list of regulations also found in the Charter. According to the UN Charter, the exceptions to the general prohibition on the use of force are:

- Collective measures against a disturber of the peace on the basis of Chapter VII;
- The right of self-defence against an armed attack according to Article 51; and
- Measures taken against former 'enemy states' according to Articles 53 and 107.

The general prohibition on the use of force cannot but be regarded in connection with the collective security system described in Chapter VII, either from the regulations laid down in the Charter or from the perspective of actual UN practice. The prohibition on the use of force and the duty to secure peace constitute legal duties laid upon the members of the UN, the observance of which is to be overseen by the international community and the organs commissioned by it for that purpose – namely, the Security Council. In the logic of a collective security system, one member's violations of common norms must draw proportionate and appropriate measures of retaliation, up to and including the use of military force.

Article 39 of the Charter defines, normatively and procedurally, the conditions under which such forceful measures may be used. First, the Security Council must determine whether a threat to or a breach of the peace, or an act of aggression, has in fact taken place. Should this be the case, the Security Council is authorized to issue non-binding recommendations to the member states with respect to their behaviour towards the disturber of the peace. The Security Council may also decide to take forceful measures that are binding on both the target state and all other members of the UN. It may do this, however, only if it believes that measures provided for in Article 41 'would be inadequate or have proved to be inadequate' (Art. 42) in bringing about a change in the peace-disturbing behaviour of the states involved. Should this be the case, it may invoke Art. 42, under which measures of military force under the leadership of the UN, or individually-named member states, or specified international organizations (Art. 48), may be carried out. It is necessary for such decisions to be taken that a quorum (as defined for the taking of substantive decisions) of nine votes in the Security Council – including the votes of all five permanent members – be forthcoming. The Security Council may also choose to implement enforcement action under its authority through regional arrangements as addressed in Chapter VIII of the Charter (Art. 53). These Chapter VII regulations make it quite clear that, except for the purposes of individual or collective self-defence as set out in Article 51 (see below), force may be used only on the basis of a Security Council determination to that effect. The Security Council may thus be said to possess a monopoly on the legitimization of the use of force.

The Security Council is not a world court, but a political decision-making committee, bound in its competences to the Charter and customary international law. Thus it is necessary to take a closer look at the situations listed in Art. 39 as being the basis of the Security Council's realm of responsibility: threat to the peace, breach of the peace, and act of aggression. A breach of the peace occurs when at least two states undertake acts of armed combat. It is also taken to be a breach of the peace when an independent de facto regime which has not been recognized as a state uses or becomes the victim of armed force. In spite of this relatively clear criterion, the Security Council has as yet seen fit in only four cases (Korea, 1950; the United Kingdom/Argentina, 1982; Iraq/Iran, 1987; and Iraq/Kuwait, 1990) to base its activation on the existence of a breach of the peace.

Every act of aggression also constitutes a breach of the peace, but a finding of an act of aggression requires additionally that the aggressor be named. In order to produce a more precise definition of the situation of 'act of aggression', on 14 December 1974 the General Assembly produced a definition of the concept, which contains in Article 3 a non-exhaustive list of seven types of action, each of which constitutes an act of aggression (UN General Assembly Resolution 3314 (XXIX): Definition of Aggression). As a General Assembly Resolution, this definition is not binding on the Security Council, but it may certainly be used by the Council to evaluate the facts of a situation. In fact, the Security Council has in a large number of cases determined that certain actions constituted acts of aggression, including Southern Rhodesia's incursion into Zambia in 1978, Israel's aerial attacks on PLO targets in Tunisia in 1985, and the South African intervention in Angola in 1985. The Security Council went on, however, to determine that each of these acts had the character of a threat to the peace. Thus far, even in relatively unambiguous cases such as Iraq's invasion of Kuwait, the Security Council has not seen fit to find an act of aggression in the sense of Article 39.

Of the three situations named in Article 39, that of 'threat to the peace' offers the Security Council the widest margin for interpretation. In spite of its conceptual fuzziness and lack of straightforward legal and political intelligibility, it is none the less the key situation of fact for the collective maintenance of peace, as it extends its reach to situations and actions lying in the zone just short of an open breach of the peace. Thus it is capable of offering a non-violent solution to brewing conflict, rather than being constrained to wait until a conflict has already erupted into violence. How flexible the Security Council is willing to be with this concept has been demonstrated by its practice in the 1990s. Internal events including civil war, mass expulsion and other large-scale human rights violations, the breakdown of state apparatus leading to the unrestrained use of force by armed bands and militias, and the state support of terrorist activities, were all labelled threats to international peace, justifying the implementation of collective counter-measures. In principle, all actions a state could take that might possibly call forth an armed reaction can be considered threats to the peace, including such as have no connection with immediate military or otherwise physical force – for example, the damming of a river. If the members of the Security Council agree, they can conceive of the notion of a threat to the peace in extraordinarily broad terms. Through the consistent and expansive use its freedom to interpret the UN charter over the course of the 1990s, the Security Council extended its scope of responsibility and action significantly. The practical effectiveness of the UN collective security system, however, has lagged somewhat behind the vistas of possibility opened up by this practice.

The UN Charter's second exception to the prohibition on the use of force consists of the natural right of a member state to defend itself – either alone or together with other states – against an armed attack (Art. 51). However, the wording of this provision makes it immediately obvious that the framers did not intend to allow even this natural right to stand completely unrestrained. Thus a gap opens up between Article 2(4) and Article 51: the right of self-defence does not obtain against any and all forms of threat or use of force; only against an armed attack. What constitutes an armed attack is left open by the Charter. Even the General Assembly's definition of Aggression does not fully elucidate the matter, because it relates only to the phrase 'act of aggression' in Article 39, and is expressly not intended to regulate anything respecting the right of self-defence against an armed attack (Definition of Aggression, Art. 6). However, the definition can at least aid in clarifying the relationship the concepts 'act of aggression' and 'armed attack' have with one another: an armed attack is a particular type of act of aggression, from which it follows that not all acts of aggression can necessarily be taken to justify an invocation of the Article 51 right of self-defence. This strict construction is in full harmony with the spirit and logic of the Charter, the central purpose of which is to reduce to a minimum the occurrence of the use of force by states. In political practice, however, as will be shown below, problems in the observance of this rule are practically guaranteed.

In the classical view, an armed attack has occurred when a state employs military force to a significant extent and over a protracted period of time. Short-term border incursions and the small-scale battles that may accompany them constitute acts of aggression in the sense of the Definition of Aggression, and thus violations of the Article 2(4) prohibition on the use of force, but not armed attacks in the sense of Article 51. Forceful defensive measures are in fact permissible against such acts of aggression, but these measures must remain of a nature short of military operations. In order to exercise its right of military self-defence, a state must in fact have been the victim of an armed attack; a generally threatening situation does not justify the use of military force. Pre-emptive defensive measures against an obviously and immediately imminent attack, such as in the situation in which Israel found itself on the eve of the Six Day War (1967), are, however, justified according to customary international law. The 9/11 attacks made clear that that not only states but also non-state actors such as terrorist groups can lead armed attacks against a country. In its resolution 1368 of 12 September 2001, the Security Council made it clear that states are authorized to defend themselves under Art. 51 against non-state aggressors. Article 51 thus reinforces the natural right of self-defence, but limits it at the same time by tying it to the requirement that an armed attack must be either under way or imminent. The preventive use of armed forces on the basis of abstract threats and risks, as well as military reactions against other violations of human rights and the forceful implementation of even legitimate rights upheld by arbitration proceedings or international courts, remain all alike forbidden. The security strategy of the USA since September 2002, and its military operations in Iraq in 2003, however, have caused this understanding to come under discussion (see Chapters 4 and 8).

Furthermore, even a state that has been attacked and may exercise its right of self-defence legitimately is not unrestricted in its choice of means. Military operations in self-defence against an armed attack are bound by the law of war principle of proportionality as much as is any other military action. The further limitation in Article 51, that the state undertaking measures in self-defence must inform the Security Council of their actions, and that those actions remain permissible only until collective security measures have been taken by the Security Council, has become rather meaningless. This condition was meant to emphasize the subsidiary character of self-defence within the framework of a collective security system. In practice, however, no country's self-defence measures have ever been suspended through the UN's entrance into the fray.

Article 51 promises the right not only to individual, but also to collective, self-defence. This means that even states that have not themselves been attacked may hurry to the aid of a state that has been attacked, including initiating military operations, without violating the general prohibition on the use of force. The right to military support from other states is, of course, bound to the same prerequisites as the exercise of self-defence for the affected state, and above all to the existence of an armed attack and the principle of proportionality. Thus preventive use of force is still forbidden even as a measure of support. Article 51 does not, however, prevent the formation of preventive defence alliances such as NATO or the former Warsaw Pact. The right to collective defence of a state falling victim to an armed attack does not depend on whether or not that state was already part of such a defensive alliance. However, it is absolutely necessary for this kind of international emergency support that the affected state must request, or at least agree to, such aid. The right of collective self-defence may also be appealed to only by states, so that the support of parties to civil war or domestically displaced ethnic groups may not be justified through this exception to the general prohibition on the use of force.

Over the course of the United Nations' history, the so-called 'enemy state clauses' of Articles 53 and 107, which were to have been the third exception to the general prohibition on the use of force, have become utterly empty of meaning. Enemy states were those that had, during the Second World War, been enemies of one of the signatories of the United Nations Charter (Art. 53(2)), so that not only Germany, but also Bulgaria, Finland, Italy, Japan, Romania and Hungary fell into the category. Should it become necessary to take certain measures against these 'enemy states', regional arrangements (Art. 53) and 'the governments having responsibility for such action' (Art. 107) – that is, the founding members of the UN, were granted special rights to exemption from the general prohibition on the use of force. These special rights related to the taking of preventive forceful measures against the 'renewal of aggressive policy on the part of any such state' (Art. 53(1)), and to the implementation of such measures as normally follow a war, such as the creation and specific formulation of a peace treaty. The 'enemy state' clauses contain – as the heading of Chapter XVII shows – merely transitional security arrangements, explicable by the general uncertainty attending the effectiveness of the newly-formed world organization. The 'enemy state' label was not meant to be an enduring stigma, and could be dissolved by a state's entry into the United Nations Organization. Although neither Article 4 nor Article 53(2) contain such regulations in express form, it may be concluded from the principle of the sovereign equality of all member states (Art. 2(1)), as well as from the Article 4 prerequisite that a state be 'peace-loving' to become a member, that once a state has entered the organization as a member, it may not suffer discrimination as an 'enemy state'. Since, in the intervening time, all the former 'enemy states' have become members of the UN and have, in some cases repeatedly, undertaken responsibility for the world's peace as non-permanent members of the Security Council, the 'enemy state' clauses have become obsolete. The high hurdles to altering the Charter, set down in Articles 108 and 109, have thus far prevented the absolute removal of these clauses. Nevertheless, the General Assembly's Resolution 50/52 (11 December 1995) has instructed that, in any future comprehensive reform of the Charter, the 'enemy state' clauses are to be deleted.

Problems

As the basic constitutional norm of international law, the general prohibition on the use of force is valid worldwide and accepted formally by all states. At the same time, however, it is subject to more frequent violation than nearly any other rule of international law. Since the Charter came into force, its member states have failed to observe the prohibition on military force in more than a hundred cases. However, even in spite of the clear progress over its predecessors, the violence-reduction regime of the Charter still suffers from grey areas that make unambiguous legal and political judgements about certain forms of state use of force extraordinarily difficult to reach. Furthermore, even in cases of aggressive acts, the general prohibition imposes strict regulations and limitations on the use of force, which are difficult for the member states to accept because it is often painfully clear how ineffective the system is in providing security.

Logically, it follows from the definitional gaps between the general prohibition and the right to self-defence that there are in fact some forms of violence that states must suffer without being allowed to respond militarily. In practice, therefore, the states have attempted consistently, and not without success, to interpret their right of self-defence as broadly as possible, in order to justify military measures taken in or against other states. Above all, rescue operations on behalf of one's own citizens – without the agreement or consent of the state where those citizens are located – have been undertaken repeatedly in since the latter decades of the twentieth century. The most spectacular of these operations were those of the Belgians in the Congo in 1959/60 and 1964; the storming of a captured Israeli passenger plane in the Entebbe Airport in Uganda by Israeli commandos in 1976; and the failed attempt of the USA to free its citizens trapped in the US Embassy in Tehran in 1980. In Grenada (1983) and Panama (1989), the USA presented the rescue of nationals as one of several grounds for intervention. During the conflict in Rwanda in 1994, Belgian paratroopers evacuated their own and other nationals, and in March 1997, the Federal Republic of Germany carried out its very first military rescue operation to retrieve twenty Germans and forty nationals of other states from Tirana, Albania.

In no case could these countries point to a rule of international law allowing such actions. According to currently valid regulations and the leading opinion in the realm of international law, such interventions are not measures of self-defence, but rather violations of the general prohibition on the use of force (Pape, 1997, pp. 105 et seq; see in this source also many other supporting sources). On the other hand, no such measures have ever been condemned by the Security Council. In any case, it cannot be concluded from the execution of such illegal actions that a Customary International Law development of a right to protect nationals abroad as part of the right of self-defence has taken place. The legal and political evaluations of most of these actions were, and remain, contested, so that neither a general state practice nor a unanimous conviction of the legal rightness of the actions (*opinio juris*) has emerged. Customary International Law does not provide any grounds beyond those allowed in the UN Charter for legitimizing an individual state's use of force (Deiseroth 1999, p. 3087). This is so even when the rescue operations – because of conditions where there is an acute and enduring threat to the life and limb of nationals – the state where those nationals are located is unable or unwilling to secure them under its own protection, and only appropriate and proportional means are used, might be considered *tolerable* violations of the existing norms (Stein, 2000, 6).

In view of the general reluctance to use the right to self-defence as a justification for the use of military force on behalf of nationals abroad, the legal formula of humanitarian intervention tends to be called upon more often. Thus Dieter Blumenwitz is of the view that it makes no jurisprudential sense to differentiate between the protection of one's own nationals and the support of foreign nationals in the case of massive human rights violations (Blumenwitz, 1994, 7). It must be seen immediately, however, that the very invocation of a right to humanitarian intervention contains within itself difficulties that strike to the very core of the general prohibition on the use of force and the peace-maintenance mechanism of the United Nations.

The shift in global conflict patterns from classical inter-state to intra-state disputes that occurred with the end of the Cold War placed before the United Nations new and grave challenges. The responsibilities of the UN and the shape of its organs had been designed to prevent or limit inter-state war, because that was the most important form of disturbance of the peace that existed at the time of its founding. Domestic occurrences such as civil war, human rights abuses, humanitarian catastrophes, and even the genocide in Cambodia fell into the common understanding under the scope of Article 2(7)'s prohibition on intervention, and were not amenable to interference by the UN. In the 1990s, in view of the quality and intensity of violence being used in these internal disputes, the Security Council occupied itself with a large number of them, from Iraq and Somalia through Rwanda and Haiti to East Timor and the former Yugoslavia. The Council determined that these cases constituted threats to the peace according to Article 39 of the Charter, and thus approved forceful measures and authorized humanitarian interventions using military means.

This aggressive enlargement of the Security Council's competence is usually seen as having happened within the bounds of the Charter (Fink, 1999, 877), and sometimes even as having been inevitable. If the Security Council is in fact authorized to determine that an internal conflict constitutes or results in a threat to the peace, then its decision to take collective measures for the purposes of eliminating that threat is in accord with both the regulations and the logic of the Charter. The Charter does not, however, recognize any subsidiary right of self-defence (analogous to that of states) for the affected groups of people in the case of internal conflicts or massive human rights violations. A group of people forced into a threatened position may, of course, defend themselves, but they may not appeal for help to other states in any way that might justify an exception to the general prohibition on the use of force. Forceful humanitarian interventions may thus take place only as collective measures under the authority of the Security Council. This also means that the possibility of military protection of fundamental human rights or aid to a group of victimized people depends entirely on the effectiveness of the UN regime. In view of the ever-recurring inability of the Security Council to reach decisions because of the threat or use of a veto by one of the permanent members, there is clearly a large discrepancy between the need for an effective regime in the protection of human rights, and the legally permissible means available to achieve such a regime.

The member states of NATO attempted to fill in this gap in 1998 and 1999, when they first threatened and then used massive force to compel the Serbian armed forces to leave the province of Kosovo and cease the grave human rights violations being carried out there. The Security Council had already imposed an arms embargo in March 1998 (Resolution 1160, 31 March 1998). It then went on to describe the situation as a threat to the peace in two further resolutions (Resolution 1199, 23 September, 1998; and Resolution 1203, 24 October 1998). Because of Russian and Chinese opposition, however, no authorization for the use of military force was forthcoming, so NATO acted alone. The broad public, political and academic discussion about the permissibility of this non-authorized use of force that followed the action cannot be expanded upon here. What is important for us to note is that, even if the dominant opinion is true and NATO's actions were morally justified as emergency aid, the damage to the effectiveness of the general prohibition on the use of force and the collective security system cannot be overlooked. With barely a respite, the general prohibition was faced with a whole new set of challenges in spring of 2003 by the military intervention of the USA and its allies in Iraq, which also took place against the will of the Security Council (see Chapter 4).

In fact, for quite some time now the prohibition on the use of force has been developing regressively in the case-law. This has been happening not only in humanitarian cases, but also in other grey areas of international relations: retaliation against terrorist attacks, for example, as in the cases of the USA against Libya in 1992 and against Afghanistan and the Sudan in 1998, or pre-emptive use of force against imminent attack, as in the case of Israel against Egypt in 1967. Even though the general prohibition on the use of force is legally valid independently of the effectiveness of the collective security system created to enforce it, violations of it – no matter how justified they may be as individual cases – cannot but have serious consequences for the credibility of this central constitutional norm. Every violation brings that much more harm to the prohibition and puts one more crack in the Security Council's monopoly on the legitimization of the use of force. The UN's attempt to make the system of international relations more stable and secure through legal regulation, which has prospered surprisingly well despite all the setbacks, would be doomed to ultimate failure by a further weakening or dissolution of the general prohibition on the use of force. The possibility of developing a customary norm that would derogate from the prohibition and partly eliminate, partly complement the norms fixed by international treaty, seems to hold little promise. The violent interventions of individual states or groups of states are nearly always guided by particular interests, along with the pretended or real orientation on general humanitarian goals and standards. The formation of an *opinio juris* consistent with general state practice is thus most unlikely.

The general prohibition on the use of force has proved unable to remove war from the international scene. It has, however, become a basic norm against which both the individual and collective behaviour of states have been able to orientate themselves, and thus it is hardly possible to conceive of an international system without it. In any case, the constant divergence of state practice and rules of international law leads to significant problems. Tolerating violations of the prohibition on the use of force leads only to the lowering of the threshold for violating it again, thus eroding the norm. It is imperative, then, that the collective security structure of the UN is strengthened, if the system of international relations is not to be thrown back on the doctrines of *ius ad bellum*, or just war. Thus the following sections will first explain and discuss the collective security system contained in the UN Charter, and then explore the management of this system in political practice (Chapter 4) and the possibilities available for its reform (Chapter 8).

From the League of Nations to the United Nations: The Organizational Evolution of Peace-maintenance

It is nearly impossible to have a full understanding of the intentions informing the founding of the United Nations collective security system without at least a brief look at the League of Nations. The connection in which the two organizations are usually mentioned is that the United Nations was designed to address the normative and structural weaknesses and deficits of its predecessor. Although on the one hand this is true, on the other, such a perspective makes it too easy to overlook the far-reaching developments set in motion by the League of Nations, and the organizational conditions it created, on which the United Nations was able to anchor itself. This is true particularly for the basic mission of the League of Nations: to create a regime for the prevention of war based on norms of international law, and to place the responsibility for peace with an international organization.

The catastrophe of the First World War made the ultimate failure of the Westphalian state system in Europe obvious to everyone. Even during the war, a number of peace societies (for example, the Union of Democratic Control, the *Schweizer Friedensbureau*, or the League of Nations Society) as well as individuals (such as Léon Bourgeois, Henry Noel Brailford, or Matthias Erzberger) had already begun to lay plans for a post-war order on the basis of an international federation (Schücking and Wehberg, 1924, pp. 7–10). The American president, Woodrow Wilson, relied in part on these ideas when he gave his famous 'fourteen points' speech before both houses of Congress on the occasion of the USA's entry into the First World War. In this speech, he outlined the American objective for the war, and demanded that 'A general association of nations must be formed under specific covenants for the purpose of affording mutual guarantees of political independence and territorial integrity to great and small states alike' (Wilson, 1918, p. 367/Point 14). Parallel to the Paris Peace Conference, a League of Nations Commission comprising representatives from fourteen states worked on a draft for a League of Nations Statute, which was heavily influenced by Wilson's ideas. The work lasted from February 1919 until 28 April 1919, when the full assembly of the peace conference adopted the statute.

With only a few changes, this statute then became an integral part of each of the four peace treaties signed on 28 June 1919 at Versailles, St. Germain, Trianon and Neuilly. This close connection between the peace treaties and the statute of the League was not only criticized by the defeated Central Powers, but also failed to conform to the expectations of the neutral states, which had been unable to carry their own suggested contributions to the statute. The Covenant of the League of Nations was thus 'introduced into a set of circumstances which removed much of its sacredness in the eyes of the world' (Schücking and Wehberg, 1924, p. 27). These connections to the peace treaties were in fact largely external, and the Covenant remained a stand-alone work with universal goals. The circumstances, however, that only the colonies and territories of the defeated powers fell under the mandate government system of Article 22, and that a number of the areas given up as part of war liquidation were transferred to the League (Eupen-Malmedy, Saargebiet, Danzig, Memel), had the effect of eviscerating the Covenant's chances of acceptance.

Membership of the League was open in principle to all states, but there was a clear differentiation made between founding members and those who joined later. The original members were the signatory powers of the peace treaties (with the obvious exception of the defeated powers – Austria, Bulgaria, Germany and Hungary), along with thirteen neutral countries. Of the thirty-two signatory states to the peace treaties, Ecuador, Hedjas (a part of which was later to be Saudi Arabia) and the USA decided not to ratify the peace treaties, and thus did not enter into membership of the League. A two-thirds majority in the federal assembly was required for the admission of new members. Furthermore, permission for membership was contingent upon the hopeful state's acceptance of an armed forces and armaments arrangement determined by the League. Since such arrangements could be decided upon only by unanimity, the differentiation of member status became a matter of significant political relevance. The original members were able to place requirements on new members that they themselves did not have to observe. Nevertheless, over the course of time, twenty-one states – including all the defeated powers of the First World War – became members of the League of Nations. A right to withdraw from membership in the League with a two-year term of notice was contained within the statute. Nearly a third of the members (nineteen in total) eventually made use of this provision, including the German Empire (1933), Japan (1933), and Italy (1937). According to the Covenant, 'any Member of the League which has violated any covenant of the League may be declared to be no longer a Member of the League by a vote of the Council concurred in by the Representatives of all the other Members of the League represented thereon' (Art. 16), so that even members of the council could be expelled from the organization. The only state to be so treated was the Soviet Union, on 14 December 1939, because of its attack on Finland. By that time, however, the League was already essentially defunct.

According to its Covenant, the League's primary bodies were the Assembly, the Council, and the Permanent Secretariat (Art 2). The Permanent Secretariat had its seat in Geneva, the official seat of the entire League, and where the sessions of both the Assembly and the Council generally took place. All members were represented in the Assembly by a delegation, each delegation having one vote. Non-members who were parties to a dispute that the League wished to address could be invested with a vote and involved in the Assembly's sessions. The Assembly possessed comprehensive competence with respect to all the League's areas of activity and to all questions touching on world peace, so that it was able to deal with any issue and make recommendations on it. The Council consisted of both permanent and non-permanent members, the total number of which changed several times in the course of the League's history. For the year 1920, when the Covenant came into force, it was intended that there would be five permanent members (the 'representatives of the allied and associated powers' of the peace treaties: France, Great Britain, Italy, Japan and the USA), and four non-permanent members, which were to be chosen by the Assembly according to its free judgement. Because the USA declined to enter the League, its permanent seat remained free. A permanent seat was created for Germany on its entry in 1926, and for the Soviet Union when it joined in 1934, and the number of non-permanent members was increased in two phases to eleven.

The Council usually reached its decisions and recommendations through consensus, unless the Covenant specified that some lesser quorum was sufficient for particular issues. In the event that members of the Council became involved in a dispute, their votes were suspended, so they were unable to exercise a veto over any decision reached in their own cases. The Council, which usually met for five (later four) regular sessions each year (and also met for *ad hoc* sessions, when necessary), was allowed the same comprehensive competencies as the Assembly, so the two bodies were in a relationship of competitive responsibility.

This problem was alleviated to some extent through a practical division of labour: the Council, as the smaller body and the one that met more frequently, dealt with the more urgent matters (Weber, 1995), while the Assembly was left with everything else. The Permanent Secretariat, under its two Secretaries-General, Sir James Eric Drummond (until 1933) and François Joseph Avenol, constituted the administrative body of the League. The Secretary-General enjoyed the services of two Deputy Secretaries-General, three Under-Secretaries-General, and an international bureaucracy divided into departments and staffed primarily by personnel recruited from the civil service of the member states.

For the purpose of sustaining world peace and security, the Covenant created a dual system of collective security, orientated on the one hand on the prevention of war through an institutionalization of peaceful processes for dispute resolution, and on the other providing a sanctions mechanism for the purposes of ending wars already in progress. The Covenant's partial prohibition on war obligated all member states to take part in a 'cooling-off process' (see above) in any situation of dispute that might conceivably lead to war. The point of this process was to submit the matter of dispute either to an arbitration process, to the Permanent International Court, or to the Council itself. The Council had six months to investigate the situation and to complete a report, and the court or arbitration process was to have a specific time-frame within which it could operate. During this phase, and including a further period of three months after all these processes should have been carried out in full, no party was allowed to resort to war. In the case that one of the parties to the dispute should accept the judgement, arbitration or unanimous recommendation of the Council, an absolute prohibition on resort to war came into force. Should a Council recommendation be given by a mere majority, however, after the cooling-off period, it was left to the judgement of the parties to the dispute whether to pursue their objectives through war or not.

One of the gravest weaknesses of this set of regulations was that no use of force falling below the threshold of actual war came under the scope of its prescriptions. Thus the question of when a permissible use of force became (impermissible) war, had to remain open. Such ambiguities were of great significance for the effectiveness of the collective security measures. These collective measures, on a spectrum ranging from economic and political boycott to military force, were to be implemented by all the members of the League. In addition, if there was in fact a danger of war, such measures could even be taken against non-members of the League. Because of the lack of a clear definition of aggression, however, as well as the ambiguities regarding permissible versus impermissible uses of force, discussed above, there existed a great deal of uncertainty about the conditions necessary for the implementation of forceful measures in general, and in particular about the scope of the member state's duty to contribute military resources. At the beginning of the 1930s, when Japan invaded northern China, the League did nothing about it. Later, when Japan withdrew from the League in 1933, the organization was even more powerless to prevent the outbreak of the Sino-Japanese war in 1935. In practice, the League exercised its ability to sanction only once: in the Abyssinia War of 1937, the Council laid an (ultimately ineffective) embargo on Italy. The Soviet aggression against Finland in December 1939 did lead to the ejection of the Soviet Union from the League, but in view of the outbreak of the Second World War in September of that same year, it was already clear that the League of Nations had failed as a collective security system.

The culprits normally blamed for this failure are the deficits and ambiguities in the normative underpinnings of the Statute, mentioned above. The special target of such criticism is the fact that the Statute contained only a partial rather than a full prohibition on war. Structural weaknesses in the organization itself, however, must also share some of the blame. The institutional connections between the League and the execution of certain provisions of the Paris Peace Treaties drew the League – fairly or unfairly – into the cross-hairs of the defeated powers' unrestrained revisionist mania (Weber, 1995), thus accelerating its demise. Above all, the League of Nations did not succeed in including all the great powers of the day. The United States preferred a separate peace to the Paris treaties. In 1933, after the National Socialists' seizure of power, the German Reich withdrew from the League, as did Japan. The Soviet Union did not even join until 1934. Thus the League was never able to become a universal organization. On 18 April 1946, at the 21st session of the Assembly, the League was dissolved.

All the same, it would be a mistake to dismiss the League of Nations as a total failure; it stands as a watershed in the history of ideas in international relations. This is so, even if states were not yet ready at the time to give a real chance to this revolutionary new idea of how to prevent war and secure peace, or even to use the global system as a clearing-house for questions of global security (Guggenheim, 1932, pp. 272 et seq). Its ultimate failure in the catastrophe of the Second World War did not lead to a general conviction that the ideas and norms at the foundation of the League were utopian or superfluous. Instead, the need for an effective system of collective security was emphasized dramatically only by the occurrence of the Second World War. With the UN Charter, the world made a second attempt to establish such a system.

The Collective Security System of the UN Charter

Just as the League had done before it, the United Nations erected its collective security system on the two pillars of prevention of war and common enforcement action against disturbers of the peace. In contrast to the League, however, the UN Charter was able to introduce a comprehensive prohibition on both the threat and use of force (Art. 2(4)) into international law, thus alleviating a significant portion of the regulatory ambiguities and normative grey zones. Beyond this, the United Nations succeeded in inducing all the great powers of the time to participate in the new organization, and in creating the Security Council as a potentially powerful and capable organ for taking on primary responsibility for peace (Art. 24).

However, the growing evidence of an East–West conflict made it clear that the consensus of great powers necessary for an effective security system would be all but impossible to achieve in practice. The Security Council, the most important main body of the organization, was to all intents and purposes hamstrung for decades. As a result, the collective security system of the United Nations could never be implemented in the way that the Charter's framers had intended. Instead, the Charter was used to create new instruments of peace-maintenance, such as observation and 'blue helmet' missions. Even after the demise of the bipolar world order, when the Security Council was able to extend its area of competence and to reach decisions on enforcement measures up to and including military force, this was always done in harmony with the relevant norms and rules of the Charter. It is, however, important to go into a brief explanation of the collective security system as originally imagined by those who drafted the Charter. All the deficits and weaknesses that attend it, in spite of all the progress it represents, are an essential part of the explanation of why the practice of the UN and its member states has deviated so much from the ideal. Above all, the Charter's weakness lies in its intentions and claims, which far outstrip the practical political possibilities offered by a world of states. The practice of both the organization and its member states will be examined in the following chapters.

Article 2(3)'s duty to resolve disputes peacefully, as well as the general prohibition on the use of force that follows logically from it (Art. 2(4)), constitute the normative core of the UN collective security system. Their relationship to the two other central constitutional principles of Article 2, the principle of sovereignty (2(1)) and the prohibition on intervention (2(7)), can thus be interpreted to mean that the state's sovereign decision on which means to use for the pursuit of political goals must be subject to the collective interest of world peace and international security. Member states accept this hierarchy of principles when they enter the organization, and thus it has become a part of Customary International Law and being effective beyond the scope of the Charter. Because such normative principles can offer no guarantee of their own observation, however, the United Nations took the opportunity of further specifying the principles and processes of pacific

FIGURE 3.1
Escalatory steps in the collective security system

UN Charter

Peaceful resolution of disputes under Chapter VI

Chapter VII measures to be taken in case of a threat to, or breach of, the peace, and in case of acts of aggression

Article 33 • 34 • 35 • 36 • 37 • 38 • 39 • 40 • 41 • 42 • 43 • 44 • 45 • 46 • 47 • 48 • 49 • 50 • 51

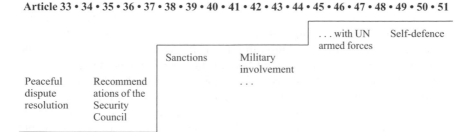

settlement of disputes in Chapter VI. In Chapter VII measures are described that can be taken collectively by the organization against a renegade member in the case of threats to the peace, breaches of the peace or acts of aggression.

The Charter situates the Security Council at the very centre of this security system, placing upon it the primary responsibility for peace. The Security Council is an executive organ with extensive authority to evaluate international and domestic events with respect to their potential to endanger the peace. It is also the only main body enjoying the authority to make decisions that are binding upon all member states (Art. 25).

Chapter VI: The Pacific Settlement of Disputes

In Chapter VI of the Charter, the United Nations set out a number of legal duties for its members, arising from Article 2(3) and regarding the forms and processes of the peaceful resolution of disputes. Article 33(1) requires that

> [t]he parties to any dispute, the continuance of which is likely to endanger the maintenance of international peace and security, shall, first of all, seek a solution by negotiation, enquiry, mediation, conciliation, arbitration, judicial settlement, resort to regional agencies or arrangements, or other peaceful means of their own choice.

This introductory Article of Chapter VI places the primary responsibility for such efforts on the member states; the role of the Security Council in this Chapter remains largely restricted to that of moderator or of catalyst to the various suggested processes. Any member of the UN may bring a matter of dispute to the attention of the Security Council. The Council may also, on its own authority and according to Article 34, undertake to examine any situation with respect to its potential to threaten the peace and issue recommendations on its resolution (Art. 36). All the same, the Council lacks in all processes of peaceful dispute resolution any right to issue binding instructions. Even a suggestion for mediation may be offered only when all parties to the dispute have called for advice (Art. 38).

In the field of tension between sovereign statehood and collective action, Chapter VI accords pride of place to the former. The essential limitation on state sovereignty – aside from the prohibition on the use of force – lies in the obligation actively to seek a peaceful resolution. There is no obligation to produce a certain result or to abide by any third-party declaration. Later statements of the General Assembly designed to clarify the processes of dispute settlement merely confirm the dominance of the principle of sovereignty, rather than indicating possible paths to new forms of conflict resolution through collective efforts. In particular, the 'Manila Declaration on the Peaceful Settlement of International Disputes' of 15 November 1982 (UN General Assembly Resolution A/RES/37/10), declares itself 'devoted to the fetish of sovereignty' (Tomuschat, 1983, p. 734) when it declares that processes of peaceful dispute resolution should not be seen as incompatible with the principle of sovereign equality. The emphasis on the sovereignty principle is surely not inappropriate for an international organization formed upon the membership of states. Intervention and external pressure are unlikely, to create a sustainable solution, especially in the early phases of a dispute.

In contrast, co-operation and institutionalized conflict settlement before an arbiter or the International Court of Justice, or the appeal to the good services of the Secretary-General are tried and tested methods of preventing war and maintaining peace. These, however, depend for their credibility on the assumption that the parties are equal. This principle of the equal rights and equal worth of states, and with it the anticipation of a lasting consensus or compromise, would be contradicted by an early third-party intervention that had not been agreed to by all parties to the dispute. At the same time, Czempiel (1994, p. 141) is to be sympathized with when he complains that the obligation to take part in the Chapter VI processes is not more clearly emphasized, and that the functions of the Security Council, not to mention the barely-alluded-to General Assembly, remain so modest. Greater obligations and more specific processes would indeed further limit the scope of judgement and thus the sovereignty of the states, but on the other hand, it is precisely in this that the nature and intent of a collective system of peace-maintenance lie. Furthermore, staggered regulations could be created in such a way as to make mediation or arbitration through the Security Council obligatory only if the parties to the dispute are to come to a peaceful solution through their own efforts, and the threat to peace continues to exist.

The objection that a higher degree of obligation in regard to processes of peaceful dispute resolution would constitute an unendurable limitation of sovereignty is less convincing because, in the case of a failure of consensus processes, the Charter anticipates the imposition of much greater limitations on sovereignty through force. Furthermore, even currently permissible measures such as trade embargoes may cause considerable damage and disadvantage to states that are not even involved in a dispute, when they must, for example, limit their political or economic relations with a state under sanction. The introduction of binding processes of peaceful dispute resolution would thus represent no unacceptable check on state sovereignty, but rather a moderating intermediate step. On this vital point, Chapter VI of the Charter is stuck far short of where it needs to be to maintain international peace. The principle weakness in the area of peaceful dispute resolution remains the often insufficient political will of states to make use of the framework at all, and to subject themselves to decisions in particular cases. If the preventive treatment of conflict is ever to be firmly anchored in the system of international relations, a thorough revision of Chapter VI will be imperative.

Chapter VII: Action with Respect to Threats to the Peace, Breaches of the Peace and Acts of Aggression

While Chapter VI builds as much as possible on the idea of consensus and compromise among equal and sovereign states, Chapter VII offers the Security Council the opportunity to implement forceful measures against the will of the state or states involved. Formal requirements for the use of forceful measures include the failure of peaceful attempts at dispute resolution and the continued existence of a threat to or breach of the peace. The spectrum of available measures ranges from non-violent sanctions all the way to the application of military force, including limitations on sovereignty up to and including the practical suspension of sovereign rights. Transitional administrations possessing state-like authority and capabilities were thus set up by the Security Council in Cambodia, the former Yugoslavia and East Timor, and the sovereign authority of the territorial state was, at least temporarily, revoked.

In order for the Security Council to become active under Chapter VII, the legal and procedural prerequisites of Article 39 (the first article in Chapter VII) must be met. First, the Security Council must determine, with the usual quorum of nine votes and without the veto of any permanent member, whether one of the three situations on which its authority is based – namely a threat to the peace, a breach of the peace or an act of aggression – exists. Should such a determination be reached, the Council may either issue recommendations or may decide to implement coercive measures under Articles 41 and 42. The difference between recommendations and such measures is that the former are not binding either on the states to which they are addressed or on the other member states of the organization. Other than that, the Charter does not differentiate them clearly from forceful measures. Thus it remains unclear whether the Security Council may recommend forms of behaviour which, if in fact followed by the member states, might take on the form of coercive measures with respect to the target state – for example, the breaking off of commercial relations. The existence of clear regulations for forceful measures in Articles 41 and 42 rather mediates against this possibility, so that the Security Council is restricted to recommendations that would not, if followed, have an adverse effect on the target-state's rights as guaranteed to it in the Charter and in general international law. One example of this might be the Security Council's recommendation that the member states cease to deliver arms and weapons to a particular state, or that they assist a victim of attack in the exercise of its right to self-defence. Another option short of coercive measures is for the Security Council to advocate the observance of preliminary measures according to Article 40. This happens quite often in practice, mainly in the form of demands that combat activities, or other activities threatening the peace, be discontinued.

The coercive measures in Articles 41 and 42 are the core of Chapter VII. They are by their very nature against the will of the target state, and furthermore do not require the agreement of any state not belonging to the Security Council at the time. Thus they constitute the narrow area in which the United Nations can in fact exercise supra-national functions. These measures are not forms of punishment, but rather of collective pressure to which the community can look when it wishes to influence a member to change its peace-disturbing behaviour. They are thus permissible only so long as the disturbance to the peace lasts, and must be lifted once it is past. Consistent with the nature of the UN as a consensus-orientated international organization, these measures are used only infrequently. In the history of the United Nations, non-violent sanctions (see Chapter 4) have been imposed in only fifteen cases (thirteen of which took place in the 1990s), and in only two cases (Korea 1950 and Iraq 1990) has resort been made to military force. Article 41 contains a broad palette of measures ranging from the full or partial interruption of economic relations, transportation and communication, to the breaking off of diplomatic relations. This non-exhaustive list may be extended by the judgement of the Security Council to include other appropriate measures. Thus, in the exercise of its authority under Article 41, the Security Council created an international criminal tribunal for the former Yugoslavia through Resolution 827 (25 May 1993), for the purposes of prosecuting various grave violations of international humanitarian law. A year later, the same step was taken for Rwanda (Resolution 955, 8 November 1994).

Should the Security Council come to the conclusion that peaceful sanctions have shown, or would show, themselves to be ineffective, it may have recourse to military measures which are necessary to maintain or restore the peace, and may employ land, air and sea forces. In other words, the Charter does not delineate any hierarchical order of escalation in which the effects of softer measures must be awaited before the Security Council can turn to military force. There are also no express regulations laid on the Security Council with respect to the intensity of military force it may employ. Since the Security Council is none the less bound to both the Charter and to Customary International Law, it is to be taken for granted that, in spite of the large space left to it for political judgement, it must remain bound to its own principles. Above all, it must keep in mind that the measures employed must be appropriate to the intended purpose, and that they must be consistent with proportionality.

Responsibility for the implementation of the measures determined by the Security Council lies either with the Council itself or with the member state or states so authorized by the Council, according to its own judgement. The latter option arises from the wording of Article 42(2), in which the use of national military forces is mentioned. It follows also from Article 48(1), according to which the actions required for carrying out the Security Council's decisions may be taken by all, or some, members of the UN, or even by one, should the Security Council so determine. In this case, the Security Council would have to confer the mission on the member, or empower it to undertake the necessary measures. The Council may also utilize 'regional arrangements or agencies' (Art. 53(1)) in the Chapter VIII sense for the implementation of coercive measures. This was done, for example, in the case of the former Yugoslavia, through the OSCE. Should the Security Council intend to carry out the forceful measures itself, it is necessary for the member states to make units and resources of their own armed forces available to it on its request, on the basis of one or more special agreements (these troops are not to be confused with the Stand-By Register, which is a later creation). The Article 43 regulations require of member states only that they enter into such special agreements with the Security Council if the latter should so request; otherwise, there is no obligation to conclude or ratify such documents. In fact, no such special agreements have ever been made, so that no member state is currently obliged to make troops available to the Security Council. Article 42 measures may thus be taken under the authority of the Security Council only on the basis of voluntary *ad hoc* arrangements. Even this, however, given the practice of the United Nations up to the time of writing, is not to be expected (see Chapter 8 on possibilities for reform). In every case in which the Security Council has decided to use military force, this was done either through the authorization of member states (as in the first Gulf War) or through other international organizations such as NATO (as in Bosnia-Herzegovina, Kosovo and so on).

Similarly to Article 43, which has remained essentially a dead letter, Article 47's provisions for the creation of a General Staff Committee have effectively been ignored. This General Staff Committee, which was intended to be composed of members (or their representatives) of the General Staffs of the permanent members (Art. 47(2)), holds a significant position as the only subsidiary organ to be mentioned by, and based specifically in, the Charter. Its remit is to advise and support the Security Council in all military questions regarding the maintenance of world peace (Art. 47(1)), as well as carry the responsibility for the strategic leadership of all the armed forces placed at the Security Council's disposal (Art. 47(3)). In practice, however, it has remained one of the more curious of all the UN bodies. For nearly forty years, at two-week intervals, defence attachés of the armed forces of the permanent members held informal meetings without ever discussing matters of substance. Since the beginning of the 1990s, these meetings have taken place among the military advisers of the respective UN delegations of each of the permanent members. Occasional suggestions to the effect that the General Staff Committee ought to be integrated into the leadership of UN peacekeeping operations have never been pursued, so that the General Staff Committee was never able to develop any substantive military or political functions.

In complete contrast to Chapter VI, on the pacific settlement of disputes, Chapter VII places great demands on the collective engagement of the member states, far outstripping the practical political realities. A certain amount of solidarity among the organization's members is necessary for the completion of special agreements on the provision of troops for collective security measures – a solidarity the member states do not wish to, and indeed probably cannot, achieve. The extent of the abstract collective interest in peace is usually too small in specific cases to cause states to be ready to endanger their own soldiers' lives for the sake of general obligations. The United Nations thus lacks a key element of a quick and effective collective security system. This still does not mean that the use of military force is impossible for the United Nations, as the practice of the 1990s since the first Gulf War has shown. The processes necessary to its implementation, however, have turned out to be somewhat more complicated and protracted than the drafters of Chapter VII had imagined. Even so, the example of the first Gulf War shows that when the political constellations are favourable and there is a high degree of convergence of interest among the acting states, even very large-scale and rapid operations fall within the realms of possibility.

The UN's dependency upon such 'coalitions of the willing', however, pierces to the heart of the principle of collective security. The fact that states must be *willing* to take part in common action, with such willingness resulting primarily from a particular interest in the matter at hand, is almost guaranteed to lead to selectiveness as to which missions are undertaken. The decision for or against collective measures thus orientates itself not upon the requirements of the current conflict, but upon the degree of interest other states have in that conflict's solution. The complex peace missions of the 1990s have shown that collective measures are dependent not only upon the availability of *willing* states to implement them, but also upon the availability of states with the technological, financial and other *capabilities* to do so. The selectivity born of interest that emerged after the failed action in Somalia, above all among industrialized countries, is impossible to ignore. It also raises the suspicion that certain countries may attempt to instrumentalize the collective security system for their own ends. These developments caused not only the effectiveness of the system as a whole, but also the legitimacy of the Security Council's decisions to slide further into crisis.

In fact, the composition, voting processes and modes of activity of the Security Council are not designed to alleviate this suspicion in any way. The power relations within this most powerful of the main bodies reflect too closely the political situation at the end of the Second World War, as though they could remain unchanged over half a century, and the Security Council's claim on the observation of its determinations could continue to be accepted by all sides. A more balanced representation of all regions of the world in the permanent membership of the Security Council is thus just as necessary a change as the modification of its voting procedures and the abolition of the veto.

Chapter VIII: Regional Arrangements

It has already been indicated that the United Nations accords considerable meaning to regional arrangements. Article 52 explains that regional organizations – in so far as they are in accord with the purposes and principles of the United Nations – should attempt to resolve local disputes peacefully on their own, before the Security Council becomes involved. The founders of the United Nations believed that organizations that were nearer to the actual occurrences would have a better understanding of the situation, and were not unaware that it would be a lightening of the UN's own burden for these organizations to do some of the work. Proximity to a situation can, however, be a disadvantage as well as an advantage. It is sometimes more acceptable for conflicting parties to suffer external intervention from neutrals rather than from neighbours. As the Article refers to the role of regional organizations only in the peaceful resolution of disputes, it is still the case that any coercive measures would have to be authorized specifically by the Security Council under Article 53. Experts in international law are not in agreement, however, on what exactly constitutes a regional arrangement in the sense of Chapter VIII. Strict constructionists decline to include military alliances such as NATO in the category of regional arrangements. In practice, however, the definition that has emerged involves merely some regional association and a membership roster more restricted than that of the UN itself. The list thus comprises such institutions as the Arab League, the Organization of American States (OAS), the Organization of African Unity (OAU), and the Organization for

Security and Co-operation in Europe (OSCE), as well as NATO. The United Nations have often authorized or empowered regional arrangements to implement peace missions. Prominent examples include the implementation of the Dayton Accords from December 1995 in Bosnia-Herzegovina (IFOR/SFOR), as well as the placement of peacekeepers in Kosovo (KFOR) since June 1999, both of which are under the leadership of NATO.

A greater involvement of regional arrangements presents risks as well as opportunities. Advocates emphasize the amount of work taken off the shoulders of the UN as well as a better international division of labour, and in fact agitate for a more serious consideration of the possibility of delegating the decision to use forceful measures to regional mechanisms. On the other hand, in a more critical view this can be seen as a hollowing-out of the United Nations' responsibilities in its very core areas, and more likely to lead to chaos and confusion than to efficiency.

Further Reading

Butfoy, Andrew (1993) 'Themes Within the Collective Security Idea', *Journal of Strategic Studies* (4), pp. 490–510.

Hurrell, Andrew (1992) 'Collective Security and International Order Revisited', *International Relations* (1), pp. 37–55.

Kupchan, Charles A. and Clifford A. Kupchan (1995) 'The Promise of Collective Security', *International Security* (1), pp. 52–61.

Opitz, Peter J. (2002) 'Collective Security', in Helmut Volger (ed.), *A Concise Encyclopedia of the United Nations*, The Hague: Kluwer, pp. 25–31.

Randelzhofer, Albrecht (2002) 'Art 2 (4)', in *Simma*, Bruno (ed.), *The Charter of the United Nations: A Commentary*, Oxford: Oxford University Press, pp. S.112–35.

Weber, Hermann (1995) 'League of Nations', in Rüdiger Wolfrum, with Christiane Philipp (eds), *United Nations: Law, Policies and Practice*, 2 vols, Dordrecht, Boston, Leiden: Martinus Nijhoff Publishers, pp. 848–53.

4

The Changing Practice of Peacekeeping

Although clearly based on the ideas laid down in the Charter, the collective security system has been changed and reformed in manifold ways in the practice of the United Nations. This practice is the object of study in the present chapter. It has already been mentioned several times that war has not, in spite of the general prohibition on the use of force, been eliminated from international relations. Before the practice of the United Nations is analysed in two steps in the following pages, therefore, it will be useful to add a brief empirical note on the development of war on the one hand, and the UN's instruments of peace-maintenance on the other.

Since the UN's founding in the summer of 1945, there have been more than 200 wars (even though the number varies slightly according to definition and research method), claiming many more dead in total than the Second World War (see Figure 4.1). From the early 1960s, the number of wars occurring worldwide

FIGURE 4.1
Number of wars conducted world-wide every year

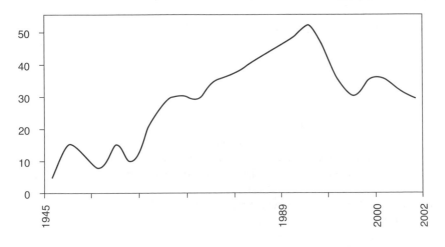

Source: Data from Working Group for Research into the Causes of War (AKUF).

89

increased almost continuously for three decades, with a peak at the beginning of the 1990s. But even the drastic reduction in the frequency of war between 1992 and 1997 did not lead to a confirmation of the optimistic assumption that the number of wars would be permanently reduced. It is true that war in the so-called 'OECD world' (the thirty member states of the Organisation for Economic Co-operation and Development) has become quite rare, and the belief that democracies do not fight wars with one another – in itself an important connection between modes of conflict resolution in internal and external behaviour – appears to have been confirmed. Seen from a global point of view, however, war as a means of settling conflicts clearly remains 'a companion to the process of social development' (AKUF, 2000, p. 11) and a 'central part of political effectiveness even in the 21st century' (Hoch, 2001, p. 17). On the edges of the 'zones of peace' there is a certain grey area to be found, characterized primarily by instability. Some analysts have even argued that the world is now finding itself on the way from a Cold War to a 'hot' one (Parsons, 1995) or 'deadly peace' (Carnegie Commission, 1998).

According to the *Arbeitsgemeinschaft Konfliktursachenforschung* (Working Group for Research into the Causes of War) (AKUF, 2000, p. 59), a war is a 'violent mass conflict exhibiting all of the following characteristics':

- Two or more armed forces take part in the combat, of which at least one is the regular armed force (military, paramilitary groups, police units) of a government;
- There must be a minimum level on both sides of centrally-directed organization of the parties to the conflict and of the combat, even when this means nothing more than organized armed defence or planned assaults (guerrilla operations, partisan warfare and so on); and
- The armed operations take place with a certain continuity, and not merely as opportunistic, spontaneous collisions; that is, both sides operate with a planned strategy of some kind, whether the combat takes place in the territory of one or more communities, and whether the engagements are long or short.

Using this definition, twenty-nine wars were waged in 2002, of which 37 per cent were in Africa, 35 per cent in Asia, 22 per cent in the Near East and Middle East, and 6 per cent in Latin America.

The AKUF differentiates among five types of war, although intermediate forms may also occur in practice:

(i)   Anti-regime wars, where the struggle is for the overthrow/defence of a government or for a change in the political system or social order;
(ii)   Wars of autonomy/secession, where the struggle is for greater regional autonomy within a state or federation, or for secession from a state or federation;
(iii)   Wars of decolonization, where the struggle is for liberation from a colonial ruler;
(iv)   Inter-state wars; and
(v)   Other internal wars.

Classical inter-state war (the prevention of which was the driving motive behind the United Nations) has become an increasingly peripheral phenomenon, even though wars of this kind still accounted for around 17 per cent of all wars between 1945 and 1995 (in 2001, it was 6.5 per cent). According to the AKUF criteria, more than three-quarters of all wars in 2002 were purely internal conflicts. Of these, the largest portion (41 per cent) were anti-regime wars, in which a violent regime change was being attempted. In second place, at 32 per cent, were wars of autonomy or secession.

In the place of traditional inter-state war, a new type of war has begun to emerge (Creveld, 1991; Kaldor, 2000), which can manifest itself in many different ways, and encompasses public and private, intra- and inter-societal, international and national, as well as regional and local parties to conflict as actors. This type of war combines elements of classical war, civil war, organized crime and planned large-scale violations of human rights. It is also characterized by the tendency to privatize the application of force. In the course of this change, the modern monopoly of the state over war is being eroded, and thus it will be more difficult in future to determine the precise locus from which a military danger arises. The nation-state's claim to be the sole authority with the right to use military force may have led to a number of wars, but it also had a stabilizing effect in so far as it limited the number and types of actors able to cause wars. The decline in inter-state war is at least partly a result of the observation of the general prohibition on the use of force. It no longer seems possible, however, to legitimize a state's use of military power for the pursuit of national interest, nor does military power seem to be a very effective tool. In the nuclear age, moreover, the risks associated with military power are just too great. The privatization of violence and war, the 'return of security politics to the Middle Ages', is eroding this newly-won stability. War and conflict are becoming even more confusing than before.

The causes of conflict have also become more diverse. The struggles of ethnic groups for independence and the violent exercise of the right to self-determination, fundamentalism and other religious or ideological extremism, terrorism, classical power struggles or regional conflicts, destruction of the environment, scarcity of vital resources, or reaching the limits of the global ecosystem and so on. are all among the most important potential future sources of conflict that might lead to violence. Added to this is the amount of global inequality, sometimes described as 'global apartheid', which seems to be an increasing source of conflict. It is no longer strong states but rather weak ones that appear to be the main problem for stability, because they offer fertile ground for the development of sub-state or private violent actors, which may become active within failed states as warlords, or export violence to other states and societies.

Furthermore, armed forces everywhere seem to be undergoing their own process of significant change. Here, the buzzwords are 'post-modern warfare', the revolution in military affairs (RMA), and information warfare (Arqilla, 1997; Morgan, 2000). Even these, however, seem to point in two different directions. On the one hand, they outline the development of ever more expensive weapons systems, which are far more precise and designed also to minimize one's own losses. Examples include unmanned aircraft, satellite-guided steering systems, and the possibilities for attacking an opponent's infrastructure through cyber-warfare. On the other hand, these can also all be gathered under the heading of asymmetrical warfare, since these technologies are not aimed at combating simi-larly-equipped opponents, and problem states and aggressive non-state actors have almost unrestricted access to the means of unconventional warfare. In the course of the proliferation of biological and chemical or nuclear weapons and their respective carrying systems, this danger has been raised to a previously unheard-of level. The basic truism of security politics, that no scenario – no matter how vile – is unthinkable, holds true here; and it is practically guaranteed that what is think-able will at some point be attempted.

It is in this context that the terrorist attacks on the World Trade Center and the Pentagon on 11 September 2001, in which thousands of people from some sixty countries lost their lives, will be remembered (see Chapter 4). The intensity of the destruction and the extent of the damage symbolize the globalization of terrorism as well as the new way of waging war. Even though it is still difficult to draw a clear picture of the current situation, because so much is still in flux, some overar-ching trends may indeed be analysed from a political science perspective:

(i)   Terrorist organizations will aim openly and consciously at the vulnerabilities of modern societies, and the damage from terrorist attacks will take on the dimensions of the results of war. The system of interdependence among open societies will be targeted: globalization has improved international terrorism's chances for success; and

(ii)   This development makes it clear that the risk-calculus at the root of classical deterrence has been made obsolete, and thus there is an urgent need for re-evaluation of established security strategies. Irrational actors such as fanati-cal terrorist groups and the states that support them include their own possible demise in their calculation, and thus are hardly – if at all – likely to be dissuaded by classical security strategies. The assassins themselves expend almost no resources on flight or concealment of their actions, but concentrate almost 100 per cent of their energies on the execution of the deed itself. The readiness for personal sacrifice present in asymmetrical wars thus requires new military-strategic concepts, which will cause a permanent change in security politics.

An important characteristic of warfare in the beginning of the twenty-first century is its variety: there are countless very different types of actors involved, forms in which conflict can manifest itself, and consequences for the international system. The spectrum of international missions has also expanded enormously; the time of one-dimensional peace and security politics is long gone. In the new peacekeeping missions, unlike in combat missions, traditional soldiering roles become mixed with police and civil administration functions. The conduct of war itself has tended to move to the background, giving way to other tasks. This has been particularly noticeable since 1995 in the Balkans missions. In these 'peace support operations' (or 'operations other than war'), totally new capabilities are required. In classic UN peacekeeping missions, soldiers are sent in not with a goal of victory against an opponent, but rather to check the violence among the conflicting parties and to oversee or protect the political solution. These missions normally take place within states affected by civil wars or ethnic conflicts. This requires the provision of civil capabilities, which might (but not necessarily) extend to forces able to take part in the creation of a new state order. On the other hand, such capabilities are not very useful for actual combat missions, such as forcing the retreat of Serbian troops from Kosovo in Spring 1999 or the Enduring Freedom mission in the war on terrorism: here, the 'soldier as combatant' is still needed, requiring different skills from the peacekeeper.

Thus the very things that increase the legitimacy and acceptance of crisis response missions can in fact be counter-productive in combat missions. This is why experiences of coalition warfare, such as that in Kosovo, are often judged so negatively – especially in the USA (Clark, 2001) – that they have little hope of being repeated. The 'lessons' of these experiences have been palpable in the anti-terror mission Enduring Freedom of the USA and its allies, which has been going on since 7 October 2001. In the American strategic community, this type of mission is known as a 'we call you if we need you war'. The USA certainly places a high value on a broad political coalition for the struggle against terrorism, but the military operations are decided as far as is possible on a unilateral basis, and allies tend to be included in the above sense only very selectively. Normally, the allies – with the exception of the UK, which has been granted the status of military junior partner – are included in the planning largely for the purposes of relieving the burden on American forces who are not involved directly in the combat mission. The avoidance of friendly casualties no longer enjoys uncontested pride of place as the highest priority, at least not in the USA since September 11. The American experience of the direct vulnerability of its territory is likely to have long-lasting effects.

The 2003 war in Iraq also constitutes a fundamental break in the recent history of warfare, with, at the time of writing, indeterminate consequences for international law and the international order (see Chapter 8).

It is obvious that changing forms of war also require a modified understanding of the instruments of peace-maintenance. The first distinction to be made in the context of the United Nations is the above-mentioned difference between securing the peace, in Chapter VI, and peace enforcement, in Chapter VII (see Table 4.1).

When it became clear that the collective security system as foreseen in the Charter would be unable to work under the given conditions in precisely the way it was meant to, alternative forms of peace-maintenance were developed. These neither went against the interests of the permanent members, nor infringed the sovereign equality of the other member states. They were, however, suitable for supporting the claims of the United Nations in the recognition of its purposes and principles. New measures for peace-maintenance emerged with the use of UN peacekeeping troops or observer missions – the so-called 'blue helmets', named

TABLE 4.1
UN approaches to preventing and managing conflicts

Collective security	Theory and practice whereby all states thwart an aggressor state by joining together against the aggressor. Attempts to prevent the outbreak of conflict, but if an attack occurs, aggression is met with force
Preventive diplomacy	Practice of engaging in diplomatic interventions before the outbreak of conflict and monitoring hot spots through the use of peace-keeping forces or surveillance technology
Peaceful settlement	Various techniques by which disputes are settled, such as adjudication, arbitration, mediation, conciliation and good offices
Peacemaking	Efforts to bring parties to agreement
Peacekeeping	The use of multilateral forces to achieve several different objectives: observation of truce and ceasefire lines; separation of forces, promotion of law and order; provision of humanitarian aid and intervention
Peace-building	Post conflict activities to strengthen and preserve peace, such as development aid, civilian administration, and human rights and election monitoring
Enforcement measures	Direct actions taken to ensure compliance with UN measures, such as imposition of economic sanctions, banning of air flights or communications, and use of force
Arms control and disarmament	Efforts to persuade states to limit, reduce or eliminate specific types of weapons

Source: Based on discussion in Mingst and Karns (2000, p. 76).

for their conspicuous headgear. Looking for a particular textual basis for the blue helmets in the Charter is, however, a vain enterprise. Because of their many-sided character, it is also very complicated to provide a precise definition of these missions. They encompass the dispatching of everything from civilian observer missions to military units. In the more than fifty years of peacekeeping, several different types of operation have developed, belonging officially to the genus of peace missions, but the concrete manifestations of them could hardly be more different.

The classic version of peacekeeping is a form of military operation that is not based on force. The central element of classic peacekeeping is well expressed by the saying 'there is no peacekeeping if there is no peace to keep'. This constitutes an important modification of the principle of collective security. The contradiction between acting 'in concert' and exercising compulsion was resolved in peace-keeping practice to the advantage of the 'in concert' side. Through the further development of this peacekeeping concept, the Charter has been enhanced by an informal 'Chapter 6½', situated between the classic consensus-orientated processes of peaceful dispute resolution such as mediation efforts and informa-tion-gathering missions, and the implementation of forceful measures of compul-sion. As has already been discussed, during the Cold War (that is, until 1989/90), the Chapter VII option existed largely only on paper. Although the Security Council had discussed the possible use of coercion in countless cases of a threat to or breach of the peace, it had in fact adopted them only in a few exceptional cases (the empowerment of specific states to undertake military operations under the leadership of the USA in North Korea in the summer of 1950, an economic boycott against Southern Rhodesia in the winter of 1966, and an arms embargo against South Africa in autumn of 1977).

The Security Council was weakened significantly by the permanent members' veto power (depending on the way it is counted, up until 1990 the veto was used some 240 times; most often by the USSR with 118, then by the USA with 69, Great Britain with 32, France with 18, and China with three (Mingst and Karns, 2000, p. 28)). Occasional attempts by the General Assembly – in cases of a self-blockade by the Security Council – to win more authority for itself, remained largely without noticeable effect. The most prominent attempt by the General Assembly to break a Security Council gridlock was the above-mentioned Uniting for Peace Resolution of November 1950, in which it attempted to recommend the use of forceful measures to the member states. However, the Security Council reasserted its primary responsibility for the maintenance of international security, enshrined in Article 24.

In more than forty years of classical UN peacekeeping (1948 to the end of 1988), the UN initiated a total of sixteen peace missions, some of which continue to the present day (see Table 4.2). Since the 1988 renaissance (the UN peace missions were awarded the Nobel Peace Prize in 1988) of peacekeeping, made possible through the East–West détente, the total number of missions both initiated and completed has grown markedly, and some of these have even been Chapter VII operations (see Tables 4.2 and 4.3). In categorizing the various UN peacekeeping missions (from 1948 to August 2003, there were a total of fifty-six such missions), Dennis Jett (2000, pp. 21–34) has identified seven phases of peacekeeping:

- In the 'nascent period' (1946–56), there were only two missions, both of which continue to the present day, and for neither of which was the term 'peacekeeping' used explicitly;
- In the 'assertive period' (1956–67), an innovative concept of peace-maintenance was developed, and used in several instances, with varying levels of success;
- In the 'dormant period' (1967–73), a certain amount of disillusionment appeared, manifesting itself in the blockade of further missions through the systemic antagonism of the two superpowers;
- In the 'resurgent period' (1973–8), a few new classic missions were begun;
- In the 'maintenance period' (1978–88), no new missions were introduced and the system suffered once again from the heightening East–West conflict;
- In the 'expansion period' (1988–93), in the course of the massive changes going on in world politics, there was an increased number of missions (there were more missions initiated in these five years than in the previous forty),

TABLE 4.2
UN peace missions, 1948–88

Mission name	Time period	Location
UNSCOB	1947–51	Special Committee for the Balkans
UNTSO	Since June 1948	Mission for the supervision of the cease-fire in Palestine
UNMOGIP	Since January 1949	Military observation group in India/Pakistan
UNEF I	November 1956–June 1967	First emergency force in the Sinai
UNOGIL	June 1958–December 1958	Observer group in Lebanon
ONUC	July 1960–June 1964	Operation in the Congo
UNSF	October 1962–April 1963	Security force in Western New Guinea
UNYOM	July 1963–September 1964	Observer mission in Yemen
UNFICYP	Since March 1964	Peacekeeping troops in Cyprus
DOMREP	May 1965–October 1966	Mission in the Dominican Republic
UNIPOM	September 1965–March 1966	Observer mission in India/Pakistan
UNEF II	October 1973–July 1979	Second emergency force in the Sinai
UNDOF	Since June 1974	Observer force for the breaking up of troop contact between Syria and Israel
UNIFIL	Since March 1978	Interim force in Lebanon
UNGOMAP	Aprril 1988–March 1990	Good offices mission in Afghanistan
UNIIMOG	August 1988–February 1991	Observer group in Iraq/Iran

Source: Data from UN Department of Peacekeeping Operations.

which exhibited, however, significant conceptual differences from and much more complex mandates than the earlier missions; and

- In the 'contraction period' (since 1993), because of the failure of several missions, disillusionment has crept in once again, and while it shows itself on the one hand in somewhat undifferentiated UN-bashing, it has also given rise to a number of ideas for reform.

The United Nations itself tend to prefer a typology of 'generations' of peace-main-tenance. Missions of the 'first generation' are traditional 'blue helmet' operations for the supervision and safeguarding of already-concluded peace treaties or cease-fires. Missions of the 'second generation', after 1988/9, are distinguished by a far more complex set of tasks; those of the 'third' mix elements of peace-maintenance and peace-enforcement; and those of the 'fourth' can involve responsibilities up to and including the exercise of civil administrative functions. Yet another way of categorizing has found its way into the discussion since the presentation of then-Secretary-General Boutros Boutros-Ghali's 'Agenda for Peace' in 1992, which differentiates among 'preventive diplomacy', 'peace-making', 'peacekeeping', and 'post-conflict peace-building'.

Tobias Debiel (2003, pp. 221–4) has argued that another criterion, as well as the scope of the tasks undertaken by a mission, should be the extent to which a peace

TABLE 4.3
Completed UN peace missions, 1989–August 2004

Mission name	Time period	Location
UNAVEM I	January 1989–May 1991	Angola verification mission
UNTAG	April 1989–March 1990	Transitional assistance group in Namibia
ONUCA	November 1989 –January 1992	Observer group in Central America
UNAVEM II	June 1991–February 1995	Angola verification mission
ONUSAL	July 1991–April 1995	Observer mission in El Salvador
UNAMIC	October 1991–March 1992	Advance mission in Cambodia
UNPROFOR	February 1992–March 1995	Protection force in the Former Yugoslavia
UNTAC	March 1992–September 1993	Transitional authority in Cambodia
UNOSOM I	April 1992–March 1993	Operation in Somalia
ONUMOZ	December 1992–December 1994	Operation in Mozambique
UNOSOM II	March 1993–March 1995	Operation in Somalia
UNOMUR	June 1993–September 1994	Observer mission in Uganda/Rwanda
UNMIH	September 1993–June 1996	Observer mission in Haiti
UNOMIL	September 1993–September 1997	Observer mission in Liberia
UNAMIR	October 1993–March 1996	Assistance mission for Rwanda
UNASOG	May 1994–June 1994	Aouzou Strip observation group (Chad)
UNMOT	December 1994–May 2000	Mission of observers in Tadjikistan
UNAVEM III	February 1995–June 1997	Angola verification mission
UNCRO	March 1995–January 1996	Confidence restoration operation in Croatia
UNPREDEP	March 1995–February 1999	Preventive deployment force in the FYR Macedonia
UNTAES	January 1996–January 1998	Transitional authority in East Slavonia (Croatia)
UNSMIH	July 1996–July 1997	Support mission in Haiti
MINUGUA	January 1997–May 1997	Guatemala verification mission
MONUA	June 1997–February 1999	Observer mission in Angola
UNTMIH	August 1997–November 1997	Transitional mission in Haiti
MIPONUH	December 1997–March 2000	Civilian police mission in Haiti
UNPSG	January 1998–October 1998	Civilian police mission in Croatia
UNOMSIL	July 1998–October 1999	Observer mission in Sierra Leone
MINURCA	April 1998–February 2000	Mission in the Central African Republic
UNTAET	September 1999–May 2002	Transitional authority in East Timor
UNMIBH	December 1995–December 2002	Mission in Bosnia-Herzegovina
UNMOP	January 1996–December 2002	Mission in the Croatian peninsula of Prevlaka
UNIKOM	April 1991–October 2003	United Nations Iraq–Kuwait observation mission

Source: Data from UN Department of Peacekeeping Operations.

operation is capable of using compulsion when consensus is not forthcoming. He thus identifies five types of military peacekeeping:

(i)   Traditional peacekeeping, as a consensus-orientated instrument of military peacekeeping;
(ii)   Multidimensional peacekeeping, in which new tasks in the realm of post-conflict peace-building are added;
(iii) Robust peace missions, as a cross between missions based on consensus and those capable of using force;
(iv)   Military peace-implementation in medium-intensity wars, in which there are actual confrontations between the UN troops and the warring parties; and
(v)   Military peace-implementation in high-intensity wars, in which extensive use of force and compulsion is made.

The next two sections will develop the central features and problem areas of peace-keeping, while current efforts at reform to the peacekeeping system will be dealt with in Chapter 8.

The First Four Decades of Peace-maintenance

The first large UN mission undertaken in the 'nascent period' (1946–56) was the UNTSO (see Table 4.1), which is still going on. Prior to this mission, in October 1947, the General Assembly had resolved to set up a special committee for the support of peaceful development in the Balkans, the UNSCOB, but it was not subject to the United Nations Organization. Although the term 'peacekeeping' had not yet been used explicitly, the original purpose of this mission was indeed the safeguarding of a cease-fire following the first Arab–Israeli war in 1948. In November 1947, the General Assembly had approved a plan for the partition of Palestine that was intended to create two states: one Arab and one Jewish . The plan was rejected by the Arab states. In May 1948, the United Kingdom ended its mandate in Palestine, the Jews living in Palestine declared the state of Israel despite the Arab rejection of partition, and rioting and violence followed between the Arab and Jewish populations of the territory. At the end of May 1948, the Security Council demanded, in Resolution 50, an end to the hostilities in Palestine, and determined that the cease-fire should be safeguarded by a UN mediator and a group of military observers. The first group arrived in the region in June 1948, and has undertaken various tasks since then. Its maximal size has hovered around 200, and by the end of the 1990s was costing around US$30 million per year.

The second large mission also took place in the context of an inter-state conflict. This time, it involved the maintenance of the cease-fire between India and Pakistan (UNMOGIP). Already by January 1948, the Security Council had determined (in Resolution 39) to create a commission for India and Pakistan to mediate between the parties. After a cease-fire was reached in June 1949 with the Karachi

Accord, the Security Council passed Resolution 91 in March 1951 that set up UNMOGIP to oversee the cease-fire. Since then, approximately fifty military observers have been monitoring the border, with the task of investigating complaints of cease-fire violations and communicating the results of their investigations to both parties to the conflict as well as to the UN Secretary-General. Although there are constant disagreements over the mandate, the mission has lasted into the present day, and the expenses (around US$8 million in 1998) are paid from the UN's regular budget.

In the 'assertive period' from 1956 to 1967, there were a total of eight new missions, ranging from observer troops (UNOGIL in Lebanon, UNYOM in Yemen, DOMREP in the Dominican Republic, and UNIPOM in India and Pakistan) to comprehensive missions that have been given complex and novel sets of tasks (UNEF I in Egypt, ONUC in the Congo, UNSF in New Guinea, and UNFI-CYP in Cyprus). The novelty of this phase is described appropriately by Dennis Jett (2000, pp. 23 et seq): '[f]or the first time, the UN assumed temporary authority over a territory in transition to interdependence, added civilian police to a PKO, became involved in a civil war, established a large-scale operation, and allowed the peacekeepers to carry arms'.

Of particular importance is the first instance of the UN's use of emergency troops, the United Nations Emergency Force (UNEF I) in Egypt. This mission, from November 1956 to June 1967, is usually regarded as the birth of classic peacekeeping. The peacekeeping troops – numbering around 6,000 at the height of the mission in February 1957 – were sent in to ensure the cessation of hostilities, including the withdrawal of French, Israeli and British troops from Egyptian territory, and to act as a buffer between Egyptian and Israeli forces after that withdrawal. As the Israeli–Egyptian conflict intensified, the Security Council – incapacitated by the French and British vetoes – was unable to condemn either the Egyptian annexation of the Suez Canal or the Israeli aggression. The General Assembly therefore attempted – with the Uniting for Peace Resolution – to enter the fray. First, with Resolution 997 of 2 November 1956, the Assembly condemned both the Israeli occupation of Egyptian sovereign territory in the Sinai and the Egyptian blockade of the Suez Canal. Second, it recommended the introduction of peacekeeping troops. This procedure was legally contested, but because of the agreement of the parties to the conflict, it did not count as compulsion in the sense of Chapter VII (in which case the Security Council would have had to be responsible), so the Security Council did not oppose the process. A further reason for the lack of opposition might have been that neither of the superpowers, nor indeed any other major power, had an interest in opposing this arrangement and insisting on the sole right of the Security Council to act. In addition, the General Assembly requested that Secretary-General Dag Hammarskjöld oversee the implementation of the Resolution and report to the Security Council and the General Assembly should further measures appear to be necessary.

Conflicts over the legal basis of these peace-maintenance measures did, however, continue to arise. The USSR and France, along with others, refused financial support to the UNEF, and later also to the ONUC in the Congo, with the argument that they were in conflict with the UN Charter because, according to Article 24(1), it is the Security Council alone that carries primary responsibility for the maintenance of peace. The International Court of Justice, when this question was put to it for clarification, defined the functional responsibilities of both the Security Council and the General Assembly (Sucharipa-Behrmann, 2001). In practice, an acceptable form of cohabitation for these two bodies has developed, although since the 1960 Congo crisis the Security Council has been more assertive in reserving to itself initiative and decisional authority.

The Secretary-General played an increasingly important role in the lead-up to the UNEF mission, with a great deal of freedom to influence how the mission took shape. In Resolution 998 (4 November 1956), the General Assembly requested that the Secretary-General produce, within forty-eight hours, a plan for how to post an international emergency force with the consent of the affected parties. On 5 November 1956, Resolution 1000 called the international peacekeeping force into being, under the command of a general designated by the United Nations. According to Ernst-Otto Czempiel (1994, p. 114 et seq.):

> The UN force could not possibly and was not intended to resolve the Near East conflict. It could not force the conflicting parties to desist from the use of force. But as long as the parties to the conflict were willing [to desist from the use of force], the UN troop could wedge itself between them, and preserve the situation for the longer term . . . The consent of the parties involved is decisive. It is not of a fixed, but rather of a flexible extent, and it can be influenced and stretched. Should it erode or break, the instrument of peacekeeping becomes unfit.

Thus the next Secretary-General, U Thant, recalled the UNEF in May 1967, because there was no longer consent by the conflicting parties, and Egypt was demanding a withdrawal. It was apparent that the conflict had not been resolved, but the region had none the less been held in a state of peace for ten years.

The UNEF entered the history of international peacekeeping above all on the strength of one particular circumstance. In the run-up to the first large-scale peace-keeping mission, Secretary-General Dag Hammarskjöld formulated important fundamental principles for an emergency force and communicated them in various reports to the General Assembly and the Security Council. This force was to become the model for further missions of classical peacekeeping:

• *Consent of the parties to the conflict.* Classical 'blue helmet' missions cannot take place against the will of the affected states. Rather, all parties involved in a process of conflict resolution must find some consensus, through a cease-fire or a peace treaty, regarding a 'blue helmet' peacekeeping mission. The agree-ment of the affected parties is the *conditio sine qua non* of this type of peace mission. A consensus decision not only eases the problem of the soldiers' acceptance in their mission area, but is also an important prerequisite for the willingness of member states to provide troops, because it minimizes the danger that the 'blue helmets' will be drawn into combat situations.

- *Direct responsibility of the United Nations.* In contrast to military operations such as those in Korea, the first Gulf War, or more recently in the Balkans, UN peacekeeping missions are as a rule not only authorized by the Security Council, but also conducted under the operational leadership of the Secretary-General. In the UN Secretariat, a special main department was created specifically for the planning and implementation of peacekeeping missions: the Department of Peacekeeping Operations (DPKO). The military leadership of the mission falls upon a Force Commander named by the Secretary-General, and the political leadership is usually carried out by a Special Representative of the Secretary-General (SRSG). As a rule, UN peacekeeping missions are financed through a unique budget, raised for each separate mission through a cost-sharing process among the member states. The deployed soldiers and civil servants are provided by the member states, while any other assistance necessary is usually acquired locally. Although the 'sending states' retain responsibility for their troops and civil servants in a general sense and for the purposes of labour law, observer missions and peacekeeping troops in the field function effectively as subsidiary organs of the Security Council. This status is of decisive importance for the acceptance of peacekeeping missions by states that might otherwise not allow the presence of troops in their sovereign territory.
- *Neutrality.* Inextricably tied to the principle of party consent is the principle of the neutrality of the peacekeepers. The 'blue helmets' constitute a buffer zone between the armed forces of the conflicting parties, thus preventing a resumption of combat activities. The provision of 'good offices', such as facilitating a meeting of negotiating delegations in buildings belonging to the peacekeeping mission, also belongs to the accepted list of tasks for 'blue helmet' operations. Involvement in the conflict – no matter of what kind, and even when one side has flagrantly violated the conditions of the cease-fire – is not part of the agenda of any classical 'blue helmet' mission. Furthermore, when the force is being composed, due attention should be given to balanced regional representation.
- *Use of weapons only in self-defence.* While observer missions are usually carried out by unarmed military experts, the members of a peacekeeping force have the use of light, hand-held weapons. These weapons are intended for self-defence only, but this can take place in relation to the implementation of the mandate. The conditions under which 'blue helmets' might use their weapons were understood very narrowly indeed, until the 1990s, in order to give the parties no pretence for drawing the UN troops into the conflict.

The initial successes of the UNEF mission meant that, by the beginning of the 1960s, there was a great deal of optimistic expectation bound up with the peacekeeping missions of the UN. This optimism was expressed *inter alia* through the ambitious deployment into the Congo (ONUC) from July 1960 to June 1964. This mission, however, did not hold very closely to Hammarskjöld's principles. Beginning with Resolution 143 (July 1960), and including a total of four further Security Council resolutions, the mandate was expanded continuously. The

ONUC mission – at its height consisting of around 20,000 troops – was originally sent in to oversee the withdrawal of Belgian troops from the Republic of Congo. Eventually, however, it grew to involve the protection of the territorial integrity of the Congo, the prevention of the outbreak of civil war, and the support of the government in its attempts to create a civil service. With Security Council Resolution 161 (February 1961), the peacekeepers were allowed for the first time to use their weapons in the service of their mission, and not just for self-defence. The result of this was that, contrary to the original concept, in the course of the mission the peacekeepers became one of the parties to the conflict.

After initial success, the ONUC became the first 'major peacekeeping failure' (Jett, 2000, p. 24). The UN was drawn increasingly into the unresolved internal conflicts of the Republic of Congo, and important member states were pursuing very different interests, which often manifested themselves in disagreements over the mission's mandate and financing. In the summer of 1964, the operation was brought to a close, because the Congolese government did not agree to an extension of the mandate. The lessons of the Congo mission, which William Durch (1993, 12) somewhat exaggeratedly called 'the UN's Vietnam', have, however, made something of the same impression on the UN as that other war did on the USA. For more than three decades, no mission of comparable size and complexity has taken place, and the goals of peacekeeping have become more modest. The United Nations recalled Hammarskjöld's principles, and sought in particular the consent of the parties involved before any mission was undertaken. The Security Council also managed to reconfirm its position as the only body that could mandate and oversee peace missions.

Another prominent example of classic peacekeeping is the UN mission in Cyprus, which at the time of writing is still ongoing. The UNFICYP mission was created by Security Council Resolution 186, in March 1964, in an attempt to prevent further battles between Greek and Turkish Cypriots. None the less, the struggles continued, and culminated in the forceful partition of the island. Since the implementation of a cease-fire in Summer 1974 (the mandate has been extended every six months since 1964), more than 1,200 soldiers of UNFICYP have overseen the agreement and secured the buffer-zone. In addition, the Secretary-General has made several attempts at mediation to resolve the conflict. The mission has suffered a great deal of criticism, most particularly the charge that the decades-long UN presence is in fact removing any pressure for the two sides to reach a lasting agreement. Despite these and other accusations, however, it is still true that since 1974 there has been no escalation of the conflict, although UNFICYP has suffered 170 fatalities.

A large number of potential peacekeeping missions were prevented from taking place by the antagonism between the Eastern and Western blocs and their blockade of the Security Council. In the 1970s, those missions that did succeed in winning approval were focused on the conflict in the Near East. Three missions in one decade were undertaken in the region: in October 1973 the second Emergency Force (UNEF II) entered the Sinai; in June 1974 an observer mission went to the Golan Heights (UNDOF); and in March 1978 the interim force in Lebanon

(UNFIL) was begun. All three missions, the latter two of which are continuing at the time of writing, are classic missions of the 'first generation'. It should be noted, however, that the consent of the parties was temporarily not forthcoming in Lebanon, and so the UNFIL was for a time restricted to humanitarian aid activities. After these three missions, and up to the end of the 1980s, no new missions were undertaken. It was not until 1988, and the UNIIMOG and UNGOMAP operations – the first of which was an observer force overseeing the cease-fire between Iraq and Iran, and the second a supervision of the withdrawal of Soviet troops from Afghanistan – that a peacekeeping renaissance took place. While UNIIMOG was an unarmed observer group, conforming to the classic peacekeeping profile, UNGOMAP was a new type of mission. This 'good offices mission' was not in fact mandated directly by the Security Council; it was merely given its approval.

If one were to add up the experiences of the first four decades of UN peace-keeping, it would certainly produce a mixed result. It must first be asserted that every mission is a special case, which cannot run according to a pre-set plan that is precise in every detail. The ideal set out in the Charter (and in particular the exten-sive regulations in Chapter VII) proved to be less than practical, which is why the innovation of 'blue helmet missions', not foreseen by the Charter, had to be devel-oped. The missions were aimed mainly at assisting the parties to a conflict in its resolution, or in 'lay[ing] the violent portion of the conflict to rest' (Kühne, 1993, p. 19), in so far as the parties were willing and able to do so. 'Blue helmet' missions were a means of damping conflict, not of solving it. This apparently unambitious goal arose not out of modesty or a lack of confidence in the UN's competence to solve conflicts, but out of conceptual restraint, strategic ingenuity, and an orienta-tion around what is practicable. In most cases, this modest goal was achieved, although often at the price (as in Cyprus) of a costly long-term presence. Should these limitations be abandoned, as they were in the Congo, the results of far more missions would probably be negative.

Peacekeeping after the Cold War

The thawing of relations between the USA and the USSR in the late 1980s and the approaching end of the East–West conflict practically catapulted the UN – after decades of relative impotence – back into the centre of international politics. The Security Council, whose permanent members had for a long time made common initiatives impossible through the practically habitual exercise of their vetoes, achieved a previously unknown level of capability to reach decisions and take action. The number of vetoes dropped to almost nil, and there was an explosion of resolutions and measures taken by consensus. Suddenly, blue helmets were no longer an 'exotic peripheral phenomenon of international peace and security poli-tics', but rather 'one of its most important pillars' (Kühne, 1993, p. 18).

The 'expansion period' of peacekeeping thus fell in an age of fundamental political upheaval on a global scale, and the lingering consequences of the Cold War had to be dealt with in Asia (Afghanistan, Cambodia), Africa (Namibia,

Angola, Mozambique), and Latin America (El Salvador, Nicaragua). Iraq's invasion of Kuwait destroyed any hope of a world free of inter-state war, and the collapse of states in Africa (Somalia) and Europe (Yugoslavia) deposited an all-new set of challenges on the UN's doorstep. Increasingly, the organization saw itself as being confronted with conflicts internal to states rather than between them. A gradual expansion of the Security Council's competences to include actions that would, a few years earlier, have been considered taboo because of the Charter's prohibition on intervention was both the result of, and a necessary condition for, the creation of a new generation of peacekeeping missions.

Between 1988 and 1992, fourteen new missions were begun – nearly as many as in the previous forty years put together. According to the UN Department of Peacekeeping Operations, in January 1988 there were 11,121 soldiers, police and civilians operating in a total of five missions worldwide, costing around US$230 million. By the end of 1992, there were nearly 100,000 peacekeepers in fourteen missions, costing around US$4 billion. In 1993 alone, there were six new peace missions, and in spite of a temporary de facto moratorium in the mid-1990s, the total number of missions had increased to fifty-six by the year 2003. In December 2003, around 45,732 personnel were active in thirteen peace missions, costing US$2.81 billion. By the end of December 2003, a total of 1,865 UN personnel had died in the course of their duty; more than 1,200 of those fatalities occurred in the 1990s alone.

If the classic peace missions were distinguished primarily by their function as a buffer between the armed forces of the (usually state) parties to the conflict, the mandates of the 'second generation' were characterized by an ever-widening spectrum of tasks. Aid for states in transitional periods or undergoing processes of national reconciliation, support for processes of democratic consolidation, disarmament and reintegration of the parties to civil wars, repatriation of refugees, and finally the temporary undertaking of quasi-sovereign competences for an entire country, were now among the tasks a peace mission might be expected to fulfil.

Clearly, composition of the personnel of these peace missions also required serious changes commensurate with this new 'to-do' list. While classical operations relied primarily on soldiers, the 'second generation' missions increasingly required the integration of civilian experts – for example, in the areas of civil policing, the administration of justice, humanitarian aid, public administration, and the organization and supervision of elections. In Resolution 632 (16 February 1989), the Security Council gave the UN Transitional Assistance Group in Namibia (UNTAG) an extensive mandate in support of the country's transition to independence from South Africa. In the brief period from April 1989 to March 1990, more than 8,000 soldiers and civilian experts escorted the country through the cessation of hostilities and the withdrawal of the South African troops, created opportunities for the repatriation of refugees, prepared elections, and supported the construction of a new legal and political order. The independent Namibia was admitted to the United Nations in April 1990. A decisive measure preceding the Namibia mission had been the sending of the first Angola Verification Mission (UNAVEM I) in January of 1989. This mission had overseen the withdrawal of the Cuban troops who had been intervening in Namibia from bases in Angola.

In November 1989, the UN began a mission in Central America that was to last for around two years. The Observer Mission in Central America (ONUCA), according to Resolution 644 of 7 November 1989, was to support Costa Rica, El Salvador, Guatemala, Honduras and Nicaragua in the maintenance of the obligations they had undertaken with respect to a peaceful coexistence with one another. The critical job of the 260 military observers, strengthened by an 800-man infantry battalion and countless civilian workers, was the demobilization of around 20,000 Nicaraguan Contras as a pre-condition for free elections in Nicaragua. The implementation of those elections was overseen by another UN mission. A separate mission in El Salvador (ONUSAL, begun in April 1991) originally had the task of supervising the observation of human rights, until it was also given the task of realizing the cease-fire that had finally been negotiated between the parties to the civil war. The Iraq–Kuwait observer mission (UNIKOM) was a more traditional peacekeeping operation, also begun in April 1991. It was created in order to guard the demilitarized zone along the border in the aftermath of a large-scale international military operation that the Security Council had mandated for the liberation of Kuwait.

The success of the operation in Namibia encouraged the United Nations to take on its largest-ever peacekeeping mission. On 28 February 1992, in Resolution 745, the Security Council gave the UN transitional authority in Cambodia the mandate to oversee the implementation of the peace agreement that had been signed in October 1991, in the hope of ending the terrible civil war that had shaken the country for so long. It was clear from the beginning that such a mission could not limit itself to the passive readiness to provide aid, but must in fact be constituted as a transitional administration. More than 22,000 soldiers and civilian experts organized free elections under UN auspices, supported the drafting and promulgation of a constitution, helped in the creation of a state administration and infrastructure, and enabled refugees and displaced persons to return to their homes. In September 1993, this mission – at US$1.3 billion the most expensive ever – was brought to a close.

The development of peacekeeping doctrine into the 'second generation' could be considered a gradual one, in so far as the missions were still taking place largely post-conflict; that is, in a relatively peaceful context and in support of an existing peace agreement or consent of the parties. A few of the post-1992 missions, however, did begin to experience difficulties with the hallowed principles of 'blue helmet' operations, thus heralding the slide into the 'third generation'. UNOSOM II in Somalia was the first time since the Congo operation that a mandate for peacekeepers was given under Chapter VII and included the use of military force. In spite of early signs of success, the mission – the UN's first humanitarian mission – failed to disarm the warring clan militias and to provide consistent humanitarian aid to the populace. After the deaths of twenty-four Pakistani soldiers, the blue helmets abandoned their neutrality and once again became a party to a conflict where they were supposed to be impartial. In November 1994, the Somalia mission was broken off with the resolution to withdraw the troops completely no later than 31 March 1995. A hundred and thirty-two 'blue helmets', and an unknown number of Somalis, died during the course of the mission. UNOSOM II suffered primarily from the fundamental contradiction that the 'blue helmets' were not going in to support an existing peace, but to compel one, and under heavy losses they joined the conflict instead of stopping it.

The UNPROFOR operations in the former Yugoslavia, on the other hand, tried for a long time to stick to the classic peacekeeping formula. It soon became apparent, however, just how useless a proven instrument becomes when it is applied to a context for which it was not designed. 'Blue helmets' were deployed despite the lack of a reliable peace agreement. The mission, begun in Croatia in 1992 to keep the conflicting parties away from one another, slowly broadened to include Bosnia-Herzegovina. Eventually, under pressure of events, the mandate evolved into an intervention to protect the civilian population from massive human rights abuses. The Secretary-General had warned several times that the peacekeepers should not be given tasks for which their training and rules of engagement (ROE) were not suitable. The new mandate, however, was not accompanied by appropriate changes either in the military outfit or in the legal and political definition of the ROE. There were several cases of 'blue helmets' being taken hostage or used as human shields. Frequently unable to tell where the 'fronts' were, because they might consist of anything from regular forces to warlord bands, the blue helmets were caught between them rather than keeping them apart. Finally, the leadership and command structure was splintered among the UN, the troop-contributing states, and other co-operating organizations. Together, these problems ensured that UNPROFOR constitutes a somewhat less than sparkling chapter in the history of the UN. In the winter of 1995/6, the responsibility for military peacekeeping in Bosnia-Herzegovina was transferred to NATO.

Experience with the peacekeeping missions of the so-called 'third generation', in the course of which the means to the implementation of 'blue helmet' mandates were expanded to include compulsion and military force, falls into two very different categories. On the one hand, the failed missions in Somalia and the former Yugoslavia symbolize the beginning of the crisis of UN peacekeeping. The pictures of dead US Rangers in Somalia or UN troops held hostage in Bosnia – seen the whole world over – caused a dramatic drop in the readiness of many states to send their soldiers into danger in difficult missions. The overrunning of the UN safe zone of Srebrenica by Bosnian Serbs in July 1995 (in which at least 7,000 Bosnian Muslims who had trusted in vain in the protection of the United Nations, were killed) became a symbol of the UN's failure in concrete situations of conflict.

The authorization of a robust intervention, such as the NATO-led IFOR (later SFOR) carried out in the winter of 1995, had been avoided in the spring of the previous year in the case of Rwanda. Operation Turquoise (Summer 1994), which was supposed to prevent the continuation of genocide in Rwanda through military intervention and for which the Security Council had empowered France as well as a small number of African countries, took place only *after* more than 800,000 people had been murdered. Instead of strengthening the 'blue helmets', as the UNAMIR Force Commander had requested, and allowing them to take action to prevent the genocide, the UN had in fact reduced the existing mission there enormously when the massacres began (Carlsson *et al.*, 1999).

These failures caused the UN to be seen by large sections of the public in a somewhat unfavourable light: it looked like an incompetent paper tiger. It became clear that a very fundamental analysis of the political and social conditions in the target-country needed to be undertaken in order to produce a clear mandate, and that the appropriate means to the achievement of these mandates must be made available before the missions could make any sense of the situation. At the time of the first Chapter VII peacekeeping mission, the UN had possessed nothing like such capabilities. Furthermore, the sobering experiences of the past few years, with UN peace missions taking place in the context of conflicts that had already broken out into violence and hostilities, have shown that the contributions of the UN and its special organizations towards the *preventive* regulation of conflicts are even more important.

On the other hand, the mission in Haiti was on the whole accomplished successfully. In 1993/4, it removed a military dictatorship and reinstated the democratically-elected president. It must also be admitted, however, that the Security Council decision to send a UN peacekeeping mission was made possible only by the actions of armed forces under US leadership. Another success was the UNTAES mission (1996–8), with a 'robust mandate' to realize the peaceful transfer of East Slavonia – a contested territory – to Croatia. The INTERFET mission, on the other hand, received a rather more equivocal evaluation: this was the international intervention force empowered by the Security Council in Resolution 1264 (15 September 1999) to restore peace and security in East Timor. The Security Council did manage to come to a speedy and unanimous decision to intervene a mere two weeks after the beginning of the massive expulsions and killings that followed the Independence Referendum of 30 August 1999. Furthermore, the force was able, under Australian leadership, to get the situation under control quite rapidly. However, even though it had hardly been doubted by anyone that acts of violence would follow the referendum, the UN had been content to trust the security assurances of the Indonesian government, and did not take any steps to outfit the UNAMET mission – which was given the task of the execution of the referendum – with its own security component. Thus the UN certainly bore a good deal of the responsibility for the emergence of a situation which then made a military intervention necessary.

Although UN peacekeeping certainly does not come out with nothing but negatives on its balance sheet, in the course of the 1990s the organization experienced a severe crisis with respect to its original areas of responsibility. The industrialized states in particular, which have their own functional security organizations, lost confidence in the UN's ability to handle the political and military leadership of complex peace missions. Hesitation or refusal to provide human, material and financial support to UN peace missions led to a removal of competences from the Security Council to regional alliances, as demonstrated by the transfer of military responsibility for the peace process in the Balkans. Here, the Security Council has restricted its authority to the granting of appropriate mandates, which essentially

TABLE 4.4
Elements of complex peace missions

Security	Creation of a secure environment which facilitates political solutions
Observation	Control of the observation of cease-fires, borders, troop withdrawals and peace agreements; possibly the creation of a buffer zone between the conflicting parties
Disarmament	Oversight of the demobilization of combatants and the collection/destruction of weapons; mine-clearing
Humanitarian aid	Protection of the transport of food, medicine and other vital goods; sometimes also the direct provision of humanitarian aid and medical care
Elections aid	Advice on election rules and the organization of elections; possibly also the physical observation, or implementation, of elections
Civilian policing	Oversight of police work; training of native police units
Administration	Execution of administrative functions in place of failed state structures

amounts to the adoption and endorsement of agreements reached outside the Security Council's procedures. In other regions, however, above all in Africa (MONUC in the Democratic Republic of Congo; UNAMSIL in Sierra Leone; UNMEE in Ethiopia/Eritrea), but also in Asia (UNAMET in East Timor), urgently-needed missions either did not happen at all, or came only after significant delays and often in an incomplete fashion.

Thus the UN's claim to be a global system for peace maintenance with comprehensive responsibility and a legitimate claim to the international observation of the norms and rules set down in its Charter was brought increasingly into question. The accusation that the industrialized countries were simply using the UN selectively for the pursuit of their own interests gained support, particularly from the developing countries' corner. The danger grew that the UN would become marginalized in the very core purposes for which it was founded. Such a development would involve more than the vague concern that an international organization might collapse. It is far more about the fundamental question of principle, whether issues of world peace and international security will in the future remain within the compass of a collective security system, or will fall back to the level of states and regional alliance systems. This question becomes even more urgent as internal conflicts with countless direct and indirect effects on the international system draw ever more military interventions on humanitarian grounds in their wake. Were this option to reside de facto with states on an *ad hoc* basis, this would sooner or later lead away from the international legal order which managed – in the face of so many obstacles – to develop itself after the Second World War. Despite all the fragility of that system, there still exists a wide consensus among states that it is an indispensable one.

Reform Attempts in the 1990s

This large number of new tasks and functions sketched out above were placed on an organization that was not ready for them. Becoming accustomed to these responsibilities involved a difficult learning process. It was imperative that the structures and procedures in place for the implementation of peace missions – none of which had been planned carefully, but had simply occurred as reactions to earlier grave mistakes – be improved. Winrich Kühne (1993, p. 93) pointed out correctly that even traditional peacekeeping did not develop overnight, but was rather 'a permanent learning process on the basis of trial and error'.

In comparison with the situation at the beginning of the 1990s, the recent efforts at reform, above all in the Secretariat, have led to noticeable improvements. On 31 January 1992, in its first session at the head-of-government level, the Security Council charged the Secretary-General with the preparation of an analysis of and recommendations on the question of how the UN's peacekeeping capabilities could be strengthened comprehensively and made more efficient. In June of the same year, Secretary-General Boutros Boutros-Ghali presented his 'Agenda for Peace'. Not least through the clarification of key terms and ideas, this Agenda created a new peacekeeping concept, and furthered the discussion of its future look in both the UN and in the member states. The Secretary-General identified five distinct but closely-related task-areas:

(i)   *Preventive diplomacy*: the goal of this is to minimize tensions and to eliminate the causes of those tensions *before* a conflict erupts. The essential elements are confidence-building measures, the creation of structures for fact-finding missions, early warning in all relevant areas of tension, demilitarized zones, and preventive missions;

(ii)   *Peacemaking with civilian and military means*: Chapter VI should be taken more seriously and improved systematically. Furthermore, sufficient means for third parties in conflict mediation must be made available. Chapter VII measures (peace enforcement) should be implemented consistently; according to the Secretary-General, this means that there must be armed forces made available to the Security Council in the sense of Article 43;

(iii)   *'Blue helmet' peacekeeping*: the preconditions for the use of this instrument should be adjusted conceptually to fit the changed types of conflicts; beyond that, it is necessary to conclude agreements with the member states regarding their readiness to provide troops, and to solidify through written agreements a much better level of financial and logistical support;

(iv)   *Post-conflict peace-building*: a cease-fire does not constitute a lasting peace. The post-conflict period must be given a great deal more attention, including the disarmament of warring parties, mine-clearing, the resettlement of refugees, political reordering, and the reconciliation of the parties; and

(v)   *A conflict-specific division of labour between the Security Council and regional organizations*: better use should be made of the co-operation with regional arrangements mentioned in Chapter VIII. That Chapter states that localized conflicts should be resolved peacefully through the active efforts of such regional organizations, before the Security Council is activated. In the case that coercive measures need to be used, however, the empowerment of the Security Council would still need to be sought.

Although the Agenda for Peace was never implemented in its entirety, the basic structure, the conceptual framework of these reform attempts, remains valid. In the course of the 1990s, the Department of Peacekeeping Operations was completely restructured and its personnel increased. This was necessary if the Department was to do justice to the challenges posed by the management of around 100,000 soldiers and civilians in seventeen different missions around the world. The planning process was streamlined through co-operation with other departments of the Secretariat. With the development of the standby arrangement system (UNSAS), a sort of data bank in which the member states log the capacities they wish to make available to the UN, it was possible to shorten the process of agreement between the UN and troop-sending states. In April 1995, a lessons learned-unit was created to draw conclusions from completed missions and turn them into recommendations for future missions. A training unit began to develop standardized guidelines for training in order to improve the co-ordination of soldiers and civilian experts from very different countries. The introduction of new logistical standards and the creation of the UN Logistic Base in Brindisi in Italy made more rapid deployment and better supply of missions in the field possible.

The original and thoroughly successful orientation of the UN on the prevention of inter-state war has been altered radically by a system-wide shift to internal conflicts. Spectacular failures such as Rwanda, Srebrenica and Sierra Leone have heightened the pressure for reform in this area. According to Chapter VII of the Charter, the UN should enjoy the use of a wide range of instruments in the case of a threat to or breach of the peace, but in practice these means have hardly ever been used. According to the suggestions of a group of experts under the leadership of a former foreign minister of Algeria, Lakhdar Brahimi, given in August 2000, UN troops (on whom around US$2.2 billion were spent in 2000) should operate only on a robust mandate and be sent on missions only when the rules are clear and practicable and when the troops are properly equipped. Furthermore, according to the concept of 'stand-by forces', a capable multi-national force should be constituted such that quick recourse could be made to it if needed.

Although some of the institutional and conceptual innovations have been successful, comprehensive reform is still lacking. Peacekeeping and peacemaking are becoming ever more closely tied to one another, and require mutual success. In cases such as Bosnia-Herzegovina, Kosovo or East Timor, the challenge lies not only in the need to prevent the resumption of hostilities through a deterrent military presence (a robust mandate), but in the need to create new structures in all relevant political, social and economic areas, and to re-create a stable community after the destruction of all order. The experiences with different kinds of peacekeeping operations make it evident that the UN as an inter-state organization

111

TABLE 4.5
Ongoing UN peace missions (as of August 2004)

UNTSO	UN truce supervision organization. Mandate: supervision of the cease-fire in Palestine. Begun: 1948. Strength: 153 soldiers, 93 UN civilians, 112 local civilian workers. Fatalities: 39. Costs 2003/04: US$27.69 million.
UNMOGIP	UN military observer group in India and Pakistan. Mandate: Supervision of the cease-fire in the Kashmir Valley. Begun: 1949. Strength: 44 military observers, 29 UN civilians, 43 local civilian workers. Fatalities: 9. Costs 2003: US$7.25 million.
UNFICYP	UN peacekeeping force in Cyprus. Mandate: Supervision of the cease-fire in Cyprus. Begun: 1964. Strength: 1,202 soldiers, 45 civilian police, 49 UN civilians, 106 local civilian workers. Fatalities: 172. Costs 2003–4: US$45.77 million.
UNDOF	UN disengagement observer force. Mandate: Supervision of the cease-fire on the Golan Heights. Begun: 1974. Strength: 1,029 soldiers, 38 UN civilians, 91 local civilian workers. Fatalities: 40. Costs 2003–4: US$41.81 million.
UNIFIL	UN interim force in Lebanon. Mandate: Supervision of the cease-fire in Lebanon. Begun: 1978. Strength: 1,949 soldiers, 112 UN civilians, 295 local civilian workers. Fatalities: 249. Costs 2003–4: US$94.06 million.
MINURSO	UN mission for the referendum in Western Sahara. Mandate: Supervision of the cease-fire in the Western Sahara. Begun: 1991. Strength: 230 soldiers, 14 civilian police, 135 UN civilians, 107 local civilian workers. Fatalities: 10. Costs 2003–4: US$43.4 million.
UNOMIG	UN observer mission in Georgia. Mandate: Supervision of the cease-fire in Georgia. Begun: 1993. Strength: 118 soldiers, 11 civilian police, 102 UN civilians, 176 local civilian workers. Fatalities: 7. Costs 2003/04: US$32.1 million.
UNMIK	UN interim administration mission in Kosovo. Mandate: Creation of a civilian transitional administration. Begun: 1999. Strength: 3,510 civilian police, 36 soldiers, 820 UN civilians, 2,737 local civilian workers. Fatalities: 37. Costs 2003/04: US$329.74 million.
UNAMSIL	UN mission in Sierra Leone. Mandate: Supervision of the cease-fire in Sierra Leone. Begun: 1999. Strength: 11,539 troops, 116 civilian police, 305 UN civilians, 526 local civilian workers. Fatalities: 137. Costs 2003/04: US$543.49 million.
MONUC	UN organization in the Democratic Republic of the Congo. Mandate: Supervision of the cease-fire and the withdrawal of foreign armed forces from the DRC. Begun: 1999. Strength: 10,576 soldiers, 139 civilian police, 692 UN civilians, 940 local civilian workers. Fatalities: 40. Costs 2003–4: US$667.27 million.
UNMEE	UN mission in Ethiopia and Eritrea. Mandate: Supervision of the cease-fire between Ethiopia and Eritrea. Begun: 2000. Strength: 4,006 soldiers, 241 UN civilians, 256 local civilian workers. Fatalities: 8. Costs 2003–4: US$196.9 million.
UNMISET	UN transitional authority in East Timor. Mandate: Creation of a transitional administration in East Timor. Begun: 2002. Strength: 1,609 soldiers, 129 civilian police, 265 UN civilians, 629 local civilians. Fatalities: 13. Costs 2003–4: US$193.34 million.
UNMIL	United Nations mission in Liberia. Mandate: Support for the implementation of the cease-fire agreement. Begun: 2003. Strength: 14,833 soldiers, 791 civilian police, 361 UN civilians, 435 local civilians. Fatalities: 15. Costs 2003–4: US$564.49 million.
UNOCI	United Nations operation in Côte d'Ivoire. Mandate: Supervision of the situation in Côte d'Ivoire. Begun: 2004. Strength: 3,036 soldiers, 60 civilian police, 93 UN civilians, 17 local workers. Fatalities: – Costs 2004/05: US$502.35 million.
ONUB:	United Nations operation in Burundi: Mandate: Supervision of the situation in Burundi: Begun: 2004 Authorized strength: 5,650 soliders, 120 civilian police. Fatalities: –. Costs 2004–5: In preparation.
MINUSTAH	United Nations stabilization mission in Haiti. Mandate: Supervision of the situation in Haiti Begun: 2004, Authorized strength: 6,700 soldiers, 1,622 civilian police. Fatalities: –, Costs 2004–5: In preparation.

Source: Data from UN Department of Peacekeeping Operations.

cannot replace the states themselves in the exercise of their responsibilities for the peace of the world. In particular, the nearly complete failure of 'third generation' peacekeeping has shown that the organization is largely incapable of peacemaking. It was therefore good advice for the UN to leave combat missions to the state coalitions which were ready and able to carry them out, and to limit its own role to the creation of a framework of legitimization. On the other hand, classical peace-keeping is not likely to become obsolete, as the continuation of several existing missions shows. Peacekeeping and peace-building will in the future be constituted less on the basis of a settled and accepted set of principles and rules, and more on the specific necessities of the target country. Complex mandates will become the rule rather than the exception, and the UN can therefore ill-afford to avoid the development of an integrated, multidisciplinary concept for peace operations (see Chapter 8).

Sanctions as an Instrument of Peace-maintenance

The Security Council's renewed will to react to threats to the peace with coercive measures has also led to the re-discovery of non-military sanctions (Stremlau, 1998). Sanctions of this kind can be used in connection with many different issue areas, from the cessation of all political or cultural contact through embargoes of every kind all the way to criminal prosecution of individuals through war crimes tribunals such as those for the former Yugoslavia and for Rwanda. The list of possible sanctions in Article 41 is not meant to be exhaustive. Within the frame-work of the Charter, the Security Council may use any measures it deems appro-priate for the prevention or ending of disturbances of the peace. Sanctions are not international criminal punishments, but a means of exercising political pressure to move states to change their policies. There are two models of how sanctions should work, based on two different basic assumptions:

- The first follows from the belief that the government of the affected country is a rational actor. Thus, if the costs of the sanctions outweigh the benefits of the sanctioned behaviour, then the state will change its behaviour to comply with the Security Council's directions; and
- The second model aims at the creation of political pressure within the target state itself. Economic sanctions, in particular, tend to affect the general popu-lation adversely; their suffering is then expected to lead to the strengthening of an opposition group or party and a weakening of the regime, thus leading to a change in policy.

Both assumptions are plausible only in connection with states that have a mini-mum level of interest in co-operative international relationships or have made some effort at a pluralistic political order. Regimes that base their power on inter-national isolation and the brutal repression of their populations are comparatively immune to sanctions of this kind.

Legal obligations for the UN member states come into force at the same time as sanctions become effective, since according to Article 25, all members accept and implement Security Council resolutions. Member states may mai. their relations with the target state only in those areas that are not limited thro the sanctions. For the supervision of such measures as it may enact, the Secur Council can create sanctions committees. In practice, these committees exist primarily to distribute permission for exceptions and to make judgements in ambiguous cases. Since the Security Council has no supervisory forces of its own, the committees may work with other organizations or with member states on a case-by-case basis.

The 1990s could, with some justification, be called the 'decade of sanctions' (Cortright and Lopez, 2000). Whereas before 1990 the Security Council had made use of its right to impose non-military compulsory measures only twice (in Southern Rhodesia in 1968–79 and South Africa 1977–94), it has done so thirteen times since then. This practice was a reaction to the increasingly complex demands of international peacekeeping. The measures were used in the classic way against Iraq, the former Yugoslavia, and Ethiopia/Eritrea, all of which were involved in inter-state wars of some kind, but also in Angola, Liberia and Sierra Leone, where the goal was to force an end to civil war. In other cases, such as Somalia and Haiti, the purpose was to improve humanitarian conditions, and Libya, Afghanistan and Sudan were targeted because of their involvement in international terrorism.

Once again, however, the balance sheet shows mixed results. The initial enchantment with this 'new' instrument of peacekeeping – more a manifestation of euphoria that the Security Council was able to make decisions at all than of a rational expectation based on examples of practical success – soon gave way to disillusionment. The very first set of sanctions, levied against Iraq for its aggression against Kuwait, failed to lead to a change in Iraq's politics. In Haiti, Somalia, the former Yugoslavia, and other cases, sanctions proved ineffective even as a less-costly alternative to military intervention. The disadvantages of sanctions, whose lack of effectiveness made it appear increasingly irresponsible to accept the grave humanitarian problems that accompanied their use, became clear very quickly. A reasonable expectation of effectiveness is an essential pre-requisite for the legitimacy of sanctions in the international community, and thus also for the support of states in their use. Ineffective compulsion loses its legitimacy quickly when the side-effects are worse than the problem that the measures were intended to address.

Many sanctions imposed during the 1990s lacked even a clear purpose, not to mention any careful targeting of the measures (Kulessa and Starck, 1997, pp. 4 et seq). The less specific the means used (above all embargoes, prohibitions on the landing of planes, and isolation), the more serious were their side-effects relative to any modest successes in the achievement of the goal. The arms embargo on the former Yugoslavia, for example, for a long time had no effect whatever on the Serbs' capacity to continue on hostilities, but it certainly made it difficult for the Bosnian Muslims to defend themselves. The lack of a supervisory body led to countless cases of evasion of the embargo provisions. This lack was partly caused by the failure to provide sufficient surveillance resources, but also to the intrinsic impracticality of a comprehensive embargo with many exceptions. The humanitarian problems in Iraq demonstrated particularly well for longer than a decade that neither of the two basic assumptions that might support sanctions are necessarily conclusive in all cases (Cortright and Lopez, 1995). In Iraq, the increasing misery of the civilian population not only did not lead to pressure on the Hussein regime for political change, but in fact increased his ability to repress his subjects. Saddam Hussein was able to use the dramatic humanitarian situation to brush the problem of his weapons of mass destruction (WMD) programme – the ostensible reason for the sanctions – under the carpet and split the Security Council on the question of the sanctions policy.

Those measures not targeted directly at a specific purpose but rather have a general effect on the economy, the populace and/or the political opposition have proved to be problematic (Kulessa, 1998, p. 32). The development of targeted or 'smart' sanctions would seem to be urgently needed. The idea behind such attempts is to have sanctions hit harder at the parties directly responsible for the offensive policies, and to keep adverse consequences for the rest of the populace and any third parties to a minimum. A sort of surgical strike of sanctions in the framework of a consistent policy of avoiding escalation, however, also requires clear legal and political rules. There must not only be a transparent decision process and a consistency in states' implementation of sanctions, but also an effort from the moment of decision to anticipate and moderate the negative side-effects. It is also a necessary part of this process to consider and address the possible limitations on the rights of third-party states. Article 50 allows states affected indirectly by sanctions to present their problems to the Security Council, but there exist neither rules of procedure nor mechanisms for compensation to address these complaints. The creation of a compensation fund could contribute to the fair distribution of burdens within and solidarity of the community of states. The experience of the 'decade of sanctions' has opened new perspectives on the use of this sensitive instrument, and it remains on the agenda for the future.

Disarmament and Arms Control in the Framework of the United Nations

Along with peacekeeping in a narrower sense, the UN is also concerned with issues of the control, limitation and reduction of the military power potential of its member states. There is a conceptual distinction to be made between 'arms control' and 'disarmament'. While 'disarmament' means the quantitative and qualitative reduction of weapon stocks and military personnel, arms control is aimed more at the political control of arms processes through bilateral, multilateral or global treaties.

One of the goals the Charter lays down for the UN is the promotion of international security 'with the least [possible] diversion for armaments of the world's human and economic resources' (Art. 26). In contrast to the League of Nations, this formulation implies that a certain level of armament is regarded as necessary, not least for the implementation of forceful measures determined upon by the UN.

In the same way, the right to self-defence as foreseen by Article 51 would be impossible without a military apparatus or armaments. In the literature of political science, the function and effect of armaments measures are a matter of debate. On the one hand, there is the view that armaments lead necessarily to less security and exacerbate the security dilemma described in Chapter 2. But on the other, it is argued that a certain level of armament is absolutely necessary for the stabilization of the international system. Depending on which view is held, the value of disarmament and arms control will be estimated differently. The deputy director of the UN Institute for Disarmament Research (UNIDIR), Christophe Carle (1999, p. 17), formulates the tension thus:

> [d]isarmament can come to fruition only if the international environment is perceived as increasingly benign. But it is also true that disarmament itself is part of the international strategic scenery. Its onset and progress can contribute to creating and reinforcing the very conditions that engender perceptions of security instead of insecurity. Unfortunately that virtuous cycle is as difficult to initiate as the opposite vicious circle is easy to fall into.

After the end of the Cold War, there were many successes in the realm of disarmament. Between 1990 and 1998, military spending in nearly every region of the world (with the exception of East Asia) went down, conventional and nuclear arsenals were drastically reduced, and countless disarmament and arms control treaties were signed or re-activated. The total share of the global product spent on military purposes, however, continues to hover at around 2 per cent – much higher than the share spent on development aid. Since 11 September 2001, several countries have again begun to increase their military spending. The US defence budget for 2001, for example, was US$296 billion, but for 2002 had climbed to US$329 billion, and by 2003 was up to US$364 billion (see Figure 4.2).

Along with the successes in the upheaval following the Cold War, however, came a number of new risks. The danger of uncontrolled proliferation of nuclear and biological weapons of mass destruction, along with carrier systems for these warheads, has grown, as has the proliferation of small arms. In addition, fifteen years after the end of the Cold War, the debate in expert circles over the thus-far preferred methods of creating armaments stability has intensified. This includes, for example, the questioning of important established arms control agreements such as the ABM treaty, and discussions about missile defence programmes.

The methods available to the UN in the realm of disarmament and arms control are both manifold and limited at the same time (for an overview, see Brauch, 1998, 2002; BICC, 2000; SIPRI, 2000; Lang and Kumin, 2001). The UN's activities consist primarily in attempts to create agreements with global reach and the participation of as many states as possible. These are not meant to be in competition with or take the place of the bi- or multilateral efforts of individual states or groups of states. There are two places in the Charter where questions of disarmament are handled explicitly: in Article 11, it says that the General Assembly may 'consider ... the principles governing disarmament and the regulation of armaments, and

FIGURE 4.2
World-wide military spending, 1987–2003 (US$ bn)

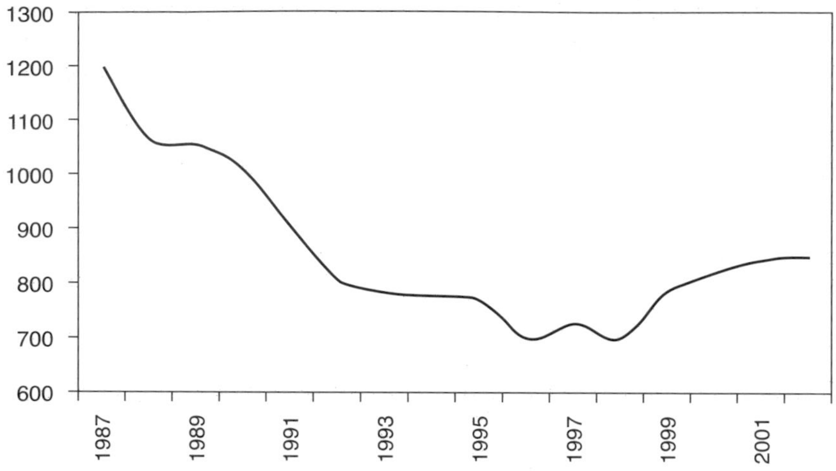

Source: Data from Stockholm International Peace Research Institute (SIPRI).

may make recommendations with regard to such principles to the Members, or to the Security Council, or to both'. In Article 26, the Security Council is given the task of the creation of plans 'to be submitted to the members of the United Nations for the establishment of a system for the regulation of armaments'.

Within the UN itself, there are a large number of committees involved with these issues. In the Secretariat, there is a department dealing with the conduct of conferences and the supervision of individual disarmament regimes, which also publishes a *Disarmament Yearbook* explaining the current status of disarmament every year. The General Assembly deals with questions of disarmament at every yearly session, has created a Disarmament Commission, and has passed several important Resolutions on the subject. In addition, since 1978 the General Assembly has met at irregular intervals as the Special General Assembly on Disarmament Issues, but without any real practical successes. Because of the need for consensus on all issues, it is often not even possible to agree on the agenda for the meeting, so that the conclusion of binding agreements on substantive issues is practically inconceivable. The Security Council has been active only occasionally on disarmament issues. The most prominent example of this was the demand placed upon Iraq in 1991 to destroy all chemical and biological weapons and to submit itself to an inspections regime; the outcome of these efforts is well known.

Of great significance is the Geneva Conference on Disarmament, in which about seventy states form a standing forum in which to discuss issues of disarmament, arms control and non-proliferation. Formally, the Conference on Disarmament is an independent construction. In fact, it is very closely tied to the

UN. Among the global disarmament agreements negotiated under the auspices of the UN are the Convention on Bacteriological and Toxic Weapons (in effect since 1975), the Nuclear Non-Proliferation Treaty (1968; extended indefinitely in 1995), the Chemical Weapons Convention (1997), the Comprehensive Test-Ban Treaty (ready for ratification since 1996), and the Agreement on the Prohibition of Anti-personnel Mines (1999). Countless special organizations belonging to the UN system supervise specific agreements (for example, the CTBTO for the supervision of the Test-Ban Treaty). In December 1991, the General Assembly decided to set up a UN weapons registry to collect information on the import and export of conventional weapons. The states are called upon to communicate data voluntarily on national weapons stocks, but only about half of all states in fact participate in the project.

The work of the United Nations in disarmament can be summarized in the following list of functions:

- The development of new efforts through non-binding exchanges of information and ideas;
- The presentation of different national positions before the broad forum of the global public;
- The articulation of concrete tasks for processes that might also take place outside the UN framework;
- The exercise of moral pressure on rule-breakers with the goal of influencing them to co-operate;
- The provision of organizational aid to interested states which will not or cannot maintain their own apparatus for disarmament or arms control;
- The introduction of a larger number of states to the obligations previously decided upon by a smaller circle; and,
- The oversight of agreements already reached, through special organizations or regimes.

The debate within the UN thus 'makes it possible for the initiators to float test-balloons, for the interested to develop an idea in discourse, and for the critics to articulate their objections and perhaps have a substantive influence on the initiators' (Barker, 1990, p. 183). It is also true, however, that many important steps taken in this realm have been at the periphery of, or even outside, the UN. The will of states to use the UN as a multilateral forum for arrangements and as a communications platform varies greatly from one to the next, preventing fundamental progress in this area.

Prevention as a Task of the United Nations

Another important field of action is the prevention of crises and conflicts. In July 2000, the Security Council requested the Secretary-General to create a report on the 'prevention of armed conflict'. This report was presented in July 2001 (Annan,

2002a). The twenty-nine recommendations contained in the report present a good guide on how to strengthen preventive thinking, and range from a demand for the creation of long-term strategies, through an increased reliance on the International Court of Justice and the Secretary-General, better co-ordination of the whole UN system with respect to the goal of prevention, and the rapid implementation of reforms in the area of peacekeeping operations, all the way to demands for increased contributions to development aid. As usual, it depends ultimately on the member states implementing these recommendations.

The term 'conflict prevention' tends to be sprinkled liberally through the strategy papers of international organizations and national governments, but this is a thankless job. When it is successful, its contribution is often ignored because it is not often possible to prove which measures had a direct causal relationship to the cessation of a crisis or conflict. But even when prevention does not work, there is rarely a serious analysis of the causes of failure. Instead, only general conclusions tend to be drawn such as 'too late' or 'not handled decisively enough'. The unique dynamic of each crisis is also usually noted – often with some justice – as being only partially amenable to external control. This, along with the rather spongy and indistinct character of what is understood under the heading of 'conflict prevention', leads to the situation that – despite rhetoric to the contrary – conflict prevention as a political concept is often not handled with the requisite seriousness. In reality, prevention is less an independent field of action than a new perspective on politics:

- First, it is a cross-cutting task, in which foreign, development, financial, trade, environment, and security policies all play an essentially equal role, and can (and must) complement one another. Trouble spots such as Kosovo, Macedonia or Afghanistan prove that a strong military component for the compulsion of peace is necessary, but that any success at stabilization may very easily be lost through inadequate civil capacities and a lack of sustained post-conflict attention.
- Second, prevention requires the co-operation of the most diverse actors, including international organizations (IGOs), non-governmental organizations (NGOs) and states. Purely national strategies not bound into a multilateral concept can thus contribute very little. On the contrary, as the crisis management in the Balkans demonstrated, differing national strategies practically guarantee ineffectiveness.
- Third, prevention in the potential conflict region must exist on several levels and be aimed not only at the political and military decision-makers, but also at various social groups. Such a structure, with multiple themes and actors, obviously requires an enormous amount of co-ordination at both national and international level in order to avoid repetition or competition and to achieve a meaningful division of labour.

What are the chances of early checks on crises having any success? Has the current understanding of prevention been a failure, or is it no longer appropriate for the new security conditions? On which levels should preventive politics be active, and is it necessary in extreme cases to understand 'prevention' in a military sense in order to be able to react to novel forms of conflict?

It is helpful first to differentiate among some of the different forms of preventive politics (Varwick, 2003):

- Crisis prevention can be understood generally as a systematic and forward-looking effort of the international community or individual states to prevent potentially violent crises, or as a contribution to the transformation of violent conflicts into peaceful modes of resolution. Prevention politics are aimed not at avoiding conflict altogether, but rather at influencing those processes which lead to the use or escalation of *force*. Whether this should be called violence- or conflict-prevention, conflict transformation, or war prevention, is a matter of secondary importance.
- Chronologically, it is possible to distinguish between early or primary prevention of the emergence of a violent conflict and the prevention of the escalation or spread of an already existing, but limited, violent conflict. The prevention of flare-ups from concluded conflicts lies more in the realm of peace consolidation. For every point on the time axis, there are appropriate and inappropriate mechanisms to be applied, and these can also differ from crisis to crisis.

A further categorization follows from the concepts of operative and structural prevention:

- Operative prevention relates to measures taken at short notice in the hope of preventing or regressing an escalation. Instruments can include civil measures, offers of mediation, sanctions, incentives and so on, as well as military measures on various levels.
- Structural prevention, on the other hand, relates to mid- to long-term measures aimed at the deeper causes of conflicts and crises. Here, also, the list of available methods is very diverse: fighting poverty, sustainable development policy, environmental policy, arms control and, the encouragement of regional integration, but also security principles such as deterrence, balance-of-power politics, collective or co-operative security arrangements, and the strengthening of the Security Council's monopoly on the legitimization of the use of force that goes along with such arrangements.

The success of crisis prevention depends primarily on the capacity to negotiate, which involves knowledge of the relationships among various effects as well as the accurate ascertainment of concrete link-points in crises and conflicts. Above all, success requires the readiness or the will to negotiate, which in turn depends on many factors. At the political decision-making level, there are the questions of 'national' interest, cost–benefit calculations and internal support. At the international systemic level, the sovereignty principle and the prohibition on interference in 'domestic affairs' set strict limits on effective prevention.

A structural problem for preventive politics is the often-lamented gap between the early recognition of a crisis (early warning) and the practicability of early action to avert it. Knowledge about the causes of conflicts, and the factors that allow conflicts to spiral into a crisis and then into a violent confrontation, is multi-faceted. This is true for both the structural and operative dimensions. Diverse offices in ministries, bureaux, services and international organizations, as well as non-state actors, prepare information, conduct analyses, and present recommendations for action, often making all this information available to the public. A crisis breaking out completely unexpectedly is the exception rather than the rule; crises usually have lead-times, amenable to analysis and usually also subjected to it. The connections among global inequality, poverty, lack of perspective and the disintegration of state structures are well known. In spite of all the discussion regarding efforts at global development, while the worldwide figure for military spending in 2002 was US$830 billion, the figure for development aid was only around US$55 billion. The goal of the industrialized countries, declared in the 1970s, to reserve 0.7 per cent of their national product for development aid has been achieved in only a few cases (see Chapter 7). Regional conflicts such as those in the Near East have been analysed from countless different perspectives, and their threat potential for international security described extensively, yet still there is no sustainable solution in sight.

The gap between early warning and early action is dramatically evident in two crisis situations, the backgrounds of which have since been well-documented:

(i)   In the case of genocide in Rwanda, there was plenty of early warning. As mentioned above, Operation Turquoise took place only *after* 800,000 people had already been slaughtered, in spite of the presence of a UN 'blue helmet' mission (UNAMIR). As has already been explained, the UN chose not to authorize the strengthening of the 'blue helmet' force or the Force Commander's request to take preventive measures, and instead *reduced* the force when the violence began. At the time of writing, it is estimated at the UN that a deployment of around 5,000 soldiers in April 1994 would have been sufficient to check the genocide.

(ii)   In the case of Kosovo, there was no lack of suggestions for solutions to the conflict, but rather a lack of a common strategy. Thus it took nearly a decade after the suspension of Kosovo's autonomy for the international community to decide on military intervention. In the efforts at peace in the Balkans, Kosovo was generally bracketed out of the discussion because it was clear that the parties would never agree over it. Too many attempts at mediation and civil mandates had already foundered on the refusal of the conflicting parties to accept any plan for peace, or on the Serbian government's refusal to accept mediation. NATO's military action in the early summer of 1999 was not a preventive effort, but a reaction to a humanitarian catastrophe that had been giving off warning signals for some time. The early recognition of the conflict at the expert level was unfortunately never implemented on the political side.

However, the international community has learned from the failure of so many efforts at prevention. It is true that structural prevention has been somewhat neglected, even after the shock of September 11. At the same time, there has been a recognition that 'black holes in world politics' (states or regions that sink into chaos without external interference) are not acceptable, and will sooner or later become a threat to the security of stable states. It has also been recognized that there ought to be some instrument well-prepared to interfere quickly in specific crises. Whether such an instrument would actually be used if available is another question.

The ways in which war can be prevented and peace secured are manifold. Our understanding of the causes of conflict is greater than it ever has been; the resources and instruments are, at least in principle, available. This does not mean that all conflicts are solvable, nor that the escalation of a conflict into a crisis is dependent solely on whether there is external engagement or not. Rather, it means simply that the prevention of crises depends to a large extent on the presence of actors ready and willing to take preventive action. For this to be the case, prevention-politics must be placed at the top of states' lists of foreign- and security-policy priorities. The main obstacle to the prevention of conflicts and their escalation into violence lies less in a lack of knowledge about potential conflicts and crises, and more in a lack of political will to act early to avert those crises. More emphasis should be laid on the consideration of how to create and mobilize this political will, and how to transform a 'culture of reaction' to a 'culture of prevention' (Annan, 2002a).

The UN and International Terrorism

The United Nations reacted immediately to the terrorist attacks of 11 September 2001 in New York, Washington and Pennsylvania. With a speed and unanimity that even UN optimists had barely believed possible, it made decisions and determined on measures with far-reaching legal and political implications. It almost seemed as if the unprecedented challenges of international terrorism were heralding a renaissance of the UN as the central actor in global crisis- and conflict-management.

The force of the attacks impressed both states and individuals with the global and comprehensive character of the threat of international terrorism. All important powers, and above all the five permanent members of the Security Council, felt themselves threatened in their very existential interests. The new respect enjoyed by the UN, at least momentarily, in the context of the fight against terror created a new starting-point for the organization in its efforts to win back lost confidence and provide lasting proof of its indispensability. The challenges of international terrorism thus also became an important test for the UN and its fundamental principle of institutional multilateralism (see Chapter 9). The result of this test will depend on how well the organization succeeds in fulfilling the two basic functions that fall to it in the global fight against terror:

- First, and in the short-term, the creation of a political and legal framework for the immediate military engagement of terrorists, their networks, and their state and quasi-state supporters. Military actions, however, constitute only one small part of a broad spectrum of measures in the proceedings against terrorism. The UN will thus also be judged by whether it manages to develop and apply appropriate legal and political instruments for the defeat of terrorism; but
- More important in the mid- and long-term, however, will be the production of sustainable strategies aimed at combating the causes, if not of terrorism itself, at least of the support and popularity of it that terrorist organizations so often find in poor and oppressed societies. Support of economic and social development, as well as of a more equitable distribution of the fruits of globalization, still belongs to the sworn central tasks of the UN.

In the weeks and months following the terrorist attacks, the concrete initiatives and activities of the UN were concentrated above all on the realm of political and legal measures to fight terrorism, as well as on the stabilization of the new regime in Afghanistan.

Legitimization of the Military Action

After the Security Council met on the very day of the terrorist attacks of 11 September, in order to allow its president to pass judgement on them, it passed its first Resolution on 12 September. While the operational portion of Resolution 1368 called on all member states to strengthen their efforts in the prevention and combating of terrorist activities, and to develop intensive inter-state co-operation for this purpose, in the general section it also placed great emphasis on the necessity of countering this threat with *all* available means. Furthermore, it reaffirmed the right of individual and collective self-defence on the basis of the Charter. It is on this basis, repeated and reaffirmed in the much more extensive Resolution 1373 of 28 September 2001, that the USA and its allies have supported their military operations against Osama bin Laden, the Al Qaeda network, and the Taliban regime in Afghanistan. Even if the Security Council did not mention explicitly a right of self-defence against terrorist acts in Resolution 1368, the whole context of the Resolution makes it clear that this was in fact the idea being expressed. A general reference to a right already mentioned explicitly in the Charter, without any connection to the object of the Resolution, would have been utterly superfluous. The Security Council made it clear that a state attacked by terrorists could use the same means against them as against a state aggressor.

Before the right to self-defence could be exercised, however, it had to be established whether or not an armed attack in the sense of Article 51 had taken place at all. Even more important was discovering who carried original responsibility for the attack, because, of course, this would be necessary in order to know against whom measures should be taken. While this sort of determination is usually relatively simple in the case of an inter-state war, the suspected opponent in this case was an amorphous, decentralized, transnational network with no openly recognized structure or form. Nevertheless, the evidence brought together by the USA and its allies, and above all the public expressions of Osama bin Laden and other spokesmen of his Al Qaeda organization, constituted sufficient grounds for the defensive measures eventually decided upon.

More difficult was the question of how to involve Afghanistan, or rather the Taliban regime, in the military action. Afghanistan had not carried out an armed attack on the USA, but it had – even according to the Taliban itself as the functional government of the country – offered bin Laden an operational base for the planning and execution of terrorist attacks, and had refused to extradite him even at the binding request of the Security Council. The state of affairs in Afghanistan had been considered a threat to peace in a long line of Security Council Resolutions preceding 11 September (the last being Resolution 1333 on 19 December 2000). The form of support for bin Laden practised by the Taliban constituted an aggressive action according to both the Declaration on Friendly Relations (24 October 1970) and the General Assembly's definition of Aggression (14 December 1974). Even though the documents, as resolutions of the General Assembly, are not binding on member states, it was according to precisely these definitions that the International Court of Justice held the USA's support of terrorists and armed bands in Nicaragua to be illegal. The arming and military training of the Contras was described as the kind of act of aggression that might activate Nicaragua's right to self-defence. An analogous use of this understanding in the case of Afghanistan makes it very clear that the USA's self-defence against Afghanistan was legitimate. That the USA and its allies did not simply handle the situation according to their own judgement is emphasized by the fact that the military measures taken since 7 October 2001 have been reported to the Security Council as per Article 51, and have been recognized and approved by the Council.

It has already been noted that the undertaking of actions in self-defence does not require authorization by the Security Council. None the less, its integration into the process and its approval of the defensive measures taken by the USA carry essential political meaning. In that Resolution 1373 states unambiguously that terrorist acts pose a threat to international peace and security, the American military actions are also placed in a context of addressing this global danger. The backing of the Security Council, as the possessor of the monopoly on the legitimization of force, is even more important in light of the fact that international law contains no regulations comparable to those in domestic law, according to which aggressors may be called to answer for their deeds. This means that military means, in particular, tend to be contested not only politically, but also legally. The support of the Security Council thus constitutes a further basis of legitimization of a special quality, not only in the Islamic world, but also among the populace of democratic societies, which usually place high demands on the legitimacy of the use of military force as a political means. The activation of the Security Council, its ongoing occupation with the problem of fighting terrorism, and not least the fact that the states involved are acting on its Resolutions and observing the Charter's provisions, have all heightened the reputation of the somewhat long-suffering central organ of the UN.

A fight against an enemy who is difficult to identify is particularly suited to demonstrating the importance of a multilateral organization for decision-making and legitimization. The determination of whether a state lies under sufficient suspicion of co-operation with terrorists to justify military action against it certainly cannot be left to the sole judgement of the state wishing to take such action. If it were, the goal of a global fight against terror would certainly slide into the mill of individual state interests and be ground to nothing. Whether the Security Council truly is on the way to achieving the authority intended for it by the Charter, as the highest custodian of international war and peace it remains dependent on the will – particularly of the 'Permanent Five' – to co-operate. The question of the legitimacy of Security Council decisions and their dependence on the Permanent Five, arising in the new course of the 'War on Terror', may also reignite discussion about the Council's reform (see Chapter 8).

Other Legal and Political Measures

Transnational terror networks constitute a global threat. At the same time, the key to their defeat lies with individual states, which must take preventive and other measures through legislation and criminal procedure to hinder the formation of terrorist groups and the conduct of attacks, as well as finding those responsible and bringing them to justice. An effective collective procedure requires the existence of internationally-accepted norms and standards, on which national regulations can orientate themselves. State efforts to create such standards have led, since the Convention on Offences and Certain Other Acts Committed on Board Aircrafts of 14 September 1963, to no fewer than twelve UN conventions, countless resolutions and declarations of the General Assembly and Security Council, and a large number of regional agreements dealing with forms of terror and ways of fighting it. Despite all this, there has still been no success in producing a binding definition of what is to be understood as 'terrorism'. A number of states that support liberation movements in 'illegally-occupied territories' want to prevent any definition that includes such 'legitimate struggles for self-determination'. It was this position, held by a small group of states centred on Pakistan and Egypt, which, in the first week of November 2001, led to the failure of four years' worth of effort to produce a comprehensive convention on terrorism. Although this convention would have been very helpful, especially in the matter of clarifying the definition, it must not be forgotten that the existing conventions provide a comprehensive legal and political instrument with which nearly all forms of terror can already be pursued legitimately.

States have, however, proved themselves exceptionally hesitant to ratify these conventions (passed by overwhelming majorities in the General Assembly) and incorporate them into their domestic law. With Resolution 1373, the Security Council made use of its authority to accelerate the implementation of a few basic regulations into state domestic law. Once it had determined, in accordance with Article 39, that acts of terrorism constitute a threat to the peace, it placed the decisions and requirements in the operative section of the Resolution under the auspices of Chapter VII, making the catalogue of measures to be taken binding on all member states. Thus it is now a state's obligation to prosecute every form of financial support of terrorism as a criminal activity, to freeze any related assets, and to forbid any and every form of direct or indirect financial support for terrorist attacks. The Security Council thereby set the International Convention for the Suppression of the Financing of Terrorism (passed in 1999 and up to the time of writing ratified by only five states) into effect. As far as the active support of terror is concerned, it is required of all states that they deny terrorists any haven or base of operations, and to ensure that acts of terrorism count as felonies in their national law. Furthermore, the Security Council appeals to states to strengthen the exchange of operational information for purposes of prevention and prosecution of terrorist acts, and to pay more attention to the close connection between terrorism and international organized crime. For the oversight of the fulfilment of these obligations, the Security Council formed a committee, which had to be informed by all member states within ninety days of any measures they had taken or had decided to take on the basis of Resolution 1373. As of February 2002, 113 states had provided their reports to this committee.

With the unanimous acceptance of this Resolution, sponsored by the USA, the Security Council advanced considerably in the direction of a substantial progressive development of international law. A broad palette of legal and political measures, supported by verbal acclaim but in fact implemented only by a minority of states, should now be implemented in national law by way of compulsion. As far as the formal legal pre-requisites go, there is nothing about this rather unusual action of the Security Council that could give cause for complaint. For the purpose of restoring peace and international security, it enjoys an extraordinarily large scope for its own judgement, and according to Article 25, the member states have all obligated themselves to accept and support the Security Council's decisions.

At the same time, this step was not without risk. If a significant number of member states had refused to follow, or had used the lack of a clear definition of terrorism to excuse themselves from following the Security Council's decision, its authority would have suffered serious damage. Even considering the apparent limitation on states' sovereign rights to legislate for themselves, many states in fact welcome this type of compulsory development of international law as it gives politicians a way around domestic political objections to the implementation of such policies. Furthermore, the deep shock left by the terrorist attacks on the USA has made many societies more willing to accept even unpopular legislation. At any rate, with Resolution 1373, the Security Council has pulled a number of goal-orientated measures out of the endless loop of the ratification procedure and thus warned the member states that they need to be conscious not only of their sovereign rights, but also of their obligations in the process of developing a workable international law.

Further Perspectives

The fight against terrorism did not end with the military defeat of the Taliban, and the struggle for a stable Afghanistan will remain a long and difficult process. It has been an express purpose of those involved there not to repeat some of the mistakes of other peacekeeping missions. Thus there is no intention to create an external transitional authority as there was in Kosovo (with 50,000 personnel), or to compel an external solution as was attempted in Bosnia-Herzegovina (with 60,000). Calculated according to the size and population of Afghanistan, such an undertaking would require several hundred thousand soldiers – an order of magnitude that could never be achieved politically or supported financially. In addition, there were good reasons to avoid any appearance of a foreign occupation. Not least, the rather ambiguous experiences of the UN with nation-building – for example, in Cambodia or Somalia, meaning the organization of completely new political, social, economic and state structures – encouraged more modest efforts.

Following the Bonn Afghanistan Conference in December 2001, where a political solution was reached under the patronage of the UN and with the participation of all major Afghan groups, the military task is primarily to secure the implementation of that solution. Equipped with a robust Chapter VII mandate by Security Council Resolution 1386 (20 December 2001), troops are to support the multi-ethnic Afghan transitional government under the leadership of Hamid Karzai with the maintenance of security in Kabul and its surroundings. Thus the International Security Assistance Force (ISAF) is allowed to employ force not only in self-defence, but also in the pursuit of its mission. The ISAF, which has been under NATO leadership since August 2003, is a mixture of robust peacekeeping and an *ad hoc* coalition, but is not a UN peacekeeping mission in the strictest sense. It is a multinational force consisting of contingents from several member states, mandated by the Security Council, but it is not a 'blue helmet' mission. The restriction of ISAF's area of responsibility to Kabul and its immediate surroundings does, however, have a negative effect on its capabilities, and causes large expenditure on co-ordination. The United Nations has named a special representative for Afghanistan – Lakhdar Brahimi – whose task is to co-ordinate and supervise all UN programmes and activities in humanitarian situations and in the protection of human rights. He is supported in this by the UN Mission on Afghanistan (UNSMA). It remains to be seen how much this will contribute to the stabilization of Afghanistan.

The 'division of labour' favoured by Washington in recent years, in which the USA accomplishes the military victory and then the UN takes on the dangerous, expensive and obstacle-strewn work of repatriating refugees and rebuilding the state, is not likely to undergo any major changes. For the purposes of the fight against terrorism, states need organizations that are capable of action, and the organizations need the active and long-term support of their members. Should the fact of this mutual dependency find broader recognition in the wake of September 11, it might indeed lead to a renaissance of the United Nations.

The UN and the 2003 War Against Iraq

Hopes of such a renaissance suffered a serious setback in Spring 2003 with the dispute over military intervention in Iraq. The Iraq Question (Berdal, 2003;

Cordesman, 2003; Kubbig, 2003) put international politics to a serious and multi-faceted test. It was not only about finding the proper strategy for the containment of dictators armed with weapons of mass destruction and the future face of the crisis-prone Near East, but also about who has the right to make decisions about the appropriateness of preventive military measures; on which international legal grounds these might be undertaken; and what relationship they might bear to the general prohibition on the use of force.

Efforts to find a solution to the Iraq Crisis within the framework of the United Nations have occupied the international community for more than a decade. After Iraq invaded Kuwait in August 1990 and ignored an ultimatum in January 1991, a broad coalition of twenty-eight states, under the leadership of the USA, intervened militarily and liberated Kuwait (Operation Desert Storm). A number of conditions were imposed on Iraq. Resolution 687 (April 1991) created a cease-fire agreement that was meant to hold only so long as Iraq co-operated with the UN. The newly-created United Nations Special Commission on Iraq (UNSCOM) and the International Atomic Energy Agency (IAEA) were given the task of the control and demolition of Iraqi weapons of mass destruction. All atomic, biological and chemical weapons, weapon parts and establishments for their production were to be destroyed, and Iraq was to remain under constant supervision so that it could not resume development, production or acquisition of such weapons.

A re-evaluation of the existing policy of international containment against Iraq was of decisive importance in the assessment of the legitimacy of any war against that country. It was here that the advocates and opponents of military action in Iraq differed in their judgements, and here that the fault line between the USA and its partners and their opponents ran, in the Security Council and elsewhere. When the UNSCOM and IAEA inspectors started their work in 1991, all members of the Council had been in relative agreement and supported their work unanimously. The inspections, however, proved to be very difficult to carry out, because Iraq did not co-operate fully as it had been required to do, and as it had agreed to do. It was supposed to disclose the questionable programmes voluntarily; it did not do this. Although the original time-plan for inspections, set for one year, were totally confounded, there were none the less an impressive number of ballistic delivery systems and combat agents destroyed and a network of surveillance cameras and measuring points installed for early warning of renewed attempts at armament in the period between 1991 and 1998. However, the unanimity of, and therefore the pressure coming from the Security Council increasingly gave way over this period, and ultimately Iraq refused all co-operation. Even Resolution 1134 (October 1997), which drew attention to Iraq's un-cooperative behaviour, was no longer supported unanimously .

Beginning in Spring 1998, after many incidents, the situation began to escalate. Only a last-minute agreement between Iraq and the UN prevented a military inter-vention by the USA and the UK even then. But the 'cat and mouse game' of the Iraqi regime went on: Iraq acknowledged openly that it no longer intended to co-operate, and the conflict over inspections in the presidential palaces finally led to the total withdrawal of UNSCOM inspectors on 16 December 1998. Following this, the USA and the UK decided, without the approval of the Security Council, to carry out Operation Desert Fox, the largest military action undertaken since the end of the 1991 Gulf War. In a four-day air operation, Iraq's military potential was hugely weakened. The Security Council was never activated; Russia, China, and France protested the attacks, and the international public discussion was also nearly unanimously negative.

Not until December 1999 was another attempt at inspection, the UN Monitoring, Verification and Inspection Commission (UNMOVIC), established. The corresponding Resolution 1284 was supported only by the USA and the UK, among the permanent five; the others abstained. For nearly three years, the UNMOVIC inspectors were unable to work on location, at least in part because of the lack of backing from the Security Council, and because Iraq refused to co-operate with it. It was only under decisive military pressure from outside once again that allowed the return of the weapons inspectors on 27 November 2002. The foundation for this was Resolution 1441, passed unanimously on 8 November 2002 after weeks of diplomatic tug-of-war. In it, Iraq was given a 'final chance' to fulfil the requirements of the 1991 cease-fire resolution, and to lay its programmes for the development of WMD open to inspection, or to provide reliable proof that such programmes no longer existed. Should co-operation not be forthcoming, Iraq was threatened with 'serious consequences'.

The Gap between Interventionists and Inspectionists

The leader of UNMOVIC, Hans Blix, and his counterpart from the IAEA, Mohamed El Baradei, presented the Security Council with regular reports on the status of the co-operation. Progress was made, but deficits still existed. The two 'camps' within the Security Council were unable to come to a common understanding of the political meaning of the reports. While the USA, the UK, Spain, and Bulgaria argued that it was clear from the reports that Iraq was *not* co-operating fully and was thus far in violation of Resolution 1441, France, Russia, China and Germany saw progress being made, and thus there were insufficient grounds to break off the inspections and take military action. They supported an expansion of the inspections, a clear time-plan with which Iraq's willingness to co-operate could be reliably evaluated, and above all an avoidance of any action that might lead to war. German foreign minister, Joseph Fischer warned urgently against war with Iraq in his address to the Security Council on 7 March 2003, suggesting that it would be better to exhaust the peaceful means available and to support the inspections. It was not apparent, he said, that a radical solution needed to be sought when less extreme instruments still existed. Germany, France and Russia claimed in their common declaration of 15 March 2003, that Iraq was, in fact, 'in the process' of disarmament.

In the end, the Security Council was deeply split between Interventionists and Inspectionists. French, German, Russian and Chinese suggestions were directly opposed to Anglo-American plans, and demonstrated moreover that there was no hope of a unanimous understanding of the situation in Iraq. It was in the context of this deadlock that the USA had on several occasions made it clear that it would act without a decision of the Security Council if necessary. The inspections needed neither more time nor more personnel, but rather the full co-operation of Iraq, which was not being provided. At a tripartite American–British–Spanish summit in the Azores on 16 March 2003, this position was re-emphasized, and Iraq given a final deadline. The USA and its partners saw the authority of both the Security Council and the UN as a whole threatened by the fact that its Resolutions could be ignored – and what was worse, ignored apparently without any adverse consequences. President Bush insisted that in matters of its own security, the USA did not need permission from the United Nations to act. If the UN could not act in such a situation, it was merely proving its irrelevance and displaying its true nature as a 'talking society'. On 20 March 2003, military intervention began, without the previous authorization of the Security Council.

What does this renewed marginalization mean for the UN? Is the rule of force returning to international politics (if it ever left), and would it result in worldwide instability because other states, too, might arrogate to themselves the right to act unilaterally without recognizing the Security Council as an authority? Is the entire international order of capable international organizations and international law, with the United Nations at its centre, at stake?

With their decision to end the months-long political tug-of-war in the Security Council, and to prepare a violent end for the Iraqi regime without the mandate of the community of nations, the USA and its coalition partners have done more than set the UN and its system of collective security to another serious test. This situation, far more than previous cases of the UN's and the Security Council's marginalization, carries with it the potential for a real existential crisis for the world organization. When, for example, NATO intervened in the Kosovo crisis in 1998/9, also without a mandate from the Security Council, at least the states of the 'Western camp' were able to maintain a unified position, which found wide global acceptance when it ended largely successfully. Furthermore, they made sure that the Kosovo question came back to the United Nations, and that the necessary civil and military peacekeeping was legitimized through the Security Council. The overt split in this powerful group of states – holding three permanent and two non-permanent seats on the Council – that occurred with the Iraq crisis has merely accelerated and brought into the open a dramatic development that has been under way for some time. In its most important core task of the maintenance of peace, the United Nations stands at a fork in the road: can the organization maintain its concept of institutionalized and norm-based multilateralism, or will a world hegemony dominate, which meets its needs for international co-operation with loose and changing *ad hoc* coalitions?

The USA and the UN – a Shattered Relationship

According to the USA's 2002 security strategy, since classical security precautions such as deterrence or arms control offer no support against terrorist organizations and despots, the USA must be in a position to strike its enemy before the enemy can attack. The 'pre-emptive measures' or 'pre-emptive strikes' mentioned in the strategy do not, however, relate only to recognized dangers or immediate threats. Even abstract risks could justify recourse to such measures (see Chapter 8). The USA is also ready, if necessary, to carry out these so-called pre-emptive (in fact preventive) measures alone. In particular, it is willing to act without involving the UN, whose functions and responsibilities are not mentioned at all in the entire US security strategy. The US administration has long insisted on the right to sovereign decision-making, independent of international norms or bodies, for the purposes of ensuring the security of American citizens – and this includes the decision to use military force.

Present in the US administration is a camp that simply considers the entire idea of an international norm- and decision-making system for the limitation or prevention of violent unilateral action to be completely unrealistic (Glennon, 2003). It is also supported in its strategy by a school of international legal thought that insists that the norms of international law are valid only for those states that have consented to them or accepted them. The 'state consent' argumentation strikes at the core of the United Nations as an organization created specifically – in the aftermath of the the the Westphalian system with its *liberum ius ad bellum*, which failed catastrophically in the humanitarian disaster of two World Wars – to *remove* states' rights to war and violence as means of international politics, and to place these instead under the control of an international body. It is also a position not shared by the majority of the international law community (Tomuschat, 2003).

It is obvious that international legal norms do not disintegrate when they are broken once or twice by a single state or power, and the competencies and procedural norms of the Security Council remain valid, even when force is used over its head. However, the USA, as by far the strongest and most capable power, can also cause such harm to the international legal order and its major organ that it comes almost to the same thing as its destruction. It is certainly not to be insinuated that the USA is deliberately trying to return the world to previous epochs of international law. It is rather that its leading thinkers assume that the USA will continue to be in a position for a long time to maintain the global balance of a *pax americana* (Kagan, 2003, p. 115 et seq.). On the other hand, there exists significant doubt as to whether this unipolar order really would function better than the existing one. The emerging over-extension of American forces in a large number of crisis regions in general, and in particular the difficulties the USA has encountered in coping with the post-war situation in Iraq, show that US estimates of its own strength may very well be a little too self-confident to gamble away a global order accepted by the overwhelming majority of states.

European states carry their own responsibility for the splintering of the unanimous position of the Security Council in February/March 2003 and the marginalization of the Council that followed the British–American action. France had originally suggested a two-step process in Iraq: after a final ultimatum (such as that in Resolution 1441), if Iraq continued to violate UN requirements, then possible military steps should be discussed. France thus signalled its willingness, at least in principle, to consider a military solution. When, however, in January 2003, France began to call for indefinite extensions for the inspections – even before the weapons inspectors' reports were received, and then escalated its opposition to any possible military action to the actual threat of a veto, this was understandably interpreted by the USA as a breach of the agreed-upon plan. At the same time, the USA and UK saw their position coming under ever greater pressure because of questionable evidence, rapidly alternating justifications for war, and an apparently more-compliant Iraq – albeit in a very feeble sense. The Cheney–Rumsfeld camp, which had been against the route through the Security Council from the beginning, regained its influence over the US president. The basis for a common solution to the Iraq problem crumbled visibly when Germany blocked itself by taking – for domestic political reasons – a strict anti-war position even if the Security Council had succeeded in passing a resolution. Furthermore, when agitating loudly against Washington's policy on the Iraq situation, Germany denied itself its traditional role as an honest broker between the USA on the one hand and France and Russia on the other.

This failure of the Security Council, brought about by its most important members, produced the worst results for everyone. The war could not be prevented, and attempts at prevention did not encourage Washington's willingness to bring the issue back before the Security Council in the foreseeable future. There was little reason for celebration in the camp of the unilateralists, however: its victory over the 'irrelevant' Security Council showed itself to be somewhat superficial as soon as it became clear that the stabilization of the region as well as the control of WMD proliferation required capable international organizations and multilateral arrangements. The damage done to the United Nations and to the principle of multilateral peacekeeping is considerable – and attempts to restore these will mean a great deal of effort from all sides.

The Reintegration of the World Hegemony

The existence of a hyperpower, of a world hegemony, is among those realities that simply have to be recognized. The principle of sovereign equality must still hold firm for the purposes of co-operative relationships in the UN, but as the privileged position given to the permanent members shows, this rather idealistic provision of Article 2(1) was always a limited one. In the Security Council, the USA has more power and capability than the four other permanent members put together. This weight also manifests itself – once again as shown by the Iraq crisis – in the determination of the world political agenda. Next to its massive technological and military lead, the USA is far ahead of the rest of the world in the identification of security challenges and the formulation of strategies to address them. While a number of European states may justifiably hold the opinion that these strategies rely rather one-sidedly on hard power, and that a set of international rules should be created for their use, they must understand that the survival of any effective international regimes at all is predicated on the reintegration of the hegemony.

The course of the Iraq crisis in 2002–3 showed that it is demanding too much of the Security Council and its individual members to exercise a policy of containment of the USA – quite apart from the question of the suitability and appropriateness of such a policy. The UN may be of use and significance to the USA, but in light of the existing power gradient, this dependency tends not to appear as immediate or as obvious to the USA as it does to other states or regions. Instead of endangering the Security Council and the UN further with continued attempts to contain the USA, it would seem to promise more success to reintegrate it into the Security Council as *primus inter pares*. That would include the acceptance of its status and the readiness of the members to co-operate more in the fields that carry particular importance for the USA. This would not be a capitulation to the right of the strongest, but a precept of political wisdom. The history of the transatlantic relationship shows that the USA is more amenable to influence from co-operative partners than from objectors. On the other hand, it lies in the nature of the 'paradox of American power' (Nye, 2002) that the USA needs friends and partners. Both sides would do well to keep this decades-long experience in mind.

This is all the more urgent as the re-establishment of good transatlantic relations also has a special meaning in the context of the UN. If no institutional renewal of the Security Council is in sight, then Europe and the USA must find their own way back to a complementary coexistence. The liberal democracies have an obligation to the world not to hamstring themselves with internal disputes. They would be better occupied in pursuing their common core processes of contributing to the spread of democratic principles as a sustainable basis for global stability. It is thus even more urgent to overcome the current split in the democratic core of the Security Council, because the world needs the leadership of both Europe and the USA in its most important decision-making body to meet the current challenges of global politics.

Further Reading

Annan, Kofi (2002) *Prevention of Armed Conflicts*, UN-Document (A/55/985), New York.

Berdal, Mats (2000) 'Lessons Not Learned: The Use of Force in Peace Operations in the 1990s', *International Peacekeeping* (4), pp. 54–74.

Bothe, Michael and Thomas Dörschel (eds) (1999) *UN Peacekeeping: A Documentary Introduction*, The Hague: Kluwer.

Boutros-Ghali, Boutros (1992) *An Agenda for Peace*, UN-Document (A/47/277), New York.

Brahimi Report (2000) *Report of the Panel on United Nations Peace Operations*, UN-Document (A/55/305-S/2000/809).

Dunne, Michael (2003) 'The United States, the United Nations and Iraq: "Multilateralism of a Kind" ', *International Affairs* (2), pp. 257–79.

Glennon, Michael (2003) 'Why the Security Council Failed', *Foreign Affairs* (3), pp. S.16–35.

Jett, Dennis C. (2000) *Why Peacekeeping Fails*, New York: Palgrave.

Parsons, Anthony (1995) *From Cold War to Hot Peace: UN Interventions 1947–1995*, Harmondsworth: Penguin.

Roberts, Adam (2003) 'Law and the Use of Force after Iraq', *Survival* (2), pp. S.21–56.

Sucharipa-Behrmann, Lilly (2001) 'Peace-Keeping Operations of the United Nations', Franz Cede and Lilly Sucharipa-Behrmann (eds), *The United Nations: Law and Practice*, The Hague: Kluwer, pp. 89–104.

Teixeira, Pascal (2003) *The Security Council at the Dawn of the Twenty-First Century*, Geneva:UNIDIR.

United Nations Department of Public Information (ed.) (1996) *The Blue Helmets. A Review of the United Nations Peace-keeping*, New York: The United Nations.

5

The United Nations and Human Rights: Normative Development, Codification and Definition

Along with the maintenance of international peace and security, the protection of human rights forms the second original area of responsibility for the United Nations. In this case, as in the other, it required a global catastrophe to bring about a fundamental change of opinion among the community of states on a matter of central importance to all humanity. Where it took the experience of the First World War to produce the idea that states should no longer enjoy the right to resort to war, it took genocide practised on European Jews (among other grave and large-scale human rights violations), to make the need for an effective protection for basic human rights dramatically clear. In this case, effective protection was thought to be achievable through binding international norms and collective mechanisms for the implementation of such norms. The content of the term 'human rights' is so unclear as to make a commonly-accepted definition barely possible, but the basic principle on which the UN is founded is that every human being has inborn and inalienable rights that demand protection regardless of age, sex, religion, ethnicity, nationality or regional or social background.

The consciousness of a close relationship between world peace and respect for human worth has had a long tradition in intellectual history, and had a noticeable effect even during the Second World War. This was evident in particular in the efforts of the American president, Franklin D. Roosevelt, to include a comprehensive catalogue of human rights in the charter of the world organization he hoped to see created. Numerous intellectual and civil organizations took hold of this idea, and a number of Latin American states brought it up at the San Francisco Conference as a possible element of the charter. However, it had already become clear at the conference of the four powers in Dumbarton Oaks in the summer of 1944 that the protection of human rights would find only a limited mention in the Charter. From the Soviet side, and also from the British, it was objected that the new organization should not be given any right to interfere in state sovereignty. Despite this, the delegates at the San Francisco Conference in the spring of 1945 did use some of the suggestions from Dumbarton Oaks to enlarge and make more precise the rather subdued formulation on human rights in Chapter IX. Still, compared to the chapters on the prevention of war and the maintenance of peace, which were written in an operative style, the protection of human rights remained programmatic and did not receive a legal or institutional formulation, either through the practice of the UN or of its member states. Indeed, in the principle of sovereignty and the Article 2(7) prohibition on intervention, the states had created strong defensive instruments for themselves, specifically in anticipation of overly-ambitious demands on the part of the organization.

The states were hesitant to outfit their newly-created world organization with constitution-like competencies in the realm of the protection of human rights. This becomes understandable when one recalls that the precarious relationship between the claims of an international organization and the principle of state sovereignty shows up even more clearly on the issue of human rights than even on that of the prohibition on war and the use of force. Hardly any other form of state behaviour belongs more immediately to the realm of 'domestic affairs' than the way that a state or society deals with individuals. It is precisely the goal of an international human rights regime to institute the legal regulation of this internal relationship, and to over-see its implementation. It is thus hardly surprising that the discussion of human rights and their protection, in spite of the great progress made since the Second World War, has taken place precisely along the fault line between collective regulatory compe-tence and the sovereignty principle. This discussion is primarily about the problem of what precisely constitute the core human rights – those subject to universally-valid norms and standards that cannot be derogated by states. The discussion is also about the question of how these standards can be created and maintained, and in what form and by what means the community of states is authorized to act against indi-vidual members of the community in the case of a breach. It would seem to be appro-priate first to regard these general problems of the protection of human rights before we address the specific way the UN has handled the situation.

In the second half of the twentieth century, the idea of human rights spread in a completely unprecedented fashion over the whole world. In declarations, treaties and conventions without number, a global normative framework was created and then further developed through regional arrangements. The Universal Declaration of Human Rights is now the most-translated and most widely-promulgated inter-national document in existence. The globalization phenomenon, not least in the realm of communication, has given human rights a prominent place on the global (media) agenda. However, in spite of the universal verbal acknowledgement of human rights (Kühnhardt, 1991, p. 29), the chain of violations still crosses the globe unbroken, and the standards of civilization that have been set at the global level have by no means found their way into positive state law in the way that the spread of international human rights documents might suggest. The reasons for this lie primarily in the still-inconclusive nature of the conceptual framework. The idea of human rights suggests a material and legal clarity which, on closer inspec-tion, simply does not exist. Borrowing from the historical development of the idea, it has become customary to speak of three 'generations' of human rights:

(i)   The first generation comprises the classical liberal rights protecting individuals against the arbitrary judgement or violence of state or society: the rights to life, liberty of conscience, speech, religion and the rule of law;

(ii)   The second generation extends to rights of individual claims on and participation in social, economic and cultural realms, such as the right to work, to humane working conditions, to a materially-secure existence, or to health; and

(iii) The rights of the third generation aim more at collective goals: the right to development, to a clean environment and to peace. These are rights of solidarity, which none the less take the individual into consideration indirectly as the original bearer of rights.

The various understandings supporting each of these 'generations' reveal categorical differences in the perceptions of human rights that grow out of the world's cultural plurality. These differences are capable not only of bringing the postulate of an indivisible and globally-accepted core list of human rights norms into serious question, but also of ideologizing the very idea of human rights and instrumentalizing it for political purposes. The Western democracies tend to promote the civil liberty rights of the first generation. During the Cold War, however,the socialist states tried constantly to redefine participation rights in connection with an ideologically-based concept of peace into socialistic human rights (Kühnhardt, 1991, pp. 251 et seq.). In the approximately twenty years that the discussion of the third generation of human rights has been going on, it has been in particular the countries of the southern hemisphere that have claimed that the realization of collective rights – especially the right to development – is a pre-requisite to the implementation of other civil rights (Howard, 1997/8, p. 99 et seq.). Many developing countries putting forward this argument are motivated by one (or both) of two goals:

(i)   They wish to decouple their material claims on industrialized states from Western conditions regarding Western conceptions of human rights; and

(ii)   The argument is to a great extent about defending against demands for participation and democratization coming from within. Collective human rights of the third generation often present – for example, in the case of 'Asian values' – legitimizations for neo-authoritarianism and the stabilization of the authority of the indigenous elites.

As accurate as these objections to the concept of collective human rights – most often raised by the Western democracies – may be, the democracies' own practice regarding human rights has hardly been such as to be convincing of their superiority. This applies first to the recognition that human rights may be violated even in mature democracies, as the annual reports of Amnesty International make clear. Even more, however, it applies to the problem of double standards, when industrialized countries on the one hand condition development aid on the fulfilment of human rights requirements, and on the other overlook serious human rights abuses when these take place in countries of great political or economic importance. The

United Nations could become the global forum where the process of human rights/civilizational standard-setting could finally be decided. It is suited to this task as is no other international organization. As in the case of peacekeeping, however, the UN is dependent on the personal, financial, material and above all political, support of its member states. In Chapter 6, the means and opportunities available to the UN in the realm of human rights protection will be analysed in the context of the discussion that has just been sketched out above.

Human Rights in the UN Charter

A universally valid list of codified norms and rules is essential for the effective protection of human rights on a global scale. However, as has already been shown, the states acted with the utmost restraint and care when framing the UN Charter's provisions on human rights and their protection, so that no inclusion of a comprehensive catalogue of human rights in the Charter was possible. Human rights did not even rate an article of their own, let alone a whole chapter. The limited number of provisions on human rights goals or obligations that did find their way into the Charter are spread out over a number of Articles dealing ostensibly with other matters. This rather less-prominent placement of human rights, based no doubt on tactical considerations with respect to the opponents of overly-obligatory formulations, none the less did no harm to the effects that such provisions were intended to produce, because, in the course of the San Francisco Conference, in spite of all the careful efforts of the states to protect their claims to sovereignty, a few epochal changes were in fact introduced:

*   First, a programmatic framework for the development of international protection of human rights was created in the Charter;
*   Second, binding norms and mechanisms were integrated into the Charter, through which the organization was also given competence to engage with concrete human rights situations inside the member states; and
*   Third, in this way it was made clear that human rights, as a collective legal good, were to be removed from the exclusive disposal of states.

Thus the Charter of the United Nations became the first international law treaty to be built – among other things – on universal respect for human rights (Boutros-Ghali, 1995a, p. 5). Even in the Preamble, 'faith in fundamental human rights, in the dignity and worth of the human person, [and] in the equal rights of men and women' is emphasized. In Article 1(3), it is named as one of the binding purposes of the organization to 'promot[e] and encourage[e] respect for human rights and for fundamental freedoms for all without distinction as to race, sex, language, or religion'. Although this goal is formulated in a rather vague way and is in obvious need of further interpretation, in the prohibition on discrimination it still contains a rule that can be applied with no need of further modification. The validity of a basic idea of rights for all individuals independent of their origins or convictions is a constitutive element of the Charter's framework for the protection of human rights (Tomuschat, 2000, p. 432). The prohibition on discrimination, which is re-emphasized in the operative provisions of Article 1(3), constitutes an independent normative element that creates an immediate legal obligation for the member states (Riedel, 2002).

The programmatic formulation of this purpose is to be found in Chapters IX and X. First, in Article 55(c), the close connections among economic, social and humanitarian welfare and world peace are underlined. Then, in binding terminology, the United Nations promotes 'universal respect for and observance of human rights and fundamental freedoms' with special attention to the prohibition on discrimination. In practical terms, this meant that the organization's first order of business was to develop a definitional basis explaining which human rights and fundamental freedoms should be included under the umbrella of international protection. The United Nations fulfilled this requirement with the creation of the International Bill of Human Rights and other treaties following from it, such as the International Convention on the Elimination of All Forms of Racial Discrimination; the Convention Against Torture; and the Convention on the Rights of the Child. A general obligation for standard-setting in the area of human rights can also be drawn from the language in Article 55(c) (Riedel, 1998, p. 25), which the United Nations has attempted to meet over the decades of its existence with an almost unimaginable number of resolutions and declarations.

The programmatic framework also answers the question of which organs and committees are responsible for the realization of this task. Article 60 places responsibility on the General Assembly and the ECOSOC, which operates under the authority of the General Assembly. Article 68 requires the ECOSOC to form functional commissions to support it in the realization of its multifaceted duties. The only commission of this kind actually specified by name is that for the promotion of human rights. In immediate fulfilment of this provision, ECOSOC formed the Human Rights Commission of the UN in 1946. Originally occupied with the development of a normative foundation in the form of the International Bill of Human Rights, the commission has evolved since the 1960s, and in particular in the 1990s, into an effective organ for overseeing the protection of human rights worldwide. It is supported in this work by the Commission on the Promotion and Protection of Human Rights, which was created in 1947 by ECOSOC as the Sub-Commission on Prevention of Discrimination and Protection of Minorities, and renamed in 1999. A second sub-commission for the protection of the freedom of information began its work in 1952. In 1946, the ECOSOC also created what started out as a sub-commission, but what then became the independent Commission on the Status of Women. The newest functional commission of the ECOSOC to concern itself with human rights is the 1995 Commission on Crime Prevention and Criminal Justice.

The Charter does not stop at the programmatic framework, however – the fulfilment of this depends in large part on the member states' readiness to take substantial steps to implement protection of human rights in their domestic realms. The General Assembly and the ECOSOC are also given competency for concrete action. According to Article 13, the General Assembly can instigate investigations and issue recommendations as a contribution to the realization of human rights and fundamental freedoms. Article 62 gives ECOSOC the right to issue recommendations regarding the observance and realization of human rights. These competencies, which are neither supported by an ability to sanction nor backed up by the authority to check the human rights situation of any particular country inside its sovereign territory against its will, seem modest at first glance. However, the decisive breakthrough is that this was the first time that an international organization had been given the right to involve itself in the human rights problems of its member states. Thus the United Nations was given a potential for action that both complements and goes beyond the treaty obligations of international law contained in the International Bill of Human Rights, which the organization was able to build upon slowly over the following decades (Boutros-Ghali, 1995a, p. 9).

This is true in particular of the gradual overcoming of Article 2(7)'s limitations on intervention. The codification of the sovereignty principle and of the resulting prohibition on involvement in states' domestic affairs helped the states to balance against the organization's claims to collective regulation, especially in the area of human rights. Furthermore, in this area the Charter placed only very weak legal requirements on the states. Article 56 requires the member states, in pursuit of the goals listed in Article 55, 'to take joint and separate action in cooperation with the organization'. This expression, however, amounts to little more than a stressing of the Article 2(2) duties of states to abide by the provisions of the Charter. Only the continued politics of obstruction in the case of discrimination was recognized specifically by the General Assembly as a violation of the duties in Article 56. In view of the weak legal obligations in the Charter, it is hardly surprising that repressive regimes could use Article 2(7) successfully as a means of defence against external criticism for decades (Weiss, 1996, p. 57), and that the operative work of the UN bodies dedicated to human rights remained relatively feeble.

As ideas of human rights grew more binding by degrees with the passing and ratification of the basic documents, the self-confidence of the General Assembly and the Human Rights Commission in dealing with human rights violations within states also grew. Their involvement has become the rule, and the burden of proof has shifted so that a state accused of serious human rights violations must now provide public proof of its progress (Baum, 1999, p. 247), instead of being able to evade its responsibilities by pointing to the prohibition on intervention. Not least, the Security Council's practice of intervention during the 1990s contributed significantly to the spreading of the belief that human rights and world peace stand in an indissoluble relationship to one another. Beginning with Resolution 688 of 5 April 1991, for the protection of the Kurds in northern Iraq, the Security Council repeatedly described large-scale human rights violations as threats to peace, against which it could intervene to the limits of its power of sanction. The character of human rights as a collective legal good transcending the state has thus been declared emphatically not only in the Charter, but also in the political practice of the United Nations.

Through a dynamic interpretation and an ever more decisive use of the rather modest tasks and authorities assigned by the Charter, the UN has succeeded in expanding its options for action in the realm of human rights to a significant degree over and against states. Correspondingly, the prohibition on intervention continues to be described in increasingly restrictive terms: human rights are no longer a part of those 'matters which are essentially within the domestic jurisdiction of any state' (Art. 2 (7); Riedel, 1999, p. 17). The United Nations has thus become not only a forum for, but also one of the central actors in, the international protection of human rights.

The International Bill of Human Rights

Although the attempt to insert a comprehensive catalogue of human rights in the UN Charter failed, the newly-founded world organization immediately began to work on the protection of human rights. During its first session in June 1946, the ECOSOC called into being the Human Rights Commission foreseen in Article 68, whose first, and for a long time *only*, task according to the will of the General Assembly was the creation of an International Bill of Human Rights. In the hopes of resolving the basic contradiction between state sovereignty and increasingly binding international human rights, the eighteen experts of the Commission – under the leadership of Eleanor Roosevelt, the widow of the US president, Franklin D. Roosevelt – determined in December 1947 on a multi-step process. First, the collection of those particular rights and freedoms that were to come under international protection should be accomplished in the form of a Declaration, in order to express a universal understanding of 'human rights'. The second step was to involve the placing of international legal duties upon the states through an international treaty. This was to contribute to the third step, which was to create the institutions and instruments that would be necessary for the implementation and protection of human rights. Partly on the basis of work that had already been done during the war, and partly supported by an international UNESCO symposium in which scientists of all disciplines participated the Human Rights Commission was able to produce a first draft of the Human Rights Statute within just one year. After intensive discussion in the Third Committee, responsible for such matters, as well as in the General Assembly plenary meeting in Paris, on 10 December 1948, the Universal Declaration of Human Rights was passed in the form of Resolution 217A (III). The Declaration was passed without opposition by forty-eight of the fifty-six members of the UN; the USSR and five allied socialist states, such as Saudi Arabia and South Africa, abstained.

The first two articles of the Declaration codify the principle of equality and the resulting prohibition on discrimination. Article 3 contains the first specific enumeration of the human rights to be protected: 'Everyone has the right to Life, Liberty, and Security of Person.' In the following articles, these fundamental rights are rounded out with a number of other civil and political rights. Included among these are the prohibitions on slavery and torture, the claim to be dealt with according to the rule of law and to a process of fair trial, the protection of privacy and property, the freedoms of conscience and assembly, and the right to form a family. Further rights to a nationality and to claim asylum – neither of which was a self-evident proposition in 1948 – were also included. Article 21 contains the right to political participation, which developed slowly over the following years into a human right to democracy. Article 22 constitutes the second main pillar of the Universal Declaration, in which it is stated that:

> [everyone], as a member of society, has the right to social security, and is enti-
> tled to realization, through national effort and international cooperation and in
> accordance with the organization and resources of each state, of the economic,
> social, and cultural rights indispensable for his dignity and the free develop-
> ment of his personality.

These basic claims, too, are explained more exhaustively in the following articles, where the rights to paid work worthy of human dignity, an adequate standard of living, education, and participation in cultural activities are all laid down. Article 28 promises all human beings the entitlement to live in a social and international order in which the rights enumerated in the declaration can be realized. One can already hear in this provision a premonition of the so-called 'third generation' of human rights. Article 29 in particular shows the influence of the Asian-Confucian culture by laying duties to society upon the individual, and making it possible to limit individual rights through laws that are in harmony with the purposes and principles of the UN. In Article 30, on the other hand, the extent to which human rights may be limited is itself constrained with the provision that they may not be abolished by any state, group or individual.

As a General Assembly resolution, the Declaration carries no legally binding effects for the member states, but it was precisely the fact that the document was not binding which made its approval possible. It was easier for states to profess their faith in the Declaration, because the method and measure of its implementation remained within the sole responsibility of the government, and the fulfillment of its claims was subject to no external control. The Declaration's real triumph was the success of the Human Rights Commission in putting together a universally acceptable inventory of human rights in the space of thirty articles.

The production of a legally binding treaty for the protection of human rights proved to be a long and difficult process. It was made even more difficult by the onset of the Cold War at the close of the 1940s, and the impossibility of consensus because of the ideological conflict of the two camps. It very soon became clear that there were differences in world-view not only in the material–legal realm, but also in the matter of mechanisms for implementation, which would make the passing of a uniform treaty completely impossible (Boutros-Ghali, 1995a, p. 43 et seq.). The Human Rights Commission had presented an 18-article draft for a Human Rights Pact in 1949, which took the suggestions of countless governments into consider-ation, but contained no provisions on economic, social or cultural rights. The inclusion of such rights had, however, been a particular requirement from the socialist states (Strohal, 2001). At the request of the ECOSOC, the General

Assembly thus decided in the following year, in Resolution 421 (v), section E, that the civil and political freedoms as well as the economic, social and cultural rights were interconnected and interdependent, and demanded the inclusion of appropriate regulations in the draft. The Commission then produced fourteen further suggested articles, as well as a further ten directives for the implementation and supervision of the legal duties in the signatory states.

However, legal problems arose very quickly. Negative civil rights on the one hand, and positive economic, social and cultural rights on the other cannot be implemented and monitored by the same mechanism. Under pressure from the Western states, the General Assembly thus revised its original position and asked the Human Rights Commission to make two separate pacts. In order to protect the unity of the International Bill of Human Rights, it required that both pacts contain as many common regulations as possible and be passed in a common acceptance process. The drafts finally produced by the Human Rights Commission were, however, not accepted by the General Assembly, but subjected instead to an article-by-article discussion in the Third Committee. This discussion, in which all the UN member states took part, covered a period of twelve years, in which it was above all the goal to win the states newly-emerged from decolonization over to the idea of the protection of human rights. This long period was necessary in order to form a consensus in a heterogeneous community of nearly 120 states. In the end, on 16 December 1966, these efforts produced the International Covenant on Civil and Political Rights, including an optional protocol for individual complaints, and the International Covenant on Economic, Social, and Cultural Rights, accepted unanimously through Resolution 2200 A (xxi). These are also sometimes known as the Civil Covenant (or ICCPR) and the Social Covenant (ICESCR), for short.

As is already clear from the names of the two covenants, they contain different sets of rights. In the ICCPR, the classical negative civil-liberal rights dominate, which build in general from the prohibition on discrimination and the equal rights of men and women. The individual guarantees can be grouped into four different categories according to the scope of their application and the extent to which they may be derogated:

- *Protection of the individual sphere*: here belong above all the rights to life, to freedom from slavery and servitude, to recognition as a legal person, to protection of the private sphere and of personal honour, to free profession of religions and world-views, to protection of the family, and to protection of children;
- *Protection of the social position of the individual*: in this group are the right to personal freedom and security, the liberty of movement and free choice of residence, to protection for aliens from arbitrary deportation, to the free practice of religion, and to freedom of expression. The freedom of expression is already specifically limited in the covenants so that war propaganda and the incitement to nationalist, racist or religious hate must be forbidden by law;
- *Protection of position in the polity*: this comprises all the political rights, such as the right to take part in governance and public affairs, the right to vote, and the right to equal access to public office. These general claims are complemented

through the right to freedom of assembly and the freedom to form political and labour parties and unions; and

- *Judicial rights*: the principle is emphasized that no one may be condemned for an activity that was not a crime at the time it took place, and the entitlement to a legal and fair trial, as well as a right to the enforcement of punishments in a humane manner. Some efforts were made to limit the use of the death penalty: it may be used only on the basis of a law and in cases of especially grave crimes. It may not be used against persons who had not reached eighteen years of age at the time of the crime. On 15 December 1989, the second optional protocol to the International Covenant on Civil and Political Rights for the Abolition of the Death Penalty was adopted. As of March 2004, it had been ratified by fifty states.

While the rights contained in the ICCPR can be transformed into state duties without further action, Article 2(1) of the ICESCR requires the state signatories 'to take steps, individually and through international assistance and co-operation, especially economic and technical, to the maximum of its available resources, with a view to achieving progressively the full realization of the rights recognized in the present Covenant by all appropriate means, including particularly the adoption of legislative measures.' For a long time, it was assumed on the basis of this formulation that states were obliged only to *promote* such rights, and that a large degree of freedom was allowed to them in this undertaking. This perspective, however, overlooks the fact that the ICESCR also includes a number of immediate positive rights, such as the protection of children, the right to unionize, and the right to equal pay for equal work. In spite of these utterly differentiated implementation obligations, the ICESCR's guarantees have been considered to be far looser than those of the ICCPR. This finds expression also in the fact that in the framework of the ICESCR, there is still no individual or group complaints process in place. The ICESCR protects three kinds of rights:

- *Economic rights*: above all the right to work, the right to just and reasonable working conditions, the right to form unions, and the right to social security;
- *Social rights*: including protection of the family and in particular protection of mothers and children. These regulations are enhanced by obligations placed on the state to create an appropriate standard of living for all people. Finally, the claim to a very high degree of physical and psychological health, implying concrete duties for the state; and
- *Cultural rights*: there is an entitlement to education, which obliges states to provide free elementary-level education. The right to take part in cultural life and in scientific progress is included, along with the right to scientific and artistic freedom.

As in the ICCPR, the general negative rights of the prohibition on discrimination and the obligation to the equal treatment of men and women are included in the ICESCR. Both covenants contain nearly identical Preambles, and the right to self-determination of peoples – as a concession to the states newly-emerged from decolonization – is also included in both.

Aside from the different groups of rights contained in each, the Covenants also differ in two further essential points, namely the extent to which the rights may be limited, and the process for their implementation. With respect to the limitation of rights, the ICESCR contains an all-encompassing general clause according to which the rights may be limited only on the basis of a law, and even then only for the purpose of promoting 'the general good in a democratic society'. The ICCPR, in contrast, contains in nearly every article individual regulations referring to the way in which, and the degree to which, each right may be restricted. States are, however, also allowed the option of suspending rights in a state of emergency. Any state making use of this provision must inform the other parties to the treaty, but it need not provide an account of its reasons for doing so, or the specific measures it has taken or intends to take. This particular limitation clause is among the most enduring weaknesses of the ICCPR. With respect to the implementation of rights, the ICESCR contains only the provision for a periodical reporting process in which the states must give an account of the status of the fulfilment of their duties to the Committee for Economic, Social, and Cultural Rights. In the ICCPR, there is a three-step process which, along with the obligatory periodical state reports also encompasses the optional state or individual complaints processes.

Both covenants came into force only after a ten-year adoption phase, on 3 January 1976 (ICESCR) and 23 March 1976 (ICCPR with first optional protocol), respectively, once thirty-five states had deposited instruments of ratification for each covenant with the Secretary-General. As of March 2004, 148 states had entered the ICESCR and 151 the ICCPR. The optional protocol to the ICCPR on the individual complaints process has been ratified by 104 states. However, it is the example of these two covenants that shows that the decades-long discussion regarding precisely which human rights are to be protected has still come to no definite conclusion. Many states, predominantly those in Asia, prefer a phased model, in which social standards must first be secured before civil rights can be considered (Thomsen, 1998, p. 25). Other states have ratified the covenants only with restrictions, such as, for example, the People's Republic of China, which ratified the ICESCR on 27 March 2001 with a reservation relating to the right to form unions. The USA has ratified the ICCPR, but not the ICESCR, which it signed in 1977.

In spite of the long period of its development and the remaining deficits in its implementation, the International Bill of Human Rights still constitutes a breakthrough in worldwide efforts for an effective protection of individuals against the arbitrary will of the state or of society. On the basis of this document, human rights have established themselves increasingly in the global public consciousness as a collective good, the protection of which falls on the same level of importance as the maintenance of global peace. The 'relativization from below of state sovereignty' (Kälin, 1998, p. 12) that has accompanied the internationalization of human rights, opens up manifold opportunities for states, international regimes and the organizations of the global community to involve themselves in human

TABLE 5.1
Selected human rights agreements of the UN

Instruments	States-party*	Signed but not ratified
International Convention on the Elimination of All Forms of Racial Discrimination	169	7
International Covenant on Civil and Political Rights	151	7
1 Optional Protocol to the ICCPR on Individual Complaints	104	5
2 Optional Protocol to the ICCPR on the Abolition of the Death Penalty	50	7
International Covenant on Economic, Social and Cultural Rights	148	6
International Convention on the Elimination of All Forms of Discrimination Against Women	174	1
Optional Protocol to the Convention on the Elimination of Discrimination against Women	53	32
Convention Against Torture and Other Cruel, Inhuman or Degrading Treatment or Punishment	133	12
Convention on the Rights of the Child	192	2
Optional Protocol to the Convention on the Rights of the Child on the involvement of children in armed conflict	57	61
Optional Protocol to the Convention on the Rights of the Child on the sale of children, child prostitution and child pornography	64	60
International Convention on the Protection of the Rights of All Migrant Workers and Members of Their Families	23	10

Source: Data from Office of the UN High Commissioner for Human Rights (March 2004)., * States which became members of the treaties by ratification or accession; current status of ratifications available under: www.unhchr.ch

rights situations in various countries, without those countries being able to appeal to a prohibition on intervention in their domestic affairs. A number of other international special protection agreements beyond the two covenants have arisen from the Universal Declaration of Human Rights, and with these, a comprehensive codification of the human rights deserving of protection has been achieved; see Table 5.1.

Comprehensive Protection of Human Rights

The early value placed on the development of a comprehensive protection for human rights is shown by the varied nature of the activities of the Human Rights Commission and its Sub-Commission on the Promotion and Protection of Human Rights, the Commission on the Legal Status of Women (also founded in 1946/7), the ECOSOC, and the General Assembly itself. In the foreground stood efforts to provide adequate help to groups of people who had been the victims of particularly frequent and/or serious human rights violations. By 1952, the General Assembly had passed the Convention on the Political Rights of Women, which had been drafted by the Commission on the Legal Status of Women. It was followed by numerous other resolutions and conventions, eventually leading to the legally binding Convention on the Elimination of All Forms of Discrimination Against Women (CEDAW) could be passed in 1979. The General Assembly and ECOSOC then turned to the problem of trafficking in human beings and the exploitation of prostitutes; became active in the protection of the rights of refugees and stateless persons; and demanded humane minimum conditions for prisoners and the execution of criminal punishments (for an overview, see Boutros-Ghali, 1995a, ch. III).

In total, the UN's activities have produced a dense web of standards and norms, which appears on the one hand so confusing as to be almost opaque, but has on the other contributed significantly to making human rights standards into one important measure of the legitimacy of state actions (Tomuschat, 2000, p. 435). Here only those international treaties will be discused that are both legally binding and include mechanisms for implementation.

Elimination of Racial Discrimination

The raw memory of the Holocaust, the continuing racial discrimination in South Africa's apartheid system, and above all the newly-independent former colonies, ensured that the International Convention on the Elimination of All Forms of Racial Discrimination (CERD) was given the highest priority. Its drafting was made even more urgent by the fact that no conclusion to the adoption process for the Human Rights Covenants, which both also prohibited racial discrimination, seemed to be in sight. Essentially drafted by the General Assembly in consultation with state offices and independent experts, the Convention was adopted on 21 December 1965, and came into force on 4 January 1969 following the deposition of the required twenty-seven instruments of ratification. As of March 2004, 169 states had joined this, the first of all the UN legal instruments to include an international supervision mechanism and provisions for individual complaints processes. Racial discrimination is understood broadly to mean every differentiation, exclusion, limitation or privileging based on race, skin-colour, descent or national origin that has as its purpose or effect the prevention or restriction of an equal recognition, enjoyment or exercise of human rights and basic freedoms in economic, social, cultural or any other area of public life. A specification of the concept of 'race' has still not been presented, for very good reasons: such a specification might restrict the spectrum of marking characteristics which may not be used to justify unequal treatment to those that are merely biological or external.

The Committee for the Elimination of Racial Discrimination, formed on the basis of Article 8 of the Convention, starts from the assumption that membership in a particular group follows from the individual feeling of belonging to that group. The Convention requires its signatory states to pursue an active policy for the elimination of racial discrimination through the abandonment of discriminatory activities on the part of the state, the legislative prohibition of discriminatory activities on the part of non-state actors, and the promotion of organizations and programmes with integrative functions. As the high number of ratifications shows, the Convention has been accepted by the overwhelming majority of the global community, and is firmly anchored in state civil and criminal law. At the same time, even in the states-party (states which became members of a treaty by ratification or accession), racial discrimination has by no means been fully eliminated. In everyday life and speech, a number of deep-rooted stereotypes and prejudices come – consciously or not – with the constructed concept of 'race', and are constantly reinforced. It thus requires particularly vigorous efforts to introduce a change in consciousness on the many social levels that cannot be regulated by legal directive. The United Nations therefore tried, with the World Conference Against Racism (August 2001 in Durban, South Africa), to give a further impulse in this direction, and to keep the problem of racism firmly on the agenda of the state community and the global civil society.

Protection of Women's Rights

With the anchoring of the equal rights of men and women in the Preamble as well as Article 1(3) of the UN Charter, a meaningful step was taken. For the first time, the principle of equal rights was included in a binding international legal document, and this at a time when such a belief was hardly to be taken for granted even in the Western democracies. That being said, the belief that the discussion of women's rights was a legitimate part of the discussion of human rights in general remained contested even in the UN right through the 1980s. It has only been since the 1990s that the relevant UN documents routinely indicate the human rights dimension of violations of women's rights, particularly in the case of violence against women (Gottstein, 1998, p. 82). Deriving from the Charter's provisions, the Commission on the Legal Status of Women has developed many activities which eventually led to various conventions, declarations, and resolutions of the General Assembly. The efforts of the Commission were aimed at the achievement of equal rights with respect to marriage, citizenship, equal position in education and employment, and political rights. A further area of activity was the creation of specific negative rights for women, for example in their role as mothers, or with respect to the fight against trafficking in women and girls, or to the exploitation of prostitutes (see for many examples and further sources, H. Wolfrum, 1995).

Along with the progressive development of standard-setting, numerous measures were taken by the UN for the mobilization of the global public consciousness in the recognition of the human rights of women. In the 'International Year of the Woman', announced by the UN in 1975, the first World Conference on Women took place in Mexico City and passed a World Action Plan for the equalizing of the position of women. At the instigation of this conference, the International Research and Training Institute for the Advancement of Women (INSTRAW) was founded as an autonomous research institute of the UN. The 'Decade of the Woman' began in 1976, and in 1980, another World Conference on Women took place in Copenhagen. As a result of the conference held in Nairobi in

1985 at the conclusion of the 'Decade of the Woman', the UN Development Fund for Women (UNIFEM) was founded and integrated into the UN's existing development programme.

The most important result of the 'Decade of the Woman' – at least in the legal codification process – was the Convention on the Elimination of All Forms of Discrimination Against Women (CEDAW), which came into force in 1981. Arising from proposals at the World Conference in Mexico City, this convention brought together all the provisions that had until then been regulated in separate instruments, including the prohibition on discrimination, the requirement of equal treatment, and the requirement for special protection. In the meantime, the convention has been ratified by 174 states, and has been confirmed in its significance as the central human rights instrument for women at both the Vienna Human Rights Conference of 1993 and the 1995 Fourth World Conference on Women in Beijing. As a strategy for the further development of the protection of women's rights and the gradual realization of equal treatment, it was suggested in the Beijing Declaration and Platform for Action – the conference's concluding document – that should there be a systematic integration of the gender perspective into all areas of life, called 'gender mainstreaming' in UN jargon. This means that all state and social measures and actions worldwide should be examined with respect to their gender-specific effects.

In view of the fact that there is hardly any field of international protection of human rights that is affected as strongly by culture-related objections as the rights of women, this is a rather complex project, creating problems even for highly-developed societies. In fact, at the 23rd special session of the General Assembly ('Beijing+5'), called together in June 2000 to examine what progress had been made on the Beijing Platform for Action, it found rather sobering results. Alongside only moderate successes were to be found renewed attempts to weaken the norms and standards developed in Beijing. Further efforts on behalf of women's rights – possibly a fifth world conference – will clearly be necessary. The long-term success of the Action Platform and its strategies will require not only state will, but also a fundamental rethinking of the traditional understanding of the role of gender in nearly all societies. The example of the gradual progressive development of the idea of human rights, however, shows that such ambitious projects are, at least theoretically, realizable.

The Convention Against Torture

Some of the most obvious violations of human worth and human rights are torture, acts of cruelty and humiliating treatment or punishments. The abolition of such practices, which are unfortunately still widely used in many states, is the goal of the Convention Against Torture and Other Cruel, Inhuman or Degrading Treatment or Punishment (CAT), which came into force in June of 1987. By March 2004, 133 states had ratified the convention. Article 1 defines torture as:

> any act by which severe pain or suffering, whether physical or mental, is intentionally inflicted on a person for such purposes as obtaining from him or a third

person information or a confession, punishing him for an act he or a third person has committed or is suspected of having committed, or intimidating or coercing him or a third person, or for any reason based on discrimination of any kind, when such pain or suffering is inflicted by or at the instigation of or with the consent or acquiescence of a public official or other person acting in an official capacity.

In the detailed provisions of its first section, the convention obliges all states-party to take effective legal measures for the elimination of torture, and excludes all 'extraordinary circumstances' such as war, internal instability, or the declaration of a state of emergency, as grounds for derogation. All instances of torture constitute crimes, which must be threatened with appropriate punishments. The criminal prosecution of suspected persons can be undertaken by any state in whose sovereign territory a suspect happens to be located. As with the other instruments mentioned thus far, a special committee was set up for the CAT, which enjoys extensive authority to investigate cases.

The Convention on the Rights of the Child

The protection of the rights of children as particularly weak and endangered persons is also among the central goals the UN has pursued since its founding. In fact, in this case the UN was able to build on the work of the League of Nations, particularly its 1924 Declaration of the Rights of the Child. With the establishment of the UN's Children's Fund (UNICEF) in December 1946, one of the most effective subsidiary organs of the UN was created, and the rights of children are expressly emphasized in both the Universal Declaration of Human Rights and the two Human Rights Covenants. As the first document of the UN to concern itself exclusively with the rights of children, the Declaration of the Rights of the Child was passed by the General Assembly on 20 November 1959, thus initiating a development that led to various activities for the mobilization of worldwide interest in the matter, and finally culminating in the Convention on the Rights of the Child. This convention, adopted by the General Assembly on 20 November 1989, quickly became one of the most-ratified international agreements. On the first day the convention was open for signature, 26 January, 1990, sixty-one governments were lined up to sign (Boutros-Ghali, 1995, p. 81). At the time of writing, 192 states have ratified the convention, but not the USA and Somalia.

Any person who has not yet reached the end of his or her eighteenth year of life is counted as a child, unless national law makes the age of majority younger than that. The signatory states have obliged themselves to guarantee or to protect through legislative precautions the rights laid down in the convention for all children within their sovereign territory. In total, the convention contains fifty-four individual provisions, in which the classical negative civil rights, but also the economic, social and cultural participation rights of the child are to be found. The states-party have agreed to take all legislative, administrative and other measures including international co-operation in order to realize these rights. The states must also submit regular reports to the Committee on the Rights of the Child to enable that body to exercise supervisory control over their progress.

There are, however, no other processes for review, making the convention a rather weak international instrument in reality. Once again, though, it cannot be overlooked that it was the very lack of hard enforcement mechanisms that made it easier for states to accept the norms laid down in the convention. It was in this way that worldwide standards could at least be introduced, then later successively expanded and realized. After six years of preparation, on 25 May 2000, the General Assembly passed two additional protocols to the Convention on the Rights of the Child, which were to improve the protection against trafficking in and sexual abuse of children, and the protection of children involved in armed conflicts, respectively. Both protocols were signed by a large number of states during their first appearance on the occasion of the UN Millennium Summit on 5 September 2000, and came into effect after a relatively short ratification process in January and February, respectively, of 2002. The additional protocols currently have fifty-seven and sixty-four states-party, respectively.

In spite of all these efforts and real progress being made, children remain the victims of grave human rights violations, particularly in the realms of sexual exploitation and child labour (Schellinski, 1998, p. 142 et seq.), as well as in military conflicts, where hundreds of thousands of them are abused and forced to become child soldiers (Kreuzer, 2001, p. 308). The UN Conferences from the 1990 World Summit for Children (New York) through the 1996 World Congress against Sexual Exploitation of Children (Stockholm, with a follow-up conference in Yokohama 2001) to the 2000 International Conference on War-Affected Children (Winnipeg) have made clear just how massive the dimensions of the problem are.

The Convention on the Protection of the Rights of Migrant Workers

Nearly thirteen years after its adoption by the General Assembly, the International Convention on the Protection of the Rights of all Migrant Workers and Members of their Families (MWC) finally came into force on 1 July 2003. The convention aims at easing the living conditions of one the most underprivileged and vulnerable groups in global economics. According to the Office of the High Commissioner for Human Rights, more than 150 million migrants worldwide live outside their home countries, often becoming victims of illicit recruitment and trafficking, exploitation and unbearable working conditions.

The MWC is an attempt to put the status and treatment of migrant workers on a stable legal basis. It applies during the entire migration process from departure to the return home (Art. 1(2)), and provides a category system for the different types of migrant worker. In Part III (Arts 8–35), the Convention unfolds an elaborate set of human rights for the workers and their family members without differentiating between documented (legal) and undocumented (illegal) workers. Additional rights for migrants with a regular status are anchored in Part IV (Arts 36–56), while Part VI obliges states-party to promote sound, equitable, humane and lawful conditions for workers and their families. Thus the convention imposes international standards binding on both host states and the states of origin. The application of the MWC is monitored by a Committee created in Part VII, consisting of ten independent experts to be elected by secret ballot by the states-parties. After the convention's coming into force for the 41st state-party, the number of Committee members will have risen to fourteen.

As of March 2004, a total of twenty-one states had acceded to the convention, but that number does not include any industrially developed countries. Without the support of the receiving countries, which usually gain considerable advantage from the migrant workers, the Convention will remain the weakest of the seven major human rights treaties.

The Interdependence of Human Rights

The concept of 'third generation human rights' refers to international solidarity rights and collective positive rights such as the right to peace, to a healthy environment, and to development, which are all far more abstract and in many ways more vague than the individual liberty rights of the ICCPR or the participation rights of the ICESCR. Although the terminology of 'third generation human rights' first began to appear in the late 1970s and 1980s, the underlying ideas are certainly much older (Esquive, 1989). Political efforts relating to these third generation rights have their roots in the process of decolonization which took place in the 1950s and 1960s, in the course of which the number of developing countries increased dramatically. Commensurate with their growing weight in the General Assembly, the new states used the forum of the UN to lay their demands for substantial support in overcoming their social and economic challenges on the doorsteps of the industrialized countries.

The December 1960 Declaration on the Granting of Independence to Colonial Countries and Peoples was aimed at establishing international standards of justice, in which the peoples' right to self-determination and to participation in economic and social development were brought into line with the UN's efforts for world peace and international security. Nine years later, the General Assembly reinforced this approach in the Declaration on Social Progress and Development (General Assembly resolution 2542 (XXIV) of 11 December 1969). This provided a catalogue of the means and methods for the formation of a development process aimed at global justice, along with a formulation of principles and purposes. The so-called 'third generation human rights' were first addressed under that name by the then-leader of the UNESCO Human Rights Division, Karel Vasak (1974) during the lively human rights and development discussion of the 1970s. It took a debate lasting nearly ten years, in which the North–South problem was overshadowed for a long time by the ideological battles of the East–West conflict, until the General Assembly was able on 4 December 1986 to pass its Declaration on the Right to Development (General Assembly resolution 41/128, 4 December 1986). In this declaration, the right to development is considered to be an inalienable human right, on the strength of which all people, and peoples, have a claim to participate in, to contribute to, and to draw use from a process of economic, social, cultural and political development in which all human rights and basic freedoms can be fully realized. In view of the polarized debate over the existence of a human right to development, the results of the vote were surprisingly unanimous: 143 votes supporting the decision and eight abstentions against one non-supporting vote (the USA).

The rights of the third generation achieved their breakthrough at the Vienna Human Rights Conference in Summer 1993. In the Vienna Declaration and Programme of Action, the conference's unanimously adopted concluding document (on 25 June 1993 by the 171 participating states), the states-party professed their belief in the universality, indivisibility and interdependence of human rights, and underlined their significance for world peace. Democracy, development and the observation of human rights were seen as mutually-strengthening goals. The right to development was given a broad interpretation, strengthened even more on the basis of the 1986 Declaration, and given precise content. A healthy environment, a general right to participate in the fruits of scientific progress – especially in medical and information technology, forgiveness of developing countries' debts, and the fight against extreme poverty were all named as goals or prerequisites for the international protection of human rights.

Although the end of the Cold War freed the discussion over third generation rights from ideological content, the results of the Vienna conference have still been the subject of serious criticism from several sides. Franz Nuscheler (1996, p. 11) asks, for example, what 'development' in fact means. He fears that the vagueness of its description will be inflated into a 'right to everything', and criticizes the 'lazy compromise' through which the Western states essentially brought the agreement of the developing countries to the universality of civil and political rights with tactical concessions regarding the right to development. There are also technical legal objections; for example, that the rights of the third generation are so extremely imprecise that they lose their legal character, because it is totally unclear to whom these rights in fact accrue, and from whom their fulfilment may be demanded. The question is also put forward of whether states, which have a duty to guarantee certain rights to their citizens, can at the same time enjoy the right to make claims of their own. This criticism overlooks, however, the fact that state-structural principles such as the welfare state or the rule-of-law state are clothed in abstract formulations and made concrete only through specific guarantees (Riedel, 1999, p. 28). In this process of concretization, the right to development functions as a representative for all rights of the third generation, even though the progress made on that particular right has remained sharply limited. Still, with their Millennium Declaration in September 2000, the heads of state and government have obliged themselves to take concrete steps in the fight against poverty and illness as well as in the promotion of education, thus once again underscoring the interdependence of the three generations of human rights. Although it is still not possible to bring suits for damages arising from these rights, as soft law they have the effect of creating standards for the further construction and implementation of the international protection of human rights.

An overview of the most important activities and instruments the UN has undertaken or produced in the course of its efforts for a comprehensive protection of human rights shows that the phase of standard-setting and codification is nearing its close. There is hardly any area of human rights for which international norms have not been developed and accepted by the overwhelming majority of states. What is just as important, however, is that in nearly all areas, the actual realization of human rights protection lags far behind the almost universal profession and recognition of these rights. Aside from the difficulties already mentioned regarding universal acceptance of a codex of human rights, and the resistance of many states and societies, on many grounds, towards following such norms, in many parts of the world the simple lack of opportunities for the ensuring of such rights – especially participatory rights – is also responsible for this state of affairs.

Further Reading

Alston, Philip (ed.) (2004) *The United Nations and Human Rights: A Critical Appraisal*, Oxford: Oxford University Press.

Amnesty International; *Annual Reports*.

Chesterton, Simon (2001) *Just War or Just Peace. Humanitarian Intervention and International Law*, Oxford: Oxford University Press.

Fields, A. Belden (2003) *Rethinking Human Rights for the New Millennium*, Basingstoke: Palgrave.

Risse, Thomas, Stephen C. Ropp and Kathrin Sikkink (1999) *The Power of Human Rights*, New York: Cambridge University Press.

Steiner, Henry J. and Philip Alston (2000) *International Human Rights in Context*, 2nd edition, Oxford: Oxford University Press.

Tomuschat, Christian (2003) *Human Rights. Between Idealism and Realism*. Oxford: Oxford University Press.

6

Human Rights Protection: Institutional Framework and Code of Practice

Effective protection of human rights cannot be limited to the codification of norms and the ethical appeal to their observation. It needs reliable mechanisms for integrating human rights standards into national legal systems, for supervising their observation, and for enforcing it, where necessary. The basic problem intrinsic to the protection of human rights – the relationship between the claims of international organizations to collective regulation and the sovereignty principle – has already been discussed. The states' fear of impermissible interference in their domestic affairs allowed them to remain for years in the belief that inspections and implementation mechanisms in the realm of human rights had to be based on a treaty. The competencies of the UN human rights committees were consequently essentially limited to normative work, and could be expanded only gradually, beginning in the 1960s. Here we shall first examine the three most important treaty instruments of supervision and implementation of the agreed-upon standards, in order to explore their application and the extension of the practice of their various organs and committees.

The basic controversy over inspections of human rights standards within states was first addressed through an agreement on the process of state reports. Through this modality most protective of sovereignty (Tomuschat, 1995c), the states-party obliged themselves to report regularly on the status of the implementation and observation of the agreed-upon norms in their sovereign territory to one of the committees formed by the provisions of the treaty. The state reporting process was developed during the negotiations on the Civil and Social Covenants, but given an effect as an obligatory instrument for the first time with the Convention Against Racial Discrimination, which was in fact passed earlier than the two covenants. All six of the pacts that followed the CERD subjected their signatories automatically to the duty to report. This control procedure through the responsible committee is not regulated expressly in any of the treaties. In practice, however, the procedural regulations of the various committees have all come to contain provisions that the reporting states may be represented by their own deputies in any investigations processes, and may give additional information or statements. The process is concluded with 'general remarks', and each committee handles the writing of its own reports and recommendations differently. Respecting the suitability of the state reporting process for the effective protection of human rights, it may be objected that it leaves it up to the states how openly and honestly they choose to report. It must also be kept in mind, however, that because of the public treatment of the reports and the opportunity to collect other information – for example, through NGOs (Otto, 1996; Liese, 1998) – that any state even remotely concerned with its international reputation will have an interest in handling its reporting duties seriously.

In contrast to the duty to report, the process for state complaints is obligatory only in the CERD. In the ICCPR and the Anti-Torture Convention, the possibility for state complaint is tied to a voluntary subjection clause, and it is not present at all in the other human rights conventions. The state complaint process is one in which one state may accuse another of neglecting or violating the obligations arising from the charter. The complaining state should not – at least according to the intention of the process – have primarily its own interests in mind, but should be functioning as a watchdog for the observance of an objective order (Partsch, 1995). For the confidential handling of this complaint process, the Civil Covenant and the Anti-Torture Convention each have a committee and the CERD an arbitration commission. This state complaints process has to date never been used in the area of human rights. The instrument has, however, found its way into various regional human rights agreements, such as the European Convention on Human Rights or the most important African human rights document: the African [Banjul] Charter on Human and Peoples' Rights, of 27 June 1981.

The efforts to protect human rights by making individuals the subjects of international law find expression in the individual complaints process. Through a wish to avoid the term 'complaint', the UN has introduced the term 'communication' in its place. This process is intended to give every individual the opportunity to present him or herself before an international committee to inform it of violations of his/her personal rights and to seek help from it. Of the seven most important human rights treaties, there are now four that include the individual communication process, although it is not obligatory and is subject to the voluntary self-subjection of the states. In the cases of the Civil Covenant and the Women's Rights Convention, this self-subjection takes place by way of the ratification of an optional protocol; in the Anti-Torture Convention and the CERD, it takes place through a simple declaration of agreement.

In the UN Charter, the right to personal petitions is mentioned only in Article 87b. It allows the inhabitants of trustee territories to go before the Trusteeship Council, which can then investigate violations of their individual rights in co-operation with the responsible government. Since the independence of the majority of trustee territories in the mid-1960s, this already seldom-used process has played no role at all. With respect to the Human Rights Commission, the UN declined (through ECOSOC Resolution 75 (v) of 5 August 1947) to give itself the ability to look into individual communications. The state of de facto powerlessness of the UN in the sphere of monitoring and implementation of human rights standards lasted for more than twenty years, until the ECOSOC, under pressure from the Human Rights Commission, and revised its position in Resolutions 1235 (XLII) of 6 June 1967 and 1503 (XLVIII) of 27 May 1970. It finally allowed the Human Rights Commission to accept and investigate, under specific conditions, individual communications and public statements (in the resolutions: Chairman's Statements) on those communications (Tomuschat, 1995a).

Treaty-based Bodies

As has already been described, committees were set up under the provisions of the human rights treaties, which have the task of overseeing the application of the above-mentioned instruments for the implementation and maintenance of the agreed-upon norms. The procedures, decisions and reports of these committees are detailed exhaustively in the Treaty Body Database at the office of the UN High Commissioner for Human Rights in Geneva. In spite of their obvious commonalities, the committees also exhibit a number of differences in their practices, and each of them will be examined individually here.

The Human Rights Committee of the ICCPR

After the ICCPR came into force, the Human Rights Committee, under the International Covenant on Civil and Political Rights, was called into being in 1976. The committee consists of eighteen members elected by secret ballot from a list of suggestions submitted by the states-party in a special assembly called by the Secretary-General, and serve a four-year term. Each state-party may nominate two of its own nationals. The members of the committee are not there as representatives of their states, and are not bound to follow the instructions of their states. Because of the requirement to carry out their UN-related work conscientiously and impartially, it would be impossible for members of the committee to fulfil the duties of a political office or government position at the same time. As a rule, the committee meets three times a year in New York or Geneva, and is supported in its work by a secretariat located with the High Commissioner for Human Rights in Geneva. The overwhelming majority of the committee's work is concentrated on the examination of the reports submitted by the states-party. Every new signatory state must present a report within six months of the time the treaty came into effect for that state, detailing the measures it has undertaken for the realization of the rights contained in the treaty. After that, the state is subject to the committee's requests for further reports at five-year intervals. Furthermore, the committee may require additional reports at other times, should it become aware of possible human rights violations. In the process of examining the reports, the statements of NGOs are given a great deal of weight – on the one hand for the purposes of additional information, and on the other, to encourage greater openness and honesty in the reports themselves. Discussion of the reports is public and closes with the publication of the Concluding Observations, in which both the achieved progress and the outstanding deficiencies and points of criticism are stated frankly.

The examination of individual communications against a state is possible only if the state has ratified the first optional protocol to the ICCPR. This procedure makes it possible for individuals or groups of people to apply to the Human Rights Committee with their complaints, but only under very strict conditions. The right to complain ('communicate') accrues only to persons who have themselves experienced a violation of their human rights, and these persons must have exhausted the domestic processes available to them. Even then, a communication will be accepted only when the matter is not currently under consideration by any other international body such as, for example, the European Court of Human Rights. The examination of the communication takes place in confidence. The committee communicates its decision to the complainant and to the state involved through the so-called 'views', which do not have the character of binding judgements, even though they are modelled as such, and include recommendations for restitution along with a finding of the facts and legal appraisal. The Human Rights Committee publishes its 'views' as an annex to its yearly report to the General Assembly, thus contributing to the mobilization of public pressure on the states involved to observe the legal evaluation and recommendations of the committee. In comparison with regional human rights regimes such as, for example, the European Convention on Human Rights, and the binding judgments of the European Court of Human Rights, the competencies of the Human Rights Committee appear to be limited. They are, however, of decisive importance for the overwhelming majority of people, and peoples, who have no access to more effective regional regimes.

The Committee for Economic, Social and Cultural Rights

Unlike the ICCPR, the ICESCR did not contain provisions for the creation of a special treaty body for the supervision of its own implementation. Instead, the states were meant to submit their reports to the ECOSOC through the UN Secretary-General. Before 1985, ECOSOC reviewed the reports with the assistance of the Human Rights Commission and in co-ordination with other specialized agencies. It then decided to create a Committee on Economic, Social and Cultural Rights (CESCR) to deal with this task. Since the members of this committee come not from the states-party, but rather are elected from among the fifty-four member states of the ECOSOC regardless of their membership or non-membership in the ICESCR, the CESCR is in reality a charter-based subsidiary body. The committee meets twice a year, for three weeks at a time, and is supported by the Office of the High Commissioner for Human Rights. The CESCR's only control instruments are the state reports. After the initial report, which must be presented within a year of the treaty's coming into effect for the member, the reports are to be presented at five year intervals. The examination of the reports is carried out first by a pre-sessional working group comprising five experts, which drafts a number of questions relating to the report, taking into consideration additional information (from, for example, NGOs). The state submitting the report must respond to these questions within six months. Following an oral presentation by a government delegation, the committee then addresses the primary problems regarding the implementation of the covenant and discusses these with the delegation. After a non-public advisory phase, the committee presents its Concluding Observations. In further General Comments, the committee attempts a more concrete interpretation of the provisions of the treaty, which create standards for the application of the relevant norms, but are not legally binding (Riedel, 1998, p. 40).

Two circumstances make the CESCR a rather weak instrument of control: first, the participatory rights of the covenant are difficult to adjudicate upon, because their boundaries are defined by the capabilities of the state involved rather than any objective criterion. This problem is exacerbated by the fact that many states ratified the covenant with reservations, through which certain rights, such as, for example, the formation of unions, are removed from the authority of the control mechanism. Second, the committee's only weapon in its task as a monitoring instrument is the state reporting process – even if it does receive additional information from independent sources – and the usefulness of that process depends in large part on the states' willingness to co-operate. Furthermore, the labour-intensive procedure of examining these state reports is threatening to overwhelm the committee. An optional protocol to enable individual complaints has been under construction for some years, but there exist significant doubts as to whether the protection of the rights in the ICESCR could be improved meaningfully by such a procedure, because of the difficulty of litigating on them.

Committee on the Elimination of Racial Discrimination

On the basis of the Convention on the Elimination of All Forms of Racial Discrimination, eighteen independent experts were called together to form the Committee on the Elimination of Racial Discrimination (CERD), which began its work on 10 January 1970 as the first of the six important treaty bodies. As with most of the other treaty bodies, the members of the Committee are elected from among the states-party for a four year period of office. Again, the Office of the UN High Commissioner for Human Rights in Geneva is responsible for supporting the committee's work. For the exercise of its monitoring functions, it enjoys the use of the state reports, as well as procedures for both state and individual complaints. Although this is the only treaty in which the state complaint procedure is in fact obligatory, no use has ever been made of it. As at the time of writing, only about a quarter of the 169 states-party have made a declaration submitting themselves to the individual complaints procedure. The confidential treatment of the individual communications leads to a non-legally-binding statement, delivered to both the complainant and the state involved.

The reporting system requires parties to submit comprehensive reports every four years, as well as additional reports on any particularly important developments. A member of the committee is named as the *rapporteur* for each report; the *rapporteur* must present his/her evaluation of the status of the Convention's goals in the state involved, and may make use of the aid of independent experts and organizations. During the public discussion of the reports, the respective governments may also present their perspectives. The committee's Concluding Observations, including mention of both progress and deficiencies, is forwarded to the General Assembly's Third Committee for further advice. One of the newer developments of the CERD is that it now attempts public proceedings against states that fail to submit their reports, or whose reports evince a drastic need for action.

Committee on the Elimination of Discrimination Against Women

The Committee on the Elimination of Discrimination Against Women (CEDAW), created in 1981, consists of twenty-three independent experts elected by the states-party. The centre of the CEDAW's work lies, unlike the other treaty bodies, not in Geneva at the UNHCHR headquarters, but in New York. The primary instrument of the Committee's work is once again the state reports, which are examined in a process similar to the ones described above for the other bodies. The Committee's yearly reports go through ECOSOC to the General Assembly's Third Committee, or through the Secretary-General to the Commission on the Status of Women. Since 22 December 2000, the long-overdue optional protocol for the enabling of an individual communications procedure has been in effect, but it has been ratified at the time of writing by only fifty-one of the 173 states-party, and thus plays only a secondary role in the work of the Committee.

On the basis of the reports made and subsequent recommendations, a number of substantial improvements have been undertaken in a number of countries regarding the legal protection of women. Measures for the temporary preferential treatment of women, as foreseen by the Convention, have also been strengthened in several countries. This being said, the CEDAW is hemmed in to a far greater extent than any of the other treaty bodies by the many reservations that the states made at the time of ratification. Even in states that have no official regulations debarring women from certain rights, many of the CEDAW's recommendations are not implemented, on the grounds of cultural peculiarities or customary law. Article 20 of the Convention throws a revealing light on the states' lack of will to create an effective monitoring and implementation organ for women's rights: it states that the committee 'shall normally meet for a period of not more than two weeks annually' in New York for the purposes of reviewing the state reports. Every conceivable extension of the committee's competencies is *ex ante* drastically limited by this regulation.

Committee Against Torture

Like the other monitoring bodies, the Committee Against Torture (CAT) is based on treaty provisions (Article 17 of the Convention Against Torture), and consists of ten experts chosen *ad personam* by the states-party. Next to the obligatory state reporting procedure, the CAT enjoys both the state complaints and individual communication procedures, although the former is, in practice, completely meaningless. Both

procedures can occur only upon appropriate declarations on the part of the signatory states. The CAT is similar to the other committees described above in its
modus operandi and procedural rules. However, the grounds on which the CAT
may become active go somewhat beyond those found in the other treaty bodies.
For example, the CAT may examine 'reliable information' that indicates the existence of systematic torture in a state-party.

This clause enables NGOs to apply directly to the CAT with information and to
instigate its investigation. There is also a Working Group on the Optional Protocol
to the Convention Against Torture, which is drafting an optional protocol meant to
enable sub-commissions to make investigative visits to correctional facilities or
other facilities of signatory states in which people may be held under arrest. The
competencies foreseen in the draft protocol for the sub-commission are broadly
constructed. It would thus constitute a great improvement in the protection against
torture if a large number of states were to ratify such a protocol. Experience with
other such voluntary mechanisms of submission to specific procedures, however,
leads one to expect that the ratifications will be given primarily by those countries
in which, in any case, torture plays no role. Those states that might potentially be
implicated are likely to be rather more reluctant to enter into such self-imposed
obligations.

Committee on the Rights of the Child

The ten experts who form the Committee on the Rights of the Child (CRC) monitor the gradual realization of this most widely-accepted of the human rights
treaties. Commensurate with the co-operative holistic approach of the Convention
on the Rights of the Child, the CRC works together with the other human rights
committees from its seat in Geneva, but above all with UNICEF. As a treaty body,
however, the only monitoring tool the CRC has at its disposal is the state reporting
process. The two optional protocols, passed on 25 May 2000 and coming into force
at the beginning of 2002, on the rights of children involved in armed conflicts and
protection against child-trafficking and prostitution, both contain their own
requirements for state reports to the CRC. The committee may also require additional reports, should it think this necessary, and thus it has what approaches a right
to investigation. Unlike the Convention itself, the far more concrete optional
protocols have been ratified by only about a quarter of the signatory states. The
protection of children's rights thus remains very under-developed.

Committee on the Protection of the Rights of All Migrant Workers

After the coming into force of the Migrant Workers Convention (MWC) on 1 July
2003, the committee monitoring its application had to be established within six
months. Ten independent experts were elected by the assembly of the states-party,
to be increased to fourteen when the 41st state accesses the MWC (Art. 72). The
committee meets annually at the UN Headquarters in New York (Art. 75). The
states-party are obliged to submit reports to the UN Secretary-General on the

legislative, judicial, administrative and other measures they have taken to put into effect the provisions of the Convention. The Secretary-General then forwards the reports to the committee for consideration. The initial report must be submitted within one year of the Convention coming into force for the state-party concerned. The follow-up reports are to be presented every five years or upon the committee's request (Art. 73). The states-party can make a specific declaration accepting the competence of the committee to receive and consider communications from states-party claiming that another state party is in violation of its obligations under the MWC (Art. 76). Article 77 also provides for the voluntary acceptance of individual communications to the committee. As of March 2004, the committee has been established, but has not yet had time to consider any of the state reports.

Summary

Unlike the Declarations and Resolutions of the General Assembly, the human rights treaties constitute binding international law. However, the rather weak monitoring mechanisms in these instruments show that the implementation and monitoring of human rights standards are in serious need of further development. A few procedures, such as the bodies preparing state reports or field missions to various states, have become accepted practice, while other efforts, such as the attempt to have local investigations or to grant a right of initiative to the treaty bodies, are still stuck in their embryonic phases. In the future, these efforts should be concentrated primarily on a stronger integration of the protection of human rights into regional arrangements and national law. At the global level, the bundling and harmonization of the various instruments is on the agenda, in the hope that this will accelerate the examination process. In view of the now-comprehensive inventory of human rights norms, it seems that the emphasis of future efforts should be placed on the improvement of the monitoring mechanisms rather than on the suggestion of ever more refined rules with very questionable prospects of realization (Riedel, 1998, p. 54).

Human Rights Protection by UN Organs

The decisive advantage of human rights treaties – their legally binding effect – naturally applies only to those states that have submitted themselves to the respective regimes. In order to close the gap between the universal claims of basic human rights standards and the rather more limited membership in the treaty systems, and to augment the none-too-effective implementation mechanisms of the treaties, the UN has gradually expanded its own monitoring competencies with respect to the member states. This required no emendations to treaties or drawn-out ratification processes. The UN was able to work through simple General Assembly and ECOSOC Resolutions, in which more extensive interpretations of Charter provisions were given. It is a result of this ability to re-interpret the jurisdictional scope that the Charter-based protective mechanisms are considered 'political' processes of human rights protection, as opposed to the 'juristic' processes of the international law treaties (Alston, 1994, pp. 1–21). The political character of the protection of human rights through organs of the UN is underscored by the fact that their work is carried out by representatives of the various state governments, who are bound to follow their governments' instructions, as opposed to independent experts, as in the treaty bodies. The UN committees are thus rather more flexible than the treaty bodies, but also more susceptible to the temptation to orientate their work along considerations of political opportunity, and thus to the problem of double standards.

Aside from the main bodies, to which the Charter gives an original jurisdiction over questions of human rights, it is mainly subsidiary bodies that are concerned with the protection of human rights. First among these is the Human Rights Commission, which functions as a commission of ECOSOC, but also works closely with the General Assembly's Third Committee on the drafting of Declarations and Resolutions. The High Commissioner for Human Rights (UNHCHR), attached to the Secretariat, plays a somewhat different role. The UN Human Rights Centre in Geneva belongs to the office of the High Commissioner. Although this office was created by a political decision, specifically a General Assembly Resolution, the High Commissioner him/herself, along with his/her colleagues, are members of the International Civil Service of the United Nations, and thus not bound by any instructions from a member state. The High Commissioner acts on behalf of the Secretary-General, and in the name of the UN.

The Human Rights Commission

The UN Human Rights Commission (HRC), founded in 1946, consists in the early twenty-first century of fifty-three members, chosen by ECOSOC on the basis of the principle of balanced geographical representation and serving a three-year term of office. Africa occupies fifteen seats; the Asian-Pacific group of states has twelve; Latin America, eleven; Eastern Europe, five; and the Western European and Other States group, ten. Since immediate re-election is allowed, it is possible for quasi-permanent memberships to emerge. After the USA was not selected in 2001 (although it was returned to a seat the following year), only two states have been members of the Commission since its inception (Russia and India). The member states of the HRC are represented by delegations that are bound by the instructions of their home governments. All other UN members have observer status and can – just like the hundreds of NGOs with consultative status in the ECOSOC – take part in the debates without a right to vote on the final outcome. Nearly all member states make regular use of their right to participate. The six-week session every spring at the Commission's seat in Geneva is thus a forum for more than 3,000 participants from states, civil society, UN organs and other international organizations. The work of the Commission is supported by the Sub-Commission on the Promotion and Protection of Human Rights, created in 1947 as the Sub-Commission on Prevention of Discrimination and Protection of Minorities. This sub-commission consists of twenty-six experts who are not bound to state instructions like their colleagues in the Commission, and are appointed by ECOSOC for three-year terms with the possibility of re-appointment. The Sub-Commission conducts studies and produces recommendations for the HRC, but also has a five-person working group as a first instance for the review of individual communications submitted to the Commission.

In comparison to the 1950s and 1960s, when the HRC was concerned largely with the development of human rights standards, and held itself closely bound to the restrictions of Resolution 75 (v) with respect to the protection of human rights, its current mandate is much more extensive. It can concern itself with all questions relevant to the issue of human rights, from the further development of standards, through the investigation of human rights violations to the issuing of recommendations for the better implementation of human rights norms in domestic law (Baum, 1999, p. 242). This expansion of competencies was made possible by ECOSOC Resolution 1235 (1967), which permitted the Commission to deal with the human rights situations in a few specified countries, and ECOSOC Resolution 1503 (1970), which allowed individual petitions. Like the remarks of the treaty committees, the resolutions of the Human Rights Commission are not legally binding, and are not backed by the power to sanction. One of the HRC's most important weapons is thus the mobilization of public interest and consciousness. The formal work of the HRC is characterized primarily by the use of the following instruments.

- *Debate*: the HRC is a forum of public discussion in which NGOs as well as state representatives may take part. Debate serves the public discussion of important human rights themes, but also addresses the actual human rights situations in member states;
- *Resolutions*: specific issues in the debate are usually concluded by the HRC in the form of resolutions. They may relate to thematic issues such as the death penalty or racial discrimination, or may contain – as country resolutions – general remarks on a country's human rights situation, recommendations for its improvement, or proposals for more far-reaching actions;
- *Chairperson's statement*: as an alternative to the rather judgemental resolution, a consensus between the HRC and a particular state may be so handled that the chairperson of the HRC openly addresses the human rights situation in a particular country, and indicates at the same time the concentrated efforts of the HRC and the state involved to eliminate whatever deficiencies are in evidence;
- *Special reporters*: the HRC can deploy special reporters for the observation of the human rights situation in specific states, who then work with that state's government, with other state actors and with NGOs. Furthermore, theme-based special reporters or working groups can be assigned to problems involving several countries, such as disappearances, torture, child-trafficking or the right to development;
- *The 1503 procedure*: this procedure, named after the above-mentioned ECOSOC Resolution, opens up the option to individuals and groups of individuals of submitting a complaint or communication in cases of well-founded

suspicion of massive and systematic human rights violations in a particular country, when the complainant has exhausted all measures available to him/her in the relevant country for redress of his/her grievance. In contrast to the other remarks of the HRC, this procedure is confidential. It has become regular practice accompanying the procedure, however, for the HRC chairperson to publish a list of the countries involved; and

• *Norm development*: although the primary work of the HRC since the 1990s has been the monitoring of the implementation of treaties that have already come into force, it also continues to work on the further development of norms. Among the most recent results of this work are the Declaration on the Protection of Human Rights Defenders (9 December 1998) and the two additional protocols to the Convention on the Rights of the Child.

As a political committee, the HRC is also a forum for the settling of controversies in which the still widely differing understandings of the type and scope of international protection of human rights find lively expression. Thus it is not only in the USA that the question is raised of how the membership of states such as Sudan can be reconciled with the operations of the Human Rights Commission. The discussion of the practice of tasking stubborn and habitual violators of human rights with their protection, while at the same time voting the USA out of the Commission (even if only temporarily), received yet another impetus when Libya took over the chair in 2003. A large number of countries, especially those from the Asian and African continents, argue that national and cultural peculiarities should be given more consideration in the way that the agreed-upon norms are actually guaranteed. Western democracies in particular tend to accuse these states of practising human rights relativism under the cover of cultural differences. These countries' answer to this accusation is that the West also practices an inconsistent politics of double standards, and that it ignores human rights violations in its own spheres of interest. None the less, it must also be admitted that it is precisely the Western countries that hold to the HRC mandate to concern themselves with grave and systematic human rights violations everywhere in the world and to be able to name the states involved. The intrinsic tension between the principle of sovereignty and collective implementation of rights has also been a major theme of discussion in the HRC, particularly since the latter half of the 1990s. Here it has been shown, however, especially by the example of China, that the avoidance of a confrontational discussion of the human rights situation – as has for example, been the practice of the European Union towards the People's Republic of China since 1997 – can open new and possibly more promising options for action. China signed both human rights covenants in 1998, and ratified the ICCPR in March 2001.

It is in controversies such as these that not only the HRC's character as a political body, but also the limitations resulting from this political composition, become painfully obvious. Against the interests of influential members, human rights standards simply cannot be implemented in the short term. The special significance of the HRC thus consists above all in its continual insistence on the execution of the agreed-upon duties, and the constantly recurring theme of still-existing deficiencies. However, the HRC, like the treaty bodies, finds itself increasingly confronted with the problem of over-extension. Ever more difficult and differentiated processes are faced with stagnation, or even reduced financial and personal resources. The effective protection of human rights through the HRC is thus greatly dependent on the political will of the states to outfit the Commission with the means necessary to overcome its growing challenges.

The UN High Commissioner for Human Rights

Shortly after the founding of the UN, the Secretariat formed its own human rights department, with its original seat in New York, but has been in Geneva since 1974. However, this department lacked, and still lacks even after its standing was enhanced in 1982 to the UN Human Rights Centre, a mandate that would have allowed it to develop into an operative organ with its own competencies for action. The member states took steps to strengthen the UN's capacities for the protection of human rights during the 1993 Vienna Human Rights Conference. They not only recommended that the Human Rights Centre's capabilities for co-ordinating UN-wide activities on human rights should be improved, but also argued for the creation of a new office for a UN High Commissioner for Human Rights (UNHCHR). The international push that human rights experienced after the end of the Cold War and in the wake of the Vienna World Conference helped to bring the General Assembly to the point where, after short but intensive negotiations, it was able to pass Resolution 48/141 (20 December 1993), creating the proposed office of UNHCHR. The Resolution formed a mandate for the High Commissioner and his/her office (OHCHR), and specified a long list of responsibilities, which can be split into four main categories (Boekle, 1998, p. 12 et seq.):

(i)   *The promotion and protection of all human rights*: among the core purposes of the OHCHR is the promotion of fundamental rights as set down in the Universal Declaration of Human Rights, but also as contained in the human rights covenants and other treaties. The right to development is mentioned specifically, and the OHCHR may also act in support of the work of other UN organs and programmes, such as the UNDP, in pursuit of that goal;

(ii) *International co-operation*: for the improvement of the human rights situation worldwide, the OHCHR is engaged in strengthening co-operation among governments, national and international human rights institutions, and NGOs;

(iii) *Crisis management and prevention*: this includes primarily the creation of field missions and human rights offices in countries with precarious human rights situations, but also support for countries in transformation processes; and

(iv) *Co-ordination and rationalization*: to a certain extent, the OHCHR is the supervision- centre of all the UN's human rights activities, and its duties are to give this cross-cutting set of tasks a framework and a coherent strategy.

This particular role is underscored by the High Commissioner's member-ship in the Secretary-General's Senior Management Group.

The High Commissioner occupies the rank of an Under-Secretary-General, and is nominated by the Secretary-General and approved by the General Assembly for a four-year term of office with the option of extension. S/he is supported by the Office of the High Commissioner for Human Rights (OHCHR). After the first High Commissioner, José Ayala Lasso of Ecuador, left office in early March 1997, the former Irish President, Mary Robinson, was named the new High Commissioner for human rights on 15 September 1997. From 12 September 2002 until his tragic death in a bomb attack in Iraq on 19 August 2003, the former leader of the Office for the Coordination of Humanitarian Affairs in the UN Secretariat, the Brazilian Sergio Viera de Mello, held the office. Since de Mello's passing, the office has been led by the acting High Commissioner, Bertrand Ramcharan. In July 2004 Louise Arbour from Canada became the new High Commissioner for Human Rights. Although the UNHCHR acts under the authority of the Secretary-General and the General Assembly, s/he also enjoys a large measure of autonomy, which finds expression above all in his/her extensive rights of initiative. Under his/her own competence, s/he may enter into dialogue with governments, offer them help, offer recommendations to UN organs, and call public attention to exist-ing problems and deficiencies. An important step in the improvement of the OHCHR's capabilities was accomplished in 1997 with the integration of the UN Human Rights Centre. At the same time, the office of a Deputy High Commissioner was created, intended to free the High Commissioner from admin-istrative tasks to enable him/her to concentrate more on the operational side.

As of the end of 2003, the OHCHR comprised 564 staff, with 284 people work-ing at the office's seat in Geneva, nine liaison staff in New York, and 271 in offices, missions and so on elsewhere in the world. Of particular importance for the work of the OHCHR are its field presences, which have multiplied since the beginning of the 1990s. Even more important than the quantitative increase is the qualitative change that accompanied them. While field missions, such as that in Rwanda in 1994, were mainly reactive measures to catastrophic situations, at the beginning of the new century the emphasis of the office's activities has turned to prevention. Furthermore, the UNHCHR has been able to integrate human rights components in ever-increasing number into the complex peacekeeping missions of the late 1990s. Here, it is easy to see the OHCHR's significantly improved co-operation with other departments of the Secretariat, such as the DPKO and the Department of Political Affairs (DPA) (on the work of the field presences, see OHCHR, 2004 [www.unhchr.ch]; Martin, 1998).

The primary activities of the High Commissioner consist in the main of quiet diplomacy and co-operation with various governments. The mandate obliges the High Commissioner to respect state sovereignty and national authority, thus forc-ing him/her often to walk a very thin line between co-operation and the exercise of public pressure. The discretion with which, in particular, the first High Commissioner, Ayala Lasso, carried out this task subjected him to many accusations of a lack of transparency and too much consideration of the states. Many NGOs also complained of a lack of co-ordination with, and attention to, their information and perspectives. Mary Robinson thus put a much greater emphasis on the country reports, an integration of fact-finding trips with a larger country strategy, and showed a much greater willingness to make the results of any activities public. Viera de Mello had only just been named High Commissioner when he was made the UN's special representative for the reconstruction of Iraq and sent to the Middle East, where he was killed.

Even when the improvements in co-ordination between the OHCHR and the individual subsidiary organs, programmes and specialized agencies seem to come only gradually, the creation of this office constituted a massive qualitative leap for the UN in the strategic bundling of its human rights activities. Its work now has a central promoter, who brings global publicity and attention to his/her area of responsibility, and at the same time functions as a peer contact for both governments and NGOs. All the same, this office, too, suffers under the UN's financial difficulties. Less than 2 per cent of the UN budget goes to fund the OHCHR, totalling about US$54 million for the years 2004–5. Extra allocations from the UN are hardly to be expected in light of the states' less than robust tendency to want to pay more into the organization's coffers. OHCHR has therefore had to rely increasingly on voluntary contributions, which grew from US$15 million in 1994 to an expected US$55 million in 2004.

Human Rights Protection: New Fundamentals and Perspectives

In the 1990s, the discussion of human rights and their effective protection took one of the top places on the global agenda. The end of the Cold War indicated that the ideological blockade that had for years stood in the way of a worldwide concentrated strategy for improving the protection of human rights might now be overcome. Above all, many of those who had fought for democracy and human rights were able to reach high political office and leading social positions in the formerly socialist countries, where before they had been subject to imprisonment and persecution. After the great changes in 1989–90, the Western states found in Central and Eastern Europe allies in rather than opponents to their view of human rights. In Africa and Asia, too, more and more movements arose to demand multi-party systems, rights of political participation, and human rights standards. In Latin America, most of the military dictators were toppled (Martin, 1998, p. 148).

Catalogues of human rights were to be found in numerous new constitutions, and the ratification of already-drafted human rights treaties received a new impetus. On the other hand, a wave of violence barely conceivable in its scope flared up all over the world in countless civil wars and wars of secession as well as in the activities of majority populations toward national minorities. This included everything from large-scale human rights violations to 'ethnic cleansing' and genocide. Through the rapidly-developing global network of information media, the pictures from countries in crisis found their way ever more quickly into the households and consciousness of the world public (Debiel and Nuscheler, 1996, p. 19). Above all, in the Western states, mainly because of the so-called 'CNN effect' (the usually selective pressure on decision-makers created by mass media news portrayals of crisis) there arose considerable internal political pressure to act to avert massive human rights violations.

These developments also found expression in the practice of the political decision-making centre of the UN: the Security Council. There, the détente between the USA and the Soviet Union at the end of the 1980s had already led to an increased capacity for action. With the common proceedings against Saddam Hussein in the first Gulf War, optimism grew regarding a multilateral 'new world order', the central axis of which was to be the UN, and in the framework of which the global protection of human rights was to be pushed forward. The UN engaged itself in new ways for the protection of human rights, going well beyond the mechanisms to be found in its Charter and associated treaties. In the following paragraphs, two of the most important new UN instruments of the 1990s – the humanitarian interventions carried out under the authority of, or by mandate of, the United Nations (analysed above in Chapters 3 and 4) and the International Criminal Tribunals – will be explained and discussed.

Humanitarian Interventions

Beginning with its Resolution 688 (5 April 1991) on the situation of the Kurds in northern Iraq, the Security Council continued throughout the 1990s to involve itself with human rights and humanitarian situations in various countries, demanded steps for their improvement, and undertook measures up to and including the use of military force. While the situation in northern Iraq could still be viewed plausibly as a possible international concern because of the potential involvement of Turkey in an interstate war, only a year later the Security Council had declared with respect to the situation in Somalia that the very scale of the human catastrophe there constituted a threat to international peace and security (Resolution 794, 3 December 1992). This unanimously-passed Resolution marked the first time a purely internal affair was qualified as a threat to international peace without even making mention of the – certainly present – possible international consequences such as mass migration of refugees as a constitutive part of the justification for such a qualification. The military action UNITAF (Restore Hope) authorized by this Resolution under Chapter VII was thus the first UN military intervention on purely humanitarian grounds. The Somalia Resolution represents a progression in the gradual expansion of the Security Council's functional responsibilities.

This process led to an increasing weakening of the principle of sovereignty and opened up to the UN extensive opportunities for interference on humanitarian and human rights grounds. As has already been explained, the Article 2(7) prohibition applies only to intervention in matters that are essentially within the domestic jurisdiction of a state. Furthermore, it does not apply when the Security Council decides to take enforcement measures under Chapter VII. Of course, the prerequisite for the use of such measures is an Article 39 determination that international peace has been threatened or broken, or that an act of aggression has taken place. The concept of a threat to the peace is not clearly defined, so leaving the Security Council a great deal of freedom to use its own judgement (for several sources, see Pape, 1997, p. 128). Events which the Security Council believes constitute threats to the peace are automatically withdrawn from the *domaine reservée* of the states. The use of an expansive interpretation of Article 39 thus allows the Security Council such broad powers of action that Dieter Blumenwitz (1994, p. 7) described it as the 'key element for an effective protection of human rights within the framework of the UN'. Bartl (1999, p. 133) remarks correctly that the language in Resolution 794 is of international humanitarian law, not violations of human rights. However, as Pape (1997, p. 44 et seq.) has shown, human rights law and international humanitarian law build off the same basic norms and have the same purpose: to protect the individual. Ebock (2000, p. 263 et seq.) claims that six Security Council Resolutions of the 1990s on humanitarian intervention show that the Council's decisions were premised in large part on human rights considerations.

On the basis of this broadened understanding of possible threats to the peace, in the 1990s the Security Council determined on a number of humanitarian interventions conducted either by 'blue helmets' or through the armed forces of an authorized state or states. The record of these operations is rather mixed. The hope of the early 1990s to be able to contribute to the worldwide implementation of human rights through military intervention very quickly gave way to the recognition that such a task went well beyond the UN's competencies and capabilities. Along with the conceptual and technical problems attending collective military action (discussed above in connection with peacekeeping missions), new questions arose, such as how permissible it was to endanger or sacrifice human life on the side that was supposed to be receiving aid (Smith, 1998). Furthermore, the high losses on the side of the intervening states, above all in Somalia and the former Yugoslavia, significantly reduced their readiness to endanger their own citizens' lives in selfless engagements for the abstract notion of human rights. Democratic regimes in particular must be able to justify to their constituencies the grounds on which they are risking the lives and welfare of their soldiers and civilian mission workers. The Security Council's decision to intervene or not, and a state's decision to support the UN or not, are both largely dependent on states' national interests and considerations. This leads to a selectivity in the missions undertaken that to be appears to be quite incompatible with the inalienable and indivisible nature of human rights. This selectivity has grave consequences both for the 'forgotten regions' and for the moral integrity of the intervening powers.

The core legal, ethical and political problems of military intervention for the protection of human rights merged into an all-encompassing dilemma with the Spring 1999 NATO operation in Kosovo. Although the Security Council had described the humanitarian situation in Kosovo more than once as a threat to the peace (in Resolution 1199 of 23 September 1998 as well as several other statements), any authorization of the use of military force was made impossible by the veto threats of Russia and China. In weighing the goods of securing elementary human rights to the Kosovar Albanians and of observing the law's general prohibition on the use of force, NATO made the decision to undertake an action *praeter legem*: that is, outside the formal prescriptions of international law. The worldwide discussion of the legal permissibility, the ethical responsibility and the political opportunism of this step cannot be reviewed here (see Chesterton, 2001). However, the incident showed just how complex the decisional situations regarding humanitarian interventions can be, both for states and for inter-state bodies, and furthermore just how unstable the *normative* basis still is, not to mention the legal one. The reform of the Security Council's decision structure and the development of clear criteria for the permissibility of military measures for the protection of human rights are indispensable prerequisites for the consistent use of this instrument. Specific attempts at this type of reform will be discussed in Chapters 8 and 9. Until progress is made in this area, it is likely that the UN, states and regional arrangements will undertake humanitarian intervention only in exceptional cases, otherwise they will rely on political and economic measures.

International Criminal Jurisdiction

The treaties and procedures for the international protection of human rights are characterized, as has been shown, by their efforts to bring the individual to the centre even of international law. Human rights violations, however, do not simply 'occur'; they are carried out by people. This is the case whether it be through the ordering or the actual execution of specific measures. The question of who the victims are is bound up closely with the question of who the perpetrators are, and thus it is clear that in complement to international law provisions protecting human rights, there must also be international criminal norms according to which perpetrators can be called to account for their individual guilt.

It was not by chance that the first efforts to codify international criminal norms appeared at the same time as the prohibition and ostracism of war in the 1920s. The victims among the civilian population were too numerous and it had become far too evident that modern war constituted the most horrifying violation of humanitarian norms that could be imagined. The attempt to bring the German Emperor Wilhelm II to justice for unleashing the First World War and for the violations of the Hague Conventions and other laws and customs of warfare that had been committed in the course of that conflict failed. Thus it was not until the international military tribunals at Nuremberg and Tokyo that war criminals were condemned on the basis of international law crimes. Through the introduction of the offence of 'crimes against humanity', it became possible to prosecute crimes that had been carried out by a state against its own civilian population – for example, the murder of German Jews by the Nazi regime – before an international court. At the same time, the traditional conceptualization of sovereignty, already weakened by the partial prohibition on war by the Charter of the League of Nations and the total prohibition of the Kellogg–Briand Pact, was dealt a further blow by the Nuremberg and Tokyo processes, in that these proved that actors responsible for international crimes could no longer rely on sovereign immunity to save them from punishment.

The UN's efforts at a further formulation and codification of the Nuremberg Principles, however, remained unsuccessful for a long time against the backdrop of the Cold War. A further obstacle was the reluctance of states to allow their political activities to be judged and possibly condemned according to international criminal norms. Thus, shortly after the passing of the Convention on the Prevention and Punishment of the Crime of Genocide of 9 December 1948, two attempts by the UN International Law Commission (ILC, founded by the General Assembly in 1947) to create a statute for an international criminal court failed. In 1954, the ILC presented a code of crimes against the peace and security of humanity, but its discussion was postponed indefinitely by the General Assembly, and its development was not resumed until well after the passing of the Definition of Aggression in 1974. It was not until the mid-1990s that the ILC was able to present another statute for setting up an international criminal court (1994) and a criminal code for international crimes (1996) (on this development, see Ferencz, 2001) which in fact found their way into the Rome Statute of the International Criminal Court, passed in 1998 and coming into force on 1 July 2002.

While the consultations were going on in the ILC, the development of international criminal law was accelerated by a forward-looking decision of the Security Council. In view of the massive human rights violations committed during the battles in the disintegrating Yugoslavia, the Security Council created an International Criminal Tribunal for the Prosecution of Persons Responsible for Serious Violations of International Humanitarian Law Committed in the Territory of the Former Yugoslavia since 1991 ('ICTY', Resolution 827, 25 May 1993), based in the Hague. Preceding this decision, in October 1992, an independent expert commission had been sent to investigate the humanitarian situation in the former Yugoslavia, on whose report the Security Council had relied heavily in its determination that the situation represented a threat to the peace (Resolution 808, 23 February 1993). With Resolution 808, the Security Council gave the Secretary-General the task of examining the possibility of creating a criminal court. On 3 May 1993, Secretary-General Boutros-Ghali presented a report that was composed partly from the ILC drafts, and in which the statements of thirty states, the OSCE, the International Committee of the Red Cross and a number of NGOs were also integrated. He recommended that the Security Council should create an international criminal tribunal on the basis of Chapter VII as a non-military sanction for the restoration of peace. The draft statute appended to the report was put into effect by Resolution 827 (ICTY Statute). One of the ways in which the Security Council reacted to the genocide in Rwanda the following year was the institution of another international criminal tribunal, based largely on the ICTY. The ICTR (Resolution 955, 11 November 1994) is based in Arusha, Tanzania.

As *ad hoc* courts, the jurisdictions of both tribunals are restricted in many senses. This is especially true in terms of which crimes they are able to prosecute: the ICTY may prosecute grave violations of the 1949 Geneva Conventions, violations of the laws and customs of war, genocide, and crimes against humanity. The jurisdiction of the ICTR includes genocide, crimes against humanity, and violations of the general Article 3 of the Geneva Conventions as well as the second Protocol Additional to the Geneva Conventions. Since the Security Council has no competence to legislate, the crimes over which these tribunals were to have jurisdiction had to be carefully worded so that they were firmly rooted in existing international law. In order to avoid violating the principle of *nullum crimen sine lege* (no *ex post facto* crimes), only Customary International Law crimes could be included (see numbers 33 et seq of the Secretary-General's report of 3 May 1993). According to Article 24 of the ICTY Statute and Article 23 of the ICTR Statute, only prison sentences, either of limited duration or for life, may be handed down for the punishment of the indicated crimes. In contrast to the International Military Tribunals of Nuremberg and Tokyo, the death penalty is not allowed. For the safekeeping of the accused during the pre-trial detention period, the states where the tribunals' bases are located provide the use of prison space to the UN. The serving of any sentences handed down is to be in prisons of UN member states that have declared themselves willing to accept the prisoners. As a result of this, those already sentenced by the ICTY are serving their sentences in Finland, Germany and Norway.

Both tribunals have the same structure. They consist of a jurisdictional organ with three Trial Chambers and one Appeals Chamber, an Office of the Prosecution, and a Registry. The Rwanda Tribunal does not have the use of its own Appeals Chamber it has been sharing that of the ICTY. The judges are nominated by the Security Council and confirmed by the General Assembly for a four-year term with the option of reappointment. The fourteen full-time justices of the ICTY can count on the assistance of up to nine *ad litem* justices, should the caseload increase significantly. The Prosecutor is named by the Security Council on nomination by the Secretary-General. Following Richard Goldstone and Louise Arbour, this most prominent post in both tribunals has been held since 15 September 1999 by Carla del Ponte (for details on the structure and functioning of the ICTY, see Morris and Scharf, 1995). On 15 September 2003, del Ponte's mandate was continued by the Security Council only for the ICTY. For the Rwanda tribunal, Hassan Bubacar Jallow from Gambia was appointed Prosecutor.

Following an initial phase of only the most hesitant progress, for which the blame fell mainly on the reluctance of states to deliver accused citizens, both tribunals have evolved into effective courts. On 28 June, 2001, the 39th indicted suspected war criminal was brought into pre-trial detention in Scheveningen in the Netherlands. That suspect was Slobodan Milosevic, the first head of state ever to be held answerable before an international court. As of March 2004, more than fifty trials are pending before the ICTY, twenty-five accused have been sentenced, and five acquitted. Eighteen suspects are still being sought. There are fifty-seven accused before the Rwanda Tribunal, and twenty trials have already been concluded, among them that of the former Rwandan prime minister, Jean Kambanda. With the Appeals Chamber's 19 October 2000 confirmation of the Trial Chamber's judgment, Kambanda became the first head of government to be sentenced to life imprisonment for the crime of genocide.

The 'legal intervention' of the Security Council through the founding of criminal tribunals as a non-military sanction for peace-maintenance led to fundamental debates in political science and legal circles, as well as in the public sphere. A few authors have questioned the authority of the Security Council to create courts. The particular criticism from this corner is that no state has given the Security Council sovereignty over criminal affairs, and that the Security Council had therefore arrogated to itself a legislative competence which, according to the Charter, it does not possess. Against this, it may be maintained that the Security Council did not create any new law with the statutes of the tribunals, but simply made use of existing Customary International Law. It must, however, be admitted that the group of crimes known as 'crimes against humanity', referred to in Article 5 of the ICTY Statute, is still highly contested. The scarcity of state practice with respect to this type of crime allows serious doubts as to its CIL status. Jana Hasse (2000) questions the entire Customary International Law basis of the Security Council's actions. The Secretary-General's report (see no. 48), on the other hand, started from the assumption that the relevant norms had been part of Customary International Law since the Nuremberg and Tokyo tribunals. Both the Trial and Appeals Chambers of the ICTY shared this opinion in their judgment of the Tadic case.

There has also been scepticism regarding the ability of an international criminal tribunal to contribute to international peace at all. However, it must be presumed that the threat of punishment will have at least a general deterrent effect on potential perpetrators who might earlier have counted on the protection of their sovereign immunity. The objections raised in particular against the ICTY – extending on the part of the Serbs to accusations of subordination to arbitrary political will and to the humiliation of an entire people (Hinic, 2001) – are answered by the growing recognition that the tribunal has won from the states affected by it. A number of high-ranking functionaries such as the chair of the Croatian Defence Committee, General Tihomir Blaskic, or the former president of the Republika Srpska, Biljana Plavsic, had to submit themselves to the tribunal's jurisdiction, and some of them were in fact sentenced. With the delivery of their former head of state, even the then Federal Republic of Yugoslavia recognized the tribunal's legitimacy.

The International Criminal Court

The increased significance that the criminal prosecution of those responsible for grave violations of human rights has taken on, not least through the work of the two tribunals, was demonstrated by the overwhelming majority that passed the Statute for a Permanent International Criminal Court at the conclusion of the Rome Conference on 17 July 1998. Of 148 participating states, 120 voted for acceptance, twenty-one abstained, and only seven voted against, among whom were the USA, Israel, China, Iraq, Yemen, Qatar and Libya. After the unexpectedly swift ratification by more than sixty states, the Statute came into effect on 1 July 2002. In March 2004, ninety-two states were full members of the Statute, and a further forty-eight had signed but not ratified it. From the perspective of the international protection of human rights, the importance of this development cannot be overestimated. Through the court created on the basis of this statute, the decades-long process of trying to bring the individual to the centre of international law, both in the person's need for protection and in responsibility for his/her actions, has been taken a step further. This is tantamount to a further weakening of the central value of international law: state sovereignty. Article 1 of the Statute gives the new Criminal Court complementary jurisdiction, when the legal apparatus of the relevant state is either unwilling or unable to prosecute and punish adequately the international crimes laid down in the Statute (see also Article 17 of the ICC Statute). The authority of the ICC is thus not quite as far-reaching as that of the ICTY and ICTR, which may in fact take over processes in progress in the respective states if they should consider it necessary. If one remembers, however, that the *ad hoc* tribunals were in fact called into being as Security Council enforcement measures under Chapter VII, while the ICC is a treaty in which the parties agreed voluntarily to transfer some of their sovereign rights to the Court, it is clear how meaningful a step this has been.

Article 5 of the Statute lays down four core universal crimes: genocide; crimes against humanity; war crimes; and the crime of aggression. The first three are explained in more concrete detail in Articles 6 to 8. The provisions of Article 6 correspond largely with those of the 1948 Genocide Convention. Article 7, on crimes against humanity, is based on the provisions in the ICTY and ICTR statutes, with the major difference being that these crimes are no longer bound to the coexistence of a conflict for their objective criminality (Kaul, 1998, p. 127). Article 8, on war crimes, goes far beyond the existing terms of Customary International Law. By extending war crimes to apply also to conflicts internal to states, this article has created an entirely new area of criminal law. For the crime of aggression, there has still been no success in creating a commonly-accepted definition and translating it into concrete criminal activities. The practical introduction of this criminal norm thus remains contingent on a decision of the assembled states-party. Article 25 states that the jurisdiction of the Court is over natural persons who can be called to answer for their individual criminal responsibilities. With exceptional clarity, Article 27 denies immunity to sovereign actors, including heads of state, and Article 28 regulates the criminal responsibility of military superiors. According to Article 77, the punishments available are prison sentences up to and including life terms. In addition to prison sentences, fines may be levied, and criminally-acquired properties may be confiscated. Article 11 states that the Court is responsible only for crimes that take place after the Statute's entry into effect. For this, it was necessary (Article 126) for sixty states to ratify the Statute.

In contrast to the *ad hoc* tribunals, the ICC is to constitute a permanent international court with obligatory jurisdiction. At the same time, the ICC's jurisdiction is also subject to certain regulations. Automatic jurisdiction for the crimes mentioned in the Statute can occur only when, according to Article 12(2), either the state in whose territory the crime took place or the state to whom the suspected perpetrator belongs is a party to the ICC. Thus, crimes that take place in an internal conflict in a state that is not a party to the ICC are not subject to the ICC's jurisdiction, even if the victims of the crimes were citizens of a state-party. With respect to war crimes, Article 124 provides that the states-party 'may declare that, for a period of seven years after the entry into force of this Statute for the State concerned, it does not accept the jurisdiction of the Court with respect to the category of crimes referred to in article 8 when a crime is alleged to have been committed by its nationals or on its territory'. These limitations are somewhat mitigated by the fact that non-parties to the Statute may accept the jurisdiction of the ICC for a particular case, and that the Security Council may refer a situation to the ICC under Chapter VII, when it suspects that a large number of crimes have been committed. Since such a step by the Security Council would have to be considered a compulsory measure of enforcement, the question of whether the state involved is a party to the Statute has no role at all. This could prove to be a very important provision for the effectiveness of the Court, should it in fact prevent states or their leaders from attempting to escape responsibility by simply refusing to sign or ratify the Statute. At the same time, the permanent members of the Security Council remain in a privileged, practically untouchable position.

Whether the ICC will in fact be able to begin its work in the foreseeable future is still an open question. The work on its organizational set-up is largely done, the eighteen justices chosen, and in the person of the Argentinian, Luis Moreno-Ocampo, a world-class lawyer is at the head of the prosecutor's office. However, the US government has turned its passive resistance into an open struggle against the ICC, taking the unprecedented step of withdrawing the signature of its predecessor. On 12 July 2002, in Resolution 1422, the USA achieved the practical suspension of ICC jurisdiction for citizens of non-states-party engaged in peace-keeping missions, and has been working with considerable political pressure on the realization of a series of bilateral agreements for the non-extradition of US citizens to the ICC. Although the likelihood is extremely low that US citizens would ever be prosecuted in the ICC, because of the merely complementary nature of its jurisdiction, the Court is likely to suffer serious harm from the USA's behaviour.

Summary and Further Challenges

In spite of all the progress described in the foregoing chapters, the global discourse on human rights still faces the task of producing a universally-accepted understanding on a comprehensive and consistent code of the human rights to be guaranteed and protected. Concretely, this would mean the integration of the standards and norms set up in international covenants and treaties into national law, the breathing of real life into them, and the decisive and effective use of the available instruments for their implementation. There are good chances that this might all, in fact, be brought to fruition. In the 1990s, the fall of socialism showed the unbroken attractive power of a Western understanding of human rights in combination with democratic forms of government. The course of the economic crisis in Asia following 1997 also showed that democratic states, such as South Korea and Thailand, are able to bring their problems under control more quickly and in a more sustainable way than can authoritarian systems such as Indonesia. On the other side, even in the industrialized countries the awareness is gaining strength that humankind cannot live on liberty alone. What could come out of all this is the global acceptance of a non-hierarchical inter-dependence of all three generations of human rights. This requires inter-cultural dialogue and a willingness to learn from all states and cultures involved in the human rights discourse. At the political level, this also means that there must be a progressive re-evaluation of the classical notion of state sovereignty. Elementary human rights, as a global legal good, are removed from the realm of control of individual states. The nexus between human rights and international stability in the globalized world imposes duties on states that are on the same level as the obligations to peaceful resolution of disputes and the prevention of war. This excludes isolation with reference to sovereignty rights just as much as it excludes the instrumentalization of human rights in the pursuit of national interest.

In the 'war on terror' following 11 September 2001, however, new problems have emerged. Should one happen to look at the 2004 agenda of important themes in world politics, it quickly becomes clear that the protection of human rights has lost its high position in the public's attention, at least temporarily. It is not only in the USA that questions of security have dominated the political discussion since the terrorist attacks in New York and Washington DC (Robinson, 2002). Even in democratic states, the need to guarantee basic individual rights to their own citizens, and in particular to foreign citizens, has taken a back seat to the exigencies of public safety and security. Standards for basic rights are lowered, and new hurdles for refugees or asylum-seekers are constructed. In states where the human rights situation was already precarious, such as China, Russia, or Pakistan, the fight against international terrorism serves as a pretext for the further aggravation of their handling of minorities and political opposition. Many Western democracies are not only overlooking this fact, but are also positively accepting as partners states and regimes which, a few years before, were pariahs of the international community because of their human rights practices. Inevitably, the question arises of just how serious Western democracies are about the standards they are always advocating. Is it possible that another consequence of international terrorism will be permanent damage to the idea of human rights, because its most powerful supporters will loosen their adherence to it? The advanced state of normative development in human rights reached after decades of effort, and the global infrastructure created to monitor their observation, tends to disagree with such a conclusion. Even when it has recently become evident that human rights, too, are subject to the trends of international politics and are not sacrosanct, they are still deeply rooted in the political culture of a growing number of states and societies. Human rights thus have a stable foundation, capable of bringing them back in the foreseeable future to the status of a central political concern.

The development of an integrative universal understanding of human rights will in the long-term be the most effective protection of this collective legal good. Although monitoring mechanisms have been created on the basis of the various treaties and pacts codifying human rights, under the sovereignty principle it has remained possible to establish only 'rudimentary attempts at real and effective implementation mechanisms' (Riedel, 1998, p. 52). More work to convince states of the usefulness of preventive diplomacy, as called for by former Secretary-General Boutros-Ghali in his 'Agenda for Peace', indirect strategies, such as the strengthening of democratic potential in various countries, or the creation of national human rights commissioners and commissions, are all strategies that could be effective in consistently broadening the basis of a universal understanding of human rights. Supervision through collective organs of both states and civil societies, and the public denunciation of human rights violations, are part and parcel of the process of implementing human rights standards.

That this process of gradual conviction promises eventual success is shown by the ever-growing readiness of states to enter into and ratify human rights treaties since the 1993 Vienna Conference, as well as by the broad majority of states favouring the ICC. Compared to compulsory duties, obligations entered into freely have a far greater chance of becoming embedded in the political consciousness of a state or a society. Interventionism of whatever kind for the protection of human rights will remain subject to the suspicion of unilateral pursuit of national interests as long as the causes for intervention are determined selectively by the active and powerful states. This does not mean that military intervention for the protection of human rights could never be necessary or justified, but it does mean that, as in the area of peacekeeping, they should be exceptional instances and carried out by the community of states as a whole.

Further Reading

Broomhall, Bruce (2003) *International Justice and the International Criminal Court. Between Sovereignty and The Rule of Law*, Oxford: Oxford University Press.

Nowak, Manfred (2003) *Introduction to the International Human Rights Regimes*, Leiden, Boston: Martinus Nijhoff Publishers.

O'Flaherty, Michael (2002) *Human Rights and the UN: Practice before the Treaty Bodies*, Leiden, Boston: Martinus Nijhoff Publishers.

Ramcharan, Bertrand G. (2002) *The Security Council and the Protection of Human Rights*, Leiden, Boston: Martinus Nijhoff Publishers.

Robertson, Geoffrey (2003) *Crimes Against Humanity. The Struggle for Global Justice*, New York: New Press.

Steiner, Henry J. and Philip Alston (2000) *International Human Rights in Context*, 2nd edition, Oxford: Oxford University Press.

7

Economic, Development and Environmental Questions in the United Nations: Problem Areas and Institutional Design

Next to peacekeeping and the protection of human rights, activities in the socioe-conomic and development areas constitute a third major complex of duties for the UN. In his Millennium Report to the General Assembly, Secretary-General Kofi Annan (2000, p. 9 et seq.) used the metaphor of the 'world as global village' to emphasize the extent of global interdependence. He suggests imagining that this village has only 1,000 inhabitants, and all the current characteristics of the world are reflected there in precisely their actual percentages. Around 150 of the inhabitants would live in the 'nice part of town', with 780 in the poorer quarters, some of them with insufficient nutrition, and a further seventy in a neighborhood that is in transition. Two hundred people would possess more than 86 per cent of the total wealth, while nearly half of the inhabitants would have to survive on barely two US dollars a day. Two hundred and twenty of the villagers would be illiterate, fewer than sixty of them would own a computer, only twenty-four would have access to the internet, and more than half would never have used a telephone. Some areas of the village would be relatively safe, but others would be plagued by orga-nized violence. In the last few years, there have been an increasing number of natural disasters, which hit the poorer quarters comparatively hard, and at the same time the average temperature has climbed, which is likely to create further envi-ronmental catastrophes.

According to UNDP data, the gap between industrialized and developing coun-tries tripled between 1960 and 1993; the richest fifth of the world population controlled more than 82 per cent of the world product, and the poorest fifth less than 1.5 per cent. The difference in income between the richest fifth and the poor-est was 74:1 in 1997, whereas it had been 60:1 in 1990. The developing countries' share of world trade has gone from around 0.7 per cent in 1980 to around 0.4 per cent in 1998. The share of the poorest states in world-wide direct investment was a mere 0.4 per cent in 1998. In 1999, the total debt load of developing countries was around US$2.5 trillion. The forty-one countries with the highest debt loads must pay around US$200 billion every year in interest; in twenty-nine states the interest payments are higher than state expenditures for education and health care. Although there have been improvements in individual issue areas and countries, socio-economic indicators such as life expectancy, infant mortality rate, literacy rates, nutritional situation and so on show such a degree of global inequity that some have named it 'global apartheid'.

In any case, the North–South conflict, which can be defined as a relationship of structural conflict between developing and industrialized countries, arising from the different economic, social and political opportunities for development in developing societies on the one side and industrialized societies on the other, constitutes a central problem of international relations, and thus a challenge for the United Nations. Development aid, however, can fulfil the expectations placed upon it – usually far too high given the realities – only 'when it is conceptualized and organized as a cross-cutting task, and bound up with foreign and human rights policy, trade and international finance policy, and environmental and agricultural policy in a coherent politics of the whole' (Nuscheler, 2002a, p. 7). In political science, there are a number of different competing ideas about the causes of under-development, as well as about which strategies would be appropriate to address them. The old argument between 'modernization theories' – the belief that development will catch up to modernization and economic growth – and 'dependence theories' – the belief in independent development through disengagement from the world market – has essentially been outgrown. Today, the argument turns on a different key question, one that is also of essential importance to the conceptualization of development politics in the UN: are free trade and the promotion of market structures an appropriate path to the dismantling of developmental differences, or do these only serve those who are already more capable?

A number of different concepts are used in the discussion on development policy to describe the problem that cannot be discussed in full here. Along with the current transition from the concept of 'development aid' to 'development co-operation', the term 'third world' has come under increasing criticism. In connection with the decolonization process of the 1960s, this term came from the analytical division of the world into three groups of states: the 'first' world (the industrialized states), the 'second' (the socialist states); and the 'third' (the developing countries). With the collapse of the bipolar world order in 1989–90, this analytical concept has become rather outdated, and the increasing heterogeneity among developing countries provides a further reason why a new conceptual differentiation is necessary.

What remains contested is what exactly lies behind the often-described phenomenon of the 'end of the third world'. In particular, there is a controversial debate over whether it is about the approach of encouraging countries to reach a Western standard and the strong internal differentiation among developing countries, or if this phrase is simply a cover for the still extremely unequal levels of development on a global scale. The controversial ends and means in development politics in general are reflected in the different understandings of what is a 'developing country'. One common characteristic they can be considered to have is that developing countries are not in a position to satisfy the basic needs of existence for large portions of their populations. The following criteria can also be found in differing levels in most developing countries, although how these criteria are to be weighted has still found no consensus in the academic literature:

- *Economic characteristics*: very low average per capita income together with extremely unequal income distribution, low saving and investment rates, low productivity, insufficient infrastructure, a dominant traditional sector partly orientated on providing for itself, export dependence on a few products aimed primarily at industrialized countries – predominantly raw materials – and a high level of debt;
- *Socio-demographic characteristics*: comparatively low life expectancy against a background of a broad absence of overall good health and very bad medical care, a high illiteracy rate and low levels of education, very high population growth, and a large transitory element in areas surrounding urban centres;
- *Ecological characteristics*: ecological over-exploitation because of poverty, and the destruction of particularly delicate ecosystems; and
- *Socio-cultural and political characteristics*: an orientation on primary groups such as the extended family or ethnic group, together with a low level of loyalty to institutional structures such as the state, low mobility, authoritarian but weak states, weak political legitimization for the leadership, inadequate protection of human rights, a lack of practicable political programmes, high rates of corruption, and often a tendency to violent resolution of both internal and external disputes.

The different levels of development in evidence have led the UN and its various associated institutions to use different criteria for sub-grouping developing countries. The World Bank, for example, categorizes based on per capita income, thus distinguishing countries with middle income levels (MICs) from those with low income levels (LICs), but it also differentiates into further sub-groups based on a wide range of criteria such as the level of a country's external debt. The UNDP, on the other hand, produces a Human Development Index every year, which is a combination of life expectancy, literacy rates and buying power, and produces a three-way grouping of countries with high, medium and low human development. In the year 2000, there were forty-six states in the high human development category, including Canada, Norway, the USA, Australia, Sweden, Belgium, Japan, Germany, Spain, Singapore, Israel, Slovenia, Argentina, Bahrain and Estonia. In the second group, there were ninety-three states, such as Croatia, Mexico, Russia, Brazil, Peru, Turkey, Jordan, Iran, China, Tunisia, Morocco and Kenya. Only thirty-four states were in the third group with low human development, including Sudan, Bangladesh, Haiti, Nigeria, Uganda, Burundi and Ethiopia. This group of least developed countries (LDCs) is of particular significance in the development work of the United Nations (see Table 7.1).

This group is marked by a low income level (less than US$800 per person per year), low development of so-called 'human capital' (measured on an index of

TABLE 7.1
Least developed countries (2002)

Afghanistan	Republic of Congo	Madagascar	Senegal
Angola	Djibouti	Malawi	Sierra Leone
Bangladesh	Equatorial Guinea	The Maldives	Somalia
Benin	Eritrea	Mali	Sudan
Bhutan	Ethiopia	Mauritania	Tanzania
Burkina Faso	Gambia	Mozambique	Togo
Burundi	Guinea	Myanmar (Burma)	Tuvalu
Cambodia	Guinea-Bissau	Nepal	Uganda
Cape Verde	Haiti	Niger	Vanuatu
Central African	Kiribati	Rwanda	Yemen
Republic	Laos	Solomon Islands	Zambia
Chad	Lesotho	Samoa	
The Comoros	Liberia	Sao Tomé	

Source: Data from United Nations Development Programme (UNDP) *World Development Report.*

various indicators such as health, education, life expectancy and literacy rates), and a highly vulnerable economy (measured on an index of various indicators such as economic instability, insufficient diversification of the economy and small state size). When at least two of three categories have been matched, then the ECOSOC may include that state on the list of LDCs, bringing particular advantages such as special conditions for development aid and forgiveness of debt. When the General Assembly undertook this division for the first time in the early 1970s, there were twenty-five states on the list. In 2002, there were forty-nine states, comprising 630 million people, or one tenth of the world's population.

The then-Secretary of State for the USA, Edward Stettinius, noted poignantly after the signing of the UN Charter in 1945 that 'the fight for peace must be waged on two fronts. On one front, it is about security, and on the other, it is about the economy and social justice. Only a victory on both fronts will present the world with a lasting peace' (cited by French, 1995, p. 6 et seq.). Even the terrorist attacks of September 11 did not merely show up the vulnerability of the global infrastructure, they also removed 'from the islands of prosperity the illusion that the world's crises brew on at a safe distance' (Nuscheler, 2002a, p. 2). In countless documents and Declarations, the UN has stated the connection between peace, development and the environment. In the 'Agenda for Peace' from June 1992, for example, it was stated that problems such as uncontrolled population growth, crushing debt, barriers to trade, and the ever-increasing disparity between rich and poor constitute causes as well as consequences of conflict, and require that the United Nations dedicates unflagging attention to them, and gives them the highest priority in its activities. 'Agenda 21', agreed in June 1992 at the Conference for Environmental Protection and Development, calls for a global partnership for sustainable development, which would find its expression in meeting the development and environmental needs of present and future generations. In the 'Agenda for Development' of June 1997 it is claimed that a prerequisite for an effective multilateral system of development is the recognition and support of the unique role of the United Nations: its universality, its global network of relationships which no other institution enjoys, and its ability to create consensus, to shape politics, and to aid in the rationalization of public and private development efforts.

It has already been discussed that the UN, and in particular its numerous specialized agencies and subsidiary organs, are active in practically all sub-areas of this issue, with global implications. Commensurate with this, the organization has grown greatly: 'For years now, the recipe for solving new challenges seems to have been the founding of a new committee or body' (Dicke, 1994, p. 115). This brings with it, however, the problem of growing confusion and dwindling transparency, as well as a lessening of the maneuverability of the system as a whole: 'The more the UN in New York built up its own battalions, the less capable its policy bodies became of providing an interdisciplinary framework: it became even more difficult for the UN to put brakes on inter-agency rivalry when it was competing in the game itself' (Righter, 1995, p. 49). Because of its institutional complexity, the UN system is often described as 'ungovernable'. The organizational expansion was accompanied by an increase in substantive areas of responsibility. Whereas at first peacekeeping held pride of place, at the time of writing the economic, development and social areas constitute a central pillar, accounting for some 80 per cent of the organization's total spending.

This chapter is not intended to give a detailed structural description of all the activities of the entire UN system in economic, social and development issues. Rather, selected areas of activity will be analysed, and particular problems worked through. Chapter 8 will go into more detail about the environmental aspect, which has become closely connected to the question of development.

Responsibilities and Fields of Action

The express will of the founders of the UN that socio-economic and development issues should be addressed, is found first in Article 1(3). In contrast to the League of Nations (which had tried in vain with various plans for reform to bring a similar aim to realization), it is one of the listed purposes of the UN to introduce international co-operation for 'solving international problems of an economic, social, cultural, or humanitarian character'. At the basis of this lies the broad concept of peace already discussed above, which recognizes expressly that particular conditions must be created under which peace and international security can be better, and more permanently, maintained. The Preamble of the Charter lists some of these conditions as the promotion of social progress and better standards of life. The assumption is thus that of an indissoluble connection between peacekeeping on the one hand and inter-state co-operation in economic and social questions on the other. Klaus Dicke (1994, pp. 87 et seq.) points to the fact that this has become possible only against the backdrop of a particular understanding of politics and the state in which 'international organizations are allowed much more access to member states' societies than was imaginable at the time of the League of

Nations'. Klaus Hüfner and Wolfgang Spröte (1994, p. 101) even argue that a precondition for this ambitious catalogue of activities was that, in the place of the 'night-sentry state on the basis of a liberal laissez-faire conception', the social-political responsibility of the state in the form of the 'intervention-orientated welfare state' had assumed precedence. Whether this trust in state (respectively supra-state) action in the age of globalization is still maintainable is a matter of controversy.

The mission of solving international problems of an economic, social, cultural and humanitarian nature is regulated in a separate Chapter (Chapter IX: International Economic and Social Cooperation) of the Charter. Here, the distinction between specialized agencies and subsidiary organs must once more be called to mind (see Chapter 1). It must also be noted that, over the years, the UN system has differentiated substantially internally, and was less confusing in its original construction than it is now. The subsidiary organs are created by the General Assembly; some of them reporting directly to the GA and some via other organs. The General Assembly, however, unlike the Security Council in the area of peace-keeping, does not have the competence to issue binding decisions; it can only give recommendations. The work of specialized agencies is thus somewhat more inde-pendent than that of the subsidiary organs, but these also are unable to act against the will of their members.

In Article 55 of the Charter, the central message is formulated thus: '[w]ith a view to the creation of conditions of stability and well-being which are necessary for peaceful and friendly relations among nations based on respect for the principle of equal rights and self-determination of peoples', several fields are listed in which the UN should promote the goal of stabilizing the international system. These include an improvement of the standard of life, solving economic, social, health and other related problems, as well as co-operating in the areas of culture and education, and respect for and realization of human rights and basic freedoms. Article 56 contains the obligation on all states 'to take joint and separate action in cooperation with the organization for the achievement of the purposes set forth in Article 55'. In Articles 57 to 59, the specialized agencies are mentioned, which have 'wide inter-national responsibilities, as defined in their basic instruments, in economic, social, cultural, educational, health, and related fields, [and] shall be brought into relation-ship with the United Nations in accordance with the provisions of Article 63'. Article 58 states that the UN is to 'make recommendations for the co-ordination of the policies and activities of the specialized agencies'. Article 59 expressly autho-rizes the creation of new specialized agencies in so far as this may be necessary for the fulfilment of the purposes laid down in Article 55. The work of the specialized agencies goes back to Article 22, which gives the General Assembly the right to create subsidiary organs in so far as it may see this as being necessary to the carry-ing out of its duties. Since 1997, administrative tasks in the economic and develop-ment areas have been carried out primarily by the Department of Economic and Social Affairs of the Secretariat under the leadership of an Under-Secretary-General; this does not, however, affect the possibility of creating other independent secretariats for individual programmes, commissions and subsidiary organs.

Chapter X (Articles 61–72) regulates the competencies of the ECOSOC as the organ responsible for the work of the specialized agencies. The ECOSOC is supposed to work under the responsibility of the General Assembly as a co-ordinating instance in the economic and social realms. According to Article 62, it may 'make or initiate studies and reports with respect to international economic, social, cultural, educational, health, and related matters, and may make recommendations with respect to any such matters to the General Assembly, to the Members of the United Nations, and to the specialized agencies concerned'. Furthermore, it may call international conferences on matters within its jurisdiction. According to Article 63, it 'may enter into agreements with any of the agencies referred to in Article 57 . . . subject to approval by the General Assembly, and may co-ordinate the activities of the specialized agencies'. The following Articles also give ECOSOC the right, among other things, to request reports from the specialized agencies and to perform other tasks not specifically mentioned. Article 68 enables it to set up commissions, of which right it has made comprehensive use. Thus, the subsidiary machinery of the ECOSOC now consists of a completely incomprehensible web of thirty units and a further sixty-one sub-units (Glanzer, 2001).

Among the most important of these sub-units are the functional commissions, of which there are currently nine (Statistics; Population and Development; Social Development; Human Rights; Women; Drugs; Crime Prevention; Science and Technology; and Sustainable Development), in which states are chosen for a maximum term of four years. Beyond these, ECOSOC has created five Regional Commissions, each of which have established large numbers of functional sub-committees. As early as 1947, in order to provide help for those countries hit especially hard by the Second World War, the Economic Commission for Europe (ECE) was founded in Geneva to support intra-European co-operation on all levels. With the same purpose, and at the same time, the Economic and Social Commission for Asia and the Pacific (ESCAP) was founded, based in Bangkok, and has since 1974 also included a statistical institute and a centre for the transferral of technology. One year later (1948), the Economic Commission for Latin America and the Caribbean (ECLAC) was founded, based in Santiago de Chile; in 1958 the Economic Commission for Africa (ECA) based in Addis Ababa; and in 1973, the Economic and Social Commission for Western Asia, based in Beirut. Even though the work of the Regional Commissions has to some extent been taken over by other regional organizations (in Europe, for example, by the European Union and the European Council), and they tend to play only a secondary role, their significance is to be seen in the fact that they promote inter-regional exchange and provide an impetus for co-operation. Furthermore, within their frameworks it has been possible to hold a number of macroeconomic studies and technical conventions. Not least, the ECOSOC maintains a number of permanent committees and expert committees, some of which have their own secretariats.

The 'proliferation of sub- and subsidiary organs' (Boutros-Ghali, 1994, no. 227), which has only been hinted at here, has been the target of much criticism. In particular, the ECOSOC has been accused of failing to carry out fully its duties of co-ordination, and of being barely able to reach coherent decisions. Even more basic is the question of whether the expansion of its areas of operation constitutes an over-stepping of its capabilities.

The United Nations and Multilateral Co-operation on Development

The United Nations and its specialized agencies are an important pillar of multi-lateral development co-operation. They have 'contributed substantially to making the development problematique visible and [to] letting the interests of the South influence their own definitions of "interest" ' (Brock, 1995, p. 68). A large number of bodies are concerned with these questions, including:

*   First, as organizations connected with the UN, the World Bank and the International Monetary Fund (IMF). These two are not integral parts of the UN system and are not subject to its instructions, but they do exercise important functions in the politics of multilateral development; and
*   Second, of the UN programmes and funds for development as well as the specialized agencies, the UN Conference on Trade and Development (UNCTAD), the UN Development Programme (UNDP), the World Food Programme (WFP), the UN Children's Fund (UNICEF), the Food and Agriculture Organization (FAO), the International Fund for Agricultural Development (IFAD), the International Labour Organization (ILO), the Industrial Development Organization (UNIDO), and the World Health Organization (WHO).

The existence of two largely separate systems of organizations is the most impor-tant premise for the analysis of this issue-area. The so-called Bretton Woods Organizations (named after the US location of the 1944 international conference on a new ordering of the world economy and the global finance architecture) comprise the World Bank Group (consisting of the International Bank for Reconstruction and Development (IBRD); the International Finance Corporation (IFC); the Multilateral Investments Guarantees Agency (MIGA); and the International Centre for the Settlement of Investment Disputes (ICSID)) and the International Monetary Fund (IMF). From the experiences of the global economic crises of the 1930s, the lesson was learnt that international economic issues should be drawn more firmly into an institutional framework and subjected to common rules.

The Bretton Woods Organizations are dedicated to the principles of free trade, the convertibility of currencies, and an open market economy. Their organiza-tional relationship to the United Nations is complicated. Formally and legally, they belong to the UN system, but in practice they occupy a special position, char-acterized by high independence, their own by-laws, budgets and structures, and a very rudimentary connection to the UN system. The purposes of the World Bank, which has in the meantime collected 180 members, are the stabilization of economic development in the member states through capital investments and credit, the promotion of private international investment, the expansion of international trade, and the stabilization of the balance of payments. Recently added to the list of important goals has been the promotion of growth in developing countries and those in transition. The most important instrument of the World Bank is its ability to grant credit, primarily for the purposes of project financing. Moreover, so-called 'sector operations' are sometimes carried out for the stabilization of entire economic sectors. The primary targets of financing are investment projects, technical aid and programmes for economic reform (structural adaptation credit). An important difference to classical development aid under the UN system is thus the strict orientation on economic criteria, and the granting of credit is tied to very specific conditions (conditionality), which sometimes require drastic and often controversial adaptation measures on the part of the receiving country.

The International Development Association (IDA), on the other hand, formed in 1960 as an offshoot of the World Bank, offers credit – primarily for the purposes of fighting poverty – under much less stringent conditions. The International Finance Corporation (IFC), founded in 1956, primarily promotes private sector investment in developing countries. The purposes of the International Monetary Fund (IMF) are closely related to those of the World Bank group – particularly as entry into the IMF is a formal pre-requisite for membership of the World Bank. The IMF promotes international co-operation of the area of currency politics, with the purpose of expanding trade and exchange stability; provides funds for individual states in balance of payments difficulty; and plays an important role in member states' decisions on exchange rates. The IMF's area of competence has grown markedly since the 1970s. On the one hand, the volume of credit has expanded enormously, and on the other, the IMF has developed into the guarantor – for public and private actors alike – of the willingness of countries in crisis to adopt reforms. The concluding of a structural adaptation programme with the IMF symbolizes a seal of good faith, guaranteeing subsequent access to the international capital market (Metzger, 2002). Their sometimes considerable interference in the economic and social systems of the developing countries has made the Bretton Woods Organizations subject to the accusation that they are representatives of a 'radical market turbo-capitalism', and that they pay far too little attention to a country's social stability.

This is not the place to probe this debate more deeply. The differences between the Bretton Woods Organizations and the rest of the UN system of development cooperation do however have consequences for the UN's work (see Table 7.2). In the Bretton Woods Organizations, voting rights are weighted according to financial contribution and economic capacity, which means that the Western industrialized countries dominate not only de facto (as they do in much of the rest of the UN system), but also structurally.

At first, the newly-created specialized agencies and programmes of the United Nations restricted themselves to the analysis of economic development, the collection of data, and the occasional giving of advice. Very quickly, however,

TABLE 7.2
Basic principles of the UN and the Bretton Woods Organizations

Basic principles of the UN specialized agencies and programmes	Basic principles of the Bretton Woods Organizations
Membership for all peace-loving states by a decision of the General Assembly	Membership depends on financial contributions, economic prerequisites and the consent of important states
Every member state has one vote	Voting rights weighted depending on economic strength and financial contributions
All member states treated as equals	Special treatment for poor members
Members subjected to punishment only if they violate provisions of the Charter	Members who fail to meet certain economic requirements are subjected to punishment
Programmes and measures apply to all members	Programmes and measures are tailored to particular states
Coordination with the main UN organization (in many cases only rudimentary)	Co-ordination with the main UN organization is largely neglected
No economic measures taken against members with the exception of sanctions in the case of a breach of the peace	Access to international capital markets depends on the evaluation of a state's credit-worthiness
Development aid funds either need not be repaid at all, or are levelled out by a long repayment period with very low interest rates	Development help conducted primarily according to the conditions of the market for capital

Source: Based on discussion in Childers and Urquhart (1994, p. 78).

the demand for some integration of the world trade order and development aid measures found its way onto the General Assembly's agenda. Even then, the conviction remained for a long time that the Bretton Woods institutions would address the needs of the developing countries, and that special development institutions and organizations within the UN thus seemed superfluous. (Ferdowsi, 2002, p. 156)

As the number of sovereign nation-states, and thus the number of UN members, grew rapidly within the space of a few years in the wake of decolonization, the General Assembly's priorities changed accordingly. Between the founding in 1945 (fifty-one states) and 1954, only nine new members joined. In 1955 alone, there were sixteen; from 1956 to 1959 a further seven were accepted; and in 1960 the number was increased by another sixteen. This development led to a significant lessening of the dominance of Western industrialized states – and above all, of the USA. The majority of the new members believed that the world economic and financial status quo was not in their interests, and they fought for radical changes. Moreover, the difference in prosperity between the industrialized and developing countries increased, and the need for trade became more evident. The General Assembly and the ECOSOC certainly appeared to be the appropriate forums for debating these questions.

A milestone was the founding of the UN Conference on Trade and Development (UNCTAD) at the beginning of the 1960s, the first important subsidiary organ in the area of development (see below). In the mid-1960s, it was followed by the UN Development Programme (UNDP) and the Industrial Development Organization (UNIDO). But also within the General Assembly itself, the affairs of developing countries received a greater share of the attention. For example, the General Assembly's declaration of the 'UN Decade for Development' in 1961 and the 1974 'Charter of Economic Rights and Duties of States' constituted strong accents on the theme. In the 'Declaration for a New International Economic Order' (NIEO), passed in May 1974 by a majority in the General Assembly, but against the opposition of the industrialized countries, there are extensive demands for the transformation of the world economy. It claims that the economic status quo stands in unmitigated contradiction to the developments in international relations; the developing countries have become a power that can make its influence felt in all areas of international politics. This 'irreversible shifting of the world balance of power requires the active, unlimited, and equal participation of the developing countries in the formulation and implementation of all decisions affecting the international community.' The interests of the developed countries can no longer be separated from those of the developing countries, the document claims, and there is a close relationship between the prosperity of the developed countries and the growth and development of the developing countries.

A number of principles were laid down for the new world economic order, among them easier access to markets for goods from developing countries, full sovereignty over natural resources, fair conditions for trade, the granting of active aid to developing countries free of political or military conditions, and free access to technology. These declarations, however, remained largely without effect. The industrialized countries did not institute structural reform or increase their engagement in multilateral development aid. The developing countries then became more radical in their demands, which 'again met with criticism and rejection from western publics, and prejudiced them increasingly against the world organization' (Ferdowsi, 2002, p. 159). The countless well-intentioned declarations of the General Assembly, specialized agencies and subsidiary organs were simply paid very little attention. Another reason pointed up by thoughtful observers is 'that the great political debates have always led to stylization of reality, to self-delusion about the complexity of problems, to the suppression of uncomfortable realizations, and to the denial of [the General Assembly's] own responsibility' (Brock, 1995, p. 79). In October 1970, the General Assembly determined on an obligation of the industrially developed countries to provide annually – starting within the following five years – a minimum contribution of 0.7 per cent of each country's GNP in the form of public development aid. Thirty years later, this goal had been reached only by Denmark, Norway, the Netherlands and Sweden. Germany, for example, provided only 0.27 per cent in 2002. This largely missed target exemplifies the disparity between needs, flowery declarations and reality.

The inadequate financing of the UN's development activities is a constant topic of international discussion. In the 1960s, one analyst wrote that 'in recent times, there has been an observable lessening in international efforts at development, and development aid is in a state of acute crisis' (cited in Martens, 2001, p. 52). From 1994 to 1998, the contributions of the Western industrialized countries to the developing countries in the form of public development aid sank by nearly US$10 billion. At the same time, however, private direct investment in many developing countries rose rapidly. In March 2002, after a ten-year preparation phase, a large-scale UN conference in Monterrey (Mexico) on the financing of development addressed this problem directly. The goal of the conference was the creation of a new basis for the mobilization of adequate resources for fighting poverty and establishing sustainable development. There is more to this, however, than simply raising the amount of financial resources. Under debate far more was the

(re-)conceptualization of the role and responsibility of states and the private sector in the financing of development aid. In the end, the question that must be answered is: what, in view of the failure of the state- and market-centred ideas for development of the last few decades, the rather urgently needed new paradigm for development aid should be. (Martens, 2000, p. 103)

In the so-called 'Monterrey Consensus', it was agreed not only that a new partnership for the fight against poverty should be the primary task of peacekeeping in the twenty-first century, but also that new and concrete obligations should obtain for industrialized countries to raise their levels of development aid, and for developing countries to implement good governance practices. In consequence, there has been a renewed upward trend in public funding for development aid.

Beyond all the declarations and announcements, there are a large number of committees within the framework of the UN engaged with issues of development (on the right to development, see also Chapter 5). Out of the tightly woven web of specialized agencies, subsidiary organs, funds and programmes, the central bodies will be described briefly here (detailed information is to be found e.g. on the various organizations' web-pages, which are usually formed by the name of the organization with the addition of '.org', for example, www.undp.org. A complete overview of the UN bodies is to be found under www.un.org.).

UN Conference on Trade and Development (UNCTAD)

The developing countries' dissatisfaction with the economic status quo and the dominance of the industrialized states in the world economic institutions (for example, the GATT, which was replaced in 1995 by the non-UN-affiliated World Trade Organization (WTO) and which had 146 member states in 2003 (Priess/Berrisch, 2003)) led to the demand that the numerical superiority of the developing countries in the General Assembly should be institutionalized. With this goal in mind, in 1962 the ECOSOC called for a world trade conference with the purpose of improving the position of the developing countries in the world economy. Since 1964, the UN Conference on Trade and Development has met every four years (the last time in Thailand in February 2000) as a subsidiary organ of the General Assembly financed out of the UN budget. In the meantime, 190 states have become members of UNCTAD. Between the conferences, the Trade and Development Board functions as the executive organ, and the secretariat, with around 400 personnel, is based in Geneva. The basic function of the UNCTAD is the promotion of the integration of developing countries into the world economy and the creation of a forum for the comprehensive treatment of trade and development issues. Thus, for example, the third LDC conference in May 2001 was organized by UNCTAD. Moreover, the UNCTAD publishes a yearly *Trade and Development Report* which promulgates important information for development politics. Although UNCTAD's focus is not in the operative realm, it co-ordinates around 300 projects in more than a hundred countries. The purpose of these projects is the strengthening of political institutions in developing countries and those in transition as well as the further education of decision-makers in the areas of trade and finance politics.

Compared to the original extremely ambitious list of goals (raising the rate of economic growth in developing countries, raising their share of world trade, improving the terms of trade, the abolition of all limitations on trade for developing countries, and the co-ordination of trade and development politics), the current list seems much more modest. Opportunities for real action are restricted because binding orders cannot be made. Decisions tend to command a two-thirds majority (with every state having one vote), but the results remain merely recommendations. Furthermore, it has not been possible to establish the UNCTAD as the central forum of the North–South dialogue, among other things because many of the industrialized states consider the Bretton Woods Organizations (World Bank Group and IMF) to be far more effective. The development of the UNCTAD stands

> for the fate of the whole debate over a new ordering of the world economy. The policy of the developing countries fails for a number of reasons. First, they have attempted to bridge their differing interests simply by lengthening the list of their demands. Second, the self-critical discussion of those barriers to development which come from the developing countries themselves has been bracketed out of the whole conversation on a 'new world economic order'. Third, the developing countries' bargaining position was worsened by falling prices for raw materials. (Brock, 1995, p. 72).

The UN Development Program (UNDP)

The UNDP emerged in 1965 from the combination of two preceding programmes in the hope of creating an independent instrument for the financing and co-ordination of technical aid. The UNDP has no formal membership. With more than 5,000 personnel worldwide, it administrates the greater part of all technical co-operation taking place in the framework of the UN, and plans, finances and co-ordinates development projects, which are then implemented by other organizations or state structures. It has offices in more than 130 countries (the central office is in New York), and at any given time is involved in directing around 5,000 projects in 150 states and regions. The project co-operation is orientated primarily towards fighting poverty and based on grants that do not need to be repaid. Often, projects will be financed which no market-criteria-based credit institution (such as the Bretton Woods Organizations) would support. Strong emphasis is laid on the improvement of living conditions in developing countries. Additionally, the UNDP administrates a number of funds and programmes of the UN, such as the Capital Development Fund and the Development Fund for Women. The UNDP has drawn special attention since 1990 with the yearly publication of the *Human Development Report*, which lends an important if often controversial impetus to the debate. The UNDP is supervised by an executive council of thirty-six member states (eight from Africa, seven from Asia, four from Eastern Europe, five from Latin America and the Caribbean, and twelve from the OECD countries), and reports to the General Assembly through ECOSOC. Decisions are reached by consensus.

The UNDP is financed through the voluntary contributions of member states, which are decided at yearly conferences. In 2000, the monies available stood at around US$2.2 billion, of which US$1.1 billion came from the OECD and other multilateral organizations, and US$900 million from states which had developed their own projects through the UNDP. Thus, for the core organization the funds stood at around US$600 million – a sum significantly less than the US$1.1 billion goal, and one that is about half of what it was at the beginning of the 1990s. For the UN's work on development, however, the UNDP plays a key role despite the fact that it has not been able to fulfil its co-ordination and steering roles adequately. The International Labour Organization (ILO, also based in Geneva) works closely together with the UNDP. The ILO, along with other important fields of concern in the area of labour protection, has been involved in projects of technical aid since the 1960s. In March 1997, after Kofi Annan's became Secretary-General, the UN Development Group (UNDG) was created to bring the work of the specialized agencies and subsidiary organs into better alignment with one another. The UN Office of Project Service (UNOPS) and the UN Development Assistance Framework (UNDAF) have a similar purpose.

The Food and Agriculture Organization (FAO)

The Food and Agriculture Organization, founded in 1945, with 3,700 personnel in five regional and nearly eighty state offices, is the largest specialized agency in the UN system. It has 180 member states and one member organization (the European Union). In the budget for 2000–1, financed out of the regular contributions of the members, there were US$650 million available. The FAO's goals are, *inter alia*, to raise the nutrition and living standards of the members, to raise efficiency in the production and distribution of foodstuffs, to improve the living conditions of rural populations, and to fight acute hunger. For these purposes, comprehensive expertise in agricultural issues (agriculture, forestry and fisheries) is developed, strategies for the securing of foodstuffs are expanded, and practical help is given to developing countries through technical aid projects. Furthermore, the 1996 World Food Summit was organized in the framework of the FAO, which presented a programme of action for halving the number of malnourished people (at that time around 800 million) and co-ordinated its implementation. A conference of all the member states takes place every two years, in which the organization's budget and priorities are set. The executive organ is a council with forty-nine seats, in which seven regions are represented by states delegated by the regions themselves. The Council also forms a number of functional sub-committees, while a secretariat with its seat in Rome takes care of the day-to-day business.

A further organization in the area of agriculture, an independent specialized agency not connected to the FAO, is the International Fund for Agricultural Development (IFAD), founded in 1977. It is financed through the voluntary contributions of member states, and primarily supports projects and programmes for the improvement of the nutritional situation in developing countries.

Other Specialized Agencies, Subsidiary Organs, Programmes and Initiatives

The UN Industrial Development Organization (UNIDO), founded in 1966 as a UN programme, became the sixteenth specialized agency of the United Nations in 1985. Its purpose is to promote industrial development in developing countries and those in transition. Thus, it supports partnership agreements among various actors in the public and private sectors by acting as a forum, organizes the global dialogue in this area, and offers services. It also develops and implements programmes and projects for technical co-operation. The secretariat, located in Vienna, has 700 personnel dealing with daily business. The member states, of which there are 169 at the time of writing, meet every two years in a general conference, to determine the budget (in 2000–1, around US$133 million plus additional means for special programmes) and priorities of the organization by a two-thirds majority. It also chooses the fifty-three (primarily developing countries) members that are to form the Industrial Development Council, which oversees the implementation of the various programmes.

The UN International Children's Emergency Fund was founded in 1946 for the purpose of supporting children suffering from the after-effects of the Second World War. It has been a subsidiary organ of the UN since 1953, reporting to the General Assembly through ECOSOC, and has shifted its focus to work in developing countries. Along with general lobbying for children's rights (it was on a UNICEF initiative in 1989 that the General Assembly passed the Convention on the Rights of the Child), there are programmes for the improvement of health, nutrition and education, as well as for the basic improvement of the living conditions of children, young people and mothers. Moreover, along with the initiation and support of long-term projects, UNICEF conducts emergency aid projects in cases of disaster, and in the wake of armed conflict. At the political level, UNICEF is particularly active in the fight against the use of child soldiers and for the protection of refugees. In the year 2000, the budget was around US$1.1 billion. Around two-thirds of the monies come from voluntary contributions from governments, and the remaining third comes via the thirty-four national UNICEF committees, which undertake private fund-raising. The main administrative seat in New York controls the numerous delegations in countries where programmes are being carried out. Alongside this internal review, the administrative council – the highest control organ, made up of thirty-six government representatives – also monitors the programmes. In the countries where programmes are running, the UNICEF workers regularly monitor the work of their local partners in order to ensure that the means being provided are being used for the intended purposes.

Beyond the work of the subsidiary organs, programmes, funds and specialized agencies, in the course of the 1990s a new milieu emerged in which the UN played an important role as a central space for dialogue. The 1990s were 'characterized by a heretofore unimagined level of international dialogue, in which the problems of developing countries were increasingly recognized as global problems for which all states and their peoples carry some responsibility' (Bundesministerium für Wirtschaftliche Zunammenarbeit und Entwicklung, 2001, p. xv). In these so-called world conferences (for example, on children, education, social development, AIDS), there come together several thousand representatives of governments, civil society and private business. The output of these conferences, as measured by concrete results, varies from one to the next, but 'a decisive improvement over the international dialogue of earlier decades was that the themes the UN addressed in the 1990s increasingly came to determine the agendas of other multi-lateral organizations' (Bundesministerium für Wirtschaftliche Zunammenarbeit und Entwicklung, 2001, p. xvi).

Dirk Messner and Franz Nuscheler (1996a, p. 164 et seq.) also evaluate these conferences positively on the whole. They constitute an important forum of international communication and co-operation, ease learning processes – and thus also create the necessary prerequisites for a fair balancing of interests – and with the media attention they draw, fulfil an important function of providing information on world problems. Furthermore, the history of the world conferences shows that non-binding declarations constitute part of a gradual process of building up normative strength, and that they can increase pressure on governments to observe non-binding self-imposed obligations. These summits belong to the 'theatrical direction of globalism', and that of the future of world politics. Their weakness remains the actual implementation of their determinations and announcements, because if the member states do not make rather more significant changes to their behaviour and begin 'to implement their declarations and determinations from the world conferences of the 1990s, then these conferences are likely to appear to the backward-looking eye of history as nothing but a huge waste of money' (Zumach, 2001, p. 24).

The institutional weaknesses of the UN in the area of development have led to many suggestions for reform, running like a scarlet thread through the organization's history (Hüfner and Martens, 2000). The high point of this development so far has been the passing of the above-mentioned 'Agenda for Development' in Summer 1997. According to the ambitious list of goals in Article 42 of the Agenda, the document should define a new framework for international co-operation as well as the future role of the UN in development work. Furthermore, the future development priorities and a time-frame for their realization are to be marked out. The road to the 'Agenda for Development', however, was anything but smooth. In December 1992, the General Assembly had requested of the Secretary-General that he present an 'Agenda for Development' building on the well-received 'Agenda for Peace'. It was another five years, however, before the 51st session of the General Assembly accepted the document without a formal vote. An important intermediate step was the presentation of a first draft in May 1994. In that draft, five closely interconnected main areas of development politics were differentiated from one another, picking up on the evolution of the international debate over development. Without peace, there could be no development ('peace as a foundation'); without economic growth, there could be no sustainable improvement of living conditions ('the economy as the motor of progress'); without protection of the environment, no lasting development was conceivable ('the environment as the basis of existence'); and without social justice on a global scale ('justice as a pillar of society') and free political participation ('democracy as good governance'), there could also be no stable development. The Secretary-General's draft was criticized as being not binding enough to the member states, and no consensus among the main actors could be reached on the question of the document's practical meaning for the UN's work. Therefore it was another three years and many more hurdles before the final version was accepted.

The 'Agenda for Development' attempts a comprehensive stocktaking of development policies and the constitution of concrete development policy perspectives. In the first section ('Settings and Objectives'), the opportunities and risks of the globalization process are described, and the global political post-Cold-War situation, in particular with respect to developing countries, is analysed. More intensive international co-operation is urgently needed under a totally new concept of development policy. In an integrated approach, economic growth, social development and protection of the environment must be seen as inter-dependent goals. In the second section ('Policy Framework, including Means of Implementation'), the various aspects of development issues are aligned with each other (*inter alia* economy, social development, strengthening of the rights of women and children, population development, migration and environment), and some of them are subjected to detailed analysis.

In the third part ('Institutional Issues and Follow-ups'), the document's character as a compromise becomes very obvious. On the one hand, the UN's uniqueness and its enormous potential for action in the realm of development are emphasized once again, but at the same time there is an insistence that the system of international development co-operation must have new life breathed into it. A new and comprehensive re-ordering, however, is not foreseen in the document itself, and 'aside from empty formulas about continuing necessities, this section merely says that according to the principle of hope, reform would be necessary, but there is no consensus over which reforms should be realized when or how' (Hüfner and Martens, 2000, p. 182). The status quo is not really called into question: there is no attempt to address the separation between the Bretton Woods Organizations and the UN system, the General Assembly is reaffirmed as the most important forum, the ECOSOC is given the usual co-ordination tasks, and the competencies of the various funds and programmes are left, in principle, in their existing form. At the most, a better voting process among the existing organs has been promoted, using the motto 'better inter-institutional co-ordination within the system is absolutely indispensable'. Finally, greater efforts with respect to financing are advocated, and the famous 0.7 per cent goal reiterated: 'New qualitative recognitions or extra obligations which go beyond the non-binding statements from the world conferences are not to be found in the Agenda. At its core, it remains a catalogue of platitudes as they are to be found in all the Action Programmes from Rio to Rome' (Martens, 1998, p. 52).

The UN's Balance Sheet on Development Policy

Since the end of the 1980s, the conditions for development policy have changed fundamentally. With the collapse of bipolarity, the instrumentalization of particular political arguments became less common, market economies and free trade established themselves as the central paradigms, and globalization brought with it a fundamental change in global economic relationships, which makes both the control of economic processes and the practicability of political intentions more difficult (Glanzer, 2001). At the same time, the necessity for an active politics of development remains as urgent as ever, in view of rising poverty, global financial instability, and a global inequity pregnant with the seeds of conflict.

Many problems of development co-operation are not specific to the UN, but hold for all forms of multilateral action in the area. Thus it is necessary to distance oneself from unrealistic expectations 'based on the fundamental error that development can be created through the external impetus of money, expertise, and personnel' (Nuscheler, 2001, p. 7). The UN, however, as an important pillar of development co-operation, must submit itself to such criticism. Its balance-sheet on development politics presents a rather mixed picture. On the one hand, it is attributable to the work of the UN 'that the second-most central conflict after that of the East versus the West, the North versus the South, has thus far experienced no further escalation. This [attribution] appears particularly plausible as it was hardly to be expected that the international relations conflicts over development policies could have been handled in a comparably cooperative fashion without the global negotiating system of the UN' (Rittberger *et al.*, 1997, p. 80). Furthermore, the UN plays a vital role in public consciousness-building and in the promotion of internationally agreed-upon principles in the area of development politics. Its universality, its global presence and its integrated mandate with respect to the interconnection of human rights, development, environment and peace are indispensable in international relations, and this fact is also widely recognized.

On the other hand, criticism of the execution side of things flares up constantly. Rosemary Righter, for example (1995, pp. 87–242), formulates doubts about a meaningful operative role for the UN and calls instead for the UN to remove itself largely from this area. In a world in which governments must compete as never before with other economic and social actors, it is imperative to concentrate the UN's energies on those aspects of the international agenda in which inter-state co-operation and the mediation of common institutions are absolutely necessary. Moreover, she raises a number of principled objections to a competency for the UN in these questions, and describes even the goals in the Charter as utopian and hardly practical. Along with these objections of principle, the institutional splintering in the area of development politics is also loudly criticized, and it is insisted that the countless organizations should be gathered together under one roof, or at least better organized with respect to one another (on reforms, see Chapter 8).

These objections still do not alter the fact that the UN, on the basis of its singular universality and impartiality, as well as its presence in all parts of the world, takes on a central function among all these organizations, whose potential could be used to far better effect than it is currently.

Protection of Refugees, Humanitarian Aid and Population Issues

Flight and expulsion are among the central problems with which the UN occupies itself. Following controversial debates in the General Assembly, the International Refugee Organization (IRO) began its work in 1947 as a specialized agency of the UN designed to last for only three years. In January 1951, the UN High Commissioner for Refugees (UNHCR) was established as a successor organization, whose mandate can be renewed for five-year periods by the General Assembly (the last renewal was for the period 1999–2003). At the beginning of the 1950s, concurrent with the debates on the organizational composition of protection for refugees, negotiations were taking place on the holding of a conference on the protection of refugees. At the UN Conference of Plenipotentiaries on the Status of Refugees and Stateless Persons in July 1951, the signatory states were able to agree on the Convention Relating to the Status of Refugees (the Geneva Refugee Convention), which came into force on 22 April 1954. The convention establishes the rights and duties of refugees, as well as the duties of the signatory states with respect to refugees. A refugee is any person who, 'out of a well-founded fear of being persecuted for reasons of race, religion, nationality, membership of a particular social group or political opinion, is outside the country of his nationality'. People who have fled or been driven out of their homes but have not left their own country (internally displaced persons) do not fall under this international law definition. The right to asylum, which is contained in the Universal Declaration of Human Rights of 1948, is not mentioned here, but the heart of the convention is the prohibition on expulsion or deportation. Every signatory state obligates itself not to force any refugee to cross a border into an area in which his/her life or freedom would be threatened. The original limitation of this protection to people who had become refugees because of events happening before 1951 was removed by a protocol in 1967. As of February 2002, 140 states had signed the convention, and 136 the protocol.

The UNHCR currently protects and supports more than 21 million people who have fled across state borders because of war, persecution and massive human rights violations. In addition to the refugees matching the definition in the Refugee Convention, the UNHCR is also responsible for a comparable order of magnitude of asylum-seekers, returning refugees and internally displaced persons. The absolute number of internally displaced persons is estimated to be around 25 million. In the year 2000, the countries producing the largest numbers of refugees were Afghanistan, Burundi, Iraq, Sudan and Bosnia-Herzegovina; while the countries accepting the most refugees were Pakistan, Iran, Tanzania, Uganda and Congo.

As a subsidiary organ of the UN, the UNHCR took on the task of guaranteeing the observance of the Geneva Refugee Convention, protecting refugees and providing humanitarian aid. The High Commissioner for Refugees (since 2001 the former prime minister of the Netherlands, Ruud Lubbers) is chosen by the General Assembly and heads a division of 4,900 personnel, of which 700 work in the Geneva headquarters and 4,200 in the 123 UNHCR offices around the world. Apart from marginal allowances from the UN budget, UNHCR is financed through voluntary contributions from the UN member states (the 2001 budget was US$852 million), which have dwindled perceptibly since the 1990s despite the rising number of refugees. These contributions are managed by an executive committee consisting of fifty-four states. According to its bylaws, the UNHCR's mandate relates to the guaranteeing of international legal protection and the observation of basic human rights standards in the treatment of refugees, as well as the long-term search for solutions to the problem of refugees. In addition, concrete aid programmes help countries to finance emergency help for refugees in the form of food, shelter and medical services. The UNHCR is sworn to impartiality and restricted to purely humanitarian activities.

Although the mandate has not been changed, the UNHCR's activities have altered somewhat since the 1950s. Along with new regional focuses, primarily in developing countries, the group of those receiving aid has expanded beyond refugees according to the definition in the Convention to include asylum-seekers, refugees seeking to return home, internally displaced persons, and populations affected by armed conflict. In the 2000s, the UNHCR often works as the UN lead organization for humanitarian issues, not only with diverse UN bodies, but also with more than 500 NGOs, and has thereby become more active in unstable conflict regions.

The UN relief and Works Agency for Palestinian Refugees in the Near East (UNRWA) occupies a special position, with its own budget and structure, and deals exclusively with refugees from the 1948 Arab–Israeli conflict. Within the mandate area of the UNRWA there are currently around 4 million people receiving aid.

Humanitarian Aid in the Framework of the UN

The politics of humanitarian aid has developed into a very complex area since the 1950s. Under this heading are found all the measures 'aimed at mitigating the acute need of any population group', and which 'are clearly separated from politi-cal, economic, or military aid in that they have a humanitarian motivation and pursue exclusively humanitarian goals' (Swamy, 2002). Along with the prepara-tion, implementation, and evaluation of humanitarian aid, the various organiza-tions participating in humanitarian actions must also be co-ordinated.

Thus, in 1997, an Office for the Coordination of Humanitarian Affairs (OCHA) was set up within the Secretariat, led by an Under-Secretary-General and intended to streamline the politics of humanitarian aid work in the UN system and related organizations. In order to be able to react more quickly to emergencies, a fund was also set up with an initial US$50 million, for the short-term financing of urgent projects. The World Food Program (WFP) also plays an important role in this area. It was founded in 1961 as a common programme of the General Assembly and the Food and Agriculture Organization, and in 1963 began its work as the Food Aid Organization of the entire UN system. Its primary goal is the provision of food-stuffs for countries whose populations suffer from widespread malnutrition, as well as emergency aid in cases of natural disaster and other emergency situations. This kind of emergency aid has been increasing steadily since the 1990s, and at the time of writing accounts for some 80 per cent of the stores given out.

Part of the WFP is the International Emergency Food Reserve (IEFR), which is supposed to have 500,000 tonnes of grain available every year. In 2000, with around 5,000 personnel, the WFP provided aid for more than 80 million people in eighty-three countries, and is thus the largest food-aid organization in the world. Contributions to the WFP's budget (around US$1.4 billion) are made on a volun-tary basis, and can also be made in kind. An executive council of thirty-six states (chosen by the ECOSOC and the FAO, and answerable to those organs) controls the work of the WFP and meets around four times a year. At the head of the perma-nent secretariat, based in Rome, is an executive director. The focuses for the coming years are on the areas of emergency aid (Food for Life) and the longer-term support of those most affected by food shortages: children, mothers and the elderly (Food for Growth). A further important pillar of the work of the WFP is the financing of programmes aimed at improving the total situation, among other things by paying for work on infrastructural projects with food (Food for Work).

Population Issues in the United Nations

Population development is one of the most important questions for the future of the human race. The question of the ecological, social, economic and political conse-quences of population growth (in the end, the question of how many people the Earth can support) is an extremely difficult one to answer. In general, the rate of population growth can be considered to be too high 'when – even with a subsis-tence-oriented lifestyle for the affected people – there is over-exploitation of the available natural resources or the available capital is not sufficient to finance the investments necessary for an appropriate quality of life' (Leisinger, 2000, p. 57). It is extremely difficult to state objectively when this point has been reached. What is clear, however, is that the life-style of the industrialized countries could not be transferred to all the people of the world without forcing a collapse of the global ecosystem. The UN declared 12 October 1999 as the day the six-billionth citizen of the Earth was born. It was not until the beginning of the nineteenth century that the billion-threshold was reached at all. One hundred and twenty-five years later, the world's population had doubled to two billion; only thirty years after that, the third billion had been reached, and fourteen years later there were five billion people.

In 2003, the world population was estimated to be around 6.2 billion. The population of India alone was over one billion people, that of China 1.3 billion. The UN projects – granted the uncertainty of the underlying assumptions – that by the year 2050, the world population will be anywhere from seven billion (low estimate), to nine billion (middle estimate), to eleven billion (high estimate). Should the middle estimate come to pass, it would mean that the world's population would grow in that time period by the same number of people that comprised the total world population in 1960. The regional distribution of population growth varies greatly. While the populations of industrialized countries are in fact shrinking dramatically in some cases, more than 90 per cent of the population growth is taking place in developing countries. This means, of course, that the problems appearing as a consequence of population growth are also distributed unevenly.

The United Nations is the switchboard for international population politics. In 1946, the UN Population Commission was created as a consultative sub-organ of ECOSOC, and in 1994 was renamed as the Population and Development Commission. This represented more than a simple change of name. It points to the fact that population politics have been integrated into the broader context of development politics. The centre for population issues is the UN Fund for Population Activities (UNFPA), which has been a subsidiary organ reporting to the General Assembly since 1969. The UNFPA, with its base in New York but represented in 150 countries, is the world's largest and most important structure for population issues with a yearly budget of around US$280 million, trade up of voluntary contributions from governments and private donations. There is no formal membership of states. The mandate includes a number of activities in the areas of family planning and population politics, as well as the co-ordination of population issues within the UN system. Beyond that, the UNFPA publishes a yearly report on world population and conducts large conferences on this theme (the most recent of which have been the Conference on Population and Development in Cairo in 1994, and the 1999 special session of the General Assembly on population issues in New York). These have usually had a significant number of concrete results. Together with the UNDP and UNICEF, the UNFPA constitutes the UN Development Group (UNDG).

Health Issues in the United Nations

The central organization for health issues is the World Health Organization (WHO), based in Geneva (a specialized agency of the UN since 1948). The WHO is not a development aid organization in the strict sense – although the health aspect is, of course, given high priority within the larger framework of development politics – but rather has the purpose of improving the health conditions for all human beings. In the 1946 WHO statute, health is defined as a state of complete physical, psychological and social wellness and not merely the absence of illness. Thus the organization's concept of health is very broadly understood, and the responsibilities derived from it are comprehensive. According to Chapter 2 of the Statute, the WHO's primary tasks are:

- The co-ordination of international health policy;
- Active co-operation with other UN organs, national health administrations and professional groups on health issues;
- Support for the fighting of epidemics, research on illnesses and the promotion of research, health education and standardization of diagnostic procedures; and
- Improvement of the health systems of the member states and the elucidation of health issues.

Thus the organization is both a co-ordination point for international health work as well as an instrument of technical support and advice for governments that may request such assistance. The 191 member states meet yearly in Geneva at a World Health Assembly in order to make basic decisions and to agree the budget (for 2001, around US$420 million). The executive council, with thirty-two members, implements the assembly's decisions. At the head of the secretariat in Geneva is a general director, and around 3,500 personnel are spread over the headquarters, the six largely independent regional bureaux (in Washington, Harare, Alexandria, Copenhagen, New Delhi and Manila), and the 130 country bureaux.

A particular challenge for global health politics is the rapid growth in the numbers of people suffering from HIV infection. In sub-Saharan Africa, AIDS is already the number one cause of death, is threatening to destroy the entire social system and to damage substantially the political systems. In sixteen countries, more than 10 per cent of adults (between the ages of 15 and 49 years) are infected; in seven countries – all in southern Africa – one in five adults is living with AIDS. The number of those infected worldwide is estimated to be over 30 million. UNAIDS was founded in 1986, and is now supported by eight organizations (UNICEF, UNDP, UNFPA, UNESCO, WHO, ILO, the World Bank and UNDCP). At the beginning of the year 2000, the Security Council met for the first time to discuss health issues that are confronting a number of countries – primarily in the southern hemisphere – with challenges they simply cannot meet alone. In 2001, the General Assembly took up the theme. The purpose of UNAIDS is to bundle the capacities of the various organizations and use them in a concentrated way in the fight against AIDS. To this end, UNAIDS has around 140 personnel and a yearly budget of approximately US$100 million. In addition, in 2002, the 'Global Fund to Fight Against AIDS, Tuberculosis, and Malaria' was established, which, as a 'public–private partnership organization', enjoys the use of around US$4.6 billion, of which US$1.6 billion has been provided by the USA (data as of August 2003).

Protection of the Global Environment as an International Challenge

At the founding of the United Nations in June 1945, it could not have been foreseen that a new challenge for the survival of humanity – unimaginable in its dimensions – would arise beyond the 'scourge of war' and force itself on to the international agenda. Thus, environmental concerns are not mentioned in the Charter. None the less, the protection of the global environment has in the meantime become one of the most important issues confronting humanity and commanding a large portion of the UN's resources. The central image in this is so-called sustainable development, by which in the ideal case the needs of the present could be satisfied in a way that the opportunity of future generations to meet their own needs is not destroyed. This particular expansion of UN jurisdiction goes back to the broadening of the concept of security mentioned above, and demonstrates the flexibility of the UN system to react to new challenges on the understanding of all member states without any need to change the Charter.

Things such as the ozone layer, species diversity or the global climate are known as global public goods. They cannot be divided, no one can be prevented from using them, and they cannot be protected through the individual actions of nation-states (Oberthür, 1997; Kaul *et al.*,1999a). However, such global public goods can indeed be used by individual actors without their having to pay a particular price for them. This can lead to over-use, which can have lasting ill-effects for all the other users. Another possible problem is the so-called free-rider phenomenon, in which an actor draws some benefit from the behaviour of others without itself contributing to a solution of the problem. For example, were all states apart from one or two to agree to a drastic reduction of carbon dioxide emissions, thus stabilizing the world climate, it would also benefit the state(s) that had not participated. Independent of the fact that some individual actors might in fact profit from global ecological crises:

> in the end they are all victims, and constitute a community of risk who are all sitting metaphorically in the same boat. The inmates of this boat, however, do not conduct themselves rationally in the collective sense, i.e. with respect to common survival, but in the individual sense, meaning that they try to win small advantages for themselves. The product of such individual activities is a catastrophe which no one wanted, but which after a certain point in time, no one could prevent from happening, either. (Wöhlcke, 1992, p. 8)

The institutional design for the protection of collective global goods contains at least two problem areas, which can also be seen as fundamental problems of international co-operation:

(i)   A responsibility vacuum is created by the discrepancy between an increasingly global set of problems and the decisional competencies and possibilities for action, which are still based primarily on the structure of the nation-state; and

(ii)   Under the current conditions of international environmental politics, there is a deficiency of motivation, in that actors are not sufficiently rewarded for behaviour that is to the benefit of all, and in some cases may even be punished for a politics of sustainability because it may cause them to suffer competitive disadvantages (Kaul *et al.*, 1999b, p. 466–98).

Global environmental concerns have developed into a new scourge for humanity that demands a central place in the world's attention (see an outline of the problem in Simonis, 1998; Oberthür and Ott, 2000; and a great deal of data on the global environmental situation is to be found in the *Global Environmental Outlook* published annually by the UNEP, and the reports of the Foundation for Development and Peace, the World Watch Institute, and the World Resources Institute). UN Secretary-General Kofi Annan (2000, p. 42), in his Millennium Report to the General Assembly, expressed it succinctly: at stake is

> the freedom of future generations to sustain their lives on this planet. We are failing to provide that freedom. On the contrary, we have been plundering our children's future heritage to pay for environmentally unsustainable practices in the present . . . Nevertheless, we must face up to an inescapable reality: the challenges of sustainability simply overwhelm the adequacy of our responses. With some honorable exceptions, our responses are too few, too little and too late.

Whereas such a statement would have been regarded as an expression of apocalyptic fear of the end of the world a few years ago, today, science and to a growing degree politics are close to agreeing unanimously that the statement is accurate. Global climate change, in particular, has become one of the most explosive of the world's problems. In its report from January 2001, the Intergovernmental Panel on Climate Change (IPCC), set up in 1998 by the UN Environmental Programme and the World Meteorological Organization, takes for granted that a dramatic change in climate caused by human activities is already under way. The IPCC predicts that, unless there is a drastic turnaround, there will be a long-term worldwide warming of up to 5.8°C, which would have formidable consequences such as weather extremes, soil erosion, desertification, flooding and more. The developing countries would bear the brunt of the suffering (Bangladesh, for example, would be existentially threatened by the predicted rise in sea level), but even the industrialized countries would not be able to escape the negative effects.

Were one to extrapolate the current global use of energy and resources into the future, taking into account the probable population growth to nine billion by 2050 and using the figures of energy use by people in industrialized countries as the basis for calculation, the world's resources would quickly be depleted. The Western model of prosperity is not feasible for the whole world. The world, as the director of the UN Environmental Programme, Klaus Töpfer, has said (1999, p. 87), is 'on a course that cannot be sustained. The time for a rational, well-thought-through transition to a workable future is quickly running out.' For example, the industrialized countries – with about 20 per cent of the world's population – account for about 60 per cent of the world's carbon dioxide emissions (closely correlated with the economic performance of a country, and a primary cause of world climate change). India's emissions lie at around one tonne of carbon dioxide per person per year, while Japan's are nine times that, Germany's eleven times more, Russia's sixteen times, and the USA's twenty times that rate. That said, the rate of increase of emissions from developing countries is considerable. Should India or China, with populations of more than one billion each, reach Germany's level of per person emissions, the world climate would collapse irrevocably. It is still estimated, however, that global energy use is likely to double in the next few decades, possibly leading to conflicts and – under certain circumstances – to war over access to scarce resources. Similar calculations can be made for nearly all ecologically relevant criteria including industrial production, degree of mobility, standard of consumption and so on.

In order to prevent irreversible damage to, or even the collapse of, the global ecosystem, there would need to be an ecological restructuring of the economies of industrialized countries, and an ecologically sound type of development in the developing countries, which is hardly realizable at a global level without international regulations and implementation instruments. The necessity for the internationalization of environmental politics, however, comes not only from the increasing economic–ecological interdependencies, the complexity of physical–chemical cause-and-effect relationships, the long-term nature of the effects and the possible irreversibility of the damage to the environment, but also and in particular from the large number of political actors, the contradictory nature of their interests, and the differences in their economic and technical capacities. Global or universal environmental problems require a politics that does not release the nation-state from its responsibilities as the traditional primary political actor, but which is beyond its individual capabilities (Simonis, 1998).

From Stockholm to Johannesburg

The UN's involvement with environmental issues affecting the whole of humanity can be seen as a classic case of international agenda-setting. Well before the urgency of the theme was recognized in most member states, at the end of the 1960s the General Assembly was demanding greater attention to be paid to environmental problems. For this purpose, a conference was called, which met in June 1972 in Stockholm and passed a 'Declaration of the Conference on the Human

TABLE 7.3
Main Outcomes of the Rio conference

Major principles adopted	Main institutional outcomes	Main financial outcomes
Sovereign right of states to exploit their resources	Adoption of two treaties: the Convention on Climate Change, and the Convention on Biological Diversity	Commitment by developed countries to commit 0.07 per cent of GNP ratio to foreign assistance by the year 2000
Right of states to develop	Creation of the Commission on Sustainable Development	Agreement to strengthen the Global Environment Facility
Priority of the needs of the less developed countries	Charge to states to produce national reports and action plans for sustainable development	Pledge of developed countries of new financial assistance to less developed countries at a rate of US$607 billion per year to implement the conventions
Responsibility of developed countries for global environmental problems	Integration of non-governmental organizations as partners in sustainable development efforts	
Implementation of Agenda 21 based on principles of universality, democracy, cost-effectiveness and accountability		

Source: Based on discussion in Mingst and Karns (2000, 151).

Environment', including a large number of direction-setting environmental principles, and leading among other things to the founding of the UN Environmental Program (see Chapter 2). Stockholm can be seen as the beginning of an increasing environmental sensitivity on the part of decision-makers in politics, the media and business, even when the growing pressure of the problem itself since the 1970s has contributed to keeping it on the agenda, and when the concrete contributions to a solution lag far behind what the problem requires (on the development of UN environmental politics, see Birnie, 1993; French, 1995; Conca and Dabelko, 1998; Esty, 2002). Twenty years after the Stockholm Declaration, the UN set a new milestone with the UN Conference on Environment and Development (UNCED), which has become a significant reference point for the global political debate on environmental and development issues.

With 178 governments and 1,400 NGOs (with advisory status) taking part, the conference initiated diverse institutional changes in international environmental politics and passed (after two years of preparation) a large number of legally non-binding agreements as guidelines for future work. In the 'Rio Declaration', for the first time, principles for a politics in the interests of future as well as present generations was formulated, and fundamental environmental and development principles were set down. Thus the right to development was reinforced by treaty, the fight against poverty named as a necessary precondition for sustainable development, and the responsibility of the industrialized countries as the source of the main cause of the current environmental damage recognized. The 'Climate Framework Convention' signed by more than 150 states in Rio set a process in motion which attempted through numerous conferences of the signatory states (the sixth conference met in July 2001 in Bonn) to stabilize or reduce the concentration of greenhouse gases in the atmosphere. Furthermore, conventions for the maintenance of bio-diversity, for the prevention of desertification, and for the protection of forests were also set in motion. The central document of the Rio Conference was 'Agenda 21'. This consists of around 800 pages, in forty chapters, and more than 2,000 recommendations for action on the social, ecological and economic problems and challenges of future global development, and 'aspires to be seen as *the* list of duties for the road into the 21st century' (Waldmann, 1999, p. 73).

An important test for the UN's efforts in this area was the Johannesburg summit ('Rio Plus 10 Summit'). The 'World Summit on Sustainable Development' met in late summer of 2002 to take stock of the obligations which the participating states had undertaken ten years earlier in Rio. This mammoth summit – the UN's largest to that point – included more than 21,000 representatives of 191 states, among them 104 heads of state and/or government, 9,000 official delegates, 8,000 NGO representatives and 4,000 journalists. The most important goal was the re-emphasis of the concept of sustainable development. On the agenda, among other things, were the maintenance of fish stocks, protection of the oceans, prohibition of the most dangerous environmental toxins, promotion of non-fossil-fuel sources of energy, and debt relief for the very poorest countries (see Table 7.4). For these purposes, two documents were passed: the 'Johannesburg Declaration', comprised thirty-seven guiding principles which the member states should observe when formulating policies on sustainable development, and the 'Johannesburg Plan of Action', with 153 sections devoted to the environment and development. Once again, the results have been mixed. In the concluding declaration, more than 180 states obligated themselves to implement the comprehensive programme of action passed at the summit and to engage themselves more actively with sustainable development, but whether these efforts will be successful must remain in question, to be viewed in the light of experience.

At the same time, at least the concept of sustainable development has been firmly established in the mind of the world public since Rio. It had in fact been developed long before in expert circles, in particular in the wake of the 'World Commission on Development and Environment' under the chairmanship of the then-prime minister of Norway, Gro Harlem Brundtland, but first found its way into the view of the general public through the work of the UN. In spite of all the weaknesses, stemming primarily from the non-binding nature of the provisions and the insufficient realization of financial promises, Rio and Johannesburg still mark a new phase in international environmental concerns. Since then, 'no nation-state and no national or international organization [can] deny the existence of the

TABLE 7.4
Selected time goals in the Johannesburg plan of action

Target date	Goal
2005	Development of integrated water resource management and water efficiency plans
2005	Reduction by a quarter of the occurrence of HIV in people between 15 and 24 years old
2005	Progress in the formulation of national sustainability strategies and their implementation
2010	Improvement of developing countries' access to alternatives to ozone-damaging substances
2010	Reduction of the present rate of destruction of biological diversity
2012	Creation of protected ocean areas
2015	Reduction by one half the number of people in absolute poverty
2015	Reduction by one half the number of people suffering from hunger
2015	Reduction by one half the number of people with no access to clean drinking water
2015	Reduction by one half the number of people with no access to proper sewage and sanitation
2015	Reduction of the infant mortality rate by two-thirds and the maternal mortality rate by three-quarters
2015	Creation of an opportunity for all children to have a basic education
2020	Improvement of the living conditions for 100 million inhabitants of slums
2022	Access to energy sources for at least 35 per cent of the population of Africa

Source: Adapted from Martens and Sterk (2002, p. 12).

problems being discussed, and above all the relationships between them. Thus, in the future policies may be judged by their compatibility with the recommendations of the Agenda 21' (Waldmann, 1999, p. 80). It would not, however, be the first time in international politics that attractive-sounding agreements commanded little attention in practice.

The Functions of Relevant UN Bodies

Diverse bodies of the UN system are involved with environmental issues. According to the concept of sustainable development, environmental politics is integrated into a broad spectrum of international economic and development politics, and is not the exclusive task of any single institution. This philosophy, however, the so-called 'sectoral approach', often leads paradoxically to the problem that the protection of the environment is often left hanging in the midst of jealous spats among the various groups and contradictory interests (French, 1995, p. 31).

With this limitation, the UN Environmental Programme (UNEP), with its base in Nairobi and offices in other regions, has been the formal central UN organ in the area of environment politics since 1972, although its structure and resources are insufficient for the task. The UNEP often plays the role of driving force or catalyst for the environmental activities of other institutions. It functions as the environmental co-ordinator in the UN system, and also ties in related NGOs. The UNEP is not a specialized agency in the sense of the UN Charter with its own legal personality and membership, but a programme or subsidiary organ of the General Assembly and ECOSOC. An administrative council consisting of fifty-eight states, chosen for four-year terms according to a regional key by the General Assembly, is the highest decision-making organ. The administrative costs are paid out of the regular UN budget; individual projects are usually paid for out of voluntary contributions (in the year 2000, this came to around US$96 million). The purposes of the UNEP are the support of national activities in environmental protection, advising governments on global environmental issues, and the development, evaluation and supervision of global environmental law. Beyond that, there are a number of convention secretariats established within the UNEP. Another important task is the review and registration of data and the creation of reports on the state of the environment.

A second central building-block of UN environment policy is the UN Commission on Sustainable Development (CSD). It was founded at the conclusion of the Rio Conference in December 1992 under Article 68 of the UN Charter. The breadth of the environmental and development tasks addressed in Agenda 21 determines the scope of its competencies. Its treaty-defined purpose is to secure the process following from Rio in the sense of a cross-cutting undertaking, to push forward the integration of environmental and development politics, and to guarantee the implementation of Agenda 21 at national, regional and international levels. The CSD is classified as a functional commission of the ECOSOC; the work of a secretariat is carried out by the Division for Sustainable Development in the Department of Economic and Social Issues in the New York secretariat. The high-ranking representatives of fifty-three states, chosen according to a regional key, meet yearly to set political guidelines for Agenda 21. A certain amount of overlap with the UNEP is impossible to ignore and has been much criticized.

Along with the UNEP, the CSD and the relevant specialized agencies (especially the FAO, IMO, UNESCO, WMO and WHO), there are other subsidiary organs of the UN involved with environmental issues, mainly in monitoring the environmental effects of other projects; among these are UNCTAD and the UNDP. The regional commissions have also integrated environmental issues into their work in the meantime, although with not so much of a global focus. An Inter-Agency Committee on Sustainable Development, comprising representatives of the various UN bodies, is meant to improve co-operation and co-ordination among all UN actors participating in environmental politics – a task congruent with the original function of the UNEP. Not least, the Bretton Woods Organizations have also begun to draw environmental aspects into their work, but that will not be addressed here.

Above and beyond all this, the UN framework also includes many conventions and programmes that have given rise to their own secretariats and offices. Every individual convention needs the ratification of the participating states, and the legal hurdles and regulations in the various conventions are handled very differently. There are also regulations on dispute settlement to be made, implementation to be monitored and compliance to be regulated. Furthermore, a differentiation must be made between framework agreements and protocols. While the former, as soft law, simply lay down general basic principles, concrete duties are usually laid down in the protocols (hard law). This often leads to a great deal of confusion for observers not trained in the law. In the case of climate protection, for example, the UN Framework Convention on Climate Change (UNFCCC) was signed and ratified by 186 states in 1992, but the Kyoto Protocol, containing concrete measures for the reduction of carbon dioxide emissions, was not forthcoming until 1997. The negotiation of a protocol, however, still does not mean that protocol is in fact in force, as the difficult ratification process of the Kyoto Protocol amply demonstrated.

Since no enforcement measures are available in international environmental politics, a few guiding principles have been developed for the conventions:

* They should be conducted in a non-confrontational manner, and conflicts should be avoided to the furthest extent possible;
* Decisions should be transparent, made by the states themselves, and documented by a reporting system; and
* The signatory states themselves should determine which concrete technical and financial measures should be considered necessary for implementation (Loibl, 2001).

Among the most important conventions within the UN framework are the above-mentioned Framework Convention on Climate Change; the Protocol on the Reduction of Greenhouse Gases; the Convention on Biological Diversity; the Convention on International Trade of Endangered Species; the Law of the Sea Convention; the Vienna and Montreal Conventions on protection of the ozone layer; the Convention Against Desertification; and the Forest Agreement. Currently in production is an agreement on soil protection and the problems of water. The secretariats, some of which enjoy a well-developed administrative and scientific base, are located in various cities and states. They administrate and monitor the conventions, and may also establish subsidiary organs for scientific advice and technical support. Furthermore, when necessary they organize conferences of the signatory states, which take place at irregular intervals and are focused on a detailed reworking of the conventions as well as discussions on implementation problems.

International environmental politics is an area rife with failed attempts and missed opportunities, but there have also been positive developments. The model for difficult but finally successful environmental politics on a global level is the so-called 'ozone regime'. At the beginning of the 1970s, evidence was growing that the ozone layer was being damaged by the use of chlorofluorocarbons (CFCs), and that this constituted a serious health risk for human beings. Not least through the studies and conferences that took place under UN auspices, as well as the enduring lobbying of countless NGOs, in 1987, at a conference of the UN Environmental Programme, the Montreal Protocol was signed. This contained a full prohibition – which has been further strengthened since that time – on the use of all the damaging substances. Although the UN has no direct ability to implement norms and is thus far dependent on the goodwill of the signatory states, the concentration of ozone-depleting substances was drastically reduced over the course of the 1990s and beyond, to such an extent that this problem can be considered to be largely solved. All the same, it was an important background condition of this successful agreement that viable alternatives to CFCs existed, and only one branch of industry was hit very hard by the prohibition.

The treatment of the climate problem has been less successful. After the coming into effect of the Climate Framework Convention in 1994, the states-party agreed in 1997 to the Kyoto Protocol, which obliged the industrialized states to bring their total emissions of the most important greenhouse gases down to at least 5 per cent below their 1990 levels, between the years 2008 and 2012. For the fulfilment of this goal of climate control, a very complicated process was developed. The so-called 'clean development mechanism' made it possible for industrialized and developing countries to carry out joint implementation of climate control projects in developing countries. The projects would be financed by the industrialized countries, and the emissions reductions thereby achieved in the developing countries could be credited to the industrialized countries. Furthermore, a certain amount of emissions trade was to be allowed. However, this still extremely minimalist and complicated protocol can come into force only once at least fifty-five states, accounting for at least 55 per cent of the world's emissions have ratified it (on climate control in general, see Oberthür and Ott, 2000).

When the USA declined to ratify the Kyoto Protocol because it believed the provisions would damage its economy too much and did not place enough responsibility on developing countries, it meant that practically all other industrialized countries would have had to ratify the protocol for it to come into effect. In comparison with the original 1997 version, the protocol in fact contains a number of compromises that water down the goal of climate control. So-called 'sinks' (such as forests) are to be reckoned more strongly as users of carbon dioxide, and the trade in emissions to be interpreted more broadly, than was originally planned. The actual reduction of greenhouse gases is thus much less than the UN experts regard as the necessary level for the stabilization of the world climate. Even though the number of states required was long since reached, the necessary level of total emissions has not yet been reached because Russia has also declined to ratify. Thus the protocol's coming into effect remains in doubt. Furthermore, it has become clear that it took a full decade, from the first agreements on climate control in 1992, to even produce noticeable concrete measures at the international level. In view of the urgency of the problem, this is an unacceptably long period of time. Of course, none of this should hinder any state from taking speedier and more drastic measures at a national level than is possible with 200 states all at once.

TABLE 7.5
The difficult road to climate control

Conference	Results
Rio de Janeiro 1992	At the World Summit for Environment and Development, the Framework Convention on Climate Control was created as a basis in international law basis for international climate control. It came into effect in 1994, and had been ratified by 186 states by 2001
Berlin and Geneva 1995 and 1996	The first two conferences of states-party tried in vain to reach agreement on a binding timeline with concrete goals for reductions
Kyoto 1997	At the third conference of states-party, the industrialized states committed themselves to reducing their emissions by the year 2012 to 5 per cent below their 1990 levels. Specific reduction goals for individual states were also laid down
Buenos Aires 1998	At the fourth conference of states-party, a timeline for future meetings was agreed upon
Bonn 1999	At the fifth conference of states-party, a system for the review and monitoring of greenhouse gases was discussed
The Hague 2000	The sixth conference of states-party ended without agreement on the important questions, and the conference was postponed until 2001
Bonn 2001	The question of monitoring remained open despite 180 states agreeing to a compromise
Marrakesh 2001	At the seventh conference, further compromises were negotiated in detail
New Delhi 2002	The eighth conference produced agreement on, among other things, rules for trade of CO_2 emissions among developing countries.

Source: Data from conference concluding communiqués.

Financing of the UN's Environmental Politics

Alongside the project resources of the specialized agencies, subsidiary organs, programmes and individual agreements, an important financial tool for environmental protection projects was founded in 1991 through a common initiative by the World Bank, the UNDP and the UNEP: the Global Environment Facility (GEF). The means (which are not meant to replace those of any of the existing financing programmes, but rather to supplement them) are used for the protection of environmental global public goods, such as climate control, the ozone layer, international waters, bio-diversity and the soil. The GEF's means are thus available exclusively for global environmental protection; projects with only local or regional significance are not supported. Since a fundamental reform in 1994, the GEF has been an independent body with a general assembly, council and secretariat (which is supervised administratively by the World Bank). The decision-making structures are complicated and are the result of an admixture of UN principles (one land, one vote) and Bretton Woods principles (one dollar, one vote – see Table 7.2). The 165 member states meet every three years as a general assembly and choose a council of thirty-two states (sixteen developing countries, fourteen OECD countries and two countries in transition), which then decides, on consensus when possible, on how to distribute the finances. In case of disagreement, a majority is formed when 60 per cent of the countries also representing 60 per cent of the contributions are in agreement. The GEF has around US$700 million available to it every year.

Environmental Politics in the UN: The Balance Sheet

In spite of close to 900 bilateral and multilateral environmental treaties, the global situation continues to get worse. This is where the UN's work in environmental politics comes into the picture. It neither wants to, nor can, solve every environmental problem there is, and is not intended to replace bilateral or regional agreements, to say nothing of national efforts at environmental improvements. Rather, it is meant to concentrate on strategically important aspects with global significance, and to offer a forum for the handling of environmental issues.

As in other political areas, the balance sheet here comes out neither as uniformly positive nor entirely negative. This is in part because problems have become far more urgent in recent years, and the UN does not possess the means to rectify the environmental sins of its member states. If all the declarations of principle and self-inflicted obligations the states have given or undertaken under UN auspices were in fact observed and implemented, the global environmental situation would have to have shown improvement by now. That this has clearly not been the case is demonstrated in part by the great need of the UN to reform its environmental politics. Just as in the area of protection of human rights, it is not a lack of norms and conventions that is the problem, but rather a lack of effective instruments for their implementation. Just as in the area of development, in UN environmental politics there is 'a dilemma between the capacities and the duties undertaken' (Mingst and Karns, 2000, p. 153). Increasingly, criticism is also falling on the UN mammoth conferences (Martens and Sterk, 2002, p. 11). The model of consensus-orientated multilateralism appears to have reached its limits at the very latest with the Johannesburg summit, but as yet no alternative to this type of political co-operation has been developed.

In any case, the UN has performed an important service in linking the issues of environmental protection and development co-operation in the public consciousness. Global environmental problems require a global negotiating framework, which, given the state of affairs, can be provided only by the United Nations. At the same time, the institutional fragmentation and lack of co-ordination among the various UN bodies has been criticized strongly. One possibility for improvement lies in an increase in the efficiency and co-ordination of the already-existing bodies.

Whether such a minimalist strategy is sufficient to improve the effectiveness of the existing institutional system of international environmental and development politics is, however, in doubt. What might make more sense in this perspective could be institutional proposals, such as the founding of an environmental security council or of an international environmental court. Also under discussion is the creation of a new specialized agency: the World Organization for Environment and Development, which would bind the existing agencies (the UNEP, CSD and the various relevant convention secretariats) into a new organizational structure.

Further Reading

Agenda for Development (1997) New York UN-Document (A/Res/51/240).

Conca, Ken and Geoffrey D. Dabelko (1998) *Green Planet Blues: Environmental Politics from Stockholm to Kyoto*, Boulder, CO: Westview Press.

Esty, Daniel (ed.) (2002) *Global Environmental Institutions. Perspectives on Reform*, London: Royal Institute of International Affairs.

Glanzer, Hans-Peter (2001) 'An Agenda for Development', in Franz Cede and Lilly Sucharipa-Behrmann (eds), *The United Nations: Law and Practice*, The Hague: Kluwer, pp. 215–30.

Grunberg, Isabelle (ed.) (2000) *The United Nations Development Dialogue: Finance Trade, Poverty, Peace-building*, Tokyo: UNU Press.

Kaul, Inge, Isabelle Grunberg and Marc A. Stern (eds) (1999) *Global Public Goods. International Cooperation in the 21st Century*, New York: Oxford University Press.

Malone, David M. and Lotta Hagman (2002) 'The North–South Divide at the United Nations: Fading at Last?', *Security Dialogue* (4), pp. 399–415.

Righter, Rosemary (1995) *Utopia Lost. The United Nations and World Order*, New York: Twentieth Century Fund Press.

United Nations Development Program, *Human Development Report*, New York (published annually): Oxford University Press.

Urquhart, Brian (2000) 'Between Sovereignty and Globalization – Where Does the United Nations Fit In?', *Development Dialogue* (1–2), pp. 5–14.

World Commission on Environment and Development (1987) *Our Common Future*, Oxford: Oxford University Press.

8

Reforms for the Twenty-first Century

The dramatic changes in international politics, along with the obvious weaknesses and insufficiencies of the United Nations itself, have given the theme of reform a prominent place on the international agenda. UN reform is a constant issue in political, and political science, debates. If the international community were to found the entire organization anew tomorrow, according to Secretary-General Kofi Annan (Annan 2000: no. 352), 'it would certainly look different from the organization we have today'.

The question of whether and how the United Nations is to be reformed must be answered first and foremost by the member states, as only they have the power to implement changes. In that sense, the UN is still a classical inter-governmental organization, meaning that it can act only in so far as the member states allow after the weighing of their own interests. At the same time, however, demands are placed increasingly on the UN to fill a political gap in the globalized world community, and it is precisely this contradiction between the real capabilities of the organization and the often far too ambitious expectations placed upon it that creates a climate of over-extension.

Thus are reflected in practice the theoretical understandings of the function and structure of international relations that were addressed in Chapter 2. For the Realists, the UN plays a subordinate role, and attempts at reform will largely exhaust themselves in a negligible raising of the organization's efficiency. Institutionalists and Idealists, on the other hand, see a realistic opportunity with a fundamentally-reformed world organization to create and stabilize an international milieu in which conflicts are not resolved through force, and co-operation takes place according to rules made in the long-term interests of all participants.

In practice, efforts at reform appear modest. A distinction must be made between internal reform of the organization's by-laws, which can be achieved without amending the Charter, and 'constitutional changes', which would require changes to the Charter. The hurdles in the way of the latter are extremely high. Many of the themes that have been under discussion for years have been postponed and put on the back burner because of these hurdles. Thus, some of the suggested reforms appear as regularly as clockwork on the agendas of diverse working

TABLE 8.1
Typology of suggested reforms

Increased efficiency	Institutional reforms	Fundamental changes
Reforms aim at greater capability and more effectiveness in the classical central responsibility	Reforms aims at institutional remodelling and adjustment to new challenges	Reforms aim at basic and fundamental remodelling of the current principles on which the UN is founded and on which it operates
(Example: rationalization in administrative and financial areas)	(Example: reform of the Security Council, creation of new panels such as, for example, a World Environment Organization)	(Example: lifting of the prohibition on intervention in domestic affairs; supra-nationalization of the UN)

Source: Based on discussion in Unser (2003, pp. 395–405).

groups of the General Assembly and Security Council, without any consensus ever being achieved (see Table 8.1).

In his report on reforms to the Millennium Summit in the autumn of 2000, Secretary-General Kofi Annan argued that the member states needed to reorganize the UN so that it could better meet the challenges of globalization. He named specifically three strategic goals as having the highest priority: 'Freedom from Want' (development agenda), 'Freedom from Fear' (security agenda), and 'Sustaining our Future' (environmental agenda). Although the General Assembly – meeting for only the second time in its history at the level of heads of state and government – was able to accept the report by consensus, it remains unclear how these very ambitious goals are to be realized. Two years after the publication of the Millennium Report, in September 2002, the Secretary-General evaluated the reforms that had been completed and those that were still outstanding. Much had been accomplished, he said, but further changes were necessary. According to Annan (2002a; p. 33), the 'critical criterion for success in a world in rapid flux is the ability to manage change'. Without basic reform of the UN carried out through the member states, the realization of these goals will be very difficult indeed.

Reform as a Long and Difficult Process

The UN's history has been a process of constant change and reform. Within this time-span, the world saw both the beginning and the end of the Cold War, and the completion of the process of decolonization, which not only increased the number of UN members, but also created new challenges for the organization in the management of relations between north and south. New global questions, such as the scarcity of natural resources, destruction of the environment, the changing climate, the rapidly increasing population, weapons of mass destruction, and new threats to peace from internal conflict crowded in upon the classical risks and problems that had been recognized and anticipated at the UN's founding.

Through all of this, the UN has shown itself to be an integrative organization capable of development and adaptation. Along with the gradual realization of its claims to universality with its increasing member rolls, it also accrued enlarged competencies and capacities to deal with these new challenges. At the same time, the UN limited its learning and reform processes largely to the expansion of existing panels and the creation of increasing numbers of subsidiary organs, programmes and specialized agencies. Thus the mechanism the founders had regarded consciously as an ordering principle of the organization slowly slipped out of control. The UN was meant to be constructed as a sort of 'solar system', whose core organization was meant to co-ordinate a rather loose web of institutions and organizations in pursuit of effective co-operation. The core organization would have the aggregate wisdom of the entire system at its disposal, be able to formulate comprehensive strategies, and then to implement these in an agreed fashion (Childers and Urquhart, 1994, p. 14 et seq.).

What this original concept underestimated was the centrifugal force of such a system, resulting from the divergent interests of individual states and groups of states, which led to extensive autonomy for the specialized agencies, as well as a growing consciousness of independence on the part of other subsidiary organs. The result was a UN system in which both vertical co-ordination and horizontal co-operation were extremely difficult, and whose available potential could not be used to anything like its full extent. The impotence caused by the East–West conflict worked for a long time to conceal the underlying dysfunction of this inflationary organizational development, as well as strengthening the states and blocs in their own activities. The essential absence of the Security Council as the powerful, decision-making centre of the UN led to an increased significance for the General Assembly, in which the developing countries of the 'Third World' held a majority. For these newly-emerged states, the General Assembly was the decisive forum for a formally equal articulation of their interests and affairs. Their striving towards the creation of new institutions to deal with the specific problems of developing countries was supported in the end by both great powers and their blocs for a common purpose: the newly-created panels were appropriate in a probationary capacity for the diversion of the developing countries' demands for greater participation and fairness into an institutional activism which could not bring the basic structure of the global balance of power into question. A discussion of reforms that would reach deep into the fundamental principles and new tasks of the organization as well as a new structuring of its instruments and procedures did not take place.

This situation changed with the end of the Cold War, as the UN began in a large number of areas to exchange its role as a forum for the community of states for one as an actor in international politics. In view of the Security Council's newly-won capacity to act, and of the organization's emerging structural deficiencies, a debate sprang up in which two different directions for suggested reform could be distinguished:

(i)   The members of the Non-Aligned Movement (NAM), more than a hundred states primarily drawn from the group of developing countries, were forced to recognize the weakening of their influence following the re-emergence of the Security Council. Therefore, since the beginning of the 1990s, they have pushed harder than ever for greater opportunities to participate in the essential decision-making processes of the organization, as well as for more extensive consultation in the Bretton Woods Organizations, which are still completely dominated by the industrialized countries (Saksena, 1993; South Center, 1996); and

(ii)   The industrialized states, and above all the USA, continued to criticize the UN's lack of effectiveness, and to demand more streamlined, transparent and cost-effective structures. The effectiveness argument was quickly indicted by developing countries as being nothing but a cover for the instrumentalization of the UN for the pursuit of the industrialized countries' interests (Bourantonis, 1998).

The key-words 'participation' and 'effectiveness' have developed in the course of this discussion into mutually exclusive demands. In the USA more than anywhere else, in the mid-1990s, the UN became the 'whipping-boy of politics'. It is complained on New York's East River that UN-bashing is all too popular. The organization developed over decades of co-operation – not least that of the USA itself – now found itself to be the object of pointed criticism. It was described as an institutional jungle, a ponderous apparatus with a personnel strength that was too big, and incompetent to boot, trapped in ossified structures and anachronistic working procedures, throwing the money of its member states around in a totally irresponsible fashion. The USA's prescription for overcoming these problems was for the organization to concentrate on its original core areas of responsibility in international peacekeeping, and to reduce the size of its entire apparatus. The US attempted, by withholding its contributions to the regular budget as well as to the peacekeeping missions' budgets, to force the UN into some of the reforms it considered to be necessary. Behind the institutional scolding, however, was the remaining superpower's unconcealed retreat from multilateralism as an organizing mechanism of international relations. The consensus forming the basis of the United Nations, that global problems were to be solved together through the setting aside of individual national interests, began to be questioned, and the 'Wilsonian utterances' were confronted by a neo-realist renaissance of the ascendancy of the nation-state (Eban, 1995, p. 50). Ives-Marie Laulan (1996, p. 51) compared the United Nations with the corpse of one who has died of an illness: it can no longer be healed, only reborn in some other form.

The suggestions for reform coming from more institutionally-oriented experts, who want to overcome the constructed contradiction between 'participation' and 'effectiveness' (Childers and Urqhart, 1994; Kennedy and Russett, 1995;

Weizsäcker and Quereshi, 1995), were not able to be pushed through. These proposals began from the assumption that the member states had both the political will and the endurance to discuss and come to a conclusion on a systematic reform of the world organization. Such a procedure would begin with an analysis of the global challenges and the addressing of a few basic questions about the ordering of the international system (Russett, 1996, p. 261 et seq.):

- To what degree can the states be expected to allow the erosion of their sovereignty for the sake of collective mechanisms?
- How far do states hold themselves to commonly-agreed-upon determinations, and what level of violation, non-observation or lack of support is acceptable?
- How can power and law be brought into a balanced relationship with each other, and conflicting interests be resolved in a constructive manner?
- What do global governance processes look like with states, international organizations, NGOs and the global economy as central actors?

With these questions in mind, it would have been conceivable to produce a completely new institutional design for a 'world organization of the third generation' (Bertrand and Warner, 1996), and to give its organs the necessary competencies given the internal structures and modes of work. However, the international political situation in the 1990s – unlike that in 1945 – offered no framework in which the creation from the ground up of a new world organization could have been successful. In 1945, a significantly smaller community of states was sharing common suffering after the trauma of two destructive world wars. However unwillingly, these states recognized that it would be both necessary and appropriate to give up some rights of sovereignty and accept the privileges of a small group of powers in order to avoid a third catastrophe. The global problems of the 1990s, in contrast, were far too abstract and multi-faceted to provide the pressure necessary for unity on the questions of a new orientation for the organization and a new formulation for the Charter.

Against the backdrop of many fundamental disagreements on the future form and function of the United Nations, it is hardly surprising that the ideas for comprehensive reform have remained rather vague. That *some* reform is necessary is agreed on unanimously. After six decades, it is admitted on all sides that both the Charter and the Organization as a whole are in need of a thorough overhaul:

- Many of the Charter's provisions have shown themselves to be impossible to implement (such as portions of Chapter VII, for example), or have become obsolete (such as the enemy state clauses);
- New areas of activity such as crisis prevention, environmental protection and population issues are either addressed inadequately in the Charter or not mentioned at all;
- The composition of the Security Council with regard to the permanent members reflects the situation at the end of the Second World War, and with regard to the number of non-permanent members, the situation of the organization at the beginning of the 1960s;

- The veto is increasingly regarded as discriminatory and no longer justified in its function;
- One of the principal organs – the Trusteeship Council – has suspended its work because of a lack of areas needing supervision;
- The work of the General Assembly is complicated and labour-intensive, while the role of the ECOSOC continues to lose importance; and,
- Effective co-ordination of the whole system, with its committees within committees and redundancy, is hardly possible.

In its diversity, in its many subsidiary organs and specialized agencies, in its funds and programmes and highly complex structure, the UN reflects the disjointed wills of its member states, which are so often influenced by trends and particular interests. Attempts to introduce basic administrative reform are certainly motivated by the desire to lessen overlapping jurisdictions, redundancy and waste of resources. The system, despite this dense web, is highly fragmented. The various state foreign ministries are responsible for the formulation of instructions for the permanent delegations at the UN headquarters in New York. At the same time, the delegations working with the subsidiary bodies and specialized agencies receive their orders from the relevant Departments. What this can sometimes lead to is a situation in which a member state may be demanding cut-backs in the General Assembly while its delegations in individual sub-organs are insisting on an increase in spending. Thus one may hear the admonition from the foreign ministries that co-ordination must begin at home.

What is common to all the requirements for reform mentioned here so far is that the measures to implement them can only be agreed upon and implemented by the member states themselves. While the operating procedures in the main bodies and several co-ordination problems could be addressed easily through new provisions in the relevant by-laws or through resolutions, the majority of the important reforms would require revision of the Charter. However, Articles 108 and 109, which deal with the amendment process, deliberately set very high hurdles for such changes. Every amendment needs a two-thirds majority in the General Assembly, plus the ratification of two-thirds of the member states, including all five permanent members. The permanent five thus enjoy a blocking minority and can prevent any reform. By the same token, for any of their own projects to succeed they would need the agreement of more than 120 UN members. In view of this complicated procedure and the uncertainty of its results, even completely uncontroversial changes, such as the elimination of the enemy-state clauses, have been left undone. The overwhelming fear is that such initiatives might be linked to currently insoluble issues such as the veto privilege. In this continuing situation, prognoses on the chances of realizing central intentions such as reform of the Security Council are purely negative. The reform process may thus progress only by smaller steps, and must remain limited to measures that lie within the competence of the General Assembly or the Secretary-General.

That such small steps, when added together, may indeed create substantial changes is demonstrated by the structural measures taken during Kofi Annan's term of office – both in the Secretariat itself and in the UN system as a whole. The General Assembly, too, achieved an important step in placing the UN's finances on a new basis in December 2000 after years of extremely difficult negotiations, thus paving the way out of one of its most pressing crises. We shall first address these successful attempts at reform before we analyse the issue of still-unrealized Security Council reforms. Following that, the options for reform and various perspectives on them will be examined in the three areas of peace-maintenance, protection of human rights, and economics, development and environment. Finally, we shall look into the question of the role of the UN in the international politics of the twenty-first century.

Institutional Reforms

When the USA used its veto to prevent the re-election of then-Secretary-General Boutros-Ghali on 19 November 1996, it based this step primarily on the grounds that he had proved incapable of reforming the UN apparatus. In fact, the first signs of successful streamlining and modernization of the management and labour structures were already becoming visible during Boutros-Ghali's term of office.

The changes made in the Department of Peacekeeping Operations have already been discussed. Beyond that, in the Secretariat as a whole, 2,500 positions were cut, yearly spending increases were halted, and a new Integrated Management Information System was introduced to facilitate a networked, computer-supported personnel-, issue- and budget-administration. Through a new Performance Appraisal System (PAS) for the better evaluation of individual performance, an important impetus was given to the organization's long-neglected human resources management, which is especially dependent on the quality and motivation of the personnel. The rather opaque acquisitions body of the UN administration was reorganized and made more cost-conscious. Finally, in summer of 1994, at the instigation of the Secretary-General, the General Assembly created the Office of Internal Oversight Services (OIOS) with an Inspector-General at its head, through which the UN was to be subjected to an effective internal review for the first time (on these measures, see Paschke, 1996).

That these first steps did not enjoy early success cannot be surprising in view of the UN's personnel composition and decades-long development. Corresponding to its membership structure, the UN's international civil service includes officers from more than 170 states, whose qualifications, mentalities and understanding of public service are extremely different: 'To develop the streamlined management culture of a business undertaking [in such a] multicultural environment is a thing of pure impossibility' (Paschke, 1996, p. 42). Efficiency thus cannot be understood in a pure sense of economic rationality. Above all, through the General Assembly and the Security Council, the member states convey to the Secretariat and its subsidiary organs sometimes unclear and sometimes completely contradictory mandates, and use the existing regulations to micromanage the Secretariat's various Departments (Paschke, 1999, pp. 189 et seq). Added to all this, the financial crises produced by states' refusal or failure to deliver the required contributions do not create a friendly climate for self-renewal.

However, the Secretariat could indeed have done more to prove its capacity for reform. Boutros-Ghali's successor, Kofi Annan, who entered office under a great deal of pressure to reform, was able to reorganize the Secretariat as early as March 1997, by assigning to each of the Departments as well as some of the subsidiary organs and programmes run by the Secretariat one of the five core tasks of the United Nations. For each of the fields of Peace and Security, Economic and Social Issues, Humanitarian Affairs, and Development, so-called Executive Committees were formed; the area of Human Rights Protection was designated to cut across – and thus touch upon – all of the other four areas. In his reform programme for the renewal of the UN, presented in July 1997, the Secretary-General came up with a list of decisions which altogether amounted to a 'quiet revolution' (Mingst and Karns, 2000, p. 208). Along with an abundance of suggestions for his own areas of competence, Annan gave recommendations to the member states and offered his thoughts on how the system as a whole might be better managed and directed. The only thing missing from the programme was reform of the Security Council.

With this programme, Kofi Annan drew the member states into the circle of responsibility for realizing the suggestions he had made, which – considering the fate of his predecessor – must be considered a very courageous move. The steps for which he himself could take responsibility were quickly put into practice once the General Assembly had approved his suggestions for administrative reform (Resolution 52/12A, 12 November 1997). For the realization of a new leadership and management culture, a 29-member (as of March 2004) Senior Management Group (SMG) was created – a sort of cabinet chaired by the Secretary-General, to which belong the convenors of the Executive Committees as well as other senior managers of the UN system. A Strategic Planning Unit consisting of five experts was created to be the personal labour staff of the Secretary-General, for the purpose of anticipating global trends and approaching challenges. The Office of the High Commissioner for Human Rights was strengthened by its integration into the UN Centre for Human Rights, and a new Department for Disarmament and Arms Control was formed in the Secretariat. A further reduction of the Secretariat's personnel by 1,000 posts, as well as a 5 per cent reduction of the budget, rounded out this reform package.

Of Annan's recommendations to the General Assembly, two were passed in full in Resolution 52/12B of 19 December 1997: first, the office of a Deputy Secretary-General was created, and the Canadian diplomat Louise Fréchette took office in the spring of 1998. The Deputy Secretary-General relieves the Secretary-General of much of the administrative work. Second, a Development Account was created, into which the internal savings were to flow as a 'development dividend'. One suggestion the General Assembly did not choose to implement was the supplementary financing of the UN's running costs through a 'revolving credit fund'. The Secretary-General had envisioned this fund to be one where the member states paid in voluntary contributions, which the UN could then borrow. Security was to be had through the open requirements for contributions to the regular budget and to the peacekeeping missions. Equally unsuccessful were the Secretary-General's attempts to streamline the General Assembly's agenda through a concentration on yearly themes of global importance, the reduction of the Secretariat's workload through the automatic expiration of mandates that had not been formally renewed (the 'sunset clause'), and the reintroduction of the original division of labour among the main bodies, through which the General Assembly's accrual of influence over the daily work-order of the Secretariat would have been reduced.

In the reforms accomplished at the close of the 1990s – and above all in those which were not accomplished and in some cases not even attempted – a clear pattern emerges: the Secretariat and its sub-bodies have shown themselves both ready for and capable of substantial reform in order to adjust their competencies and capacities to new challenges. The member states, in contrast, still lack the capacity to reach a consensus on those areas of reform for which their agreement is absolutely indispensable (Paschke, 1999, p. 190).

Finance Reform

The only success that the member states may chalk up to themselves over the past several years was the reorganization of the contributions scale for the regular budget and the peacekeeping activities. In December 2000, after years of the most harrowing negotiations (Koschorreck, 2000), a solution was found that took into account both the USA's wish to reduce its contributions and the realistic financial capacities of the poorest countries. The spectrum of contributions ranges from 0.001 per cent of the programme budget, which was a total of US$14,360 in 2004, to the 22 per cent that the USA is obliged to provide. The contributions must be paid on time, in full, and without preconditions. While the whole UN system enjoys a yearly budget of around US$10 billion, there is a gross disparity between the responsibilities placed on the UN and the member states' willingness to mobilize the necessary financial resources. The UN suffers considerably for the want of outstanding contributions. In August 2003, for example, only ninety-eight states had paid their contributions for the year in full. The only sanctioning instrument the Charter offers the organization in this area is found in Article 19: that states which owe the UN more than two full years' worth of contributions lose their right to vote in the General Assembly. Since contributions to peacekeeping missions are not included in that provision, and the most notorious debtors tend to keep their debts just under the critical limit and make last-minute payments, this sanction has shown its effectiveness to be less than impressive. In March 2004, twenty-four of the poorer countries were in arrears under the terms of Article 19, although eight of them were granted temporary voting rights by a GA resolution anyway.

One way out of the permanent financial crisis that has been discussed is the creation of a reserve fund that would provide funds quickly if needed. Other ideas tend in the direction of a kind of 'world tax' for the UN, which might be paid on arms spending, foreign exchange transactions, or the use of space or the oceans. The so-called Tobin tax (after James Tobin, the Nobel Prizewinner for Economics) on international currency transactions could, if levied at only 0.5 per cent on these primarily speculative transactions, lead to an income of several billion dollars. The refusal to co-operate of important member states, however, leaves such a plan with no real chance for realization, as shown by the fate of the Secretary-General's comparatively modest suggestion of a revolving credit fund. The UN will simply continue to have to appeal to the member states to take their payment obligations more seriously.

The contributions for peacekeeping operations are in addition to those for the regular budget, and for these a roster with ten categories has been developed by which the poorest and the very poor member states enjoy differentiated rebates of up to 90 per cent of their contributions (for details see A/RES/55/235). On the one hand, this agreement has had lasting significance for the stabilization of UN finances, not least from the perspective of the USA's readiness to make a reliable settlement of its liabilities. But on the other hand, such an agreement is more of an exception – the general rule being the member states' inability to reach compromises on the essential issues of the organization's future. A perfect example of this rule is the question of the modernization of the Security Council, which has been floating around unresolved for years.

Reforming the Security Council

The modernization of the most important main body of the UN constitutes one of the organization's greatest challenges, and is thus also a decisive test of its capacity for comprehensive reform of any kind. In this task, all the difficulties and obstacles of institutional remodelling are collected together in microcosm. Article 23 of the Charter states that the Security Council shall consist of five (specifically named) permanent members and ten non-permanent members chosen according to the principle of equitable geographical distribution. The non-permanent members are chosen by the General Assembly for a term of two years, and may not serve two consecutive terms. This article was changed once in 1963, when the 28th General Assembly recommended that the number of non-permanent members be raised from six to ten. The Article 108 amendment process took a surprisingly short two years, and the change came into effect in 1965. With this change, the UN indicated that the size and composition of the Security Council should keep pace, at least to some extent, with the increasing total membership of the organization. Whereas in 1965 this number stood at 115, it had grown to 191 by 2004, and there have been constant initiatives since the 1970s to further increase the numbers of non-permanent members. Such efforts have continued to be sidelined.

With regard to the permanent members, there have been two changes. In 1971, the People's Republic of China replaced the Republic of China (Taiwan) both as a member of the UN and in the permanent seat on the Security Council. In December 1991, the permanent representative of the Russian Federation communicated to the Secretary-General that his country would be replacing the dissolved Soviet Union in the General Assembly and the Security Council. Although the Soviet Union is named specifically in Article 23 as a permanent member, both the

General Assembly and the other permanent members accepted this simplified rule of succession without changing the Charter.

Furthermore, with the renewed effectiveness of the Security Council in the post-Cold War era, energetic noises came both from important financial contributors (such as Japan and Germany) as well as the Non-Aligned Movement, that the Security Council's composition, decisional mechanisms and operating procedures (which had remained unchanged since the provisional rules of procedure from 1946), should be altered. In contrast to earlier initiatives, these attempts aimed not only at the addition of more non-permanent members, but also at changes to the permanent members' circle. The privileges that the permanent members enjoy through their permanent representation and veto right are no longer considered appropriate to the times. As understandable and sensible as this elevated position for a few states may have been in the year 1945 and during the Cold War, the constellation seems less appropriate half a century later. The massive developments of the last few decades, the end of the Cold War, the process of decolonization and the appearance of new states, have created a new global order to which the power distribution in the Security Council no longer corresponds. New political groupings have emerged, and new forms and centres of conflict have arisen. Africa and Latin America, however, continue to lack any representation among the permanent members, and the entire Asiatic region is represented by only one country – the People's Republic of China.

At the 47th General Assembly, India proposed a resolution for the reform of the Security Council, which the General Assembly passed in November 1992. In it, it was determined that the 48th General Assembly should concern itself with a comprehensive discussion of this issue. The Secretary-General was given the task of requesting written statements from the member states to serve as a starting-point for the debate. Initially, in the summer of 1993, there were fifty more-or-less constructive suggestions for the future size and composition, decision-making structures and operational procedures of the Council. Eventually, the number of suggestions grew to 140. Following a rather short first discussion, in the autumn of 1993 the General Assembly delegated the negotiation of proposals as well as the further reform work to a working group created specifically for the purpose and open to all member states.

The very diverse proposals coming from the member states cannot possibly be addressed in full here (see Kühne and Baumann, 1995). Neither can the working group's reports, which essentially communicate the general helplessness to be expected from a situation where all possible arguments are put forward, but no decisions can be made. Instead, we shall attempt to sketch out the lines along which some compromise appears possible, and to discuss the most prominent obstacles. This discussion will be based on a proposal made by the President of the 51st General Assembly, Razali Ismail from Malaysia, on 20 March 1997 in his function as the president of the working group (Press Release GA/9228). His initiative was planned to be included in December 1997 in a framework resolution of the General Assembly on Security Council reform, but this was prevented by a small group of states under Italy's leadership. In spite of its initial failure, this proposal can still be regarded as the basic model for Security Council reform most likely to meet with real success.

According to this suggestion, the Council should be expanded by a further five permanent and four non-permanent members, to reach a total strength of twenty-four. The new permanent members should include two industrialized states as well as one representative of the developing countries from each of the African, Asian and Latin American–Caribbean regions. The four new non-permanent member seats should be dedicated to one African, one Asian, one Latin-Caribbean and one Eastern European state. The five new permanent members should be chosen together, in order to avoid a so-called quick fix – that is, the rapid inclusion of a smaller number of new permanent members. With respect to the veto, it was suggested that the new permanent members should not enjoy that right, and that the original permanent five should begin to use it less and less frequently. Razali Ismail's idea accords with the state of the discussion both in the UN bodies and among the member states themselves. With respect to increasing the number of non-permanent members, the USA has in the meantime given up its objection that an overly-large Council will be incapable of making any decisions at all.

On the veto issue, the proposal makes concessions to the current political and legal realities. The provisions of Article 27 that form the basis for the veto can be changed only by changing the Charter, which would require the ratification of all five permanent members. It can hardly be expected that the permanent five will willingly give up their most important privilege. It is equally not to be expected that they will want to share this right with other states. Furthermore, the admission of even more veto players into the Security Council would make the already diffi-cult process of interest-balancing into one of practical impossibility. On the other hand, the creation of a third member category of permanent members without a veto would also lead to status and prestige problems, which could have negative effects on the Council's work. If the ideal solution of a complete abolition of the individual veto and the introduction of a quorum that would make it impossible for a substantial minority to be outvoted by the majority simply cannot be achieved, then the 'second-best' Razali solution should be given preference over the status quo.

There is widespread belief in the necessity for reform, and there has been a great deal of convergence in various state positions in recent years. Nevertheless, the realization of most of these reforms is still nowhere in sight. This is primarily because of two still-unanswered questions. First, there has been no agreement on which states should become the new permanent members. While Japan seems to be widely accepted as the choice for the Asian group, a number of nations from the Western European and Other States group, under the leadership of Italy, have set themselves against a permanent seat for Germany. They fear a relative weakening of their own influence in Europe as well as in international politics if Germany is allowed entry to the exclusive club. The situation in the other three state groups remains thoroughly unclear. The further permanent seat for Asia is being fought over energetically by India, Pakistan and Indonesia, while Brazil, Argentina and Mexico tussle over the seat for Latin America. In Africa, the ambitions of Egypt,

Nigeria and South Africa must all be taken into account. Because, on purely domestic political grounds, none of these states can afford to give up its struggle for a permanent seat, no end to this discussion is in sight. Germany's suggestion of rotating several countries from a particular region through a permanent seat could conceivably be accepted by the African, Asian and Latin-American countries only if the two seats for industrialized countries were also subjected to the rotation principle. However, when states that co-operate as closely with one another as those in the EU cannot agree on a rotation principle because of divergent interests and status, it is hardly likely that other state groups will manage it.

The second, and perhaps even more serious problem, is that of the veto. The 1997 line of compromise, first to have a two-step process of expansion and then further discussion of a modification or abolition of the right of veto, appears to have been destroyed by the 'all-or-nothing' position taken by the developing countries. Their stance is understandable when one considers that the point of reform is to deconstruct current forms of discrimination. On the other hand, two-step reform can be seen as the lesser of two evils when it is compared to the status quo in which only the permanent five have the privilege of both permanent representation and veto.

Reform of the Security Council remains vital for the continued acceptance of its authority and the legitimacy of its decisions. This was shown by the Kosovo crisis in 1998–9, when the blockade of the Security Council by the threats of Russian and Chinese vetoes led NATO to simply bypass the Council altogether and take military action. The Iraq dispute of 2002–3 underscored this necessity once again. In a rule-based system of international politics, and above all in a collective security system, in which states make decisions with far-reaching consequences and existential significance for other countries, it is essential that the exercise of power be limited and brought under control (Fassbender, 1998a, 1998b). Even without a right of veto, states with permanent representation on the Security Council can exercise more influence over decisions than non-permanent members, and contribute to a broader basis of acceptance for such decisions. Even the possibilities of encouraging the current permanent five to limit their use of the veto voluntarily (Fischer, 1999) would be more nuanced and realistic coming from a permanent member than from any other member state. However, the fear remains that in the wake of the Iraq debate, any reform of the Security Council will be impossible for a long time. While the right of veto once more demonstrated its problematic side, the five holders of it will now cling to it even more insistently. Hopes that the USA might contribute to a strengthening of the Security Council through active co-operation in reform now seem completely illusory. Reform of the Security Council must be considered postponed until further notice.

Reform of the General Assembly

In comparison to the discussion of the modernization of the Security Council, considerations of how to improve the General Assembly are rather on the sidelines of the mainstream reform debates. Although the General Assembly did indeed gain influence during the Cold War, it still does not really play a central role. Article 14 merely makes it possible for the Assembly to recommend measures for the peaceful resolution of any situation which it considers likely to have a negative impact on peaceful international coexistence. In practice, however, all peace-maintenance activities are decided on by the Security Council. Doubts have been expressed as to whether this procedure is effective. Ernst-Otto Czempiel argues (1995, p. 42) that the leading role of the Security Council seems much more efficient than it in fact is. The decisive medium of the United Nations is co-operation, but it cannot be forced; it must be nurtured. The General Assembly, with its many committees, is a far more appropriate instrument for that, Czempiel claims. In it, 'the political consciousness of the world' is formed and articulated. The votes of the General Assembly as the 'public opinion of the world' constitute a sort of global legitimacy, and the hope is that it would increase the legitimacy and acceptance of UN decisions if they were taken by a General Assembly with a much enhanced status.

That said, the General Assembly in its current form is hardly the democratic counterpart to the Security Council. It, too, is primarily a panel of executives – that is, a collection of national delegations. One way that has been discussed of obtaining more democratic legitimacy is to have a parliamentary assembly along the lines of the OSCE or NATO. Such a two-chamber system need not necessarily lead to bureaucratic inflation. While one chamber would continue to be constituted by government representatives on the 'one state, one vote' principle, the other chamber (for which the title 'Assembly of the Peoples of the United Nations' has been suggested) would consist of delegations from the various Parliaments. If every national Parliament were to send an average of three delegates, such a 'World Parliament' with 570 members would still be smaller than many national Parliaments; that is, fully capable of meaningful activity. Furthermore, it might be considered whether the specialized agencies and subsidiary bodies ought not also to be outfitted with parliamentary delegations. The European Union, for example, suggested in a March 1999 resolution on world politics that parliamentary panels should be created, made up of the chairpersons of the various parliamentary committees of the national and regional parliaments. On the other hand, this position neglects the fact that most government representatives are legitimized democratically, and that the United Nations cannot be organized like a state with a separation of powers. Furthermore, the UN cultivates intensive co-operation with non-governmental organizations. What an increase in the General Assembly's status would do for the acceptability of its decisions with the great and mid-sized powers, however, tends not to be taken into consideration. It is hard to imagine that the USA, China or Russia would bow themselves to the will of the General Assembly if the majority were against them.

Reforms in the Area of Peace-maintenance

Corresponding to the dramatically changing challenges, UN peacekeeping has found itself in a process of permanent change and adjustment since its renaissance in 1988. Within only a few years, under the pressure of international political events, the organization had to develop a new task profile and operational form for peacekeeping missions which little had in common with the missions of the first generation other than the word 'peacekeeping'. However, as is usual with the UN, this process of adjustment was not the result of forward-looking conceptual considerations and planning, but rather a collection of reactive measures, to meet the need of the moment, and often implemented only hesitatingly. Added to this, since the middle of the 1990s, the UN has been entrusted with peace missions whose complexity goes far beyond that of the classical type. Peace-maintenance with military means and post-conflict consolidation through a civilian workforce are bound up inextricably with one another in these new missions in such a way that one might almost be justified in talking about 'fourth-generation peace missions' (Kühne, 2000b, p. 1357). With these new missions came new difficulties in their planning, set-up and execution, which again increased the need for reform.

The Brahimi Report on Reforms for Peace-maintenance

With all this in mind, in Spring 2000, Secretary-General Kofi Annan charged an independent committee of experts, under the chairmanship of the former Algerian foreign minister Lakhdar Brahimi, with a comprehensive analysis of the abilities and capacities of the UN in the field of peacekeeping. The committee was also requested to formulate recommendations on how to address the existing deficiencies in UN peacekeeping and improve its operation. The report, presented in Summer 2000 and passed on to both the General Assembly and the Security Council (Brahimi Report, 2000), is characterized by a frankness unusual for such documents. The first paragraph states that 'the United Nations was founded, in the words of its Charter, in order "to save succeeding generations from the scourge of war." Meeting this challenge is the most important function of the Organization, and, to a very significant degree, the yardstick by which it is judged by the peoples it exists to serve. Over the last decade, the United Nations has repeatedly failed to meet the challenge; and it can do no better today.'

The implementation of the recommendations internal to the UN system went on comparatively quickly, while the member states dragged their feet on the measures left to them. In October 2000, and then again in June 2001, the Secretary-General presented reports on the status of his own efforts (Reports of the Secretary-General, A/55/502 and A/55/977), the decisions already taken, and the remaining obstacles. Included in the second report, from Summer 2001, were also proposals from the Special Committee on Peacekeeping Operations and the recommendations of an external group of professional management consultants. This latter group had also conducted (on the DPKO) the first tests of effectiveness and economic viability to be undertaken on a UN department. These rapidly-introduced and far-reaching measures underscore the priority the UN gives to the reform of its peacekeeping activities. The fifty-seven recommendations of the Brahimi Report can be grouped into three categories, which will now be briefly described:

- First, reminders that a fundamental reorientation in the creation of the political and strategic framing conditions for peacekeeping missions is necessary;
- Second, demands that the DPKO create the necessary personnel and structural preconditions for the execution of complex peace missions; and
- Third, demands for tangible results from the member states.

Complex peacekeeping missions have often failed in recent years because their mandates were unrealistic and could not possibly be fulfilled by the troops deployed. The parameters used to formulate the mandate and to determine the scope of the missions were often best-case scenarios, while the realities on the ground were worst-case. Added to this was the fact that it was often hard to differentiate the precept of neutrality – eminently important for the success of peacekeeping missions – from mere indifference. The Brahimi Report emphasized that no failure had shaken the credibility of UN peacekeeping missions more seriously than their constant hesitation to differentiate between victim and aggressor.

What is striking is that nearly all Security Council resolutions that had anything to do with peace and international security have cited 'threats to' the peace – that is, using the weakest category in Article 39, while the term 'breach of the peace' has been used in only four cases, and acts of aggression are mentioned only where they are also seen to constitute a threat to the peace. The panel members thus stressed to the Secretary-General the imperative need to avoid telling the Security Council only what it wants to hear, and being forthright about what it must know when it is determining the scope of a mission. The co-ordination between the decision-centre of the Security Council and the planning and implementation centre of the Secretariat must be improved and intensified, and the states contributing troops must be included not only in the preparation of the missions, but also earlier, during the phase of creating the mandate in the Security Council. More than just having a clear mandate, the peacekeeping troops must also be in a position where they can execute that mandate with robust measures if necessary. The experience of a number of UN- or NATO-led peacekeeping missions has shown that a force with deterrent effect against potential disturbers of the peace becomes involved in far fewer combat situations and is more successful in fulfilling its mandate than does a poorly-armed force with convoluted rules of engagement.

The panel recommended a new structure for the DPKO for the purpose of more effective task realization. The Secretary-General adopted a large number of these suggestions as his own, and presented an appropriate plan in June 2001, which was in fact – with certain limitations – put into effect over the next couple of years. Instead of the proposed three offices under the leadership of an Assistant Secretary-General, the current two-office structure will be retained. The Office of Operations will remain largely unchanged, with its three regional divisions and the Situation Centre. Under the newly-altered Office of Mission Support are the Logistics Support Division and the Administration Support Division. The Military Division and the now higher-status Civilian Police Division are – together with the Mine Action Service – directly under the head of the DPKO. Furthermore, the Civilian Police Division also received the addition of a group of legal experts.

Thus the DPKO's structure now reflects more closely the complexity of the operations it must undertake.

For the improvement of the integrated efforts of the system as a whole, the Brahimi Report recommended setting up an Information and Strategic Analysis Secretariat (EISAS) within the Executive Committee for Peace and Security (ECPS), in order to make the Executive Committee and the departments represented within it capable of forward-looking and long-term strategic action. This Secretariat should bring together the diverse political, military, socioeconomic and cultural dimensions of peacekeeping operations in the formulation of mid- to long-term strategies. It was envisioned that the EISAS would play the role of a service centre for the UN workers involved in the planning and implementation of peace-keeping missions. Its role was planned to offer them access to information and evaluations that might be of special significance for their individual task areas. The Security Council and troop-contributing countries were also meant to benefit from the information and analysis provided by this Secretariat. EISAS was due to begin work, with around thirty personnel, in January 2001. In the summer of 2001, however, the Secretary-General was forced to bow to political and budgetary pressure, so this central secretariat eventually existed only in a much-reduced form.

In order to squeeze the most comprehensive capacities possible for mission-specific planning out of the UN system, the panel encouraged the creation of inte-grated Mission Task Forces, working as project management teams with extensive responsibility and technical competence. What was accomplished was the creation of 184 new posts, thus enabling the long-awaited personnel expansion necessary to make these and other urgently-needed planning and implementation instruments more effective.

Privatization of Peacekeeping?

One suggested reform for UN peacekeeping, which has no current chance of real-ization, but is discussed increasingly and will therefore be mentioned here for the sake of inclusiveness, is the so-called 'privatization of peacekeeping'. The back-ground for this is the trend that has become increasingly evident since the 1990s to privatize the security sector, understood as the increased execution of police and military functions through private services. Such firms have existed for many years, offering everything from military logistics and advice to active combat service, and have participated in military operations. What is being proposed is that the task of peacekeeping should be turned over, either as a whole or in part, to private firms. It thus might be conceivable in the future to call in private firms for the reform of the UN's military capabilities, or to develop a closer co-operation between the UN and such private firms (Brayton, 2002; Singer, 2003).

The UN's Standby Arrangement System

The period immediately following the conclusion of a cease-fire or peace treaty is of decisive importance for the success of a peace mission. The Brahimi Report therefore insists that time-plans must be created according to which classical peacekeeping operations can be fully deployed within thirty days (for more complex missions, within ninety days) of the passing of a Security Council Resolution. Connected to this ambitious demand are suggestions for the improvement of the selection and training of the leadership for peacekeeping operations, their early gathering for the purposes of the co-ordination of their tasks, and for the Secretary-General's authorization to begin recruiting personnel and using financial resources as soon as the granting of a Security Council mandate is in sight. The rapid availability and readiness of peacekeeping troops is, of course, tied to the readiness of the member states to co-operate. Speedy and effective participation by the states presupposes that they possess the necessary capacities and hold them available. The UN Standby Arrangement System (UNSAS), under construction since the mid-1990s, forms a basis for the further improvement of the situation. In particular, the actual availability of the resources and capacities foreseen for the UN in the Planning Data Sheets and Memoranda of Understanding requires constant updating. Were the states to permit the Secretariat to carry out such updating through monitoring teams, it would enable the Secretariat to have a more accurate idea of the operational readiness status of the promised resources while they were still in their home countries. The member states are encouraged to create multinational units at the brigade level, co-ordinated with each other in equipment and training, so that they can be deployed rapidly when needed.

There are currently (as of March 2004) eighty-two member states participating in UNSAS, after twenty-two states were dropped from the count in the context of a 2001 reorganization of the system. These twenty-two states had made general declarations of their readiness to support the UN with 'capacities' (not further specified), but had provided no practical assistance in the planning work of the DPKO. The UNSAS participants are organized into four levels according to the principle of the increasing specificity of their offers of help:

- The states of *Level 1* have presented a list of capabilities to the Secretary-General which they are willing to make available should they be needed. Since there is in the military realm generally a common understanding of what, for example, comprises a mechanized infantry battalion, such reported capabilities are relatively concrete and useful for planning. There are currently twenty-five states in this group;
- The ten countries in *Level 2* have given detailed specifications in their offers. In so-called Planning Data Sheets, the states give exact information not only on the numbers of personnel and large weaponry and transport available, but also on the capacity of the transportation needed to move it all by air or sea. Furthermore, they state whether the offered contingents are capable of supplying their own logistical needs during the mission, or will need the logistical support of the United Nations. These Planning Data Sheets constitute a great deal of time-consuming planning work that has already been done by the 'sending states' and thus need not occupy the Secretariat, which of course would increase the rapidity with which such resources may be employed;

- With forty-five states, *Level 3* is by far the largest group. These have given their express readiness to support the organization not only through Planning Data Sheets, but in actual Memoranda of Understanding, in which the specific conditions of the support activities are regulated. The signature of an MoU is a self-imposed obligation for a member state; the UN cannot require such an agreement; and
- Only Jordan and Uruguay have declared themselves willing to be on a *Rapid Deployment Level*, in which they promise to have their forces available within the 30- or 90-day periods (depending on the complexity of the mission) after the passing of a Security Council Resolution.

The resources registered by the member states can be differentiated into operational units – above all infantry, air-defence and artillery units, support units such as command and signal troops, logistics units, and all the other forms of support troops, and specially-qualified individuals such as military observers, refugee aides, infrastructural experts, medical specialists, administrative experts, or judges. In total, the member states have declared around 150,000 persons to be available to the UN as Standby Forces. In spite of this impressive number, there still exist serious deficiencies with respect to particular specialties and equipment. The overwhelming portion of the forces available consists of operational units, and of these, most are light infantry. Most of these forces, coming from developing countries, have only the most skeletal equipment of their own, and an extremely limited or non-existent capability to supply their own logistical needs. The support units – very expensive because of the qualifications and specialized technical capabilities they need – can usually be supplied only by the wealthier industrialized countries. They are desperately needed, but have not been supplied in the necessary numbers.

One successful model of standby arrangements is the Scandinavian SHIRBRIG (Standby High Readiness Brigade). It was registered with the UN in January 2000 as being available to the UNSAS. There are eleven states involved in this project, which is an exemplary one for the future organization of peace missions: Argentina, Austria, Canada, Denmark, Finland, Italy, the Netherlands, Norway, Poland, Romania and Sweden. Along with three infantry battalions, the brigade includes all the necessary support elements for a possible deployment. At the brigade's seat in Hovelte, just north of Copenhagen, the so-called Planning Element (a multinational core staff of fifteen people) is represented, while the other fifty members or so of the brigade staff as well as the actual troop units remain stationed in their home countries. The brigade's first mission was as a part of the UN Mission in Ethiopia and Eritrea (UNMEE) in early 2001. At the time of writing, SHIRBRIG is the only military formation with the capability of carrying out independent operations to be offered to the UN by its member states.

Complex peace missions, particularly where they are to set up transitional civil administrations, need a large number of specialized personnel who can carry out the administrative and juridical work. This group of people must not only be in a position to exercise the appropriate functions for the duration of the mission, but also to undertake advisory, educational and monitoring tasks for the offices and institutions being created. The member states, however, have practically no reserve personnel capable of such tasks, so that every individual administrative or police department must be depleted, and every state prosecutor or judge removed from his normal duties, in order to carry out such missions. The experience of building up civilian police missions in the Balkans or in Haiti made the serious recruiting problems in this area painfully clear. In order to be able to deploy future peace missions quickly and effectively, the member states will need to build up the necessary capacities.

Mission organization and planning will be further improved when the member states make the so-called 'on-call lists' available to the DPKO. These lists name military and civilian experts who can be made available within the space of seven days for mission preparation. The 'on-call list' concept is in the process of implementation. With thirty-nine states participating in the Mission Headquarters On-Call List there have been 154 positions identified for the military division, and around 100 for the civil police division. The 'core positions' are to be filled by the member states within seven days; and the others within fourteen.

In the end, adequate and reliable financing is the decisive factor in the success of a peacekeeping mission. In the past, the refusal to deliver funds – especially by large industrialized countries – contributed significantly to financial crises in the UN's peacekeeping activities. The UN has been in debt to a number of personnel-contributing states for considerable sums for many years. Peace missions are all financed through their own individual budgets, which must be established by the member states in a co-operative procedure. In December 2000, after years of difficult negotiations, the member states finally succeeded in reforming the financing regulations for peacekeeping missions (which dated from 1973) to reduce dependency on a few main contributors, and to distribute the burden according to a ten-part scale. This new regulation was possible only because a number of states declared themselves willing to pay more into the UN's coffers. After the USA was able to push through its demand to reduce its part in financing peace missions to 25 per cent of the overall costs, it is to be hoped that in the future the USA will not only pay off its still outstanding arrears, but will be reliable in its payments of the regular contribution. This would constitute a serious improvement in the future operational capacity of the UN in the area of peacekeeping.

In sum, very significant efforts at reform have been undertaken in the realm of peacekeeping. Peacekeepers should in principle receive a robust mandate, and be sent only on those missions that have clear rules, adequate management capacities and appropriate equipment. Furthermore, according to the concept of Standby Forces, a capable multinational armed force should be made available to be used at short notice when necessary. In total, the UN system for peacekeeping should be made more effective, and preventive diplomacy and post-conflict consolidation should receive more attention. All this having been said, the question remains as to whether the Security Council in fact has a monopoly in the area of peacekeeping, or whether NATO's actions in the former Yugoslavia (1999) and the actions of the USA and UK in Iraq (2003) have made that a hollow claim. There is also another practice that may determine the UN's relevance in the area of peacekeeping: the tendency, especially of the more capable industrialized countries, to allow themselves to be mandated only with peacekeeping missions that they can then carry out under their own responsibility. This leads to a concentration of their forces in countries and regions that are of immediate interest or significance for the state involved. This threatens to leave the United Nations with a sort of rump competence for forgotten conflicts and regions, in which it is likely to receive only lukewarm support from the industrialized countries (as was to be observed in Congo and Liberia in 2003).

The Brahimi Report's numerous suggestions to the member states are certainly a test of the seriousness and consistency with which they are prepared to treat their self-imposed obligations in peacekeeping. It would be nothing new for the member states to behave reluctantly in the implementation phase, thus preventing even well-thought-out reforms from accomplishing anything in practice.

Reforms in the Area of International Law

The war against Iraq in the spring of 2003 constituted a fundamental break with established international law. The USA justified its actions, undertaken without a mandate from the UN, with the need to free a country from a cruelly repressive regime and to remove the Iraqi regime's access to, or capability to produce, weapons of mass destruction. The goal – which was in fact achieved – was thus a forceful regime change, which is not permissible under international law (see Chapter 4). According to some, such as the American international lawyer Michael Glennon (2003), this has made it clear once again that states in general – and not just the USA – are not primarily interested in the question of whether the use of force is lawful, but whether it will serve their national interests. The international law regulations for the limitation of war, as found, for example, in the UN Charter, are claimed to have failed, and it is said to be time to reform international law and adjust it to the new realities.

Before we look at this debate over the reform of international law provisions on war and peace, a few brief general remarks on international law should be made. The most important sources of international law are treaties and agreements, Customary international law and general principles of law. Customary international law in particular is based on the idea that states observe it in their practice. In the case of non-observation by a few individual states, however, there is no effective and fair instrument available that is equivalent to a national criminal law system. Rather, how to react lies with the judgement of the various states themselves. The most important difference between national and international law is that there is no effective authority that can implement international law. International law as a whole is obviously not perfect, but over the twentieth century, and in particular since the catastrophe of the Second World War, it has exhibited extremely dynamic development. The leading international law paradigm is no longer that of unlimited state sovereignty weakened only in isolated and individual instances. In that sense, the Westphalian order has been shot through with many holes. The large number of international law treaties that affect the bases of international trade, economic exchange and the protection of human rights, are unaffected by a debate over the general prohibition on the use of force. Every well-informed person knows 'that the vast majority of international law regulations are followed without difficulty by the states affected by them, and that they thus constitute, just like national law, a secure framework for worldwide activities' (Frowein, 2003).

Thus the consideration of a reform of international law does not mean that international law as a whole system has failed or is being brought into question. The reform discussion relates primarily to the question of how to deal with dangerous risk-combinations of the future without – as happened with the Iraq war – ignoring the UN Charter. The debate thus turns on the question of 'how normative-legal principles on the one hand and political interests and problems on the other can in the future be brought into harmony with one another in a dramatically changed world environment with new crisis scenarios' (Rechkemmer, 2003, p. 2 et seq.).

The Debate Over Preventive Security Politics

Under which conditions, and for which cases, military intervention should be allowed are controversial questions, bound up in the debate over the so-called pre-emptive security politics as represented, for example, in the American National Security Strategy of 17 September 2002. There, along with the development of a broadly-conceived, multi-dimensional strategic answer to the changed security situation, which also allocates a great deal of importance to non-military elements, it is argued that today's threats must be met in a different way from those of the past. The concept of 'immediate threat' must be aligned with the capabilities and goals of today's opponents.

The background to these considerations is the changed strategic landscape, which has been under discussion in security circles for some time. One of the central security challenges lies in the combination of terrorism and weapons of mass destruction. The concept of deterrence that formed the basis of security strategies during the Cold War can no longer function under the new conditions. In individual cases, 'deterrence by punishment' must in fact progress to 'deterrence by denial'. Should military means be understood only as the *ultima ratio*, the most favourable moment for intervention, in which involvement in a conflict with comparatively low expenditure of resources – and possibly even with nothing more than a credible threat – might create the maximal political effect, might be lost. The most auspicious moment for intervention in a conflict and the moment at which public support for such an intervention is likely to be highest are too far removed from one another. Early intervention in crises and conflicts is, however, difficult, because of the public nature of determining when a crisis is occurring. Public as well as political attention tends to be drawn only after the conflict has escalated. But the greater the threat in the age of proliferation of weapons of mass destruction, the greater is the risk posed by inaction, and 'the more compelling the case for taking anticipatory action to defend ourselves, even if uncertainty remains as to the time and place of the enemy's attack. To forestall or prevent such hostile acts by our adversaries, the United States will, if necessary, act pre-emptively' (White House, 2002, sec. v).

The distinction between prevention and pre-emption is in need of a more detailed explanation. A pre-emptive attack is one that takes place in the face of an imminent aggressive action from the opposing side. A preventive attack is an act of war based on the belief that an opponent intends to engage in aggressive actions as soon as his/her capabilities are sufficient, and is aimed at destroying those capabilities before they can reach a threatening level. As was explained in Chapter 3, self-defence is a classical legitimate right of states according to Article 51 of the UN Charter. The central question is, in this age of terrorism and weapons of mass destruction, what exactly *is* self-defence, and under what conditions can it legitimately be claimed? According to the distinction mentioned above, pre-emptive self-defence is an element of customary international law built on the so-called 'Caroline Criteria' and an agreement between US Secretary of State Daniel Webster and the British foreign minister, Lord Ashburton, dating from 1837. A country does not have to wait for an armed attack against it, but is entitled to take measures of self-defence if the necessity is 'instant, overwhelming, leaving no choice of means, and no moment of deliberation'. Furthermore, the action taken must not be 'unreasonable or excessive'. The most prominent example of an act of pre-emptive self-defence is the case of the Israeli attack in 1967. The postulate for pre-emption in the US security strategy, however, far exceeds these CIL criteria. It claims the right of action even in cases of suspicion and potential threat, and thus brings itself into the neighbourhood of forbidden preventive action. In 1980, the USA supported a Security Council resolution condemning Israel's strike against the Iraq nuclear power plant 'Osirak' as an illegal preventive attack. Israel then claimed that Iraq might have had the intention of developing an offensive nuclear programme directed against it. A lack of evidence and agreed-upon criteria for judgement seem to be the problems for both the Israeli action in 1980 and some of the central claims in the US security strategy of 2002. Clearly, there is an urgent need for further discussion.

The boundaries of the right to self-defence have always been somewhat blurred, but since 11 September 2001, it has become clear that states may be threatened in their very existence by scenarios which look nothing like the classical armed attack by State A on State B. The Security Council made it clear that the USA had the right to take measures of self-defence against these terrorist attacks. So far, the ability of international law to adjust itself to new dangers is recognized and has been demonstrated in practice. The precondition for legitimate action is still, however, that dangers are not simply asserted, but that their existence is shown to be highly plausible. While military pre-emption might be considered legitimate in individual cases, preventive actions challenge the international order fundamentally. This is because it remains undetermined as to who decides how appropriate such military actions are, on which international legal grounds they are to be conducted, and what relationship they bear to the general prohibition on the use of force. Can this, in fact, bring greater stability to the system, or would it increase the unpredictability of international politics, in the end creating less security rather than more? The possible consequences of requiring any and every use of force to be sanctioned by the Security Council must also be considered, however. Situations can certainly be imagined in which the Security Council might be blocked by veto threats – not necessarily on rational grounds – but where there is also a clear and urgent need for action. In order not to leave the definition of what does or does not constitute a threat to security to the arbitrary will or national interest of individual states, a progressive development of international law in the light of new threats has indeed been discussed (Roberts, 2003).

It might be conceivable to have a debate over where the level of tolerance should lie for the proliferation of weapons of mass destruction, the support of international terrorism, or the systematic violation of human rights. A comprehensible catalogue of criteria would have to be developed, according to which an intervention could be justified. Such attempts to create definitions are bound up with numerous difficulties, and it is rather unlikely that something like this could be accomplished. The alternative, however, is to maintain the status quo, which is equally unsatisfying. The chances for agreement may be greatest on the issue of weapons of mass destruction because of the all-encompassing threat. It should be possible for members of the Security Council to agree with each other on when – under what conditions and possessed by which actors – the capability of using such weapons should be considered to constitute an immediate threat. Terrorist organizations and failed states are obvious cases; the cases of dictators and totalitarian regimes might need a more intensive discussion. The most difficult discussion would be over whether a state's behaviour in the research and production or acquisition of such weapons consistutes a threat in itself. In the case of massive violations of human rights, on the other hand, there is very little chance for the development of a binding catalogue of criteria. The selectivity with which humanitarian interventions have been undertaken so far, and the arbitrary, self-interest-determined involvement of the Western states should not lead anyone to expect anything more than the already familiar contestable *ad hoc* decisions.

The UN and the current international legal order were not destroyed by the intense confrontations in the Security Council and the 2003 war in Iraq. Both are, however, in a serious crisis, into which they were brought by leading members, and out of which they can find their way only through the new pragmatic co-operation of those same members. The Security Council remains a decisive partner for states, also for new initiatives and modes of reaction that will become necessary in the future as precautions against complex risks. This is because the Council, at least from the perspective of most states, has something to offer that is of particular value in the strategic realm: legitimacy. The analyses and solutions contained in the USA's security strategy might have appeared far less threatening in the eyes of the world if they had come out of a process involving the United Nations and its uncontested competence in the creation of criteria and standards for a legitimate and widely-acceptable implementation of a new security concept.

The doubtless necessary adjustments of international law norms and institutional precautions cannot be decreed unilaterally if they are to have any hope of success. They need a broader basis if they are to be accepted worldwide, and the UN can offer such a basis. Even while

> there will always be situations in which the leadership of the strongest power in the world, which fortunately happens to be a democracy, is indispensable for the solution of the existing problems, the maintenance of the basic structure of multilateralism, and with it a central role for the United Nations, remains equally indispensable for the maintenance of a minimum of order in the world. (Kaiser, 2003, p. 7).

Reforms in the Areas of Economics, Development and the Environment

Changes in the areas of economics, development and the environment are firmly established elements of nearly all the propositions for reform, whether developed internally or externally to the UN. In spite of the many improvements in the socioeconomic and development areas following from Kofi Annan's 1997 reforms, the UN's work in this area suffers particularly badly from overlapping competencies and a lack of co-ordination. The ECOSOC, especially, including its nearly inconceivable number of subsidiary bodies, is a central target for criticism. It is demanded that the entire system be put through a fundamental examination. In its current structure, the ECOSOC is simply not in a position to fulfil its co-ordinating function, and its work is often overly-bureaucratized and ineffective. While its complete dissolution has been suggested, others would prefer to raise its efficiency with stronger directive authority. Suggestions range all the way from the creation of a new Economic Council with competencies analogous to the Security Council (that is, the right to make binding determinations), all the way to the creation of a dovetailed triple-council system, with three Councils, being responsible for Security, Economics and Social Affairs/Development, respectively. Such suggestions have not as yet, however, been put forward officially by any UN panel, or been introduced into the debate in a serious fashion.

In his programme of reform, accepted by the General Assembly, the Secretary-General (Annan, 1997, no. 129) pointed out one function of the UN that tends to be under-estimated or even disregarded. The UN's contribution as a forger of innovative ways of thinking and a place of consensus-building at a global level has special significance – especially at a time of changing paradigms and conceptions of socioeconomic development. Through its norm-setting activities, the organization could contribute to the creation of an environment that 'would allow all countries and their enterprises to compete in international markets on an equal footing; and, through its advisory and operational activities, it can help develop the tools and human resources capabilities which would address the supply-side constraints faced my many countries'. In the future, the UN must also concern itself with using its influence on behalf of developing countries on economic decisions that are to be made in other forums:

> The United Nations must continue to endeavour to affect economic decisions taken in other fora from the perspective of the developing countries and remains best placed to build consensus based on the perspective of interdependence between issues, and to identify the means by which sustained and sustainable development can be realize by all countries.

At the same time, this system of countless specialized agencies, subsidiary organs and programmes with similar task profiles, is often accused of a level of inefficiency that can, in extreme cases, in fact lead to mutually contradictory mandates. Another especially difficult problem is the lack of co-ordination between the UN panels and the increasingly significant Bretton Woods Organizations. Thus it has been suggested that the multilateral development work of the UN should be integrated more closely with trade and finance policy, or even to merge the UNCTAD with the WTO. The German Minister for Development Aid, Heidemarie Wieczorek-Zeul (2000), has called for all these organizations to be brought together under one roof, based on the UNDP and the World Bank. The decisional competencies, however, should not be orientated solely on the economic power of the members; the weaker states must be represented appropriately. Concrete plans for reform with realistic perspectives for implementation are, however, still not in sight in this particular field.

One fundamental objection to extensive reform-euphoria in the area of economics and development is the dramatic structural change in the world economy. The time when state actors had relatively exclusive influence over the global economy and development politics ended with the onset of globalization. Therefore, demands such as that in the UN Millennium Declaration of September 2000, that the number of people living in extreme poverty should be cut by half by 2015, seem of rather dubious worth. As desirable as this intention may be, it is questionable whether it is a goal that can be reached through international organizations. Such expansive promises remind one far more of the self-imposed obligation of the industrialized countries – mockingly empty for decades – to contribute 0.7 per cent of their GNP for development aid. Energetic UN optimists may still come to the conclusion that such demands are not absolutely impossible, but even they must admit that experience teaches that they should be approached 'at best with scepticism, at worst with cynicism' (Williams, 2000, p. 166). The critical question is whether the increasing 'clichéing' of international politics (that is, the trend of making sweet-sounding promises without any real hope of implementation behind them) will not lead to a significant loss of credibility for the UN.

Reform of the International Trade and Finance Architecture

In view of the increasing divergence between developed and developing countries, and the worldwide instability resulting from it, the reform of the international trade and finance structures has also come under discussion. But here, too, no effective new regulations have been developed.

Beginning with the 1994 Mexico crisis, there has been a thoroughgoing discussion on reforming the international finance architecture in the G-8, the IMF, the World Bank, the national governments, the private finance economy, the sciences, and countless NGOs. Among the various suggestions for reform are a separation of the tasks in the IMF and the World Bank, and a refocusing of the IMF on its original purpose; the reduction of IMF credit and a less-automatic guaranteeing of credit; the introduction of pre-qualification measures, whereby only countries that have actually implemented certain reforms should receive emergency credit without further review in case of a crisis; a departure from the one-size-fits-all approach and a stronger consideration of national conditions; and heightened transparency in the international finance markets. Among the innovations discussed for the international finance architecture are the creation of a World Central Bank or an international bankruptcy court, the creation of target zones for the most important exchange rates in order to reduce fluctuations on the foreign exchange markets, or the introduction of taxes on foreign exchange transactions (the Tobin Tax). Such a tax is promoted in particular by those NGOs most critical of globalization, and is meant to lower the attractiveness of short-term speculations and reduce the high volatility of the financial markets.

With respect to reform of the world trading order, there has been a new attempt in the WTO to liberalize world trade in goods and services. After the failure of the so-called Millennium Round in late 1999, the WTO member states met again in Qatar in November 2001 for their fourth summit of ministers, hoping to breathe life into yet another round of liberalization talks. The Doha Development Agenda put together there had the goal of determining the details of a comprehensive liberalization, especially in the areas of agriculture, services, market access (for non-agricultural products) and other rules (anti-dumping, subsidies) by January 2005. The focus of the new round was to be the better integration of developing countries into the global economy.

The Debate over an Umbrella Organization for the Environment and Development

One particularly intensive debate has taken place over the idea of an umbrella organization for the environment and development. Such a 'World Organization for Environment and Development' (Biermann and Simonis, 1998, 2000) could incorporate certain existing institutions into a new, overarching structure, and amalgamate the UNEP, CSD and other relevant environmental convention secretariats into a single organization. Were this to take place, the new organization would have to work closely with the Bretton Woods Organizations, the WTO and the related UN specialized agencies. Such an organization could lead national governments, IGOs and private actors to accord a higher value to environmental and development needs, and to place these problems more prominently on their own agendas. This would in turn create better political conditions for the success-ful implementation of solutions.

The central problem of such an organization would be the decision-making process, as both administrative effectiveness and political acceptability must be achieved. Proponents argue that 'North' and 'South' would have to be given equal status, constituting something of a middle road between the 'South'-orientated procedure of the UN General Assembly and the 'North'-dominated Bretton Woods Organizations. This would be the key to the widest possible political acceptability. Furthermore, NGOs could be allowed to participate, as in the ILO. With respect to financing, a combination of the UNEP and UNDP budgets and an integration of all the existing programmes would save a huge amount in expendi-tures; another possibility might be a tax on aircraft fuel or a tax on financial or stock market transactions. Critics of the idea of an umbrella organization (Gehring and Oberthür, 2000) argue that they see no specific contribution to the improve-ment of global environmental problems coming from such an institution. There could, in fact, be good reasons why no such organization exists as yet. Effective international organizations tend to be characterized by specialization and simpli-fied decision-making processes, thus being capable of action on their own. There are, in fact, already numerous organizational elements in global environmental politics. It is therefore far from obvious why states would be more likely to give up their sovereignty to a new organization and make it any more capable of action than all the organizations that already exist. It is not likely that an international environmental politics would emerge in the framework of a world environmental organization. Should one still wish to think about possible models for a world environmental organization, three suggest themselves. Analogous to the 'UN model', there could be an over-arching framework organization, under which the various existing international conventions and organizations could remain essen-tially independent of one another, but collected together under one roof. This sort of model would, however, possess very little problem-solving capability, and would seem to offer no decisive additional advantages beyond what exists already. On the 'WTO model', there would be a central decision-making panel which would be responsible for discussing all environmental problems. This model presents the danger of linking problems to one another that should not be linked. Along with the danger of over-complexity, there is the risk of a politics that could use the non-solution of one problem to block the solution of problems in other areas. The 'EU model' would involve the preparation of decisions in individual panels and not the connection of different problem areas as in the WTO model. This would be effective, but hardly realistic, as decisions made by strict majority would still have to be implemented by all members – implying a far more exten-sive transferral of sovereignty rights to such an organization than is at all likely.

The potential of each model varies a great deal: while the UN model would contribute little and the WTO model might in fact produce negative effects, the more effective EU model is simply impossible. Furthermore, in order to establish an institution with some promise of success, there would have to be considerable resources made available. Such resources, however, might very well produce better effects if they were invested in the existing structures rather than used to make a new one. Other suggested reforms in this area relate to the creation of an Environmental Security Council, the conversion of the Trusteeship Council into an Environmental Trusteeship Council, or the founding of a World Environmental Court. Practitioners of international environmental politics are particularly keen to point out that all this planning cannot simply remain on the drawing board: the realities of the situation must be kept in mind. This is true above all of the issue of national sovereignty rights, which states are still unwilling to give up except in very limited ways. Thus it becomes necessary to ask whether it might not be over-extending and demanding too much of the UN to give it the task of solving all the serious problems facing humanity. Besides, the mere declaration of environmental, economic or social councils or organizations achieves nothing: in the end their usefulness depends on the competencies and the type of legitimacy given to them. Because any such organization would have to be approved by the General Assembly, there are also purely procedural difficulties that would hinder their realization.

A Negative Balance Sheet for Reform in the Social and Economic Areas

Klaus Hüfner and Jens Martens (2000, p. 226 et seq.), in a broad evaluation of the various reforms both proposed and implemented in recent years, come to the conclusion that, apart from a number of administrative and organizational changes and certain structural improvements, the picture is negative. They draw a few inferences from this that are of interest for the entire reform discussion. Proposals for reform lead to success only when they are 'compatible with the knowledge and self-interests of a sufficient number of relevant decision-makers'. Influence in the UN system results from the factors of financial power and voting power, and in view of the power differences and the enormous heterogeneity of interests among the 191 member states, reform proposals will be realizable only in isolated cases. This would be possible in cases, for example, such as the 1972 founding of the UN Environmental Program, when exogenous factors created a pressure for action that the main actors could not escape. Aside from such exceptional situations, proposals for reform could succeed only if the power differential among the states were less, or if their interests were to converge.

Since it is unlikely that the power structures will change significantly at any time in the near future, and the heterogeneity of interests is also unlikely to disappear, the fundamental question arises of whether the UN can be reformed at all. The way out suggested by Hüfner and Martens (2000) is to concentrate on longer-term attempts to increase the knowledge of the decision-makers, which is a key factor in the formation of self-interest, and thus also in the alteration of the UN:

It is only when the knowledge of the concrete advantages and opportunities to be gained from a more intensive world-wide cooperation in the framework of the UN has spread itself through the respective populations that the pressure on national decision-makers will grow, and with it the chance for a change in state politics with respect to the UN. Only thus is a long-term deconstruction of the existing heterogeneity of interests among UN member states possible. (p. 234)

Also under criticism are the huge world conferences organized by the United Nations, such as the Johannesburg Summit on Sustainable Development, in August 2002. Their function as a platform for global communication and interaction is uncontested. It must, however, be asked critically whether the goal of concluding unanimous declarations and formal compromises should not perhaps be abandoned:

If one were in the future at such summits on environmental and development themes to be freed from the pressure of unanimity and use such summits instead as global fora to work towards coalitions of the willing in important issues, the interests of those people affected most by the destruction of the environment and by underdevelopment would be far better served. (Rechkemmer, 2002, p. 4)

Further Reading

Annan, Kofi (2002) *Strengthening of the United Nations: An Agenda for Further Change*, New York UN-Document (A/57/387).
Bhatta, Ghambir (2000) *Reforms at the UN: Contextualising the Annan Agenda*, Singapore: Singapore University Press.
Commission on Global Governance (1995) *Our Global Neighbourhood*, Oxford: Oxford University Press.
Kennedy, Paul and Bruce Russett (1995) 'Reforming the United Nations', *Foreign Affairs* (5), pp. 56–71.
Mueller, Joachim W. (ed.) (2001) *Reforming the United Nations: The Quiet Revolution*, The Hague: Kluwer.
Rittberger, Volker (ed.) (2002) *Global Governance and the United Nations System*, Tokyo, New York: UNU Press.

9

Conclusions

As shown by the above examinations of the three fields of peace-maintenance, protection of human rights, and economic, development and environmental issues, the UN has become an important centre of multilateral politics. However, it must once again be emphasized, as it was at the very beginning of the book, that there is no such thing as 'the' UN. In a range of fields of politics, the system has various tools available to it, with differing effectiveness and aimed at different goals. In the best-case scenario, the 'three United Nations' (Russett *et al.*, 2000, p. 282) develop mutually-supporting and strengthening synergy effects. A broad concept of human security underlines the fact that the point is no longer merely the security of states, but rather the security of the people living within these states. Therefore, elements of the traditional concept of security (which have in no way become less important) become tied in, and are even seen as mutually conditioned, with the need to guarantee human rights, the right of states to develop, and the right to a liveable environment.

This issue-linking in the framework of a universal organization presents tremendous opportunities, but its limitations must also be noted. The institutions whose basic structure was created in the aftermath of the Second World War were, according to Kofi Annan (Annan, 2000, no. 30), tailored to an inter-*national* world. At the start of the twenty-first century, however, we live in a *global* world, and in the effective reaction to this transition lies the fundamental institutional challenge of this century.

Multilateralism and Global Governance: Opportunities and Limitations of a Political Concept

Generally, multilateralism can be understood as a style of politics in which the relationships among three or more states function on the basis of certain generally-accepted principles and rules of behaviour (Ruggie, 1993, p. 11). Multilateralism is the counter-concept to unilateralism, in which individual states behave according to their own national interests, even when that means acting alone or in opposition to other states. In political practice, large and powerful states tend to prefer unilateral behaviour, because it promises them a maximization of own interests. Even if such powerful states behaved according to the principle of 'as much multilateralism as

243

possible, as much unilateralism as necessary' (that is, they acted unilaterally only in 'emergencies'), an important precondition for international co-operation would be damaged, since they who are prepared to act alone and against the will of their potential partners can hardly, even in isolated cases, be surprised if other states act in the same way. In other words, only those who are prepared to subject themselves to the norms of international co-operation can expect and demand the same of others. To behave multilaterally is to recognize, according to Ernst-Otto Czempiel (1999, p. 238), that the states, because of their interdependence, are 'no longer isolated, but relate to each other in a common context, which [understanding] must be made visible in the exercise of power.' Without the basic pattern of interdependence, however, unilateral politics are more likely (see Chapter 2, Figure 2.1). Among the principles of multilateral politics are an unlimited prohibition on the use of force in the pursuit of political goals, and the recognition that national interests can be better realized through co-operation than through nation-state competition (Brenner, 1995, p. 9 et seq.). The emphasis on common interests is decisive for multilateral politics.

In these very different concepts, basic theoretical assumptions about the composition of the international system are reflected. These were explained in Chapter 2, and now that we have a better understanding of the structure and activities of the UN, we return to them (see a schematic representation in Table 9.1). While the multilateral concept relies on a broadly-conceived rationality on the part of the various actors, the unilateral concept is concentrated more on the anarchical nature of the international system. From a unilateral perspective, states are the central actors in the international arena, and international organizations play a secondary role. From the position of the multilateralist, on the other hand, countless international processes can be explained only with reference to the motives and behaviour of international organizations. Unilateralists see international politics as the result of the actions of individual states. The violation of rules through the use of force for the maximization of one's own short-term interests (sometimes even when one knows better) is seen as an iron rule of world politics, and it cannot be expected from this perspective that future international politics will be norm-guided, peaceful, and interdependence- and consensus-orientated. Even if one or two actors confined themselves to multilateral rules of play, it would by no means indicate that they could count on anyone else to do the same. Multilateralism is seen as a utopian ideal that has nothing to do with the true nature of international politics. In extreme cases, unilateralism is the only kind of behaviour that can accomplish anything. Multilateralists, on the other hand, see international politics as the result of border-crossing activities by many different kinds of actors, and see international influence as arising from competent handling of the circumstances of interdependence.

Whether unilateralism or multilateralism is more likely to be considered promising is thus heavily dependent on which theoretical paradigms are dominant in the relevant states. The United Nations can play an important role in international politics only if its members privilege multilateral strategies for addressing problems and challenges over unilateral ones. In other words, the success of the

TABLE 9.1
The unilateralism–multilateralism debate

Unilateral premises	Multilateral premises
Anarchy is the reigning basic pattern and structural principle of international relations	Interdependence is the reigning basic pattern and structural principle of international relations
States are the only meaningful actors of international politics; other actors take on meaning only in their functions as means or agents of states	Many international processes can be explained only with reference to the motives and behaviour of IGOs and NGOs
International politics are the result of the interactions of individual states, which have as their goal the retention of power in the sense of classical national security	International relations are the result of the border-crossing activities of countless international actors, which (who) have comprehensive security as their goal
International relations are a zero-sum game; that is, an increase in one actor's power can only mean a decrease in another's. Standard mode of interaction is conflictual	International relations are not a zero-sum game; that is, the advantage of any given actor results from the increased overall sum of the good(s) to be distributed. Standard mode of interaction is co-operative
International influence results from the use or threat of force, defined as actual or potential military and/or economic capability	International influence arises from the competent handling of the circumstances of international interdependence; the ability to persuade others is an aid to influence
International politics is like a game among self-contained, independent billiard balls constantly moving and running into each other on the world stage (the 'billiard-ball model').	International relations are a web-like network of various interwoven decisions, which overlayer successively the world of states.

Source: Adapted from Meyers (1997, p. 342).

United Nations is highly conditional. It is clear that, in the real world, the appropriate conditions cannot always be counted upon. Member states are all too seldom prepared to place the UN at the top of their foreign policy priorities, and even more rarely prepared to change their thinking about the proper way for a 'sovereign' state to conduct foreign policy.

The United Nations and Global Governance

One particularly far-reaching form of multilateralism is the concept of global governance. It has already been indicated that it is one of the unsolved puzzles of political science how binding commitments for the solving of international problems may be created (and made viable over the long-term) in a way that goes beyond mere inter-state politics. There is, however, a consensus on the idea that some type of international governance, extending traditional governance beyond existing borders, is absolutely necessary. The classical perspective that the state is the only source of governance is being challenged increasingly by the notion that not only 'hierarchical governance through states, but also horizontal governance with states as equal partners, or even governance without any states at all, is possible' (Zürn, 1998, p. 25; see also Rittberger, 2000, pp. 198–209). According to Michael Zürn, only the recognition of all three possible forms of governance (through states; with states; and without states) creates the possibility of a 'project of complex global governance'. Franz Nuscheler, a strong proponent of such a project, claims that the construct of global governance arises from the insight that the governability of even powerful nation-states is being overtaxed by the increasing quantity and density of cross-border transactions, the decreasing significance of the borders of territorial states, and the growing challenges of global risks Furthermore, the forms of international management of crises and conflicts that have constituted normal practice thus far are no longer up to the task, as shown, for example, by the amount of turbulence in the international finance market. Nuscheler (2002a, p. 182) argues that global governance 'is not a romantic project aimed at a safe and tidy global neighborhood, but a realistic response to the challenge of globalization and global risks. It is an evolutionary project, developing step by step'.

Positive governance beyond the nation-state – which need by no means indicate the *end* of the nation-state – is theoretically possible, but hindered by countless practical problems. There is in particular a lack of collective binding effect in international governance. Classical nation-state governance is based on the ideas that there is a fundamental correspondence between those affected by something and the space within which the actions to be regulated are taking place, and that decisions once taken (at least theoretically) are also capable of being implemented in practice. International co-operation is, in comparison to classical unilateral governance, a process requiring a great deal of time and effort. This is because of the primary structural characteristic of the international system, namely anarchy: that the state is the highest instance, recognizing no authority higher than itself. That is equally true for both the making of decisions and their realization in practice. This is why these governance models suffer from the double problem of practicability and legitimacy:

- First, given a heterogeneous interest structure in a system of overlapping and inter-penetrating partial sovereignties, how is a voluntary process of self-coordination to take place? and
- Second, if this co-ordination does not happen voluntarily, how can it be guaranteed that any process attempting to create such co-operation would correspond to democratic principles?

It therefore appears downright audacious when advocates of multilateralism claim that

in the international system of tomorrow, only multilateralism will provide an answer to the challenges of globalization. Our world will always be plural, and it is precisely because of that that, in the long run, no form of unilateralism will work. This is why the 21st century, with its over six billion people and their states, will need a United Nations capable of real action (Fischer, 1999, p. 109)

From the teleological perspective, one can only assent unconditionally to this claim. That said, the world in the 2000s is going through a process of tension and transformation in which the trends of globalization and fragmentation struggle against each other, and movement is taking place on many different levels (Kühne, 2000, pp. 447 et seq). Unfortunately, no global 'domestic politics' has emerged in the tension between these two opposing tendencies, only 'small islands of developments similar to domestic politics' which must be stabilized and expanded.

In spite of all the conceptual, and above all practical, difficulties associated with such a perspective, it is still necessary to conceive of a political model that can stand up to the attractions of the nation-state-organized world of the past. What is needed now is 'institutional imagination projecting beyond the nation-state' (Zürn, 1998, p. 28). In the same spirit, the Independent Commission on International Development Issues – the so-called 'North–South Commission', under the chairmanship of the former German federal chancellor, Willy Brandt – in the early 1980s and under completely different global conditions, noted the main points of a debate that is becoming relevant again today. According to the Commission's concluding report, humanity increasingly sees itself as being confronted with problems that concern humanity as a whole, leading to the logical conclusion that the solutions to these problems must also be increasingly internationalized. The globalization of dangers and challenges requires a sort of global domestic politics that goes far into the future, and far beyond national borders.

Although there is a great deal of agreement on this particular claim, the conclusions to be drawn from it vary considerably. The discussion of global governance is one attempt to meet the global challenges that gained prominence through the work of the Commission on Global Governance (also instigated by Willy Brandt). This independent commission under the chairmanship of the former Swedish prime minister, Ingvar Carlsson, and the former foreign minister of Guyana and Secretary-General of the Commonwealth, Shridath Ramphal, built upon the debate already taking place in academic circles (see, for example, Rosenau and Czempiel, 1992) and attempted to give the concept some content. The Commission on Global Governance (1995, p. 4 et seq.) defined global governance as 'the sum-total of the many ways in which individuals as well as public and private institutions regulate their common concerns'. The concept includes formal institutions and systems of government with implementational competence as well as informal arrangements. The basic recognition remains that the globalization of problems requires a globalization of politics. This means not only more classical inter-state co-operation, but also the development of a new model of politics that goes beyond simple demands for 'more' multilateralism and global thinking. Such a model would have to make it possible for state and non-state actors to work together in new ways and on many different levels.

This concept has roused many academics to make attempts to define it more precisely and to clarify its content (see, for example, Muldoon, 2004). The primary thing that all these attempts have in common is that they all consciously stop short of federalist visions of world government. According to Shridath Ramphal (1998, p. 3), the world possesses no government in the sense of a central supra-national authority, 'and only a very few consider such a world government either necessary or desirable'. The idea of such a monolith ruling the world is frightening rather than confronting, yet at the same time 'the world needs governance: formal and informal agreements to regulate common affairs, promote common interests, and pursue common goals'. Thus global governance means:

- First, the redefinition of state sovereignty, placing the basic principles of the sovereignty concept (inviolability of borders, prohibition on interference in 'internal' affairs, the state's sole authority over social behaviour) in question;
- Second, the 'thickening' and legalization of international relations through international organizations and regimes, understood as institutionalized forms of norm- and rule-guided behaviour in the political handling of conflicts, and which build on common principles, norms, rules and decision-making processes; and
- Third, a focus on the expansion of the circle of actors beyond the state and classical international organizations, and a development of a new style of politics.

In the centre of these global strategy concepts stands the UN system, along with other international organizations such as, for example, the WTO, international regimes such as those for nuclear non-proliferation or climate control, regional arrangements such as the European Union (which could conceivably function as the seeds of the desired development), and various global networks. The main actors in such global networks are the NGOs of the so-called international civil society. The insight of the insufficiency of pure inter-state co-operation, and the often modest results of the politics of classical international organizations, should form the foundation for the emergence of new forms of co-operation between public and private actors: the beginnings of a global public policy. The UN should, as has been demanded of it, work more closely with these international political networks, support their creation, and promote the participation of state and non-state actors (Reinicke and Deng, 2000).

The UN's relationship with organizations of the so-called international civil society is nothing new, and has in fact been the rule for decades in such realms as humanitarian and development work. NGOs play a key role in numerous areas of UN activity, so much so that some authors see an impending 'privatization of international politics' (Brühl *et al.*, 2001). The approximately 2,000 NGOs accredited with consultative status for the ECOSOC according to Article 71 of the UN

Charter certainly influence the decisions taken at international conferences and negotiations, and have become indispensable in development, environment and other operative fields. Co-operation with private undertakings (the so-called 'business international non-governmental organizations' – BINGOs) is also becoming increasingly common. One example is the Secretary-General's initiative calling for a 'global compact' in which multinational corporations would co-operate with the UN to promote just labour norms, the observation of human rights, and the protection of the environment.

These initiatives show that such international processes are gaining a significance that 'cannot be classified unambiguously as taking place in an inter-state milieu in the sense of the [traditional] models of international politics'. That this sentence was formulated in the late 1960s by the German political scientist, Karl Kaiser (1969, p. 80), and that the concept of 'transnational politics' associated with Kaiser also comes from the late 1960s shows that not all ideas packaged and sold as new really are what they claim to be. It also demonstrates, however, that the idea of strengthening international civil society still has an unbroken power to attract adherents. Whether it is the case, as Jessica Mathews (1997) and Ulrich Beck (2003) argue, that there has already been a fundamental power shift from the world of states to a transnationally-networked civil society, must remain in doubt for the time being. At the very least, such a statement must be qualified by differentiation among regions of the world and among political fields. Even the globalized world still does not allow itself to be painted with a single brush.

Outlook: The United Nations in the Twenty-first Century

What role will the UN play in the twenty-first-century world? The first obvious problem is the tension between the goals and principles of the organization on the one hand, and the political reality on the other (see Table 9.2). As shown in the table, important principles of the Charter are based on rules that, in the practice of international politics, are constantly becoming relativized, changed or simply systematically ignored (see also Chapter 1).

What does all this mean for the UN? This book has, we hope, made clear that differentiation is necessary, and that there is no such thing as 'the' United Nations. In conclusion, however, we would like to focus the argument even more. Based on the structures, processes and actors in the UN and in international politics analysed above, three possible scenarios for the UN's further development emerge. These are not meant to be predictions, but rather to show what kinds of future development are possible, under which conditions they are likely to obtain, and what their implications are. These scenarios are summarized in Table 9.3.

The first scenario (marginalisation) assumes a substantial weakening or even a mid- to long-term downfall of the UN. If important states were no longer to engage themselves within the UN framework, but privileged other forums for problem-solving, either on an *ad hoc* basis, on the basis of 'coalitions of the willing', or in the framework of other international organizations or regimes, other states would

TABLE 9.2
Purposes and principles of the UN versus political reality

Purposes and principles of the Charter	Political reality
Sovereign equality of all member states	Marked power differential among states and regions
Fulfilment of the obligations foreseen in the Charter	Withholding of contributions and refusal or failure to fulfil obligations based on the dictates of national interests
Obligation to the peaceful resolution of disputes	Omnipresent violence in the international system
General prohibition on the use of force	De facto practice of the right to a unilateral use of force by some states
World peace and international security as a collective task of all member states	Dominance of the interests of industrialized countries, and a wilful blindness towards conflicts in developing countries
Prohibition on interference in the internal affairs of other states	The globalization of fundamental problems forces an erosion of state sovereignty

follow this example and a gradual collapse of the UN would occur. Possible start-ing points for such a development could be spectacular failures in peacekeeping, or a systematic avoidance of the Security Council mechanism by important state actors. Such failures would be sure to have effects on the willingness of the members to grant the UN competencies in other areas of activity. In the field of the protection of human rights, the various existing pacts and conventions would remain, but there would no longer be a global forum available for debate and moni-toring. In the areas of economics, development and environment, there would be issue-specific bodies – perhaps some of the specialized agencies and subsidiary organs (for example, UNICEF) would remain in existence – but they would be completely separate from the UN system. In international politics, the UN as such would play no further role. The most likely consequences of such a development would be an increase in the frequency of war and an intensification of the security dilemma. It is hard to imagine the development of a new and more effective way to handle problems of human rights protection and economic, development and environment issues, either. The likelihood that this scenario will take place is low, but it is certainly not impossible.

The second scenario supposes that the UN could establish itself in the long term as a sort of world government. As the central actor of a federalized world republic, the UN would have to have the power to co-ordinate and sanction behaviour that could be exercised through civil, police or military measures, as necessary. The organization would form the central co-ordinating hub of the global governance process, and would broaden its competencies successively, to the detriment of those of the member states. One could imagine the organization having the right to

TABLE 9.3
Future scenarios for UN development

	'Marginalization'	'World Government'	'Muddling through'
Peace-maintenance	The UN plays no role, the prohibition on force erodes, and the frequency of war increases	The UN plays a central role, maintains the monopoly on the use of force, and a functioning collective security system emerges	The UN is used or ignored according to whether it has demonstrated competence and usefulness in particular task areas
Protection of Human Rights	Individual conventions remain, but there is no longer a global forum for debate, norm development, and monitoring	The numerous codified agreements are not only developed further, but also endowed with effective implementation mechanisms	The presumption must remain that there is a gap between the codification and implementation of norms, and that the politics of human rights remains subject to interest-guided selectivity
Economics, Development, and Environment	Issue-specific organizations besides the UN emerge with no central governing instance	The UN is the institutional centre of global structural politics with direct regulatory competence for fields previously reserved to the nation-state	The UN is only one actor among many and only inadequately equipped to reach its ambitious goals
In international politics, the UN plays . . .	No role	The role of central actor	Sometimes the role of actor, sometimes as instrument, and sometimes as an arena

levy taxes, and developing and implementing a worldwide peaceful legal order, as well as creating a form of global citizenship rights. In the area of protection of human rights, the various conventions and agreements would not only be codified, but also enhanced with effective enforcement mechanisms. As far as peace-maintenance is concerned, this would imply the exercise of a monopoly on the use of force as well as the functioning of an effective collective security system. In economics, development and the environment, the UN would be at the centre of the politics of global structure. The consequences of such a development would, however, most probably involve a power concentration that would prove highly problematic from the perspective of democratic monitoring mechanisms. The likelihood of this scenario in fact coming to pass is extremely low.

The third scenario is essentially that the UN remains what it is now: an imperfect instrument in need of reform, but also in many areas an extremely important international organization. Within this scenario, it remains an open question as to whether the development will be primarily in the direction of the organization's use as an instrument of member state diplomacy with little independent actor quality of its own, as an arena for the treatment of different political fields on different levels of co-operation, or as an actor in its own right. In peace-maintenance, the UN may indeed in some instances be by-passed, but will be included in others. If the organization can prove its ability to take meaningful action and the interests of the member states allow it, it could play an important role. Should this not be the case, it will simply be pushed on to the sidelines. In practice, the UN would have no monopoly on the use of force, although the Security Council's monopoly on the *legitimization* of the use of force might in fact be strengthened. As for the protection of human rights, it must simply be accepted that there will continue to be a gap between the codification of norms and their realization, and furthermore that the member states will allow themselves to be forced to regard such norms against their will only in isolated cases. In economy, development and environment, the UN would continue to be one actor among many, and have very limited chances of achieving ambitious goals. The member states would be convinced only to a very limited extent to invest more resources in the system, and would rely increasingly on bilateral measures.

Of these three scenarios, the third is the most likely, of course. In which form it will eventually appear will depend heavily on the general international political attitude towards multilateral arrangements – which can, of course, be subject to rapid changes – as well as from the position of important member states.

Five Theses on the Role of the United Nations

Since political science cannot predict the future, any prognosis about the role of the United Nations must necessarily remain in the realm of speculation. However, in conclusion, we would like to set up a few basic building blocks that may be decisive for the success or failure of the United Nations. We summarize them in the following five theses:

• First, everything will depend on what the member states make of the United

Nations. An international organization built on the inter-governmental principle can only ever be as active and effective as the member states allow it to be. Such an organization can offer a framework in which the interests, perspectives and strategies of the states can be modified and brought closer together, but in the end these learning processes must be internalized by the states themselves;

- Second, it is necessary to narrow the vast distance between the full-blown public rhetoric and the often far less-ambitious practical behaviour of the member states. If the goals and principles of the UN (as listed in Articles 1 and 2 of the Charter) were taken seriously as the measure of international political behaviour, the problems of international politics would be far fewer and far less serious. The member states, however, clearly tend to understand these provisions and their implied norms not as concrete duties, but as rhetorical flourishes. Examples are the broken promise of the industrial states to reserve 0.7 per cent of their national products for development aid, and the still-inadequate participation in the standby arrangements in the realm of peace-maintenance.

- Third (and while this may at first glance seem to contradict the second point, it also indicates the opposing trends in international politics), a milieu has appeared over the last few years in which – not *always*, but with the active involvement of the UN, at least *often* – the determinations and norms of the Charter have in fact become the reference-point. They are not always respected, but the pressure for justification in cases of norm violation has increased tremendously. Even great powers can hardly escape this pressure, strengthened as it is by international public opinion. So, while it can be expected that there will always be states that break the rules, this trend might indicate that such actors will become increasingly isolated;

- Fourth, it is necessary to abandon unrealistic expectations of what the UN can do. It is to be expected that the importance of multilateral arrangements in an ever-more-complex and inter-dependent world will increase, but not that a world government is in sight. Indeed, it would not even be worth working for one, since neither a democratically-controlled nor even a generally effective form of world government is conceivable. However, the problem areas that no longer admit of any hope of success for purely national solutions have expanded to such an extent that, in an increasing number of political realms, common attempts at solutions are absolutely necessary. The United Nations could be a focal point for these common attempts; and

- Fifth, in the future the UN must be especially sure which priorities it wishes to set, and then convince the member states to make available the necessary means of carrying out those tasks. Plenty of good reform programmes have been introduced, but no coherent and comprehensive reform has taken place – mainly because of the obstacles analysed above. A recognition that, at least with respect to extensive reforms, the *process* is the goal, would seem to be in order.

The organization's continuing need for reform should not distract attention from the fact that the United Nations is absolutely essential to the stability of the international system. Political practice very seldom keeps pace with an ever-more-complex list of international problems, and sound answers to the central troubles facing the human race in the twenty-first century will have to be multilateral. In the warp and woof of multilateral regimes and organizations that make multilateralism work, the United Nations plays a unique role. Even in peacekeeping, the often-criticized UN remains crucial. Anyone who does not wish international politics to return to the principle of might-makes-right; who desires to avoid the instability of a world where multiple states arrogate to themselves the right of unilateral action; and who does not want to risk a global arms race, must canvass for a mechanism that does not allow individual states or groups of states the permission to decide for themselves when the use of force is applicable.

Even a new and improved organization would certainly still find itself confronted by the task of discharging the fundamental goals and principles set out in the Charter. If the member states refuse to support the United Nations more than they have done thus far, success will remain permanently elusive.

Further Reading

Krasno, Jean E. (ed.) (2004) *The United Nations: Confronting the Challenges of a Global Society*, Boulder, CO: Lynne Rienner/International Peace Academy.

Muldoon, James P. (2004) *The Architecture of Global Governance. An Introduction to the Study of International Organizations*, Boulder, CO: Westview Press.

Nuscheler, Franz (2002) 'Global Governance, Development, and Peace', in Paul Kennedy, Dirk Messner and Franz Nuscheler (eds), *Global Trends and Global Governance*, London, Pluto Press, pp. 156–82.

Paolini, Albert J. (ed.) (2003) *Between Sovereignty and Global Governance: The United Nations, the State and Civil Society*, Basingstoke: Palgrave.

Reinicke, Wolfgang and Francis Deng (2000): *Critical Choices. The United Nations, Networks, and the Future of Global Governance*, Ottawa: International Development Research Centre.

Sucharipa, Ernst (2001) 'The United Nations Today: Its Current Status, Reforms and Perspectives for the Future', in Franz Cede and Lilly Sucharipa-Behrmann (eds), *The United Nations: Law and Practice*, The Hague: Kluwer, pp. 313–31.

United Nations Association of the USA (ed.), *Global Agenda. Issues before the General Assembly of the United Nations* (published annually) New York: UNA-USA.

Witte, Jan Martin, Charlotte Streck and Thorsten Benner (eds) (2003) *Progress or Peril? Partnership and Networks in Global Environmental Governance*, Berlin, Geneva: Global Public Policy Institute.

Bibliography

Abiew, Francis K. (1999) *The Evolution of the Doctrine and Practice of Humanitarian Intervention*, The Hague/London/Boston.

Afoaku, Osita G. and Okechukwu Ukaga, (2001) 'United Nations Security Council Reform: A Critical Analysis of Enlargement Opinions', *Journal of Third World Studies* (2) 2001, pp. 149–71.

Africa Banjul Charter on Human and Peoples' Rights – 27.06.1981, CAB/LEG/67/3.

Alagappa, Muthiah and Takashi Inoguchi (eds) (1999) *International Security Management and the United Nations*, Tokyo.

Albright, Madeleine K. (2003) 'United Nations', *Foreign Policy* (138) pp. 16–26.

Alger, Chadwick F. (ed.) (1998) *The Future of the United Nations System. Potential for the Twenty-First Century*, Tokyo.

Alger, Chadwick F., Gene M. Lyons and John E. Trent (eds) (1995) *The United Nations System. The Policies of Member States*, Tokyo/New York/Paris.

Alston, Philip (1994) 'Appraising the United Nations Human Rights Regime', in Philip Alston (ed.), *The United Nations and Human Rights*. Oxford.

Alston, Philip (ed.) (2000): *The Future of UN Human Rights Treaty Monitoring*, Cambridge.

Alston, Philip (ed.) (2004): *The United Nations and Human Rights: A Critical Appraisal*, Oxford.

Amnesty International, *Annual Report*, London (published annually).

Amr, Mohamed Sameh M. (2003) *The Role of the International Court of Justice as the Principal Judicial Organ of the United Nations*, The Hague.

Annan, Kofi (1997) 'Renewing the United Nations: A Programme for Reform', Secretary General's Report – 14.07.1997, A/51/950.

Annan, Kofi (2000) *We the Peoples: The Role of the United Nations in the Twenty-first Century*. Secretary General's Report – 27.03.2000, A/54/2000.

Annan, Kofi (2002a) *Prevention of Armed Conflicts*, New York.

Annan, Kofi (2002b) *Strengthening of the United Nations: An Agenda for Further Change, Report of the Secretary General* (A/57/387).

Anthonson, Mette (2003) *Decisions on Participation in UN Operations: Do Media Matter?*: *Danish and Swedish Response to Intra State Conflicts in the 1990s*, Göteborg.

Arangio-Ruiz, Gaetano (1979) The UN Declaration on Friendly Relations and the System of the Sources of International Law, Alphen.

Arbeitsgemeinschaft Kriegsursachenforschung (2000) (ed.), *Das Kriegsgeschehen. Daten und Tendenzen der Kriege und bewaffneten Konflikte*, Opladen (published annually).

Archer, Clive (2001) *International Organizations*, London.

Armstrong, David, Lorna Lloyd and John Redmond (eds) (1996) *From Versailles to Maastricht. International Organisation in the Twentieth Century*, Basingstoke.

Arnim, Gabriele von (2002) (ed.), *Menschenrechte 2003*, Frankfurt-am-Main.

Arqilla, John and David Ronfeld (eds) (1997) *In Athena's Camp. Preparing for Conflict in the Information Age*, Santa Monica, Calif.

Art, Robert J. and Kenneth N. Waltz (eds) (1999) *The Use of Force. Military Power and International Politics*, Lanham, MD.

Atlantic Charter (1941): Avalon Project at Yale Law School. www.yale.edu.Lawweb/avalon.

Baehr, Peter R. and Leon Gordenker (2001) *The United Nations at the End of the 1990s*, New York.

Bailey, Sydney D. and Sam Daws (eds) (1995) *The United Nations. A Concise Political Guide*, Lanham, MD.

Bailey, Sydney D. and Sam Daws (1998) *The Procedure of the UN Security Council*, Oxford.

Baratta, Joseph P. (1995) *United Nations System, Bibliography*, Oxford.

Barker, Enno (1990) 'Rüstungskontrolle in den Vereinten Nationen', *Vereinte Nationen* (5) pp. 183–5.

Bartl, Jürgen (1999) *Die humanitäre Intervention durch den Sicherheitsrat der Vereinten Nationen im 'Failed State'*, Frankfurt-am-Main.

Baum, Gerhart (1999) 'Die Menschenrechtskommission der Vereinten Nationen', in: Gabriele von Arnim et al. (eds), *Jahrbuch Menschenrechte 2000*, Frankfurt am Main, pp. 241–8.

Baum, Gerhart, Eibe Riedel and Michael Schäfer (1998) (eds), *Menschenrechtsschutz in den Vereinten Nationen*, Baden-Baden.

Baylis, John and Steve Smith (eds) (2001) *The Globalization of World Politics*, Oxford.

Beck, Ulrich (2003) 'Kosmopolitische Globalisierung', *Internationale Politik* (7) pp. 9–13.

Benner, Thorsten and Jan Martin Witte (2001) 'Brücken im globalen System, *Internationale Politik* (5) 2001, pp. 1–8.

Berdal, Mats (2000) 'Lessons Not Learned: The Use of Force in Peace Operations in the 1990s', *International Peacekeeping* (4) pp. 54–74.

Berdal, Mats (2003) 'Ineffective but Indispensable', *Survival* (2) pp. 7–30.

Bertrand, Maurice and Daniel Warner (eds) (1996) *A New Charter for a Worldwide Organization*, The Hague.

Bhatta, Ghambir (2000) *Reforms at the UN: Contextualising the Annan Agenda*, Singapore.

Biermann, Frank and Udo Ernst Simonis (1998) *Eine Weltorganisation für Umwelt und Entwicklung. Funktionen, Chancen, Probleme*, Bonn.

Biermann, Frank and Udo Ernst Simonis (2000) 'Institutionelle Reform der Weltumweltpolitik? Zur politischen Debatte um die Gründung einer Weltumweltorganisation', *Zeitschrift für Internationale Beziehungen* (1) pp. 163–83.

Biggs, David (2000) 'United Nations Contributions to the Process', *Disarmament Forum* (2) pp. 25–39.

Birnie, Patricia (1993) 'The UN and the Environment', in Roberts and Kingsbury 1993, pp. 327–38.

Blumenwitz, Dieter (1994) 'Die humanitäre Intervention, *Aüs Politik ünd teitgeschichte* (47) pp. 3–10.

Boekle, Henning (1998) 'Die Vereinten Nationen und der Schutz der Menschenrechte', *APuZ* (46–7) pp. 3–17.

Bonn International Center for Conversion (BICC), *Conversion Survey*, Baden-Baden (published annually).

Bothe, Michael (2002) 'Peace-keeping', *Simma* pp. 648–700.

Bothe, Michael and Thomas Dörschel (eds) (1999) *UN Peacekeeping: A Documentary Introduction*, The Hague.

Boulden, Jane (2001) *Peace Enforcement. The United Nations Experience in Congo, Somalia and Bosnia*, Westport, CT.

Boulden, Jane (ed.) (2003) *Dealing with Conflict in Africa: The United Nations and Regional Organizations*, Basingstoke.

Bourantonis, Dimitris (1998) 'Reform of the UN Security Council and the Non-Aligned States', *International Peacekeeping* (1) pp. 89–109.

Boutros-Ghali, Boutros (1992) 'An Agenda for Peace: Preventive Diplomacy, Peacemaking and Peacekeeping', *United Nations Press*, New York.

Boutros-Ghali, Boutros (1994) *An Agenda for Development. Secretary General's Report –* 6.5.1994, A/48/935.

Boutros-Ghali, Boutros (1995) 'Introduction', *United Nations, The United Nations and Human Rights 1945–1995*, New York, pp. 3–125.

Brahimi-Report (2000) *Report of the Panel on United Nations Peace Operations of 23 August 2000.* UN-Documents A/55/305 and S/2000/809.

Brauch, Hans Günter (2002) 'Disarmament', *Volger* 2002, pp. 82–99.

Brauch, Hans Günter, Czeslaw Mesjasz and Björn Möller (1998) 'Controlling Weapons in the Quest for Peace: Non-offensive Defence, Arms Control, Disarmament, and Conversion', in Alger (1998), pp. 15–53.

Brayton, Steve (2002) 'Outsourcing War: Mercanaries and the Privatization of Peacekeeping', *Journal of International Affairs* (2) pp. 303–29.

Brenner, Michael (1995) 'The Multilateral Moment', in Michael Brenner (ed.) *Multilateralism and Western Strategy*, New York, pp. 1–41.

Brock, Lothar (1995) 'UNO und Dritte Welt. Fünf verlorene Jahrzehnte?', *Jahrbuch Dritte Welt* 1996, Munich, pp. 62–80.

Browne, Marjorie Ann (compiler) (2003) *Iraq-Kuwait: United Nations Security Council resolution texts, 1992–2002*, New York.

Brühl, Tanja, Debiel, Tobias, Hamm, Brigitte, Hummel, Hartwig, and Martens, Fens (eds) (2001) *Die Privatisierung der Weltpolitik. Entsstaatlichung und Kommerzialisierung im Globalisierungsprozess*, Bonn.

Bundesministerium für Wirtschaftliche Zunammenarbeit und Entwicklung (2001) *Elfter Bericht zur Entwicklungspolitik der Bundesregierung*, Berlin.

Burgess, Stephen F. (2001) *The United Nations under Boutros Boutros-Ghali, 1992–1997*, Lanham, MD.

Butfoy, Andrew (1993) 'Themes Within the Collective Security Idea', *Journal of Strategic Studies* (4) pp. 490–510.

Cable, Vincent (1999) *Globalization and Global Governance*, London.

Camilleri, Joseph A. (ed.) (2000) *Reimagining the Future: Towards Democratic Governance: A Report of the Global Governance Reform Project*, Bundoora, Victoria.

Caplan, Richard (2002) *A New Trusteeship? The International Administration of War-Torn Territories*, Oxford.

Cardenas, Sonia (2003) 'Emerging Global Actors: The United Nations and National Human Rights Institutions', *Global Governance* (9) pp. 23–42.

Carle, Christophe (1999) 'Disarmament: The Next Ten Years', *Disarmament Forum* (1) pp. 13–18.

Carlsnaes, Walter, Thomas Risse and Beth A. Simmons (eds) (2002) *Handbook of International Relations*, London 2002.

Carlsson, Ingvar, Sung-Joo Han and Rufus Kupolati (1999) *Report of the Independent Inquiry into the Actions of the United Nations during the 1994 Genocide in Rwanda*, New York.

Carnegie Commission on Preventing Deadly Conflicts (ed.) (1998) *Preventing Deadly Conflicts*, New York.

Cede, Franz (2001) 'The Purpose and principles of the United Nations', in Cede and Sucharipa-Behrmann (2001), pp. 11–24.

Cede, Franz and Lilly Sucharipa-Behrmann, (eds) (2001) *The United Nations: Law and Practice*, The Hague.

Chesterton, Simon (2001) *Just War or Just Peace. Humanitarian Intervention and International Law*, New York.

Childers, Erskine and Brian Urquhart (1994) 'Renewing the United Nations System', New York.

Clark, Grenville and Louis B. Sohn (1960) *World Peace Through World Law*, Cambridge.

Clark, Wesley K. (2001) *Waging Modern War. Bosnia, Kosovo and the Future of Combat*, Washington, DC.

Claude, Inis L. (1966): *Power and International Relations*, New York.

Claude, Inis L. (1970) *Swords into Plowshares. The Problems and Progress of International Organizations*, New York.

Coleman, David (2003) 'The United Nations and Transnational Corporations: From an Internation to a "Beyond-state" Model of Engagement', *Global Society* (4) pp. 339–59.

Commission on Global Governance (1995) *Our Global Neighborhood*, New York.

Conca, Ken and Geoffrey D. Dabelko (1998) *Green Planet Blues: Environmental Politics from Stockholm to Kyoto*, Boulder, Col.

Conforti, Benedetto (2000) *The Law and Pratice of the United Nations*, The Hague.

Cordesman, Anthony H. (2003) *The Iraq War*, Washington, DC.

Cortright, David and George Lopez (eds) (1995) *Economic Sanctions – Panacea or Peacebuilding in a Post-Cold War World*, Oxford.

Cortright, David and George Lopez (2000) *The Sanctions Decade. Assessing UN Strategies in the 1990s*, Boulder, Col. and London.

Creveld, Martin (1991) *The Transformation of War*, New York.

Czempiel, Ernst-Otto (1993) *Weltpolitik im Umbruch. Das internationale System nach dem Ende des Ost-West-Konfliktes*, Munich.

Czempiel, Ernst-Otto (1994) *Die Reform der UNO. Möglichkeiten und Missverständnisse*, Frankfurt-am-Main.

Czempiel, Ernst-Otto (1995) 'Aktivieren, reformieren, negieren? Zum 50-jährigen Bestehen der Vereinten Nationen', *APuZ* (42) pp. 36–45.

Czempiel, Ernst-Otto (1998) *Friedensstrategien. Eine systematische Darstellung außenpolitischer Theorien von Machiavelli bis Madariaga*, Opladen.

Czempiel, Ernst-Otto (1999) *Kluge Macht: Außenpolitik für das 21. Jahrhundert*, Munich.

Czempiel, Ernst-Otto (2002) *Weltpolitik im Umbruch. Die Pax Americana, der Terrorismus und die die Zukunft der internationalen Beziehungen*, Frankfurt-am-Main.

Datan, Merav (2002) 'The United Nations and Civil Society', *Disarmament Forum* (1) pp. 41–5.

Daws, Sam (ed.) (2000) *The United Nations*, Aldershot.

De Wet, Erika (2004) *The Chapter VII powers of the United Nations Security Council*, Oxford.

Debiel, Tobias (2003) *UN-Friedensoperationen in Afrika. Weltinnenpolitik und die Realität von Bürgerkriegen*, Bonn.

Debiel, Tobias and Franz Nuscheler (1996) *Der neue Interventionismus. Humanitäre Einmischung zwischen Anspruch und Wirklichkeit*, Bonn.

Deiseroth, Dieter (1999) '"Humanitäre Intervention" und Völkerrecht', *Neüe juristische Wochenschrift* (42) pp. 3084–8.

Deutsches Übersee-Institut (ed.), *Jahrbuch Dritte Welt*, Munich (published annually).

Dicke, Detlev Christian and Hans-Werner Rengeling (1975) *Die Sicherung des Weltfriedens durch die Vereinten Nationen*, Baden-Baden.

Dicke, Klaus (1994) *Effizienz und Effektivität internationaler Organisationen. Darstellung und kritische Analyse eines Topos im Reformprozesse der Vereinten Nationen*, Berlin.

Diehl, Paul F. (ed.) (1997) *The Politics of Global Governance. International Organizations in an Interdependent World*, Boulder, Col.

Dobson, Hugo (2003) *Japan and United Nations Peacekeeping: New Pressures, New Responses*, London.

Doyle, Michael W., Ian Johnstone and Robert C. Orr (eds) (1997) *Keeping the Peace: Lessons from Multidimensional UN-Operations in Cambodia and El Salvador*, Cambridge.

Dunne, Michael (2003) 'The United States, the United Nations and Iraq: "Multilateralism of a Kind"', *International Affairs* (2) pp. 257–79.

Durch, W. (1993) *The Evolution of UN Peacekeeping*, New York.

Dwan, Renata (ed.) (2002) *Executive Policing: Enforcing the Law in Peace Operations*, Oxford.

Eban, Abba (1995) 'The U.N. Idea Revisited', *Foreign Affairs* (5) pp. 39–55.

Ebock, Kerstin (2000) *Der Schutz grundlegender Menschenrechte durch kollektive Zwangsmaßnahmen der Staatengemeinschaft*, Frankfurt-am-Main.

Elliot, Lorraine M. (2001) *Global Governance: A Report Card for the United Nations*, Manchester.

Esquivel, Adolfo Perez (ed.) (1989) *Das Recht auf Entwicklung als Menschenrecht*, Munich/Zurich.

Esty, Daniel (ed.) (2002) *Global Environmental Institutions. Perspectives on Reform*, London.

Fassbender, Bardo (1998a) *UN Security Council and the Right of Veto. A Constitutional Perspective*. The Hague.

Fassbender, Bardo (1998b) 'Reforming the United Nations', *Die Friedenswarte* (4), pp. 427–42.

Ferdowsi, Mir A. (2002) 'Die Vereinten Nationen und die wirtschaftliche Entwicklung der Länder des "Südens"', *Opitz* , pp. 155–77.

Ferencz, Benjamin B. (2001) 'The Evolution of International Criminal Law: A Bird's Eye View of the Past Century', in Hasse *et al.* (2001), pp. 354–64.

Fetherston, Anthony (1994) *Towards a Theory of United Nations Peacekeeping*, New York.

Findlay, Trevor (2002) *The Use of Force in UN Peace Operations*, Oxford.

Fink, Udo (1999) *Kollektive Friedenssicherung: Kapitel vii UN-Charta in der Praxis des Sicherheitsrates der Vereinten Nationen*, 2 vols, Frankfurt-am-Main.

Fischer, Joseph (1999) 'Rede des deutschen Außenministers vor der 54. Generalversammlung der Vereinten Nationen', *Internationale Politik* (12) pp. 103–9.

Fischer, Joseph (2002) 'Rede vor der Generalversammlung der Vereinten Nationen am 14. September 2002', *Internationale Politik* (11) pp. 126–30.

Fleitz, Frederick *H.* (2002) *Peacekeeping Fiascos of the 1990s: Causes, Solutions, and Interests*, Westport, CT.

Forschungsinstitut der Deutschen Gesellschaft für Auswärtige Politik (ed.), *Jahrbuch Internationale Politik*, Munich (published annually).

Forsythe, David P. (1997) 'The United Nations, Human Rights and Development', *Human Rights Quarterly* (2) pp. 334–49.

Freedom House, *Freedom in the World. The Annual Survey of Political and Civil Liberties*, New York (published annually).

French, Hilary F. (1995) *Partnership for the Planet. An Environmental Agenda for the United Nations*, Washington, DC.

Frowein, Jochen (2002) 'Ist das Völkerrecht tot?' *Frankfurter Allgemeine Zeitung*, 23 July.

Frowein, Jochen Abraham (2003) 'Issues of Legitimacy around the United Nations Security Council', *Verhandeln für den Frieden*, p. 121–40.

Galtung, Johan (1975) *Strukturelle Gewalt. Beiträge zur Friedens- und Konfliktforschung*, Reinbek.

Gehring, Thomas and Sebastian Oberthür (2000) 'Was bringt eine Weltumweltorganisation? Kooperationstheoretische Anmerkungen zur institutionellen Neuordnung der internationalen Umweltpolitik', *Zeitschrift für internationale Beziehungen* (1) pp. 185–211.

Glanzer, Hans-Peter (2001) 'An Agenda for Development', in: Cede and Sucharipa-Behrmann (2001), pp. 215–30.

Glen, Carol M. and Richard C. Murgo (2003) 'United Nations Human Rights Conventions: Obligations and Compliance', *Politics & Policy* (4) pp. 596–620.

Glennon, Michael (2003) 'Why the Security Council Failed', *Foreign Affairs* (3) pp. 16–35.

Gorman, Robert F. (2001) *Great debates at the United Nations: An Encyclopaedia of Fifty Key Issues 1945–2000*, Westport, CT.

Gottstein, Margit (1998) 'Frauenrechte – Menschenrechte?', *Amnesty International*, pp. 75–86.

Gowlland-Debbas, Vera (ed.) (2001) *United Nations sanctions and International Law*, The Hague.

Grewe, Wilhelm G. and Daniel-Erasmus Khan (2002) 'Drafting History', in Simma (2002), pp 1–12.

Griffiths, Martin (1999) *Fifty Key Thinkers in International Relations*, London and New York.

Grunberg, Isabelle (ed.) (2000) *The United Nations Development Dialogue; Finance Trade, Poverty, Peace-building*, Tokyo.

Guggenheim, Paul (1932) *Der Völkerbund in seiner politischen und rechtlichen Wirklichkeit*, Leipzig and Berlin.

Guicherd, Catherine (1999) 'International Law and the War in Kosovo', *Survival* (2) pp. 19–33.

Haftendorn, Helga (1990) 'Zur Theorie außenpolitischer Entscheidungsprozesse', in Volker Rittberger (ed.), *Theorie der Internationalen Beziehungen*, Opladen, pp. 401–23.

Hasenclever, Andreas, Peter Mayer and Volker Rittberger (1997) *Theories of International Regimes*, Cambridge.

Hasse, Jana (2000)'Resolutionen des UN-Sicherheitsrates contra Menschenrechte?' *Sicherheit ünd Frieden* (2), pp. 158–63.

Hasse, Jana, Erwin Müller and Patricia Schneider (eds) (2001) *Humanitäres Völkerrecht. Politische, rechtliche und strafgerichtliche Dimensionen*, Baden-Baden.

Heidelberg Institute of International Conflict Research (ed.), *The Conflict Barometer* (published annually)

Heinrich-Böll-Stiftung (eds) (2001) *Entwicklungspolitik als globale Strukturpolitik*, Berlin.

Herz, Dietmar (2002) Das Weltwirtschaftssystem, in: Opitz 2002, pp. 131–154.

Herz, Dietmar, Christian Jetzlsperger and Marc Schattenmann (eds): (2002) *Die Vereinten Nationen. Entwicklung, Aktivitäten, Perspektiven*, Frankfurt-am-Main.

Herz, John (1961) *Weltpolitik im Atomzeitalter*, Stuttgart.

Hilderbrand, Robert C. (1990) *Dumbarton Oaks. The Origins of the United Nations and the Search for Postwar Security*, London.

Hill, Christopher (2003) *The Changing Politics of Foreign Policy*, Basingstoke.

Hill, Ronald P. and Dhanda, Kanwalroop K. (2003) 'Technological achievement and human development: a view from the United Nations Development Program', *Human Rights Quarterly* (4) pp. 1020–34.

Hill, Stephen M. (2002) *United Nations disarmament in Intrastate Conflict*, Basingstoke.

Hinic, Dejan (2001) 'The International Tribunal for the Former Yugoslavia: A Serbian View', in Hasse, Müller and Schneider (2001), pp. 420–5.

Hoch, Martin (2001) 'Krieg und Politik im 21. Jahrhundert', *APuZ* (20), pp. 17–25.

Hoffman, Stanley (1981) *Duties Beyond Borders: On the Limits and Possibilities of Ethical International Politics*, Syracuse, NY.

Howard, Rhoda (1997/8) 'Human Rights and the Culture Wars. Globalization and the Universality of Human Rights', *International Journal* (1) pp. 94–112.

Hüfner, Klaus (ed.) (1995) *Agenda for Change. New Task for the United Nations*, Opladen.

Hüfner, Klaus (2002) 'UN-System', in Volger (2002), pp. 634–9.

Hüfner, Klaus and Jens Martens (2000) *UNO-Reform zwischen Utopie und Realität. Vorschläge zum Wirtschafts- und Sozialbereich der Vereinten Nationen*, Frankfurt-am-Main.

Hüfner, Klaus and Wolfgang Spröte (1994) 'Zur Reform des Wirtschafts-und Sozialbereichs der Vereinten Nationen', in Hüfner (1994), pp. 99–118.

Hurrell, Andrew (1992) 'Collective Security and International Order Revisited', *International Relations* (1) pp. 37–55.

International Bank for Reconstruction and Development, *World Development Report*, New York (published annually).

International Institute for Strategic Studies (IISS), *The Military Balance*, London (published annually).

International Monetary Fund (IMF), *World Economic Outlook*, Washington, DC (published twice a year).

Jakobsen, Peter Viggo (1998) 'The Danish Approach to UN Peacekeeping Operations after the Cold War: A New Model in the Making?', *International Peacekeeping* (3) pp. 106–23.

James, Alan (1990) *Peacekeeping in International Politics*, New York.

Jett, Dennis C. (2000) *Why Peacekeeping Fails*, New York.

Joint Four Nations Declaration (1943) *The Moscow Conference; October 1943*. Avalon Project at Yale Law School www.yale.edu.Lawweb/avalon.

Kagan, Robert (2003) *Of Power and Paradise. America and Europe in the New World Order*, New York

Kaiser, Karl (1969) 'Transnationale Politik. Zu einer Theorie der multinationalen Politik', in Ernst-Otto Czempiel (ed.), *Die anachronistische Souveränität. Zum Verhältnis von Innen-und Außenpolitik*, Opladen.

Kaiser, Karl (2003) 'Zeitenwende. Dominanz und Interdependenz nach dem Irak-Krieg', in *Internationale Politik* (5) pp. 1–8.

Kaldor, Mary (2000) *New and Old Wars. Organised Violence in a Global Era*, Cambridge.

Kälin, Walter (1998) 'Die Allgemeine Erklärung der Menschenrechte: Eine Kopernikanische Wende im Völkerrecht?', *Amnesty International* pp. 5–17.

Katayanagi, Mari (2002) *Human Rights Functions of United Nations Peacekeeping Operations*, The Hague.

Kaul, Hans-Peter (1998) 'Durchbruch in Rom. Der Vertrag über den Internationalen Strafgerichtshof', *Vereinte Nationen* (4) pp. 125–30.

Kaul, Inge (2002) 'Development Research, Development Theories', in Volger (2002) pp. 74–82.

Kaul, Inge, Isabelle Grunberg and Marc A. Stern (eds) (1999a) *Global Public Goods. International Cooperation in the 21st Century*, New York.

Kaul, Inge, Isabelle Grunberg and Marc Stern (1999b) *Global Public Goods. Concepts, Policies and Strategies*, in Kaul, Grunberg and Stern (1999), pp. 450–507.

Keeley, James F. and Rob Huebert, (eds) (2004) *Commercial Satellite Imagery and United Nations Peacekeeping: A View From Above*, Aldershot.

Kellogg–Briand Pact (1928) Avalon Project at Yale Law School www.yale.edu.lawweb/avalon.

Kennedy, Paul and Bruce Russett (1995) 'Reforming the United Nations', in *Foreign Affairs* (5) pp. 56–71.

Keohane, Robert O. (1989) *International Institutions and State Power*, Boulder, CO.

Kimminich, Otto (1997) *Einführung in das Völkerrecht*, Tübingen and Basle.

Kinloch, Stephen P. (1996) 'Utopian or pragmatic? A UN Permanent Military Volunteer Force', *International Peacekeeping* (4) pp. 166–90.

Knight, W. Andy (2000) *A Changing United Nations: Multilateral Evolution and the Quest for Global Governance*, Basingstoke.

Knight, W. Andy (ed.) (2001) Adapting the United Nations to a post-modern era: lesson learned, Basingstoke.

Knipping, Franz, Volker Rittberger and Hans von Mangoldt (eds) (1995) *Das System der Vereinten Nationen und seine Vorläufer/The United Nations System and its Predecessors* Vol. 1/1: *Vereinte Nationen*, edited by Hans von Mangoldt; Vol. 1/2: Sonderorganisationen und andere Institutionen, edited by Hans von Mangoldt), Munich.

Koschorreck, Wilfried (1997) 'Zahlungsfähigkeit versus Zahlungsbereitschaft. Die Debatte um die Beiträge zu den Vereinten Nationen', in *Vereinte Nationen* (5) pp. 161–7.

Koschorreck, Wilfried (1998) 'Beitragsfestsetzung weder gerecht noch transparent', *Vereinte Nationen* (1) pp. 33–5.

Koschorreck, Wilfried (2000) 'Noch mehr Rabatt für die Reichsten?', *Vereinte Nationen* (4) pp. 142–4.

Krasno, Jean E. (ed.) (2004) *The United Nations: Confronting the Challenges of a Global Society*, Boulder, Col.

Kratochwil, Friedrich and Edward D. Mansfield (eds) (1994) *International Organizations. A Reader*, New York.

Kreuzer, Christine (2001) 'Kinder in bewaffneten Konflikten', in Hasse, Müller and Schneider (2001), pp. 304–20.

Kubbig, Bernd W. (ed.) (2003) *Brandherd Irak. US-Hegemonieanspruch, die UNO und die Rolle Europas*, Frankfurt-am-Main.

Kühne, Winrich (1993) 'Völkerrecht und Friedenssicherung in einer turbulenten Welt: Eine analytische Zusammenfassung der Grundprobleme und Entwicklungsperspektiven', in: Winrich Kühne, (ed.), *Blauhelme in einer turbulenten Welt*, Baden-Baden, pp. 17–100.

Kühne, Winrich (2000) 'Die Vereinten Nationen an der Schwelle zum nächsten Jahrtausend', in: Kaiser and Schwarz (2000), pp. 442–57.

Kühne, Winrich (2000b) 'Zukunft der UN-Friedenseinsätze. Lehren aus dem Brahimi-Report', *Blätter für deutsche und internationale Politik* (11) pp. 1355–64.

Kühne, Winrich and Katja Baumann (1995) *Reform des Sicherheitsrates zum 50-jährigen Jubiläum. Auswertung und Analyse der Stellungnahmen der Mitgliedstaaten im Überblick*, Ebenhausen.

Kühnhardt, Ludger (1991) *Die Universalität der Menschenrechte*, Bonn.

Kulessa, Manfred (1998) 'Stumpfes Friedensinstrument? Zur Problematik der UN-Sanktionen', *APuZ* (16–17) pp. 31–8.

Kulessa, Manfred and Dorothee Starck, (1997) *Frieden durch Sanktionen?*, (SEF Policy Paper No. 7), Bonn.

Kupchan, Charles A. and Clifford A. Kupchan (1995) 'The Promise of Collective Security', *International Security* (1) pp. 52–61.

Lagoni, Rainer (1995) 'ECOSOC', in Wolfrum (1995), pp. 461–9.

Lang, Winfried and Andreas Kumin (2001) 'Disarmament Issues', in Cede and Sucharipa-Behrmann (2001), pp. 127–42.

Laulan, Ives Marie (1996) 'Il faut réformer l'ONU', *Defense Nationale* (12) pp. 45–53.

Le Monde Diplomatique (ed.) (2003) *Atlas der Globalisierung*, Berlin.

Lehmkuhl, Ursula (1996) Theorien Internationaler Politik. Einführung und Texte, Munich and Vienna.

Leisinger, Klaus M. (2000) *Die sechste Milliarde. Weltbevölkerung und nachhaltige Entwicklung*, Bonn.

Lewis, Patricia (2001) 'From "UNSCOM" to "UNMOVIC": The United Nations and Iraq', *Disarmament Forum* (2) pp. 63–9.

Lie, Trygve (1954) *In the Cause of Peace*, New York.

Liese, Andrea (1998) 'Menschenrechtsschutz durch Nichtregierungsorganisationen', *APuZ* (46–7) pp. 36–42.

Link, Werner (1998) *Die Neuordnung der Weltpolitik. Grundprobleme globaler Politik an der Schwelle zum 21. Jahrhundert*, Munich.

Loibl, Gerhard (2001) 'Environmental Protection and Sustainable Development', in Cede and Sucharipa-Behrmann (2001), pp. 195–214.

Luard, Evan (1982) *A History of the United Nations. Vol. I: The Years of Western Domination 1945–1955; Vol. II: The Age of Decolonization 1955–1965*, Basingstoke.

Luard, Evan (1995) *The United Nations. How It Works and What It Does*, New York.

Luttwak, Edward N. (1999) 'Give War a Chance', *Foreign Affairs* (4) pp. 36–44.

MacDermott, Anthony (1999) *The New Politics of Financing the UN*, Basingstoke.

MacWhinney, Edward (2000) *The United Nations and a New World Order for a New Millenium: Self-Determination, State Succession, and Humanitarian Intervention*, The Hague.

Malone, David M. and Lotta Hagman (2002) 'The North-South Divide at the United Nations: Fading at Last?', *Security Dialogue* (4) pp. 399–415.

Malone, David M. and Karin Wermester (2000) 'Boom and Bust? The Changing Nature of UN Peacekeeping', *International Peacekeeping* (4) pp. 37–54.

Martens, Jens (1998) 'Kompendium der Gemeinplätze. Die Agenda für die Entwicklung: Chronologie eines gescheiterten Verhandlungsprozesses', *Vereinte Nationen* (2) pp. 47–52.

Martens, Jens (2000) 'Globale Entwicklungspartnerschaft: Zielvorgabe für 2001', *Vereinte Nationen* (3) pp. 99–104.

Martens, Jens (2001) 'Möglichkeiten und Probleme in der Zukunft der Entwicklungsfinanzierung', in Heinrich-Böll-Stiftung (2001), pp. 52–63.

Martens, Jens and Wolfgang Sterk (2002) *Multilateralismüs zwichen Blockadepolitik ünd Partnerschaftsrhethorik.*

Martin, Ian (1998) 'Auf dem Weg zur verstärkten Menschenrechtsintervention? Zur Rolle der Vereinten Nationen nach dem Ende des Kalten Krieges', *Amnesty International* pp. 147–58.

Mathews, Jessica T. (1997) 'Power Shift', *Foreign Affairs* (1) pp. 50–66.

Mathson, Michael J. (2001) 'United Nations Governance of Postconflict Societies', *American Journal of International Law* (1) pp. 76–86.

May, Ernest and Angeliki E. Laiou (eds) (1998) *The Dumbarton Oaks Conversations and the United Nations 1944–1994*, Washington, DC.

Mayall, James (ed.) (1999) *The New Interventionism 1991–1994: United Nations Experience in Cambodia, Former Yugoslavia and Somalia*, Cambridge.

McDermott, Anthony (1998) 'The UN and NGOs: Humanitarian Interventions in Future Conflicts', *Contemporary Security Policy* (3) 1998, pp. 1–26.

Mearsheimer, John (1994) 'The False Promise of International Institutions', *International Security* (3) pp. 5–49.

Menzel, Ulrich (ed.) (2000) *Vom Ewigen Frieden und vom Wohlstand der Nationen*, Frankfurt-am-Main.

Menzel, Ulrich (2001) *Zwischen Idealismus und Realismus. Die Lehre von den internationalen Beziehungen*, Frankfurt am Main..

Messner, Dirk and Franz Nuscheler (eds) (1996a) 'Die Weltkonferenzen der 90er Jahre. Eine Gipfelei ohne neue Perspektiven?', in Messner and Nuscheler (1996), pp. 160–9.

Messner, Dirk and Franz Nuscheler (1996b) (eds) *Weltkonferenzen und Weltberichte. Ein Wegweiser durch die internationale Diskussion*, Bonn.

Messner, Dirk and Franz Nuscheler (1996c) 'Global Governance. Organisationselemente und Säulen einer Weltordnungspolitik', in Messner and Nuscheler (1996), pp. 12–36.

Metzger, Martina (2002) 'IMF', in Volger (2002), pp. 300–7.

Meyers, Reinhard (1981) *Die Lehre von den Internationalen Beziehungen. Ein entwicklungsgeschichtlicher Überblick*, Dusseldorf.

Meyers, Reinhard (1997) 'Grundbegriffe und theoretische Perspektiven der internationalen Beziehungen', in Bundeszentrale für politische Bildung (ed.), *Grundwissen Politik*, Bonn, pp. 313–434.

Michie, Jonathan (ed.) (2003) *The Handbook of Globalization*, Cheltenham.

Mingst, Karen A. and Margaret P. Karns (2000) *The United Nations in the Post-Cold War Era*, Boulder, Col.

Moore, John Allphin (2002) *Encyclopedia of the United Nations*, New York.

Moore, John Norton and Morrison, Alex (eds) (2000) *Strengthening the United Nations and enhancing war prevention*, Durham, NC.

Morgan, Patrick M. (2000) 'The Impact of the Revolution in Military Affairs', *Journal of Strategic Studies,* March, pp. 132–62.

Morris, Virginia and Michael Scharf (1995) *An Insider's Guide to the International Criminal Tribunal for the Former Yugoslavia*, Irvington-on-Hudson.

Morton, Jeffrey S. (2000) *The International Law Commission of the United Nations*, Columbia, SC.

Mueller, Joachim W. (ed.) (2001) *Reforming the United Nations: The Quiet Revolution*, The Hague.

Muldoon, James P. (2004) *The Architecture of Global Governance. An Introduction to the Study of International Organizations*, Boulder, CO.

Neack, Laura, Jeanne Hey and Patrick Haney (eds) (1995) *Foreign Policy Analysis. Continuity and Change in its Second Generation*, Englewood Cliffs, NJ.

Nelson, Jane (2002) *Building Partnership: Cooperation between the United Nations System and the Private Sector*, New York.

New Zealand Ministry of Foreign Affairs and Trade, *United Nations Handbook*, Wellington (published annually).

Newman, Edward (ed.) (2001) *The United Nations and Human Security*, Basingstoke.

Nordquist, Myron H. (1997) *What Color Helmet? Reforming Security Council Peacekeeping Mandates*, Newport Paper No. 12, Newport, R1.

Nullmeier, Frank (1997) 'Interpretative Ansätze in der Politikwissenschaft', in Artur Benz and Wolfgang Seibel (eds), *Theorieentwicklung in der Politikwissenschaft – eine Zwischenbilanz*, Baden-Baden, pp. 101–44.

Nuscheler, Franz (1996) *Das Recht auf Entwicklung. Blaue Reihe der Deutschen Gesellschaft für die Vereinten Nationen*, No. 67, Bonn.

Nuscheler, Franz (ed.) (2000) *Entwicklung und Frieden im Zeichen der Globalisierung*, Bonn.

Nuscheler, Franz (2001) 'Halbierung der absoluten Armut: die entwicklungspolitische Nagelprobe', *APuZ* ,18–19, pp. 6–12.

Nuscheler, Franz (2002a) 'Überforderte Entwicklungspolitik. Veränderungen nach dem 11. September', *Internationale Politik* (1) pp. 1–8.

Nuscheler, Franz (2002b) 'Global Governance, Development, and Peace', in Paul Kennedy, Dirk Messner and Franz Nuscheler (eds), *Global Trends and Global Governance*, London, pp. 156–82.

Nye, Joseph (1999) 'Redefining the National Interest', *Foreign Affairs* (4) pp. 22–35.

Nye, Joseph (2002) *The Paradox of American Power. Why the World's Only Superpower Can't Go It Alone*, Oxford.

Nye, Robert S. (2000) *Understanding International Conflicts. An Introduction to Theory and History*, New York.

Oberthür, Sebastian (1997) *Umweltschutz durch internationale Regime. Interessen, Verhandlungsprozesse, Wirkungen*, Opladen.

Oberthür, Sebastian and Hermann E. Ott (2000) *Das Kyoto-Protokoll. Internationale Klimapolitik für das 21. Jahrhundert*, Opladen.

Olsen, Mancur and Richard Zeckhauser (1966) 'An Economic Theory of Alliances', *Review of Economics and Statistics* (3) pp. 266–79.

Opitz, Peter (ed.) (1995, 2002) *Die Vereinten Nationen. Geschichte, Strukturen, Perspektiven*, Munich.

Osman, Mohamed Awad (2003) *The United Nations and Peace Enforcement: Wars, Terrorism and Democracy*, Aldershot.

Osmanczyk, Edmund Jan and Anthony Mango (ed.) (2003) *Encyclopaedia of the United Nations and International Agreements*, 4 vols, New York/London.

Otto, Dianne (1996) 'Nongovernmental Organizations in the United Nations System. The Emerging Role of International Civil Society', *Human Rights Quarterly* (1) pp. 107–41.

Otunnu, Olara A. and Michael W. Doyle (eds) (1998) *Peacemaking and Peacekeeping for the New Century*, Lanham, MD.

Paolini, Albert J. (ed.) (2003) *Between Sovereignty and Global Governance: The United Nations, The State and Civil Society*, Basingstoke.

Pape, Matthias (1997) *Humanitäre Intervention. Zur Bedeutung der Menschenrechte in den Vereinten Nationen*, Baden-Baden.

Paris, Roland (2001) 'Human Security: Paradigm Shift or Hot Air?', *International Security* (4) pp. 87–102.

Parsons, Anthony (1995) *From Cold War to Hot Peace: UN Interventions 1947–1995*, London.

Partsch, Karl Josef (1995) 'Human Rights, Petitions and Individual Complaints', in Wolfrum (1995), pp. 619–27.

Paschke, Karl Theodor (1996) 'Innenrevision in den Vereinten Nationen – eine neue Erfahrung', *Vereinte Nationen* (2) pp. 41–5.

Paschke, Karl Theodor (1999) 'Kein hoffnungsloser Fall. Fünf Jahre UN-Inspektorat: Versuch einer Bilanz', *Vereinte Nationen* (6) pp. 187–91.

Patil, Anjali V. (1992) *The UN Veto in World Affairs 1946–1990*, London.

Peck, Connie (1998) *Sustainable Peace. The Role of the UN and Regional Organizations in Preventing Conflict*, Lanham, MD.

Petterson, Thorleif (2002) 'Individual Values and Global Governance: A Comparative Analysis of Orientations Towards the United Nations', *Comparative Sociology* (3–4) pp. 439–65

Pfetsch, Frank R. (ed.) (1991) *Konflikte seit 1945. Daten – Fakten – Hintergründe*. 5 volumes, Freiburg.

Pfetsch, Frank R. and Christoph Rohloff (2000) *National and International Conflicts 1945–1995. New Empirical and Theoretical Approaches*, London.

Priess, Hans-Joachim and Georg M Berrisch, (2003) *WTO-Handbuch*, Munich

Prittwitz, Volker von (ed.) (2000) *Institutionelle Arrangements in der Umweltpolitik*, Opladen.

Pugh, Michael (ed.) (2001) *The UN, Peace, and Force*, London.

Rahman, Mahfuzur (2002) *World Economic Issues at the United Nations: Half a Century of Debate*, Boston, Mass.

Ramcharan, Bertrand G. (2002) *The United Nations High Commissioner for Human Rights: The Challenges of International Protection*, The Hague.

Ramphal, Shridath (1998) 'Global Governance', *Internationale Politik* (11), 1998, pp. 2–10.

Randelzhofer, Albrecht (2002) 'Art 2' (4), in Simma (2002), pp. 112–35.

Rao, Vinayak (2001) *International Negotiation: The United Nations in Afghanistan and Cambodia*, New Delhi.

Ratsimbaharison, Adrien M. (2004) *The Failure of the United Nations development programs for Africa*, Lanham, MD.

Rechkemmer, Andreas (2002) *Globale Umwelt- und Entwicklungspolitik in der Krise?* Berlin (SWP-Aktuell 44).

Rechkemmer, Andreas (2003) *Die Zukunft der Vereinten Nationen. Weltorganisation am Scheideweg – eine deutsche Perspektive*, Berlin.

Reinicke, Wolfgang and Francis Deng (2000) *Critical Choices. The United Nations, Networks, and the Future of Global Governance*, Ottawa.

Ress, Georg (2002) 'The Interpretation of the Charter', in Simma (2002), pp. 13–32.

Rice, Condoleezza (2000) 'Promoting the National Interest', *Foreign Affairs* (1) pp. 45–63.

Riedel, Eibe (1998) 'Universeller Menschenrechtsschutz. Vom Anspruch zur Durchsetzung', in Baum *et al.* (1998), pp. 25–55.

Riedel, Eibe (1999) 'Einleitung', in Bundeszentrale für Politische Bildung (1999) *Menschenrechte. Dokumente und Deklarationen*, Bonn, pp. 11–36.

Riedel, Eibe (2002) 'Artikel 55 (c)', in Simma, 2002, pp. 918–40.

Righter, Rosemary (1995) *Utopia Lost. The United Nations and World Order*, New York.

Risse, Thomas, Stephen C. Ropp and Kathryn Sikkink (1999) *The Power of Human Rights*, Cambridge.

Rittberger, Volker (ed.) (2002) *Global Governance and the United Nations System*, New York.

Rittberger, Volker (1994) 'Vereinte Nationen', in Dieter Nohlen (ed.), *Lexikon der Politik, vol. 6: Internationale Beziehungen*, ed. Andreas Boeckh, Munich, pp. 561–81.

Rittberger, Volker (1995) *International Organizations, Theory of*, in Wolfrum (1995), pp. 760–70.

Rittberger, Volker (1996) 'Die Vereinten Nationen zwischen weltstaatlicher Autorität und hegemonialer Machtpolitik', in Berthold Meier (ed.), *Eine Welt oder Chaos*, Frankfurt-am-Main, pp. 301–36.

Rittberger, Volker (2000) 'Globalisierung und der Wandel der Staatenwelt. Die Welt regieren ohne Weltstaat?', in Menzel (2000), pp. 188–218.

Rittberger, Volker and Bernhard Zangl (2002) *Internationale Organisationen – Politik und Geschichte*, Opladen.

Rittberger, Volker, Martin Mogler and Bernhard Zangl (1997) *Vereinte Nationen und Weltordnung. Zivilisierung der internationalen Politik?,* Opladen.

Roberts, Adam (1993) 'The United Nations and International Security', *Survival* (2) 1993, pp. 3–30.

Roberts, Adam (2003) 'Law and the Use of Force after Iraq', *Survival* (2) pp. 21–56.

Roberts, Adam and Benedict Kingsbury (eds) (1993) *United Nations, Divided World. The UN's Roles in International Relations*, Oxford.

Robinson, Mary (2002) 'Menschenrechte im Schatten des 11. September', in Arnim *et al.*, (2002), pp. 25–36.

Rochester, Martin J. (1993) *Waiting for the Millennium. The United Nations and the Future of World Order*, Columbia.

Rodley, Nigel (2003) 'United Nations Human Rights Treaty Bodies and special procedures of the Commission on Human Rights', *Human Rights Quarterly* (4), pp. 882–909.

Rosenau, James N. (1992) *The United Nations in a Turbulent World*, Boulder, CO/London.

Rosenau, James N. (1994) 'New Dimensions of Security – The Interaction of Globalizing and Localizing Dynamics', *Security Dialogue* (3) pp. 255–81.

Rosenau, James N. and Ernst-Otto Czempiel (eds) (1992) *Governance without Government: Order and Change in World Politics*, Cambridge.

Ruggie, John Gerald (1993) *Multilateralism Matters*, New York.

Rumsfeld, Donald H. (2001) 'America's New Kind of War', *New York Times*, 27 September.

Russell, Ruth (1958) *The History of the United Nations Charter*, Washington, DC.

Russett, Bruce (1996) 'Ten Balances for Weighing UN-Reform Proposals', *Political Science Quarterly* (2), pp. 259–69.

Russett, Bruce, Harvey Starr and David Kinsella (eds) (2000) *World Politics. The Menu for Choice*, Boston, Mass./New York.

Ryan, Stephen (2000) *The United Nations and International Politics*, Basingstoke.

Saksena, Krishan P. (1993) *Reforming the United Nations. The Challenge of Relevance*, New Delhi.

Salmon, Trevor C. (ed.) (2000) *Issues in International Relations*, London.

Santiso, Carlos (2002) 'Promoting Democratic Governance and Preventing the Recurrence of Conflict: The Role of the United Nations Development Programme in Post-conflict Peace-building, *Journal of Latin American Studies* (3) pp. 555–86

Sarooshi, Danesh (2000) *The United Nations and the Development ot Collective Security: The Delegation by the UN Security Council of Its Chapter VII Powers*, Oxford.

Scharpf, Fritz W. (1999) *Regieren in Europa. Effektiv und demokratisch?*, Frankfurt/New York.

Schechter, Michael G. (2001) *United Nations-sponsored World Conferences: Focus on Impact and Follow-up*, Tokyo.

Schellinski, Kristina (1998) *Ausbeutung von Kindern – Herausforderung für das gesamte UN-System*, in Baum (1998), pp. 139–54.

Schlesinger, Stephen C. (2003) *Act of Creation: The Founding of the United Nations; a Story of Superpowers, Secret Agents, Wartime Allies and Enemies, and Their Quest for a Peaceful World*, Boulder, CO.

Schlesinger, Thomas (2001) 'Financing and Financial Crises', in Cede and Sucharipa-Behrmann (2001), pp. 289–302.

Scholte, Jan Art (1997) 'The Globalization of World Politics', John Baylis and Steve Smith (eds), *The Globalization of World Politics. An Introduction to International Relations*, Oxford, pp. 13–30.

Schorlemer, Sabine von (2002) *Praxis-Handbuch UNO. Die Vereinten Nationen im Lichte globaler Herausforderungen*, Heidelberg.

Schücking, Walther and Hans Wehberg (1924) *Die Satzung des Völkerbundes*, 2nd edition Berlin.

Semb, Anne Julie (2000) 'The New Practices of UN-Authorized Interventions. A Slippery Slope or an Forcible Interference?', *Journal of Peace Research* (4) pp. 469–88.

Siedschlag, Alexander (1997) *Neorealismus, Neoliberalismus und Postinternationale Politik. Beispiel internationale Sicherheit – Theoretische Bestandsaufnahme und Evaluation*, Opladen.

Simma, Bruno (ed.) (2002) *The Charter of the United Nations: A Commentary*, Oxford.

Simmons, Beth A. and Lisa L. Martin (2002) 'International Organizations and Institutions', in Carlsnaes *et al.* (2002), pp. 192–211.

Simonis, Udo-Ernst (1998) *Weltumweltpolitik. Grundriss und Bausteine eines neuen Politikfeldes*, Berlin.

Singer, Peter W. (2003) *Corporate Warriors: The Rise of the Privatized Military Industry*, Ithaca, NY.

Singh, Swarna (2000) *United Nations and Geopolitical Reality*, New Delhi.

Smith, Michael J. (1998) 'Humanitarian Intervention: An Overview on the Ethical Issues', *Ethics and International Affairs* (12) pp. 63–79.

Sondhi, Sunil (2000) *United Nations in a Changing World*, New Delhi.

South Centre (ed.) (1996) *For a Strong and Democratic United Nations: A South Perspective on UN Reform*, Geneva.

Stares, Paul B. (ed.) (1998) *The New Security Agenda. A Global Survey*, Tokyo/New York.

Stein, Torsten (2000) 'Einsatzarten der Streitkräfte außer zur Verteidigung', *Neue Zeitschrift für Wehrrecht* (1) pp. 1–15.

Stiftung Entwicklung und Frieden (ed.), *Globale Trends. Fakten, Analysen, Prognosen*, Frankfurt-am-Main (published frequently).

Stockholm International Peace Research Institute, Yearbook Armaments, Disarmament and International Security, London (published annually).

Stoecker, Felix (2000) *NGOs und die UNO. Die Einbindung von Nichtergierungs-organisationen (NGOs) in die Strukturen der Vereinten Nationen*, Frankfurt-am-Main.

Stremlau, John (1998) *Sharpening International Sanctions*, New York.

Strohal, Christian (2001) 'The Development of the International Human Rights System', in Cede and Sucharipa-Behrmann (2001), pp. 157–76.

Strunz, Johann (1930) *Der Völkerbund*. Leipzig.

Sucharipa, Ernst (2001) 'The United Nations Today: Its Current Status, Reforms and Perspectives for the Future', in Cede and Sucharipa-Behrmann (2001), pp. 313–31.

Sucharipa-Behrmann, Lilly (2001) 'Peace-Keeping Operations of the United Nations', in Cede and Sucharipa-Behrmann (2001), pp. 89–104.

Swamy, Gita (2002) 'Humanitarian Assistance', in Volger (2002), pp. 260–7.

Tangredi, Sam J. (2000) *All Possible Wars? Towards a Consensus View of the Future Security Environment 2001–2025*, McNair Paper 63, Washington, DC.

Taylor, Ian (2003) 'The United Nations Conference on Trade and Development', *New Political Economy* (3) pp. 409–19.

Taylor, Paul and A. J. R. Groom, (ed.) 2000: *The United Nations at the Millennium: The Principal Organs*, London.

Teixeira, Pascal (2003) *The Security Council at the Dawn of the Twenty-First Century*, Geneva.

Thakur, Ramesh (ed.) (2000) *New Millennium, New Perspectives: The United Nations, Security, and Governance*, Tokyo.

Thakur, Ramesh (ed.) (2001) *United Nations Peacekeeping Operations: ad hoc Missions, Permanent Engagement*, Tokyo.

Thomsen, Bernd (1998) 'Rechtliche Grundlagen für einen wirksamen Menschenrechtsschutz', *Amnesty International*, pp. 19–30.

Tomuschat, Christian (1983) 'Neuformulierung der Grundregeln des Völkerrechts durch die Vereinten Nationen: Bewegung, Stillstand oder Rückschritt?', *Europa-Archiv* (23) pp. 729–38.

Tomuschat, Christian (ed.) (1992) *Menschenrechte. Eine Sammlung internationaler Dokumente zum Menschenrechtschutz*, Bonn.

Tomuschat, Christian (1995a) 'Human Rights, Petitions and Individual Complaints', in Wolfrum (1995), pp. 619–27.

Tomuschat, Christian (ed.) (1995b) *The United Nations at Age Fifty. A Legal Perspective*, The Hague.

Tomuschat, Christian (1995b) 'Human Rights, States Reports', in Wolfrum (1995), pp. 638–45.

Tomuschat, Christian (2000) 'Globale Menschenrechtspolitik', in Karl Kaiser and Hans-Peter Schwarz (eds), *Weltpolitik im neuen Jahrhundert*, Bonn, pp. 431–41.

Tomuschat, Christian (2003) 'Völkerrecht ist kein Zweiklassenrecht. Der Irak-Krieg und seine Folgen', *Vereinte Nationen* (2) pp. 41–6.

Töpfer, Klaus (1999) 'Rede des Exekutivdirektors des Umweltprogramms der Vereinten Nationen am 15.9.1999 in London', *Internationale Politik* (12) pp. 85–8.

Touval, Saadia (1994) 'Why the U.N. Fails', *Foreign Affairs* (5) pp. 44–57.

Trauttmansdorff, Ferdinand (2001) 'The Organs of the United Nations', in Cede and Sucharipa-Behrmann (2001), pp. 25–56.

Ul Haq, Mahbub, Richard Jolly, Paul Streeten and Khadija Haq (eds) (1995) *The UN and the Bretton Woods Institutions*, New York.

Unabhängige Kommission für internationale Entwicklungsfragen 1980: *Das Überleben sichern. Gemeinsame Interessen der Industrie- und Entwicklungsländer*, Cologne.

UNCTAD, *Trade and Development Report*, Geneva (published annually).

UNCTAD, (2000) *The Least Developed Countries Report 2000*, New York.

UNCTAD, (2000) *World Investment Report 2000*, Geneva.

UNDP, *Human Development Report*, New York (published annually).

UNEP, *Global Environmental Outlook*, London (published annually).

Union of International Associations (ed.), *Yearbook of International Organizations*, 4 vols, Munich (published annually).

United Nations (ed.) (1995) *UN Fiftieth Anniversary 1945–1995*, Dordrecht.

United Nations (2002) *Report of the International Conference on Financing Development*, New York (A/Conf. 198/11)

United Nations Association of the USA (ed.), *Global Agenda. Issues before the General Assembly of the United Nations* (published annually).

United Nations Department of Public Information (ed.) (1996) *The Blue Helmets. A Review of the United Nations Peace-keeping*, New York.

United Nations Department of Public Information, *Basic Facts About the United Nations*, New York (published frequently).

United Nations Department of Public Information, *Yearbook of the United Nations*, New York (published annually).

United Nations Library, *Monthly Bibliography*, Geneva (published monthly).

United Nations Non-Governmental Liaison Service (ed.) (1999) *Economic and Social Development in the United Nations System. A Guide for NGOs*, Geneva.

United Nations Non-Governmental Liaison Service (2000) *The Handbook of UN Agencies, Programmes, Funds and Conventions Working for Sustainable Economic and Social Development*, Geneva.

Universal Declaration of Human Rights, 10 December 1948, A/Res/217 (III).

Unser, Günther (2003), *Die UNO*, Munich.

Urquhart, Brian (1972) *Hammarskjöld,* New York.

Urquhart, Brian (2000) 'Between Sovereignty and Globalization – Where Does the United Nations Fit In?', *Development Dialogue* (1–2), pp. 5–14.

Van Krieken, Peter J. (ed.) (2002) *Terrorism and the International Legal Order: With Special Reference to the UN, the EU and Cross-border Aspects*, The Hague.

Varwick, Johannes (2003) 'Preventing War, Securing Peace', *Transatlantic International Politics* (1) pp. 11–16.

Vasak, Karel (1974) 'Le droit international des droits de l'homme', *Recueil des Cours de L'Académie de Droit International*, vol. IV, pp. 333–415.

Verdross, Alfred and Bruno Simma (1984) *Universelles Völkerrecht*, Berlin.

Victor, David G. (2001) *The Collapse of the Kyoto Protocol and the Struggle to Slow Global Warming*, Princeton, NJ.

Viotti, Paul R. and Mark V. Kauppi (2001) *International Relations Theory*, Boston, MA.

Voeten, Erik (2000) 'Clashes in the Assembly', *International Organization* (2) pp. 185–215.

Voigtländer, René (2001) *Notwehrrecht und kollektive Verantwortung*, Frankfurt-am-Main.

Volger, Helmut (2002) (ed.) *A Concise Encyclopedia of the United Nations*, The Hague.

Völkerbundssatzung (1919), in Knipping *et al.* (1995), pp. 401–25.

Wagner, Teresa and Leslie Carbone, (eds) (2001) *Fifty Years after the Declaration: The United Nations' Record on Human Rights*, Lanham, MD.

Waldmann, Jörg (1999) 'Agenda 21 – ein neuer Ansatz zur Lösung internationaler Probleme?', *Politische Bildung* (1) pp. 73–87.

Wallensteen, Peter (2002) *Understanding Conflicts. War, Peace and the Global System*, London.

Weber, Hermann (1995) 'League of Nations', in Wolfrum (1995), pp. 848–53.

Wehberg, Hans (1927) *Das Genfer Protokoll betreffend die friedliche Erledigung internationaler Streitigkeiten*, Berlin.

Weiss, Thomas G. (1996) 'Humanitäre Intervention. Lehren aus der Vergangenheit, Konsequenzen für die Zukunft', in Debiel and Nuscheler (1996), pp. 53–75.

Weiss, Thomas G., David P. Forsythe and Roger A. Coate (2000) *The United Nations and Changing World Politics*, Boulder, CO.

Weizsäcker, Richard von and Moeen Qureshi (1995) *The United Nations in its Second Half Century. A Report of the Independent Working Group on the Future of the United Nations*, New York.

Wellens, Karel (ed.) (2001) *Resolutions and Statements of the United Nations Security Council (1946–2000)*, The Hague.

White House (2002) *The National Security Strategy of the United States of America*, Washington, DC.

White, Nigel D. (2002) *The United Nations System: Toward International Justice*, Boulder, Col.

Wieczorek-Zeul, Heidemarie (2000) 'Deutsche Entwicklungs politik' in Nuscheler, Franz (ed.) (2000) *Entwicklung und Frieden im Zeichen der Globalisierung*, Bonn, pp. 131–43.

Wilenski, Peter (1993) 'The Structure of the UN in the Post-Cold-War Period', in Roberts and Kingsbury (1993), pp. 437–67.

Williams, Ian (2000) 'Eine kritische Masse an Staatskunst. Der "Millennium-Gipfel" der Vereinten Nationen vom September 2000', *Vereinte Nationen* (5) pp. 161–7.

Wilson, Woodrow (1918) 'Rede des Präsidenten der Vereinigten Staaten vor beiden Häusern des Kongresses', in Knipping *et al.* (1995), pp. 360–7.

Wissenschaftlicher Beirat der Bundesregierung Globale Umweltgefahren (ed.) (2001) *Welt im Wandel: Neue Strukturen globaler Umweltpolitik*, Berlin.

Witte, Jan Martin, Charlote Streck and Thorsten Benner (eds) (2003), *Progress or Peril? Partnership and Networks in Global Environmental Governance*, Washington, DC.

Wöhlcke, Manfred (1992) *Der ökologische Nord-Süd-Konflikt. Interessen, Argumente und Verantwortlichkeiten in der internationalen Umweltpolitik*, Ebenhausen (SWP-Studie 380).

Wolfrum, Hildegard (1995) 'Woman's Rights', in Wolfrum with Philipp (1995), pp. 1450–59.

Wolfrum, Rüdiger (2002) 'Preamble', in Simma (2002), pp. 33–7.

Wolfrum, Rüdiger with Christiane Philipp (eds) (1995) *United Nations: Law, Policies and Practice*, 2 vols, Munich.

World Bank, *World Development Report*, Washington, DC (published annually).
World Bank (2000) *Global Statistics*, New York.
World Health Organization, *World Health Report*, Geneva (published annually).
World Resources Institute, *World Resources*, New York (published annually)
World Trade Organization, *International Trade*, Geneva (published annually).
Yoder, Amos (1997) *The Evolution of the United Nations System*, Washington, DC.
Zangl, Bernhard and Michael Zürn (2003) *Frieden und Krieg. Sicherheit in der nationalen und postnationalen Konstellation*, Frankfurt-am-Main.
Ziring, Lawrence, Robert E. Riggs, and Jack C. Plano, (2000) *The United Nations: International Organization and World Politics*, South Melbourne.
Zumach, Andreas (2001) 'Globale Zukunftssicherung oder Geldverschwendung? Was die UN-Weltkonferenzen bewirken könne', *Internationale Politik* (5) pp. 21–4.
Zürn, Michael (1998) *Regieren jenseits des Nationalstaates. Globalisierung und Denationalisierung als Chance*, Frankfurt-am-Main.

Index